CW01263521

A RAILWAYMAN'S JOURNEY

DENNY ELLIS

HISTORIA NOSTRA VIA PEREGRINARI FERREA

FOR ALL WHO
ARE INTERESTED
IN RAILWAYS

AUSTRALIAN RAILWAY HISTORICAL SOCIETY
NEW SOUTH WALES DIVISION

Published by the

Australian Railway Historical Society
New South Wales Division (ACN 000 538 803)
67 Renwick Street, REDFERN NSW 2016

Typeset by J R Newland Enterprises, Birchgrove NSW 2041, using Adobe PageMaker 7™
Text and titles typeface: Palatino 9/13.5 point
Maps and diagrams by J R Newland Enterprises using Adobe Illustrator CS2™
Photos scanned by J R Newland Enterprises using Adobe Photoshop 7™
Cover design by Trisha Harris

Printed and bound by Ligare Pty Ltd, 138 Bonds Road, Riverwood NSW 2210

FIRST PUBLISHED 2005

National Library of Australia
Cataloguing-in-Publication entry:
Ellis, Denny, 1928 –
A Railwayman's Journey.

ISBN 0-9757870-0-4

1. Department of Railways, New South Wales.
2. Public Transport Commission of New South Wales.
3. State Rail Authority of New South Wales.
4. Railways—New South Wales—Employment conditions.
5. Railways—New South Wales—Operation and Working of.
6. Ellis, Denny—Autobiography.

DEDICATION

This book is dedicated to my wife, Mamie. Together we surmounted difficulties that our love, faith and respect for one another made possible. Our marriage gave to my life a meaning and purpose far beyond that which I could ever have hoped for.

I also wish to express my gratitude to our children Roy and Faye. They shared with us the heartbreak of Cathy's illnesses. Their love and totally unselfish dedication made her life happier and our task easier. Thank you to you both.

IN MEMORIAM

To Cathy, we each express our love and thank her for making us more tolerant and understanding of those to whom life has dealt the short straw.

ACKNOWLEDGEMENTS

Special thanks to Graham Bull who, with his proof reading expertise, turned rude matter into due form; and to the Australian Railway Historical Society, New South Wales Division and in particular to

John Beckhaus
Terry Boardman
Peter Clark
Graham and Lyn Harper
Graeme Henderson
Ross and Nicole Verdich
John Newland.

Artistic thanks to Warren Brown, the cartoonist for THE DAILY TELEGRAPH, Sydney, for willingly providing the front cover for this book.

TERMINOLOGY

Ku-ring-gai, situated north of Sydney, can be spelt in at least three different ways, depending upon the establishment using the name:

Ku-ring-gai Chase National Park;
Ku-ring-gai High School;
Mount Kuring-gai railway station; and
Kuringai for some other organisations.

Coalcliff, situated in the Illawarra District, was once spelt as two words (Coal Cliff) but has since reverted to the single word name, Coalcliff. CityRail refers to the railway station as Coalcliff.

FOREWORD

A Railwayman's Journey is far more than the title suggests. It could be described as life's journey of all the members of a railwayman's family through a world (railway, social and ethical) that was so different that it is hard to imagine from today's perspective. There are few rail narratives like this.

One completely unexpected pleasure for me arising from the Bicentennial Train operations was meeting Denny Ellis who had a major role in the planning of those trips. Gradually I learned of Denny's background and wide-ranging experience as a very senior railwayman but more stunning was to learn what that meant to his wife and children.

The Journey is through a railway totally unrecognisable today. Denny's early postings as Probationary Junior Porter at Canowindra, Lad Gatekeeper at Cowra (14 salaried staff and 18 wages staff at Cowra!), Porter Class 1 at Newbridge and Eugowra, Fifth Class Assistant Station Master at Borenore and Fourth Class Assistant Station Master at Linden— include positions and stations that no longer exist in today's operating railway. However, when you reflect on *The Journey*, you realise how important these junior positions were in developing in junior staff that innate judgment and understanding of safe and correct railway work, the hallmark of true railway professionals.

For those of you with a love of railway safeworking, I recommend that you work through the 57 Class failure at Linden and see if you believe that you could have bettered a 90-minute delay to traffic! It is an example of how staff were called on to use their hard gained experience without present day aids and communications.

The working conditions during and after World War II beggar belief. The ASM, Orange East Fork, was a most demanding position especially on stock train nights without being required to work 14 consecutive back shifts or 54 days out of 56 or working for over two years without any annual leave! That commitment and dedication of railwaymen has no equal today. When you realise that this was done while supporting a wife and young family, you start to see the effect on all the family of these working conditions. There was no time to take children to Saturday sport or share in school events. How do you manage a household with young children when the breadwinner is trying to sleep during the day as a consequence of long stints of back shift working? The whole family was profoundly affected by the *Railwayman's Journey*.

A Railwayman's Journey is a fascinating insight into life in another time that was underpinned by professionalism, dedication and an abiding commitment to Christian family values.

John Glastonbury.
Patron, Australian Railway Historical Society, NSW Division.

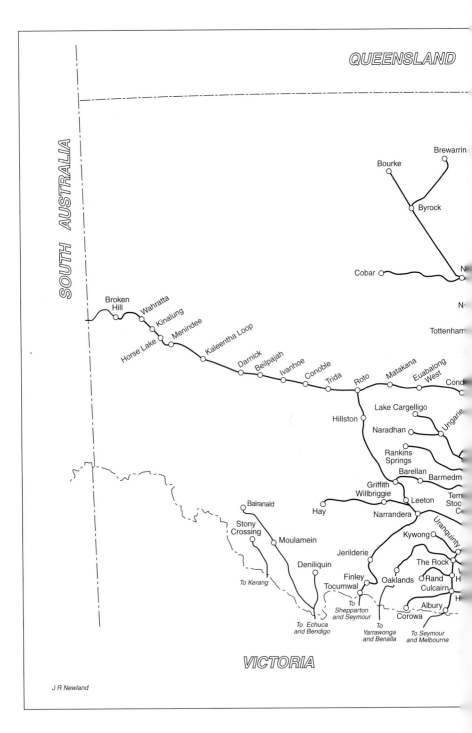

QUEENSLAND

SOUTH AUSTRALIA

Brewarrin

Bourke

Byrock

Cobar

N

N

Tottenham

Broken Hill
Wahratta
Kinalung
Horse Lake
Menindee
Kaleentha Loop
Darnick
Beilpajah
Ivanhoe
Conoble
Trida
Roto
Matakana
Euabalong West
Cond

Lake Cargelligo
Hillston
Naradhan
Ungarie

Rankins Springs

Barellan
Barmedm
Griffith
Willbriggie
Leeton
Tem
Stoc
C

Balranald
Hay
Narrandera

Stony Crossing
Moulamein
Kywong

Uranquinty

Jerilderie

The Rock

Deniliquin

Finley
Oaklands
Rand
H
To Kerang
Tocumwal
Culcairn
H

To Shepparton and Seymour

Albury

Corowa

To Echuca and Bendigo

To Yarrawonga and Benalla

To Seymour and Melbourne

VICTORIA

J R Newland

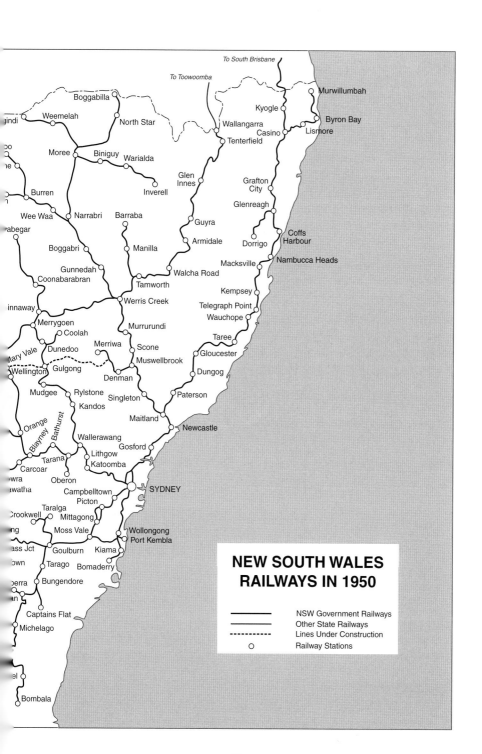

To South Brisbane
To Toowoomba

Boggabilla
Murwillumbah
Kyogle
Weemelah
jindi
North Star
Byron Bay
Wallangarra
Casino
Lismore
Tenterfield
oo
he
Moree
Biniguy
Warialda
Glen
Innes
Grafton
City
Burren
Inverell
Glenreagh
Wee Waa
Narrabri
Barraba
Guyra
abegar
Coffs
Harbour
Boggabri
Manilla
Armidale
Dorrigo
Macksville
Nambucca Heads
Gunnedah
Walcha Road
Coonabarabran
Tamworth
Kempsey
innaway
Werris Creek
Telegraph Point
Murrurundi
Wauchope
Merrygoen
Coolah
Taree
Mary Vale
Dunedoo
Merriwa
Scone
Gloucester
Wellington
Gulgong
Muswellbrook
Dungog
Denman
Mudgee
Rylstone
Singleton
Paterson
Kandos
Maitland
Orange
Bathurst
Wallerawang
Newcastle
Blayney
Gosford
Tarana
Lithgow
Carcoar
Katoomba
wra
Oberon
awatha
Campbelltown
SYDNEY
Picton
Taralga
Crookwell
Mittagong
ng
Moss Vale
Wollongong
Port Kembla
ass Jct
Goulburn
Kiama
own
Tarago
Bomaderry
erra
Bungendore
an
Captains Flat
Michelago
el
Bombala

**NEW SOUTH WALES
RAILWAYS IN 1950**

————	NSW Government Railways
————	Other State Railways
- - - - - - -	Lines Under Construction
O	Railway Stations

CONTENTS

THE BEGINNING

I WAS born at Canowindra on 16 December 1928, to parents who were, with so many others, to feel the full force of the Great Depression. My father was able to keep his job as the manager of a large holding some 14 miles from Canowindra. The closest school was in Canowindra, so going to school when I became school age was out of the question. For two years, I had correspondence lessons with Blackfriars Correspondence School. The problem was obtaining the lessons; we had no mail delivery. Because my parents drove the horse and sulky to Canowindra on alternate Tuesdays, my father, brother and I went once a month and my mother and sister also went once a month. So I received lessons only twice a month. I remember the grocer, who sold every thing from thimbles to produce, would tell the junior 'gofer' to give the horse a bucket full of chaff which he placed in a trough.

To enable my parents to buy a small farm at the location of Burdett, where a one-teacher school was located, they needed extra money. My father had two hundred rabbit traps. In the time when rabbits were in plague proportions, and their pelts were worth something in the order of a shilling a pound, he made good use of the traps. He used to rise very early and go around the traps and collect the rabbits, wring their necks, skin and stretch them over wire stretchers with the inside toward the atmosphere to allow them to dry. Every afternoon after work, he took up one hundred traps and reset them. By doing this, he always had his traps set in the same location for two nights. Every evening after dinner, he used to take a lantern and go around the traps taking out the rabbits caught and then resetting the traps. When he had finished, he used to skin the rabbits and leave the pelts until the morning to stretch; on an average he caught a hundred rabbits a night. I might say it made no impression on the numbers! I still think back over those times and am able to remember bits of them. I recall that he used to make a mark on the ground pointing to where the last trap was set. He made special markings to tell him where the next trap would be; a straight line with two bars across it meant near a fence. When he went round them, he started at the last trap he had set and followed his markings. He worked about 14 hours a day.

In January 1938, a move was made to be within one mile of Burdett Public School, my father at this time having bought the small mixed farm. My education in 1938 and 1939 was similar to that of any young boy at a country one-teacher school. The onset of war, however, changed that. With the bulk of the able-bodied work force at the war, it fell to me to assist with the planting of crops and their harvesting. In December 1941, the month of my thirteenth birthday, I pitched to the top of the 13 haystacks my father and I built. The result was that between 1940 and 1944 when I left school, I had spent approximately half the time either working on my father's farm or the farms of neighbours, and the other half was spent at school.

My last farming activity was the planting of the 1945 crop, a sorely needed source of revenue, because 1944 was recorded as one the most severe droughts of the century. There was no monetary return from harvest of 1944; the only result was some poor quality stock food.

After much discussion among my family, it was decided that the future of a farm labourer was bleak, to say the least. The appeal of a 'Government' job was magnetic. If you had one of those, you had not only a job for life, but you had financial security. The term 'job' had a far greater application to one's occupation in those days than today, when words such as career, computer analyst, manager, operator and many more all describe the occupation of a person without specifically referring to one's job. It comes down to the fact, I suppose, that in those times one's occupation was one's job and today whatever fancy name is given to the many more occupational names in the work force, one's position today is still one's job.

The appeal of a Government job outweighed any other; the thing of course was what Government job? Given my limited education, I was certainly aware, and I am sure my father was, of the limitations that placed on me. I was not interested in having a Government job that limited me to being a fettler or a labourer. So it was in June 1945, I applied for the position of a junior porter with the New South Wales Government Railways. Events then began to move quickly. I thought if I received an acknowledgment, it would be at least months before I did so. Imagine the reaction when a week later a letter arrived in the post (how else!) with a second class return pass from Orange to Sydney and return, together with a letter saying to report to the Devonshire Street Railway Institute on Thursday 21 June 1945 at 8.30am.

On Tuesday 19 June, my father and I took two mail cars to Orange, firstly to the small village of Toogong, then taking the direct mail car from Toogong, which ran Orange-Eugowra-Orange daily. We stayed overnight in Orange and caught No 26, the Orange to Sydney passenger. Can you imagine the excitement of a 16½-year old, who was further from home at Orange than he had been in his life? Can you imagine the awe in which he beheld a steam engine and its train? For he had not seen a steam locomotive before. It is incredible, in this age, to realise that this was the first passenger train I had ever seen. We

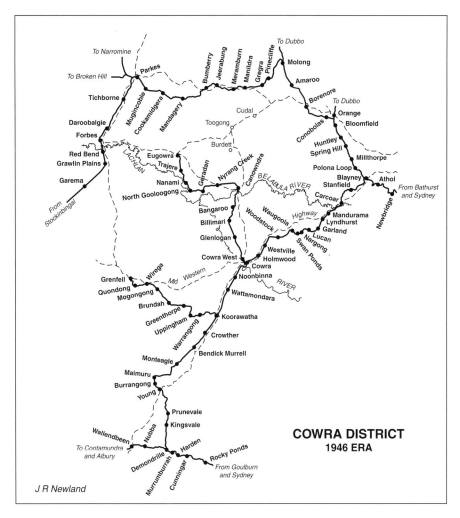

duly arrived at Sydney Terminal somewhere around 7.00pm and booked into a private hotel, opposite the People's Palace, named the Durban Private Hotel. The facade still stands, the building having been converted to apartments.

It was a wet winter's night in Sydney and as we walked down the concourse towards Pitt Street, a tram passed us. As it did, the trolley poles arced, with the resulting shower of sparks. It frightened the life out of me! The tall buildings, the street lights, the traffic, and the number of people moving left me speechless. Not in my wildest fantasising did I imagine what a city, any city, would look like. I went to bed wondering how I would ever cope in situations like this on my own. I was soon to find out.

My father, determined not to have me late, was standing outside the Institute in

Devonshire Street at 7.30am! The examination was not to commence for another 60 minutes, giving me ample time to be nervous. As I had feared from the beginning that I would not pass the examination, it was with a sense of profound relief I saw the first question, a simple addition followed by subtraction, multiplication, and division in both numbers and in money. The final questions involved fractions, which also caused no bother. The English portion was also straight forward, involving dictation and the writing of a dictated passage from a daily newspaper.

As we completed the examination, from memory there were about 20 sitting, we were told to wait outside and we would be called back if we had passed. About an hour later the examiner came out and began to read the names of those successful, instructing them to re-enter the examination room. He read and read names and the longer he read the more my father's face fell. I am sure that, by the time, my name was read out second last, that he had expected the worst. The transformation of that wizened small man's face was something to behold.

We were taken from the Institute across to the first floor of Central, entering at the entrance near No 10 platform, for our medical examinations. These were straight forward, although I was astounded with the 'confetti' eye test book. The final frightening (to me) thing for the day was to be interviewed by the Staff Superintendent, whose name I remember was F C Burgess. He was very pleasant, asked a few questions about my background, I think smelled the gum leaves and let me down lightly. His final question inquired whether I attended Church, I answered in the affirmative and today, I am still able to do that.

The next day saw us home again to await instruction, which we were told, would be 'in due course'. We took the *Cowra Mail* to Cowra, the railmotor (petrol driven *tin hare*) to Canowindra and once again fell back to the trusty mail car home.

'In due course' turned out to be a very short time, for a letter, once again with a pass, this time only for a single journey, arrived on Thursday 28 June, with a direction to present myself at the Devonshire Street Institute, again, on Monday 2 July 1945.

This time of course, the excitement of going out into the virtual unknown, was tinged with the knowledge I was leaving a home where I had been lovingly nurtured from childhood, where I had learned the values of family life, of integrity and sobriety. My father told me I should remember two things, as I went though life, the first was to treat a lady as a lady until she proved she was not and secondly, always to tell the truth, for if I did, when it mattered I would be believed. I've often reflected on the latter advice during my life, and I can say it was true, for on more than one occasion, my word was accepted when it easily might not have been. So, it was a time for a mother's tears as I left walking the mile, with my father, to a neighbour who was driving me to Canowindra. It was a Saturday evening, and he was going to town for a few beers, (no breathalyser in those days) and volunteered to give me a lift. As we arrived at the gate, my father put out his hand said " Good luck, son", wheeled and walked away. To this day, I can still see him walking away from me, with his hands behind his back, as was his wont.

I set out on my journey into the adult world with a small brown bakelite suitcase, a free pass and £5. Not very much in terms of material possessions, though I think the previous paragraph will indicate that I had something far more valuable. The standards and values I took with me stood by me all my working life. My parents, and especially my father, by instilling those values in me, contributed far more than they would have imagined to whatever successes I attained.

I do not remember much of the journey to Cronulla on that Saturday night. I was to stay with an aunt's parents, for how long I knew not.

When I arrived at the Institute on the Monday morning, I was not allowed to start. I, to say the least, was distressed. The Manpower Act was still in force, and because I had worked in a protected industry, even though I was not registered, having only recently left school, I still had to have a Manpower clearance. The Department of Railways had written to us, but posted the letter on the Friday prior to my leaving, hence we had not received it. In the end common sense prevailed, and I was allowed to stay until clearance had been arranged by the Staff Section. As a result, my official first day as a probationary junior porter was 4 July, American Independence Day, in 1945.

After the initial hiccup, I found that the Devonshire Street Institute was to be the venue for training those of us who had passed the examination. We were to have a month in a training school, to teach us how to be junior porters. I was absolutely lost, as the instructor talked of metropolitan stations and their lines. He thought I was completely dumb, when I had no idea of the geography of the Sydney area. He actually asked "where had I been all my life?" When I told him the first train I had seen was at Orange the previous fortnight, and in addition to that had never been more than 30 miles from my birthplace, his incredulity was written on his face. It did not save me from being the butt of the jokes of the place!

The language and the talk of my fellow would-be juniors left me aghast,

"My God!" I thought "did they do *that* when they were with girls!"

Being young men, they were of course quick to show off their prowess as strong men. Arm wrestling was established as the method of displaying strength. In height and stature I was just about the smallest of the group, so I was not really in contention, the big guys thought. What they did not know was for the past five years I had been carrying 180lb bags of wheat, had been involved in manual farm work and was probably stronger then than at any other time of my life since. The challenge came from the big guy who had knocked all comers over and decided he ought to be able to say he was the class champion. I had deliberately kept out of this activity, for two reasons, the first being I had done some arm wrestling with my brother and uncles and was able to hold my own with them, and the second being at this time I was reticent about joining any activity. When I was directly challenged I did not back off; the result showed I was comprehensively stronger than he was. It gained me some needed respect.

While I cannot say I learned much from the school, it did train me in some aspects— the delivery and dispatching of parcels, the calculation of fares, (with much nervousness!), and barrier duties. Each Saturday morning, I was directed to report to the station master at Cronulla for additional training, which mainly entailed the collection of tickets. It was here that I first encountered that hated task of compiling the 'Collected Ticket Return'. I probably learned more about 'life' in that month than I had learned all my life to then. At the end of the month, a dinner was held in the boardroom, on the first floor at Central. If my memory is correct, it was very close to the Chief Traffic Manager's office. I particularly remember the large oblong table. It had a green leather type surface. I do not remember which senior officers were there. However, despite being the butt of the jokes of the school, I was given the task of proposing the toast 'The NSWGR' because no one else was prepared to do so; I remember an officer named Armstrong, who was from the Staff Section, congratulating me after. I had written out a speech and memorised it.

At the dinner, we were given our postings. Mine was to a temporary extra position of Probationary Junior Porter, Canowindra. Was I jubilant, frustrated, or disappointed at returning home? My family, of course, was delighted. I, having prepared myself to leave home for good and return as time and circumstances permitted, had mixed feelings. It was necessary to find accommodation in Canowindra from Monday to Friday. The push-bike, of course, would be the means of transport between home and Canowindra, on the weekend.

On the second Monday of August 1945, I presented myself to one William Boag, the station master. He was somewhat perplexed as to why he had suddenly been sent a probationary junior porter, but assured me I was welcome and would certainly earn my pay which incidentally, was one pound twelve shillings and sixpence per week. Board was one pound ten shillings per week. I should say of Bill Boag, he was a kindly old man, but who was also a 'rogue' in many ways. Some of his antics will come to light before I leave the probationary part of my career spent in Canowindra.

The staff at Canowindra in 1945, besides the station master, included Arthur Elkington, sixth clerk in charge of the goods shed. He was responsible for the compilation of the goods accounts. Leading Porter Tom Chamberlain worked in the goods shed and wool dump, (I probably should say the *Legendary*), and Henry Harold Carlton O'Sullivan Porter Class 2 in the parcels office, (known as Carl). Tom Chamberlain spent nearly all his railway life in Canowindra. He was a bachelor and pugilist of some repute. No carrier was game to make a move in the yard without Tom's say so! In the days when the shortage of wagons was really biting, it was not unusual to see a truck of goods arrive on the pick-up in the morning around 10.00am and for the same wagon to be picked up again in the afternoon about 4.00pm by the pick-up returning from Eugowra loaded with wool or lucerne hay. The carriers all obviously worked with him to their advantage.

Carl O'Sullivan, who left Canowindra around 1948 and went as assistant station master at Clarendon, from where he eventually retired, initially trained me in the parcels office. I was also responsible for taking and sending the daily telegrams, cleaning, and assisting with unloading the parcels from the railmotor and the 'out-of-goods' from the brakevan of the pick-up which was No 47-48. Included in these 'out-ofs' on Tuesdays and Saturdays were what was known as poultry coops. They were made of cane and were quite substantial. There were larger ones made for turkeys, but they were almost unprocurable. The local turkey grower, especially at Christmas, used to nearly drive Bill Boag mad trying to get what he needed. Almost invariably he had to make his own, and there was an almost free freight return rate for them. Sometimes he got them back and sometimes he didn't! As was the case with all produce in those days, poultry moved by rail to market at Darling Harbour. My mother, on a regular basis, drove the horse and sulky to Canowindra from Burdett, with cockerels for the markets in chaff bags which had holes made in them for the head of the bird to poke through. A coop held 20 birds and that is how many she sent to market each trip. The journey in the sulky took about an hour and a half each way.

I learnt a lot in the period I was there; some of the tasks being entering inward parcels and luggage into the inward parcel book, (yes, they entered luggage in those days), the delivery of parcels and luggage, the compilation and collection of parcels storage charges, (not rigorously applied I might say), the delivery of COD Parcels, the collection of freight on to-pay parcels, the dispatching of stamped, to-pay and prepaid parcels, the compiling of the monthly parcels abstracts, daily stamp balance, the daily cash balance in the parcel office, roping and sheeting trucks of wool and fodder, the correct way to fold tarpaulins, the loading of livestock and the sealing of livestock wagons, the entering of the Guards' Road Van Waybill book, and finally sending the telegrams and receiving them on the old circuit telephones where the writing area was about 6 inches by 4 inches. The code words held some fascination for me. While I was waiting for the junior at Cowra to write down the message of the telegram I used to study the code chart next to the telephone. In the days of Morse code, especially, the code words were used as abbreviations in sentences. An example is the meaning of the code word *igol* was no trace at this, *podu* meant reply by telegram, *pedo* in reply to your telegram. A full list of the code words was printed on a large pink light cardboard measuring approximately 40 by 30 centimetres. I guess there were about 500 code words in all. Addresses of senior administrative officers were also abbreviated in this fashion.

The following are examples of the wit and wisdom of Bill Boag, who after retirement worked in the Strand Theatre, Canowindra, owned by his sons. Bill died of cancer some two years into retirement. On one bright day, old Bill let go with that famous Lady Chatterley's four-letter word, just as one of the local socialite ladies passed his door. Quick as a flash he said to me, standing near the door,

"Don't forget that bucket!"

As the lady left the parcels office, she looked into his office and said with the most wicked of smiles,

"Good morning, Mr Boag," and kept going. Poor old Bill was flabbergasted.

The obtaining of ropes and sheets was nigh impossible, but old Bill was never short for his requirements. The District Superintendent's staff knew he loaded more trucks than he had authority to load, given the amount of equipment they authorised him to use. Whatever equipment was in the brakevan when the pick-up stopped just disappeared without trace. I can remember one occasion when the traffic inspector rode the pick-up. He got out of the van and quickly came to Bill's office, no doubt to keep an eye on him. When he returned to the van the equipment for Eugowra was missing. Before he let the train depart he made a search of the premises, but found no equipment. Despite his fuming he could do nothing to Bill because he had not left him. What he did not know was that two of the carriers unloaded it on the opposite side to which he left the van and put it in the silo to which Bill had a key. Bill was given flying unexpected inspections, but never was any equipment found. They did not have keys to the wheat silos did they? The old fox Bill also had enough nous *never* to leave any equipment where it was visible; he had the carriers and old Tom well trained in this area of self defence.

The guard of the pick-up, one Walter Ramage, also a legend in his own lifetime, was, of course, party to many of Bill's, shall we say, misdemeanours. Wal Ramage had a small holding at Cowra. Grateful carriers kept him supplied in fodder for his stock. I can remember one day when he was shunting at Canowindra, and he was about to go in between wagons to couple up. He grabbed me, pulled me in between with him and gave me instruction on how to hold a coupling to avoid finger damage and how to place your feet in case of movement by the wagons. The lesson was completed with instruction in how to join the rubber Westinghouse air brake hoses together. It was a frightening experience, but in hindsight it was also a good one.

During the course of my six-month stay in Canowindra it was necessary to change boarding houses. In those times food and clothing rationing was still in force and coupons were required to purchase many foodstuffs, notably tea and butter. I relate this because when it came time for me to move on from Canowindra, I asked the landlady for my ration books. I was surprised at her reticence, but did not attach anything to it, until I was in my next boarding house. When I handed my books to the new landlady, she asked,

"What have you done with your coupons?"

I did not know what she was talking about until she showed me the books. All the tea and butter coupons as well as some of the clothing ones had been cut out. There was nothing I could do; I could not prove the previous landlady had stolen them. Fortunately, my family, living on the farm, did not have to buy butter, so I was able to replace my butter ones. As for tea, the new landlady did not worry. That was another of life's lessons learned, never assume anything.

In the field of personal relations and perhaps development, although nominally Anglican, I was a member of a Methodist Young People's group that met at Cranbury, a farming area some five miles from home. I had attended this group before I joined the railways and while at Canowindra travelled out to it with the minister, with whom I maintained a close friendship for many years. I also became friendly with the secretary of a Canowindra garage proprietor; the relationship was never more than that of a good platonic friendship, which we shared for about three years.

Canowindra railway station looking in the direction of Cowra. Although this view was photo-graphed in 1987, the scene would not have altered all that materially from the mid-1940s during the author's time there.   *I K Winney, ARHS Rail Resource Centre 8115.*

LAD GATEKEEPER, COWRA

IN LATE January 1946 I was directed to Cowra to begin my career as a permanent member of the New South Wales Government Railways staff. The usual staff consideration of those days was applied in my case; the telegram arrived Friday afternoon telling me to report on the following Monday!

Temporary accommodation was arranged with the mother of the assistant goods clerk, who ran a boarding house. On arrival on the Monday, I was told by the landlady that I had a fortnight to find other board.

Accommodation of any kind, in those early post war years, was extremely difficult to find. The fortnight stretched into a month, when an advertisement I had placed in the COWRA GUARDIAN was answered. I went to an older couple who had two other boarders plus a young married couple, who rented a room and shared the kitchen, not the ideal way to begin married life. The husband was a fireman and later a driver at Cowra.

One of the most significant events of my life occurred shortly after I arrived at this boarding house-*cum*-'home'. The two boarders I mentioned went to a party, and came home drunk. They were in such a state that one them vomited on the bed and carpet while the other defecated in

The author at Cowra, 1946.

the bedroom, in the hall, leading to the bathroom and in the bathroom. When I arrived home from backshift the stench in the room was unbearable. They had been ordered from the house by the husband and were on the verandah, still not having cleaned themselves. The landlady was inside packing (throwing?) their belongings into their cases. Before leaving they were allowed to use the outside laundry.

The significant thing was, I made a vow to myself when I saw the condition of these two young people:

"Never to drink anything or take anything that would cause me to do something I would not normally do".

I have maintained that all my life and today, more than 50 years later, I still have not tasted beer. In my latter years, I have enjoyed a glass of wine with a meal. In the early years my being teetotal was not very well accepted by my equals, resulting in, to a degree, my becoming something of a 'loner' in my early career and life. I will come back to this aspect further on in my life's story. I spent the majority of my Cowra time in this home, until the son of the lady (it was a late second marriage for both) returned home to die from tuberculosis. I then went to another boarding house where I stayed about a month.

On two occasions, the cold meat we were having for the evening meal was infested with maggots. The first time I put it down to misfortune; it was summer and the blowflies were prolific. The second time I left without worrying about the advance board and went to the Railway Hotel to stay until I left Cowra shortly after. It was here that I encountered a man whose lifestyle was homosexual. I knew nothing of homosexuality and when this guy made a tentative like suggestion to me, I was horrified. To think that another man could speak to me in this fashion was way beyond my bounds of comprehension. My face must have said it all, because he invited me to forget it and left my room. He never sat at the same table for meals nor ever spoke to me again.

Cowra was something of a culture shock for two reasons. It was my first encounter with shift work and secondly, instead of being appointed to the permanent staff as a junior porter, as I expected, I was appointed to the position of Lad Gatekeeper. I felt let down. As it turned out there were four junior porters, including the position classified as Lad Gatekeeper, at Cowra, who each in their turn manned the Brougham Street level crossing gates. Brougham Street crossed the line between the locomotive depot, the lines to Harden and Eugowra branches, and Cowra station, so that in the mornings and evenings especially, it was quite busy. The rostered hours of duty were Mondays 12.01am to 6.00am and 6.00pm to 6.00am Tuesday, Wednesday, Thursday, Friday and Saturday 6.00pm to 6.00am - 78 hours per week! The wage was that of the 44-hour week of a junior porter.

The junior porters working the station rosters signed on duty at 1.20am, 7.00am, and 3.00pm. The duties allocated to them were varied.

The 7.00am shift was required to assist with the transhipping and unloading of the brakevan of No 63 *Cowra Mail*, transhipping the Eugowra branch traffic to the railmotor, with the Canowindra and Eugowra traffic loaded in the trailer. The traffic for the unattended sidings was loaded in the area separating the first and second class portions of the motor. Five minutes before the railmotor's departure, the junior was required to ride the callboy's bicycle to the road bridge over the Lachlan River. This bridge was the extension of Kendall Street, the main street, and was the road to the Grenfell and Young districts. The gates at this crossing were closed across the line and had to be opened across the roadway to allow the motor to pass. After the railmotor passed he was required to ride to the locomotive depot and take particulars of the wagons in the locomotive depot and on the coal stage. These wagons would be either empty or still loaded with coal, which was used by the locomotives of the depot.

One of the early lessons I learnt in regard to being conscientious concerned the taking of numbers of wagons in the locomotive depot. In the Christmas period, rakes of empty wagons were stored on the coal stage road and in other roads nearby. The daily book we used, which was a guard's notebook, obviously had the previous day's wagons recorded. On the Monday of his week on day work, a junior, (who, though I remember his name, shall remain nameless) checked the wagons in loco and found they agreed with those of the previous Friday. On Tuesday, Wednesday, Thursday and Friday he did not go to loco and recorded in the book, 'unaltered' for those days. When he handed the book in on the Friday, the station master had a glance at it and asked him if he was sure the wagons on the coal stage road had not altered, the reply was,

"No, they have not".

The station master's reply was,

"They were lifted on Tuesday afternoon, and the road is empty."

The only thing that saved him from being reported to the District Superintendent, Lithgow, which may have seen his employment being terminated, was that his father, a local police sergeant, interceded on his behalf with the station master and local traffic inspector. A radical change in his attitude to his job took place!

When the junior returned to the station, if it was winter, he had to light the foot warmer boiler and maintain during the day a water temperature sufficient to heat the footwarmers. Footwarmers were heavy things; to place them in the footwarmer boiler it was necessary to stand on the edge and using a hook, place each one on a sliding hook attached to one of the twenty bars that crossed the boiler, so they were suspended in the water. I am convinced in this day and age the placing of footwarmers in boilers under these conditions would be prohibited by the Occupational Health and Safety Act. I am also sure that the Department of Labour and Industry or Workcover would not allow 16 year-old boys to carry out the task and nor should they! In the summer months, the carriage water bottles were removed and placed on a barrow and were refilled in the evening with ice water. The ice was delivered daily from the local ice works.

Generally, by the time he had completed that task, the roster clerk had finished his rostering of the guards. The junior then became a callboy and delivered the next turn of duty advices to the guards concerned. In Cowra, when I was there, there were 20 guards, who were: salaried guards Ernie Croucher, Earl Walsh; wages guards on rosters, Albert Lawrence, Wal and Jack Evans, Leo Lynch, Vince O'Brien, Walter Ramage; roustabouts, 'Snow' Anderson, Jack Bacheldor, Alf Bourke, Rod McKewan, Ben Hopping, Bill Jones, Duncan McMartin, Doug McLean, Leo Berg, Mick English, Vic Elton and Les 'Paddles' Duffy. One of the not properly explained tragedies to occur in 1946 was the death, in the Young–Monteagle section, of Rod McKewan. He worked No 155 double-headed coal train to Demondrille and, as was generally the case, was working home engine and van. For some unexplained reason, he apparently decided to leave the van and get onto the engine by walking along the outside step of the van and then climbing onto the tender. His body was found near a level crossing at Maimuru by the ganger and police who had been called out to search for him.

Interspersed with these duties the junior became a number taker. Nos 36 and 23 respectively were the pick-up trains to Blayney and Harden. One of the Evans invariably

Cowra railway station and yard looking in the direction of Blayney as photographed in 1966. Cowra was always a very busy location as is evidenced by 3665 arriving with a goods and 3008 waiting to depart with petroleum tankers in its consist.

C R Field, ARHS Rail Resource Centre 12781.

worked No 36 and guard O'Brien worked No 23. The purpose of taking the numbers was to record, on a form known as an X2010, the details of each wagon on the train. The first entry signified the type of wagon, then followed the number of the wagon, the originating station, the destination station, the contents and finally the weight. The weights and vehicle columns were added up to obtain the load and length of the train. Also included at the top of the X2010 was space for the engine number(s), the driver's name and time on duty, together with the guard's name and his sign on time. The junior was also responsible for cleaning the brakevan out. Some of the vans when they arrived were unbelievably dirty; I used to wonder how guards could let them get like they were. There were others of course, whose vans on arrival were spotless, two especially come to mind Duncan McMartin and Ben Hopping. They also demanded the vans they took out to be spotless, which was fair enough. Generally, Duncan McMartin would put an extra carbon paper and take the numbers for the junior so that he had more time to do his van. The junior was also responsible for equipping the brake van. Each van had to have six wooden sprags, two tail discs, one of which had to be exhibited on the rear of the last vehicle of the train, a kerosene tail-light and a water bucket. If the van was non-electric, it had to have three tail lights, filled ready for use. After the departure of the train, the number taker prepared a telegram with the details of the load and sent it to the station masters Blayney and Bathurst and Lithgow Control (coded *lico*).

It might have read:

"No 36 *ahab* (on time) engine No 5376 Driver Stubbs Cowra 8.50am Guard J Evans Cowra 9.45am LHG van out of traffic 27 tons 46 tons Millthorpe, 69 Orange, 23 Blayney, 90 Bathurst, 46 East of Penrith (EOP), 23 Woodstock, 23 Mandurama, 58 Waugoola and 58 Holmwood load 463 length 18/19."

The junior would give the load to *lico* over the control telephone. The ruling load Cowra to Blayney was 345 tons. No 36 was able to convey the additional between Cowra and Woodstock, the load being 640 tons.

At Cowra, a junior's work never seemed to be done, for, after completing his call boy and number taking duties, he had to assist the platform leading porter to clean and water the sitting carriages that were detached from the *Cowra Mail*. Generally it was a BS and FS or similar type carriage, but at holiday times and often of a Saturday additional carriages were detached and generally were LFX or BX. For those who do not recall them, they were side door types and I detested cleaning them. Watering was also difficult, because they had gravitational water supplied to the toilets and hand basins, therefore it was necessary to climb to the roof with the hose to water them. In the summer time, the cleaning of carriages that had been standing in the blazing sun for hours was like working in a sauna. I developed a healthy dislike for carriage cleaning that, although I cleaned carriages in other places in much more congenial working conditions, never left me. I should say that the sleeping carriage with the conductor in residence and one other carriage would fit under cover in the carriage shed. The 7.00am junior's day finished at 3.30pm with the cleaning of the carriages.

The junior who signed on duty at 3.30pm was first required to see the barracks stove fire was burning satisfactorily and that the kitchen, toilets and shower remained clean. A barracks attendant was employed in the barracks daily; her duty before finishing at 2.00pm was to have the stove alight. It generally was only necessary to keep it burning. On this shift, I used to go to the barracks about every hour. By doing this, I was able to keep the fire burning and the ash cleared without having to struggle with it. The kettles and the large hot water urn also had to be kept full of water. On the occasions when the barracks were not occupied, the afternoon and backshift juniors had a bonus. However, there were times when crews came in about midnight, and the junior then had to light the fire in sufficient time to have hot water available.

The footwarmer boiler also required his attention in the winter. The keeping of a small fire sufficient to keep the water simmering was all that was required this late in the day. In the summer months, his duty was to fill the water bottles from the cold water tub and place them on a barrow in readiness to be placed in the *Cowra Mail* carriages. He was then required to attend the barrier for the afternoon passenger to Harden.

This train ran from Blayney, connecting off the *Central West Express*. After leaving Cowra, it was also the Sydney connection at Harden for the Up *Temora Mail*. The locomotive turned, coaled at Demondrille and was re-prepared and returned to Cowra after connecting with the Down *Temora Mail* and the Up *Melbourne Express*. It continued on from Cowra to Blayney as the daylight connection for No 26, the Orange to Sydney passenger. The train then remained at Blayney until the arrival of the *Central West Express* and began its runs all over again.

I mentioned earlier the tragedy of Guard McKewan. Another tragedy, perhaps more traumatic for those concerned, involved the afternoon Harden Passenger (I think it was No 11). During an engine change at Cowra, for some reason, after giving the driver the ease up signal, the fireman walked straight between the buffers and was crushed. The engine was not moved until a doctor arrived, but in the meantime his wife had been called and arrived at the same time as the doctor. The doctor advised the assistant station master he thought when the engine was moved the fireman would lose consciousness and probably bleed to death. The fireman spoke to his wife; she was ushered away while the engine was moved. He died in the ambulance, very soon after, being unconscious before the final engine movement. The driver, whose name was Bill Plaice, committed suicide some six weeks later. I was on duty, but fortunately was nowhere near the incident and did not witness any of it. I was more upset when I heard of Bill Plaice's suicide than I was with the actual accident. He was a very tall man, with a gentle manner. Often the crews on these passenger trains changed over and they would wait in the station master's office. His character and bearing were such that 50 years later I still clearly remember him. I also heard, in later years, he was regarded as a prince among enginemen, and I remember thinking at the time 'not surprising'.

The junior was required about 6.30pm to ride to Cowra West and open the gates for the passage of the returning Eugowra railmotor. He returned directly to the station and then checked all tickets onto the *Cowra Mail*. In those times, the passenger patronage on the Mails was heavy, especially on Friday and Sunday nights. Although the junior was on the barrier, it was still his job to take the numbers of the carriages and send the train load of No 56 *Cowra Mail*. As I recall the load was sent to *lico*, *Esk*, SM Bathurst, *Coach*, *Carlights* and *Son*. Passenger train loads conveyed to the recipient of the telegram the engine number, brakevan and carriages in order from the van and the *cana*, which was the code word for the number of passengers, sleepers, first and second class. The coded addresses of *Carlights* and *Son* referred to the Train Equipment Officer, Sydney Yard, and the Yard Controller, Sydney, respectively. *Esk* was the code address of the District Superintendent Lithgow.

I do not know if coming events cast shadows or whether it was coincidence but I often thought that *Coach* (who was assistant superintendent in charge of passenger rolling stock) must almost sit at the right hand of God. I occupied the position many years later and found that was not so. I was not disappointed; if modesty permits, I will say I arrived in the senior position, with some satisfaction.

After the departure of the *Cowra Mail*, a goods train ran to Blayney leaving Cowra around 8.20pm. On Tuesdays and Saturdays this train ran as a stock train conveying stock from Cowra and off the pick-ups from Eugowra and Grenfell. During the time I was there, at least one coal train usually went to Demondrille conveying coal for Victorian destinations from the Western coal fields. The junior took the loads, cleaned the vans and sent the train loads for these trains. By the time he had finished, it was generally around 10.00pm. He worked as required until about 11.30pm, when he was required to call the guard for the Harden passenger. He signed off at midnight.

The backshift junior signed on around 1.00am. I am a bit hazy on his actual sign-on time, but his first duty was to unload the brakevan of the Harden passenger and then to give the carriages a light clean; for example, check the toilets, dust the window sills and remove any rubbish. After the departure of the train, he was required to enter the Cowra parcels and luggage into the inward parcels and luggage book. Any branch line traffic was placed on barrows to be loaded in the morning. He also swept and cleaned the parcels office.

During the night, his main job was to sweep the platform from one end to the other. A relief assistant station master, whose name was Harry Bushell, used to stand at the end of the platform as the sun rose and point out the areas, if any, that had been missed in the sweeping. When he relieved the station master, no one other than his immediate staff were allowed in the station master's office. If a junior had cause to go in or was summoned, he first knocked on the door and waited till he was bid enter. When he was bid, he took off his cap and stood by the station master's table and waited until he was spoken to. Harry Bushell was an old man at this time; he was a member of the old school, who dressed as such summer and winter. While he was actively disliked, the older members of the staff also respected him. He genuinely believed the disciplines and regulations of when he joined the NSWGR around 1895 should still be enforced.

He was a God-fearing man, who served his beloved Church of England (as it was in those days) with fervency and zeal. I have included the remarks about Harry Bushell, not as a criticism of him, but in an endeavour to show the ways in which staff, and junior staff especially, were expected to act. My time of entry into the Department coincided with that era which, in the late forties and early fifties, saw a gradual change in the relationship between station management and staff. The beginning of the postwar period saw many attitudes change, some of which I applauded, but equally as many I did not. The final straw in my view, was when a junior at Sydney yelled up the platform to the station master,

"Hey! Ron."

I have digressed from the duties of the backshift junior. During the night, he made sure the barracks fires were alight and the kettles filled, called guards for any goods trains required to run and took the numbers on an X2010. If it were winter he cleaned the ashes from the foot warmer boiler in readiness for the heating of the footwarmers off the arriving *Cowra Mail*. His final job was to attend the ticket barrier and collect tickets off the passengers from the Mail. He finished somewhere around 8.30am.

There was a junior's position in the Telegraph Office. His duty was to dispatch, to all attended stations, telegrams that were received over the Morse code. There were two Morse code operators in Cowra who spent probably 75 per cent of their shifts operating the Morse code method of communication. The area bounded by Lyndhurst (44km from Cowra), Eugowra (80km from Cowra), Grenfell (80km from Cowra) and Young (75km from Cowra) all received their telegrams from Cowra. The junior dispatched the inward telegrams and also hand wrote all the telegrams sent from these stations. It was a very busy job; I relieved in it for holidays and must confess I was hard put to keep up with it.

One of my first ventures into learning began shortly before I left Cowra, when Alec Gillies started a class in morse code operation. I was able to attend only two classes before I was transferred to the relief staff, but I learned the full morse code alphabet in the week between the classes. I did not think about this much until the night of the second class, when I found that I was the only one among a class of about 15 who had learned any more than half a dozen letters of the Morse code alphabet. It was the first time, with due modesty and humbleness, that I began to wonder if I had a capacity to learn that my colleagues seemed not to have, or whether it was simply I had no greater capacity, but a greater application. Whichever was the case, it served me well over a long period of time.

In this chapter I have covered all the duties I can recall were required of the juniors. There were always, of course, other duties required by the station master, but these as a rule were not too arduous. Once again, it was a place where I learned a lot and a place I look back on all these years later as having been an enjoyable work experience.

The roundhouse at Cowra Loco Depot during the time of the centenary celebrations on 1 November 1986 for the opening of the Demondrille to Cowra Railway. Since the author worked there, the roundhouse and depot ceased being a locomotive stabling and maintenance depot for the Department of Railways and is the home base for the Lachlan Valley Railway Co-op Society. Some of their locomotives were once rostered at Cowra. Shortly after the centenary celebrations, Cowra station was closed.   *John R Newland.*

THE WORKING OF A STEAM ERA DEPOT

IN THIS chapter I want to portray the workings of a smallish depot station in the steam era, by setting out the staff employed and the duties they each performed. I realise that this will not be biographical detail. However I believe it important in the overall context of my biography because it will give some indication of the vast difference between the operating railways of 1946 with those of the year 2005.

At about the time I was appointed to Cowra, the station master and his assistants were elevated from second class station master and second class assistant station masters to first class station master and first class assistants. Try as I may, I am not able to recall the name of the outgoing station master (who did not hold the grade) or the incoming station master. The only thing I can remember of him was that he took me aside one morning after the railmotor had departed for Eugowra and told me I was not to lift the 112lb cases of butter, which were 2 x 56lb cases wired together. He immediately issued a general order reinforcing his direction to me and at the same time nominating the leading porter and the porter shunters to tranship all two-tie cases of butter. Previously they had had a strange reluctance to do so!

The incumbent assistant station masters when I arrived were Charlie (Mr) Oliver who transferred to Taree and Eric (Mr) Riordan who transferred as Station Master, Woodstock.

The assistant station masters who replaced them were Alec Jones and Matt Cock. Alec Jones I recall had previously been at Blayney but I do not recall where Matt Cock came from. Alec Jones was an overweight man and a reformed alcoholic. He was a cantankerous man, difficult to work with, impossible to please and very critical of those with alcohol problems, but he never made any official complaints.

Matt Cock had an alcohol problem, but was entirely different. He was a gentle, kind man and, when sober, he would often share the work with everyone including juniors; he would get out with a broom and assist the junior to sweep the platform. Mind you, the next night the junior might have to take the yard for him and help him with the 6.00am

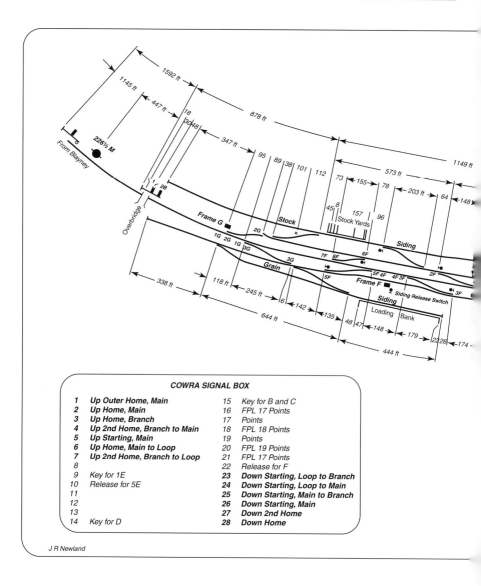

COWRA SIGNAL BOX

1	Up Outer Home, Main	15	Key for B and C
2	Up Home, Main	16	FPL 17 Points
3	Up Home, Branch	17	Points
4	Up 2nd Home, Branch to Main	18	FPL 18 Points
5	Up Starting, Main	19	Points
6	Up Home, Main to Loop	20	FPL 19 Points
7	Up 2nd Home, Branch to Loop	21	FPL 17 Points
8		22	Release for F
9	Key for 1E	23	Down Starting, Loop to Branch
10	Release for 5E	24	Down Starting, Loop to Main
11		25	Down Starting, Main to Branch
12		26	Down Starting, Main
13		27	Down 2nd Home
14	Key for D	28	Down Home

J R Newland

Traffic Report. As juniors we used to try and keep him off the telephone with Control and keep him awake. This was not something that happened on a daily or nightly basis, but it did happen quite often.

It was endemic of the railway system of the time in that some people exhibited certain disabilities, the most prevalent being alcoholism. I will return to this subject several times before I finish my story.

A RAILWAYMAN'S JOURNEY

COWRA

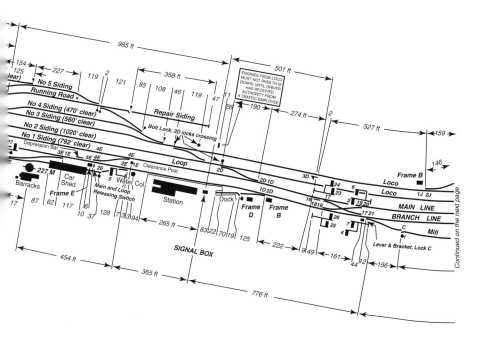

I lost track of Matt Cock when I left Cowra and years later I had contact with him when he had risen to be Special Class Station Master at Junee. I believe he still had a problem, but was he was able to conceal it because he worked in the day time only. It was a great pity; Matt Cock was a brilliant railwayman, who was greatly respected by grass roots railmen, but less so by his peers.

The staff employed at Cowra in 1946 (as my memory dictates to me) were as follows:

COWRA

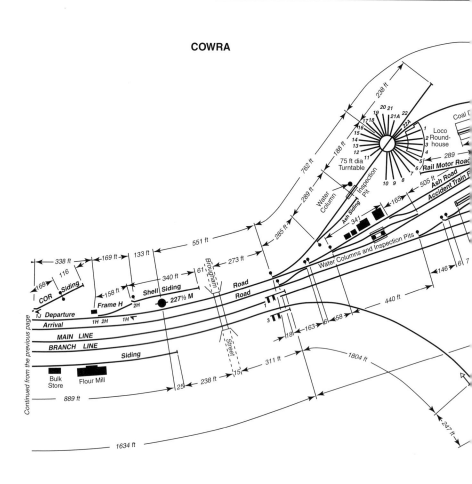

SALARIED STAFF:

Station Master, 1st Class	Name not recalled
Assistant Station Master, 1st Class	Mr A V Jones
Assistant Station Master, 1st Class	Mr M C Cock
Assistant Station Master, 2nd Class, Reducing Time* (Transferred)	Mr A J O'Donnell
Assistant Station Master, 2nd Class, Reducing Time*	Mr Ashley Gilbert
Assistant Station Master, 2nd Class, General Relief	Mr H Bushell
Clerk, 4th Class, OIC Booking Office and Telegraph	Mr J Kessey
Clerk, 6th Class, Morse operator and Booking Office	Mr 'Nick' Winter

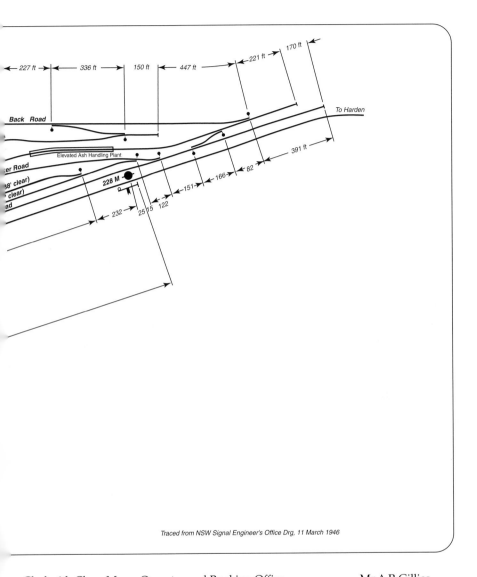

Traced from NSW Signal Engineer's Office Drg, 11 March 1946

Clerk, 6th Class, Morse Operator and Booking Office	Mr A R Gillies
Clerk, 6th Class, OIC Parcels Office	Mr R A Flynn
Clerk, 7th Class, Roster Clerk, SM's Clerk and timekeeper	Mr J Holman
Clerk, 4th Class, OIC Goods Shed	Mr S Clyde
Clerk, 6th Class, Assistant Goods Shed	Mr K Byrne
Clerk, Junior Grade, Goods Shed	Unknown

* Some positions had more hours or days in a fortnight than one officer could work without incurring overtime. The roster to cover the additional time was called a reducing time roster.

WAGES STAFF

Senior Shunter, Class 2	Jim Shepherd
Senior Shunter, Class 2	Pat Fogarty
Shunters	Two with each senior
Porter - Shunters	Bob Roots and Les Foster
Leading Porter Platform	Eric Hocking
Porter Class 2, Parcels Office	Pat Jordan
Leading Porter, Goods Shed	'Tiger' Payne
Porters Goods Shed	Two positions
Junior Porter, Telegraph	Cyril Coble
Junior Porters, General	Three positions
Lad Gatekeeper	Denny Ellis

The District Superintendent Lithgow administered the area. The superintendent was Mr C M Thomson; his Assistant District Superintendent was Mr 'Hoot' Gibson. The area traffic inspector was Mr L B Mather.

Cowra in those years was fortunate to have one of the many small refreshment rooms that scattered the State. There was a manageress and I think three other staff. My main memory of it is how polished the brasses and linos were.

The second class reducing time assistant station masters mentioned shared their time between Blayney and Cowra, working two days a fortnight at Blayney. Of the two, Jack 'Tragedy' O'Donnell was one of those unfortunate fellows whom trouble followed. If there were a major catastrophe at either Cowra or Blayney, the betting would be Jack O'Donnell would be on duty, not necessarily responsible for what had happened, in fact rarely responsible, just unlucky. He was a good officer and pleasant person, but he was very excitable, which I am afraid got him into more trouble than anything else did. After Jack was promoted to fifth class station master, to where I do not remember, Ashley Gilbert took his place. While I was not long at Cowra after he arrived, I remember a very caring, compassionate man. Ashley Gilbert only had to suggest something be done and it was. To the great sadness of all his colleagues he died of cancer about 2 years after I left Cowra. He was in his early forties. While I have never questioned my own faith, I did at that early stage in life wonder why a man of such infinite goodness should be struck with cancer. I suppose I do not have an answer yet, but am able to rationalise circumstances more sagely today. In the course of this story will be told the life of our daughter and, difficult as it was, the same rationale had to be applied to her life.

Every station had what was called Staff and Duty Sheets. They outlined the duties of every member of the staff. Directions were that they were to be exhibited for the information of all staff, (so that none could plead ignorance thereof). They were generally found in the station master's office, hanging behind the door!

The Staff and Duty Sheets for the salaried staff at Cowra are set out in Appendix A, which completes the duties as I recall of each of the salaried staff at Cowra. In listing the duties I have, of course, relied on the knowledge that I gained later in my career.

The 'Staff and Duty' wages employees, set out in Appendix B, were to be found under those of the salary staff on the same board. The wages staff at Cowra included two porter-shunters; this was the only depot I encountered them. I dare say they were employed in other depots, but not in the Western Region. There was a set rate of pay for them and an award covering the grade of Porter-Shunter. Their hourly pay rate was obviously below that of a shunter. However, I think the third year rate equalled that of a first year shunter. It was a convenient grade for porters who had no ambition to leave Cowra, but also wanted promotion to the position of guard, eventually, at Cowra. By accepting the porter-shunter position they placed themselves ahead of other porters in the State wanting promotion as shunter to Cowra. Both of the incumbents became shunters and subsequently guards at Cowra, although Les Foster later transferred to Bathurst.

Cowra railway station in the early morning of its centenary, 1 November 1986, prior to the arrival of the special centenary tourist specials. Very little would have changed to the station buildings since the author commenced his career there. Some two months after the centenary celebrations, the station was closed. The Blayney—Cowra line closed in 1988 but was re-opened on 19 April 2000.
John R Newland.

THE GENERAL RELIEF JUNIOR PORTER

L ATE in January 1946, I was called to the station master's office and was advised that because a junior porter who lived in Cowra was to be employed in his home town as a probationary junior, it was proposed that I be transferred to the general relief staff with home station Glenbrook, to make way for him. The notice of transfer on this occasion was extended to six days.

So it was: once again, I packed my few belongings into the 'Globite' suitcase. They were a few more in number because I had bought myself a light brown check sports jacket and matching trousers at the Western Stores in Cowra, the first purchase I had made of clothing for myself. The pushbike, which by this time had been upgraded, was accompanying me as an essential part of my mobility.

I departed Cowra on a Sunday night for Glenbrook, not having any idea of where I would sleep the next night, or where, indeed, I would find lodgings. When I presented myself to the assistant station master, Glenbrook at around 4.30am, his first comment was:

"You won't find any bloody lodgings in Glenbrook," which did not fill me with joy.

I think I was due to sign on about 7.30am, no shift work here fortunately. Around 7.00am I asked the dumb question,

"Where could I get something to eat?"

The response was,

"You will not find any bloody thing in this place to eat."

In due course, 7.30am arrived and shortly after so did the station master. As he walked in one door the assistant station master walked out the other, there were no words exchanged.

The first thing the station master asked was,

"Where are you staying?"

He did not ask my name or tell me what his was. When I replied I did not know and that I was totally unfamiliar with the area he replied,

"Well do not expect to look for it in working hours!"

I was somewhat staggered, to say the least, at the reception I had received thus far. I remember asking again about getting something to eat around 9.00am. He pointed me in the direction of the only shop in Glenbrook which in those days, was about 10 minutes walk from the station. Co-incidentally, a family called Balcombe owned the store; some years later I was to marry a lady whose maiden name was Balcombe.

While I was out, the station master spoke to a relief assistant station master at Emu Plains regarding lodgings. His name was Jim Hartigan. He spent more time relieving traffic inspectors, than he did SMs or ASMs and was feared up and down the mountains by juniors as much as any one else. He had in fact relieved the inspector at Cowra while I was there. Whatever Jim Hartigan was, he was a caring person and personally arranged board and lodgings for me with a Mrs Whittaker on the Mulgoa Road at Jamisontown, which was on the outskirts of Penrith on the southern side.

The station master took some pity on me and let me get an early afternoon train down to Emu Plains. From there, after meeting Jim Hartigan, I was directed how to get to the Mulgoa Road. It was not easy juggling the Globite case on the bike to ride some three miles. I found Mrs Whittaker a kindly soul who was widowed and had a son who was profoundly deaf. Because he was deaf he had not learned to speak, his mother being the only person with whom he could communicate. I enjoyed my time there with four other

Glenbrook railway station situated between Penrith and Valley Heights in the Lower Blue Mountains looking in the direction towards Sydney in September 1984. Some 10 years after the author served there, the line was electrified.					*John R Newland.*

lodgers, two girls and two boys plus me. It was the first time in my life I had lived in a house where there were young women. I was very reserved (probably shy is a better term) and found, in time, that reserve broken by the older of the two girls, who was probably in her mid-twenties, and a deeply religious person. I found it satisfying to have someone of the opposite sex who would talk to me and to whom I could talk to without being uncomfortable or embarrassed.

I used to ride the push bike to Emu Plains to catch 'Stumpy' at around 6.55am. These trains were then, and had been for a long time, and continued so for a long time, the school trains. They were worked by 32 Class locomotives and ran unassisted to Mount Victoria with a 5-car LUB–LOB–LIB– or SOB close-coupled light suburban sets and weighed about 110 tons; I think the 32 Class single load from Valley Heights to Katoomba was 125 tons. They were very slow. For example, the running time from Springwood to Linden was 27 minutes; today the XPT and Interurbans take 9 minutes. On Saturday mornings they did not run, so I was left to ride the bike to Glenbrook all the way up Lapstone Hill. I very early found what I thought was a very easy way of negotiating Lapstone Hill.

In those days the cement trucks had just started hauling cement from Kandos and Charbon, the NSWGR finally having agreed they could not keep up the demand for wagons. These trucks, like 'Stumpy' in those days were very slow and ran in almost a continuous stream on Saturday mornings. The trick was to ride the bike to the start of the

Another view of Glenbrook railway station showing the yard layout in September 1984.
John R Newland.

Emu Plains railway station situated west of the Nepean River at Penrith and the lower slopes of the Blue Mountains in September 1984. The author used to ride his push bike each day to this station to catch 'Stumpy' to report for duty at Glenbrook. John R Newland.

incline and wait for a cement truck. When it passed I was to get on the bike, catch it up and hang onto some part of the truck's table, usually a rope ring and let it haul me up Lapstone. Just before we reached the top I used to let go. The truck drivers, to my knowledge, never knew. The only thing that used to get tired was my right arm! I also remember on a Saturday afternoon returning from Glenbrook. I was riding down Lapstone, head down and tail up, when the dynamo light on the front left hand fork came loose and became entangled in the spokes, the front wheel of course collapsed and I came off at quite a pace. Fortunately I was not hurt, apart from some pretty horrendous bruising. A cement truck came to my rescue and took me into Penrith.

The duties of the junior at Glenbrook were pretty basic: attend the ticket barrier for each train, keep the station premises clean, do the collected ticket returns and attend to the signal lights. The station master was a very taciturn man who said little that was not of a sarcastic nature. The assistants and he were constantly at loggerheads for reasons that I still do not know, and I thought it was demeaning of the station master to write the most mundane directions for the ASMs in a handover book. He used to watch them walk down the steps and come in the door on the Up side of the signal box. As they passed the edge of the building the station master used to leave via the Down platform door so that he left with the building between him and the ASM.

Glenbrook won the Western Districts Garden Competition for many years. The station master was an expert gardener who spent as much time as he could in his garden. The junior of course also spent much time, digging, weeding and raking the platform, which was a daily requirement. The only time I earned his wrath was over a simple thing. No 17B the pick-up in the morning had detached a louvre van, while I was out doing signal lights. As I passed it I mentally noted the number of it. When I returned to the signal box after finishing the lights he asked me to go and get the number of the van. When I told him what it was he abused me and told me never to try and pull stunts like that on him and to go and get the right number. It was no use arguing so I went, but before I did so I wrote it down on the blotter in the train register book. I took a piece of paper with me and recorded the number and came back and gave it to him. When I did he did not say a word, but looked at the blotter. He still did not say a word, but there was however, a subtle difference in his attitude towards me for the short time I was there after that.

I should take time out at this point to mention signal lamps. At nearly every station in those days, kerosene signal lamps illuminated the signals during the night. Equally, at nearly every station it was the junior's job to fill and trim the signal lamps twice a week. The lamps would stay lit for seven days when filled with kerosene. Generally, signal lamps were changed on Mondays and checked for even flame and cleanliness on Thursdays. At some stations, a tricycle was provided with a lamp rack holding six lamps on the back of it. At other places, more particularly on busy double line sections, the lamps had to be carried. Provided for this purpose was a Number 8 galvanised wire handle that had a spring at the apex of the carrying point. They were, in fact, something like the old time handles that could be bought for carrying kerosene buckets and four gallon drums. On Mondays, the lamps were filled and cleaned, the lenses polished, the wicks trimmed and lit in the lamp room which every station seemed to have, the exceptions being small branch line stations.

I used to like to have them alight about an hour before I took them outside. By doing this I was able to set the wicks correctly and see that they were all burning evenly. Probably about half of the lamps would be out by the time the signals were reached. This was especially so in windy conditions on the mountains. The best method of relighting them was to take the old lamp out of the signal, reached after climbing the steel ladder. With two lamps in one hand and the other being used for support, it was necessary to take it off the ladder when each rung was climbed. Safe practice? Then standing on the enclosed platform at the top of the signal post, I would place the fresh lamp in the signal casing. These lamps all had a hinged copper top, which could be opened to expose the wick in the lamp. To light them, most people used to have a piece of tie wire that was shaped at one end so a match could be fitted into it. The matchbox was held at the opening of the lamp and the match struck and lowered onto the wick. This method was very effective, and in fact the only way to relight lamps high up on signals when strong winds were blowing.

I had two interesting experiences with signal lamps, the first being at Wentworth Falls. I was walking towards Katoomba to light the Up Distant signal. It was raining with a strong wind blowing that would freeze the proverbial. With my head down trying to keep the rain from my face I came across the ganger who was coming in to his ganger's shed. He asked what I was doing, and I told him, not altogether graciously. He took me by the shoulders, turned me round and pointed toward the Up Distant. I had walked passed it by about two hundred yards! Obviously, it was the first time I had been to Wentworth Falls. Equally obviously I had made the cardinal mistake of not keeping a look out for the signal wire from the signal box to the signal. I often wonder how much further I would have needlessly walked in those conditions but for the ganger.

The second experience was more exhilarating, or scary, depending upon how good your nerves were. The signal was again an Up Distant, this time at Newnes Junction. Again the weather conditions were atrocious. A gale force wind, which made riding the pull trike into it nigh impossible, was gusting from the southwest. The rails were wet as well and every time an attempt was made to pull the arm on the trike the back wheel would lose traction and drop off onto the sleepers. Very uncomfortable when you were riding it. I had therefore to walk into the wind with the two lamps, my match holder and

Springwood railway station situated between Valley Heights and Katoomba in the Lower Blue Mountains in May 1984. This was one of the several stations in the Blue Mountains where the author was the relief junior porter.   *John R Newland.*

matches. This signal mast, made of light steel, the highest one I had seen, was situated on the top of a cutting. However, access to the signal was quite easy.

When I arrived and looked up at the signal I could see that it was moving at least 12 inches at the top with every strong gust of wind. I am not afraid of heights, but climbing this signal was something that caused me to think twice. As I thought, I realised I had no option but to do so. I lit the lamps at the bottom, hoping they would be alight when I arrived at the top of the signal. With two lamps in one hand and the other used for support, it was necessary to take it off the ladder when each rung is climbed. No such luck! Both lamps were out. I put the upper light in its case and put the wire and match trick to work. To my absolute anguish when I struck the match against the matchbox it slipped from my hand and gently floated all the way down onto the Up main line. In my anxiety to retrieve it, I had let the match that was alight to go out. Of course, I had to descend to retrieve the matches and go through the process again. I might say here that a resolution was made, NEVER to leave from a lamp room without two boxes of matches in the pockets! It is also worth noting here that we were provided with no protective clothing whatsoever. There are very few places today where kerosene lamps light signals.

After leaving Glenbrook, I next relieved at Springwood. Two juniors were employed, one in the early morning and one in the afternoon about 2.00pm. Because I was still boarding at Penrith, the resident junior agreed to work the early morning shift. This was a much more harmonious station, where a station master, two assistants, a booking clerk, a safeworking porter and the two juniors were employed. The junior's duties were the usual cleaning, barrier duties and the hated collected ticket return. They also attended the parcels office, which was reasonably busy in 1947. There was one unusual duty at Springwood, which was at lunchtime, to go to the station master's residence and return with a hot meal. Because he was too proud to be seen taking the dishes home when he had finished, the junior had to return the dirties. Because of his flamboyance with the fairer sex, he was nicknamed 'Pusher'. For what reason, my then naivety did not allow me to understand. To me, his face resembled the south end of a northbound camel.

My first brush with a member of the public came at Springwood. A very well presented gentleman came into the parcels office after the arrival of *The Fish* one evening and asked for a COD parcel. I have forgotten the value of the parcel; it was a significant amount however. When the owner pulled out his chequebook to pay for it, I apologised to him and said I could not accept a cheque in payment for a COD parcel, as the regulations were very specific in this. He became very angry, accusing me of being an upstart and doubting his integrity. The reply that I was simply carrying out my directions further angered him. I then referred the matter to the assistant station master. When he entered the parcels office he greeted the gentleman by his Christian name, which did not fill me with joy. When I explained to him that the gentleman wanted to pay for the COD by cheque and that I could not accept it, the ASM turned to him, and to my satisfaction, said that I was quite right in what I had done. He also said that he would accept the responsibility and for me to accept the cheque. The guy still left the station with a poor opinion of me, I am sure.

One of the most painful and unforgettable events I have ever experienced had its beginning at Springwood. I was still boarding at Penrith and used to leave the bike at Emu Plains. The only method of getting home late in the evening was to ask the driver of one of the many goods trains that ran, all of which stopped at Springwood, to let me off at Emu Plains. The hand brakes were let off by the guard after the descent from Katoomba while the fireman took water and de-ashed the fire. If a driver agreed to let me off at Emu Plains I used to take water for the fireman, then ride on the engine to Emu Plains.

On this occasion the driver agreed to let me off, but said I should ride in the brakevan with the guard. The brakevan was an LHG which were fitted with sliding doors. As we approached Emu Plains, I thought he was going a bit hard and I tried to open the door to see exactly where we were and to try and attract the driver's attention. The door opened wide enough for me to get sideways through it but it would not budge any further, so I got both hands on the handles using my body as a lever. Suddenly it gave and I went straight out onto the platform! I was going so fast when I landed on both feet on the platform that my legs could not keep pace and I fell and slithered along the platform for some distance before stopping right at the Penrith end of it.

I had skin off on my hands, arms and knees. I was in a bit of a mess, but had no option other than to get on the bike and ride home. A bath would have been the thing but lighting a chip heater at 2.00am would have not pleased my fellow boarders. The final straw was when I went to get into bed, I found that one of the boarders had 'short sheeted' my bed! No one, possibly fortunately, owned up the next day. I was so stiff and sore the next morning every step was painful. Nevertheless I still went to work.

I worked on the mountains at various locations, such as Woodford, which was a shared job with Newnes Junction and at Leura for one day on Good Friday 1947 in the cloak room. Cloak room tickets were threepence each then. I do not exaggerate when I say two of us selling cloak room tickets filled the quite large parcel office at Leura with luggage to a height well over my head. We took something like £4 in cloak tickets. Fortunately, I was not there on the Monday when everyone started going home. The thing I did not understand, and in fact still do not, was why so many people brought luggage on the train and then cloaked it at their rail destination until they returned home.

I had moved to Blaxland and used to travel regularly up the mountains on No 23 *Caves Express*. While I was still pretty shy with the opposite sex, the head girl, who had a regular roster, invited me into the buffet for a cup of coffee and fruit cake. I discovered fairly quickly that payment for this was doing the washing up! This became a regular feature of my trips on the *Caves Express*. I enjoyed it for two reasons, one the fruit cake and two, the pleasant company, in that order!

It was around the end July of 1947 that I received a telegram to report to Warrimoo at 7.00am on a Monday. I was to obtain the keys from the station master at Glenbrook. Blaxland, Warrimoo and Faulconbridge were listed in the Sidings and Platforms book as being unattended. This information was meant to convey the stations were not open for normal transactions and were unattended. Each station was in fact manned by a lady platform attendant, who was in charge of the coaching accounts only. To all intents and purposes they were fully fledged coaching stations, selling all tickets, workman's weeklies, weekly tickets and season tickets. The controlling station for Blaxland and Warrimoo was Glenbrook, while Springwood controlled Faulconbridge. The hours of duty were from 7.00am to 7.00pm Monday to Friday, with lengthy breaks in the middle of the day, for a 44-hour week. Saturday finishing was 1.00pm.

The lady attendant at Warrimoo, who lived in the old sandstone house built in 1876, which still stands between Warrimoo and Valley Heights was, to say the least, not very mindful of her personal hygiene and somewhat erratic in her office procedures. To this point in my short career, I had not had any experience in formulating accounts or in compiling daily accounts such as blue summaries etc. The accounts were an absolute mess. There were demands from Audit* for some of the previous month's accounts.

The only records she had kept for the month were the daily ticket sales for rail, weekly and season tickets and the amount of cash remitted each day. There were no daily summaries and no daily balances kept which made a difficult task even more difficult. On the second day, Mr Mick Farrell, the Acting Chief Inspector Lithgow arrived to see if the junior at Warrimoo was capable of relieving the attendants at the three stations. He recognised me from Cowra, but had not recalled my name. As soon as he arrived he told me I would be OK and he was going to get on the next Down train, ten minutes away, and go back to Lithgow saying,

"If I had known it was you I would not have left Lithgow."

I protested about the condition of the accounts and suggested he look at them. His reply was,

"Do your best, and if you get into trouble, ring me." He still got on the train.

I spent many hours trying before I finally balanced the previous month's account current. I would have had some difficulty ringing Mick Farrell, as the poor man collapsed and died of a heart attack some days later. The station master at Glenbrook must have had some conversation with Mick Farrell, because he also took an interest, rather belatedly

---

* Audit was the name of the office to which all accounts were sent on a monthly basis. If the Audit Office found a discrepancy in the accounts which was a shortfall in cash they sent an 'AA [Audit Advice] note'. The person responsible for the shortage was called on to make good the amount.

in what had happened and what was happening at Warrimoo. The station consisted of a very small building with one room, which was disgustingly dirty.

Within a week of going to Warrimoo, I was able to get board at Blaxland, firstly with the porter from Springwood for a week. I could not get out of there quickly enough; I had never before experienced a husband and wife fighting like Kilkenny cats. Then, I boarded with a family who had originally come from Nyrang Creek near Canowindra and had known many of my forebears on my mother's side. This was really a home away from home. I enjoyed my stay there and for many years kept in contact with the family. When we were first married and went to live at Springwood, the lady who had moved there, obtained a flat for us.

For most of the next twelve months I either relieved at Blaxland, Warrimoo or Faulconbridge. I was utilised to provide for their holidays and for a lengthy time was at Blaxland vice* the lady attendant who was sick. When I had completed these, I was put on the reducing time roster that worked Mount Victoria eight days a fortnight and each of the lady attendants one day a fortnight. I moved to Mount Victoria to work this roster. It was necessary to catch 'Stumpy' (No 176 those days) at 6.00am from Mount Victoria. The Blaxland and Warrimoo days called for attending to *The Chips* which followed *The Fish* and terminated at Valley Heights. The next train to Mount Victoria was No 85, which was about two hours behind *The Chips*.

If I could not hitch a ride on the road to Mount Victoria, it made long days and short nights for these three days. One of the last jobs I had before leaving the Blue Mountains was at Mount Victoria, where I relieved the backshift Porter Class 1. Shunting was a necessary qualification for this job, because some carriage shunting with the carriages of the evening trains to form the early morning return services to the city was required. I will long remember one early morning when I had gone in between and was kneeling on my knees to couple up the hook drawgear carriages. This action was uneventful until I went to get out from underneath after doing up the airhoses. As I was getting out, I felt my head for my cap. It was not there. The peak of it was firmly held by the carriage diaphragms. Another lesson learned; keep your head down and hold the coupling over the shoulder.

To put things into perspective, I bought my first biro pen and orange slice biscuit on the same day at Blaxland from Harrison's Newsagency and General Store (long since gone) in late 1947. It was also in 1947 that the working week was reduced from 44 hours to 40 hours per week, with the ideal of five-day working weeks. This did not happen on the railways. The daily working time, almost without exception, was reduced, so that the majority of employees worked at least an eleven day fortnight. It was a very long time

---

* While this word has obvious other meanings, it was always used in Railway language to indicate a person would take the place of someone else. Hence when I went to Blaxland I was vice the lady attendant. When anyone was appointed to a position on promotion or as a transfer in the grade, the staff change advice indicated they were vice so and so transferred on promotion, or transferred in the grade.

before any thought of obeying the spirit, or indeed the Government direction, of the five-day week concept was given by the railways administration.

While I was on the mountains, I qualified in shunting and all systems of safe working. The examiner was Jim Hartigan, who became acting chief inspector after the death of Mick Farrell. He was a good examiner, who was tough and if passed by him, you possessed a reasonable knowledge. The good thing about him was that once he saw that you knew a little, he would take a different line and almost became an instructor. He would add to your answers or, as in my case at Springwood, take me into the signal box and give demonstrations on how to fill out the emergency safeworking forms. Jim Hartigan was a man I admired for his integrity and forthrightness.

The time I spent in this area was one of the happiest of my life, on my own. On the first Sunday of my time boarding at Penrith, I went to what was then the Methodist Church, which was in Henry Street. After the service, a lady named Mrs Winifred Hodgson who then was, and continued for many years to be, the church pianist, saw this stranger. She introduced herself as the gatherer of waifs and strays and wanted to know from whence I had strayed. I was invited to her home and met her two daughters and son. This kind invitation began a friendship with all members of the family that still exists today with one of the daughters.

Her husband was a fuelman at Valley Heights. In 1945 he was rushed from there after collapsing and was operated on in the Nepean Hospital for removal of his appendix, which had unfortunately burst. He died of peritonitis a few days later. She was a widow for 44 years. One of my early *faux pas* came when her sister, who lived not far away, invited me to lunch one Sunday. Now this country lad knew that in the country you had dinner at midday (or at least my family did). Tea was the evening meal and lunch was at three or thereabouts in the afternoon. It did not dawn on him that city people had lunch in the middle of the day. Imagine my embarrassment when I arrived around three!

I spent many hours with the Hodgson family. I regularly visited them for the 12 months I had remaining on the Blue Mountains. On my days off I used to help mow the lawns and cut their wood. The son at this time was still going to school and the girls both worked locally. Mrs Hodgson would have liked to see me link up with the youngest daughter. The only spark between us, however, was the friendship still existing today. Mrs Hodgson was a saintly woman who worked to great effect in the church and faced a constant struggle to maintain a home for her family when her husband died. I will forever be indebted to the family; they gave companionship and a sense of belonging somewhere that had been missing in my life away from home. They will feature again in years to come in this epistle.

PORTER CLASS 1, NEWBRIDGE AND EUGOWRA

IN mid July of 1948, when I was about 19½, I ended my time as a relief junior porter by being appointed Porter Class 1 at Newbridge. I have been back to Newbridge recently and found it has, like so many other small country towns, become only a shell of the friendly community that it once was. When my father knew I was going to Newbridge, he asked if the storekeeper was named Oscar Bennett. He was, in fact. My father told me they had fought together in France in the war. During my time there they met again and re-fought the war. I learned more from that conversation about the conditions in the French trenches than I had in a lifetime from my father.

Newbridge was an important terminus in the early railway history. The line terminated there for a short period in the late 1870s. Evidence could still be seen where a turntable had once been.

Newbridge railway station situated between Bathurst and Blayney on a very pronounced curve looking in the direction towards Bathurst photographed from the road bridge in 1987.
I K Winney, ARHS Rail Resource Centre 8102.

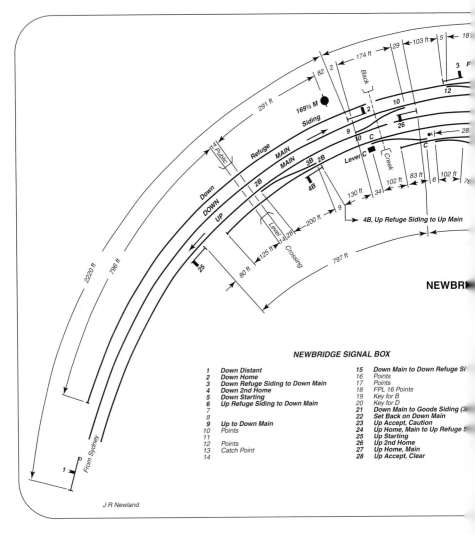

NEWBRIDGE SIGNAL BOX

1	Down Distant	15	Down Main to Down Refuge Si
2	Down Home	16	Points
3	Down Refuge Siding to Down Main	17	Points
4	Down 2nd Home	18	FPL 16 Points
5	Down Starting	19	Key for B
6	Up Refuge Siding to Down Main	20	Key for D
7		21	Down Main to Goods Siding (3
8		22	Set Back on Down Main
9	Up to Down Main	23	Up Accept, Caution
10	Points	24	Up Home, Main to Up Refuge
11		25	Up Starting
12	Points	26	Up 2nd Home
13	Catch Point	27	Up Home, Main
14		28	Up Accept, Clear

J R Newland

I was able to obtain board at the local pub, the Gladstone, named after a British prime minister who served four terms between 1868 and 1894. I determined after about a week to find something else as quickly as I could. The lodging at the hotel was satisfactory, however both the publican and his wife, especially, were determined that I was not going to live in their pub without spending money in the bar. I, of course, was as equally determined that I was not going to. After about a month, I was able to rent a semi-detached house and looked after myself. Fortunately for me, a fettler and his wife came to Newbridge and could not find anywhere to live so I sublet to them and was looked after by his wife. That beat 'batching' by a long margin!

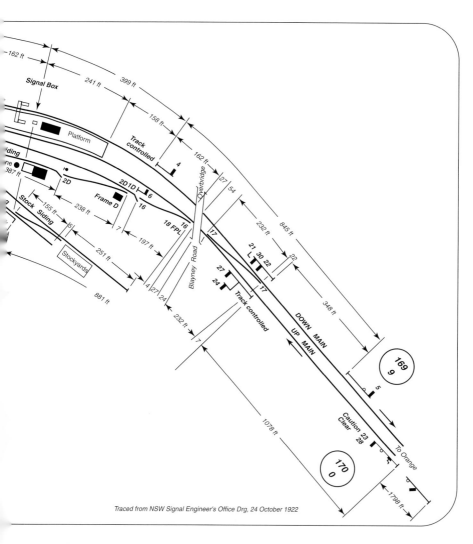

Traced from NSW Signal Engineer's Office Drg, 24 October 1922

Newbridge was a reasonable job: the usual signal lights to look after, the cleaning to do, the roping and sheeting of wool and some fodder, the unloading of the Darling Harbour truck, which was usually ticketed Blayney, out of Newbridge. This truck was attached to No 91 pick-up on Wednesdays and Saturdays. Generally, the train was taken forward and crossed over into the goods shed road on the Up side. Differences of opinion with the train controller arose when an Up train was in the Up refuge for another train to pass. Some of the Darling Harbour traffic was for the store at Hobby's Yards and had to be stored in the goods shed until delivery was effected.

In addition to that, the regulations stated that all goods traffic had to be dealt with through the goods shed. The train controllers demanded when a train was in the Up refuge, the traffic be unloaded onto the platform and then carried across two sets of lines to the goods shed. It was only on Wednesdays on stock days, that it was likely to happen. This was the cause of the senior inspector from Bathurst being at Newbridge on a number of occasions. I must say he generally agreed with the station master. It obviously was not feasible to carry bales of wool packs across the lines!

The other duty for the Porter Class 1 was to be in charge of the safeworking from 2.20pm until 4.30pm daily Monday to Friday. Safeworking at Newbridge involved Tyers one wire three position block instruments on the sections to and from Gresham. Automatic signalling was in operation westwards to Murrobo. It is necessary to note that the old Tyers block instrument in use to Gresham did not feature starting signal control, which meant that it was possible for Newbridge's Up Starting signal to be cleared at any time, even if the section was occupied. (See Orange East Fork section for more.)

I should explain for those who read this and are not familiar with signalling that the starting signal is the signal that gives a driver permission to enter into the section ahead. If the system of safeworking is based on double lines, he needs no other authority. On single line sections the driver must be in possession of the token for the section, a guarantee that he will meet no other train. Block instrument control on starting signals on double lines is where starting signals work in conjunction with the block instruments, that is the

Newbridge railway station and part of the yard looking in the direction towards Bathurst in 1987.   *I K Winney, ARHS Rail Resource Centre 8102.*

starting signal assumes the stop position when the train passes and the block instrument shows the *Train on Line* indication, they are known as starter controlled sections. It is not possible for the signalman to obtain *Line Clear* for another train until the first train has arrived at the station in advance and the signalman has given *Train Arrived* on his instrument. In automatic signalling areas, the accepting signal is the signal that controls the entrance to the signalling area controlled from the signal box in advance.

Newbridge was another station where the station master and his assistants did not get on well. The station master continually referred to his assistants as 'them floggin' nighties', a throwback to the time when assistant station masters were known as Night Officers. The station master was then probably in his early sixties and was from the old school of autocrats. I did not have any problem with him. I did, however, have little to say and kept as much as possible away from him which, given the duties, was not all that difficult. He was without doubt the worst penman I ever encountered.

The two assistants, to my mind, were both good officers, one of whom I came into contact with later and the other was a very gentle older man, whose son I later regarded as one of the most efficient railwaymen I knew in my career. There was no open hostility as there was at Glenbrook, but the attitude of the station master to them left them without any desire to be friendly to him. I sometimes wondered if he spoke to his wife in a manner similar to that he used with his staff. If he did, poor woman!

The view of Newbridge railway station and the very pronounced curve looking west, in the direction away from Bathurst in 1987.   I K Winney, ARHS Rail Resource Centre 8108.

I was still at Newbridge in the great coal miners' strike of 1949. Those who remember the strike will recall it was the time that Prime Minister Chifley finally used the army to break the strike. Train services were reduced to those that were absolutely essential. There were something like two trains a day running through Newbridge. I was firstly given my holidays. When the strike had not been settled by then, I was stood off without pay until the settlement. I was off for seven weeks. During this time I went rabbit trapping with my father and brother and digging out rabbit warrens on a property at Murga, some 20km from Eugowra. Although I made a considerable amount more than wages, I was not tempted to that life. The future in that game seemed not to be one I wanted to share in.

I remember the great day when Prime Minister Ben Chifley came to Newbridge, which was of course in his electorate. He spoke in front of the pub, as a run up to his 1949 re-election campaign to a large gathering of faithful and, I suspect, infidels to his cause. He became leader of the opposition in December 1949. The publican was happy, probably on two counts!

It was about June of 1949 that the staff wages clerk, whom I had come to know quite well when I was on the relief, rang and asked me would I like to transfer to Eugowra as a Porter Class 1. The immediate inclination was "yes"; for once again I was close to home. He warned me however, that the traffic inspector at Cowra had been instructed to go to Eugowra and find out why porters would not stay there. He was to tell the station master that his conduct was such that it would be preferable to transfer him than to keep sending porters there. That information made me hesitate, however, because while I did not mind Newbridge, there was nothing there for a young single man. I went to Eugowra. I have not yet said that there was an ulterior motive in going to Eugowra, but approximately five miles from where I had lived for many years, lived a very attractive brunette who seemed to be constantly in my thoughts.

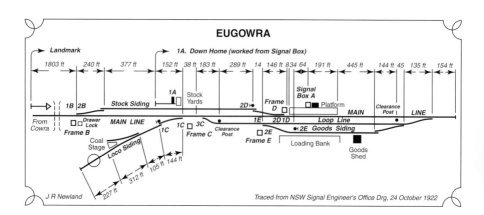

The only reason Eugowra was a Porter Class 1 position was that on alternate Saturday afternoons, he was there to dispatch the pick-up and the railmotor to Cowra and had to be qualified in electric staff working. The station master really deserved the reputation that he had. He was impossible to work with. He was disliked by the townspeople, by the carriers, by the fettling ganger and, most of all, by the traffic inspector.

An example of his bastardry was at harvest time when the silos were receiving wheat. The silos used to start operating at 7.30am and close officially at 5.00pm. The railway yard gates were officially open from 8.30am to 4.30pm. He was such a difficult person that at 4.25pm on the first day of wheat receival, he went to the trucks waiting to unload and directed their drivers to take their trucks out of the yard because the gates were closing at 4.30pm. He intimated he would not allow trucks to stand in the yard overnight. Let me assure you this caused a ruckus, because almost from time immemorial wheat trucks had stood overnight in queues in railway yards. When he was threatened by one of the local farmers, he went straight to his office and rang the police.

The local constable, after suggesting to the station master that, as it was harvest time, could he not bend the rules somewhat and, after getting a point blank refusal, had to clear the trucks. I had said nothing but guessed that at 7.30 the next morning, the trucks

Railmotor No 38 reversing into Eugowra railway station in 1978 to link up with its trailer car at the platform. The view of this terminus station displays the yard layout.
ARHS Rail Resource Centre 7803.

Another view of Eugowra railway station 1978. The single line from Canowindra to Eugowra opened on 11 December 1922. Services were suspended on 2 March 1992 due to a failure of a bridge and was never restored. The station building was later demolished.

ARHS Rail Resource Centre 7803.

would be waiting and ready to unload and the gates would be shut until 8.30am. I took one of the farmers aside during the ruckus in the afternoon and suggested that he ring the traffic inspector at Cowra and tell him what was going on. I was supplied with a key to the gates and was there to open them next morning at 7.30am. When the station master saw the trucks coming into the yard at 7.30am from his home he was less than pleased. At 8.30am when we were to sign on he went berserk and threatened me with physical violence and suspended me from duty for wilful disobedience.

The situation changed when the traffic inspector arrived on the railmotor. He first took me down to the goods shed and took a statement from me and then one from the station master. The station master was directed to forget having suspended me, because firstly, he did not have the authority and secondly, if he did not, that he, the traffic inspector, would suspend him. The gate problem was solved by giving the silo operator, despite strong objection from the station master, a key to open them in the morning and to close in the afternoon. The final indignity for the station master was, at the traffic inspector's direction, the loaded wheat trucks were allowed to stay in the yard overnight. In the afternoon, before he left, the inspector again told the station master that as he was in a small country location, that he should seek to co-operate with the local people. The response was that he would carry out every obstructive regulation there was and that nobody could stop him. The problem was he did know the regulations.

I recall one hot windy day, whilst working on a truck of lucerne hay at the dump, as I was roping and tying two tarpaulins on it, I saw a lady walk onto the platform with a small parcel and go into the office. I kept tying the tarpaulins so that they would not blow away. A few minutes later the station master came to the door and called out to me to come and serve the lady. I said nothing and went to the office. The lady was standing at the counter waiting and had stood there while he called me.

When I came in sweaty and dirty, I saw that he was reading the Salaried Officers' Gazette. I could detect that the lady was not amused, although she said nothing to me. Some time later, I saw the lady, who came from a farm some distance away, in the street. She told me he did not speak to her, but after what seemed an age, got up and called to me. She also told me she had written an official complaint to the Commissioner. In due course, there was another visit from the traffic inspector and another statement was taken in the goods shed. I was absolutely livid at the time, but I had adopted an attitude of not speaking at all if I could avoid it. That was the easiest way of surviving.

The crews of the railmotor who booked off for four hours at Eugowra refused to go anywhere near the station office. Although there was nowhere set aside for them to spend the four hours, they stayed in the motor rather than go near the station master. I renewed acquaintances again with the legendary Walter Ramage, who on one occasion threatened to clobber the station master with the Canowindra-Eugowra staff if he did not leave him alone while he was shunting. This, of course, brought a report to the District Superintendent Lithgow, from the station master. Another visit from the traffic inspector with more statements, in the goods shed from me, who funnily enough did not see or hear Guard Ramage threaten the station master (I am sure the TI would have been disappointed if I had!). Of course, no one else did either.

I was 21 on 16 December 1949. About 5 days after that, I was offered a list with 107 shunters' jobs on it. I accepted about 50 of them and was appointed to my seventh preference which was Reducing Time Shunter, Parkes.

During my Eugowra time, I bought my first motor car, a new Ford Anglia sedan. As I did not have the cash to pay for it and to get the money, my father had to guarantee me. After the Commercial Banking Company of Sydney in Canowindra had approved the loan, I had to sign 12 promissory notes of about £12 each, which were held at the Bank. Each month, after payment, one was cancelled. A far cry from the methods of obtaining and dealing with credit today. As for the car, I have to say it was not the best car I had owned. It was an 8 horsepower job with a maximum speed of 50 miles per hour. I very rarely drove it over 35 mph. At any faster speed, especially on gravel roads, it was too difficult to control. I forget the amount that I paid for it, but it was something in the order of £240. Having wheels made contact with that brunette much easier! I kept it for seven years and when I traded it in on a Hillman Minx in 1956, it did not owe me anything.

I was transferred to Parkes in February 1950 and did not have any contact with the station master of Eugowra until in 1953. When we went to live at Springwood, he was the station master at Valley Heights. I recall his name very vividly but will refrain from naming him. Up to the time that I had gone to Eugowra, my readers will have noted that I worked with some station masters who were somewhat difficult to please, but I had generally enjoyed good working relationships with them.

The Eugowra situation was different. I could not, even though I originally tried hard, work harmoniously with the station master. He was, as I said earlier, impossible for anyone to work with. He had a very stormy relationship with his wife and on more than one occasion I heard them shouting at one another while he was at lunch. I can truthfully say that Eugowra was the only place that I was pleased to leave, even if it put me another 35 miles further away from that brunette.

A goods train awaiting departure from Eugowra railway station in 1947.
J L Buckland, ARHS Rail Resource Centre 10933.

SHUNTER, PARKES

PARKES was somewhat of a shock to the system, for after having daywork for the majority of the time after leaving Cowra, the exceptions being very short periods at Mount Victoria and Wallerawang, I had not worked any backshift at all. I had worked some early morning and afternoon shifts, generally from around 6.00am and 2.00pm. This was about to change to full time shift work as a shunter which continued in all positions until 1979 when I finally completed my career of shiftwork.

I left Eugowra on a Saturday morning for Parkes where I was to commence on the following Monday. However I had to find accommodation and, after introducing myself to the station master and roster clerk, I went into the yard and enquired from the shunters where I may find board. I was fortunate and was installed in a boarding house that morning, where I stayed until I left Parkes. As boarding houses went, it was average, very noisy in the daytime, but the meals were wholesome, though the quantity was lacking at times. However, to my mind, it was far better than boarding at the 'pub' near the station where many of the railways staff boarded.

I went back to the shunting yard after unpacking my gear at the boarding house. It was usual to give a shunter a week to learn the yard and the duties associated with being a shunter. I, however, was to have 14 days because I was to relieve the senior shunters five days each fortnight. The staff was rostered 11 days, so it meant that I was to spend nearly half my time as the senior shunter. It was a tall order to go from being a Porter Class 1 at Eugowra and a fortnight later to be in charge of a shunting yard the size of Parkes.

During anyone's lifetime, there are things that stand out and stick in the memory virtually forever. One such occasion was on a Saturday afternoon when I went back to the yard. The senior shunter told me that each road (or siding) in the yard was named and that there was a daytime and a night time signalling code for each of them. He commenced by telling me that the roads in Parkes were from the main line, the weighbridge, new road, middle road, back road, Nos 4, 5 and 6. On the Up side of the line storage sidings were the long road and the short road and the access across the main line to them was known as through 31 (the number of the points lever). When he told me

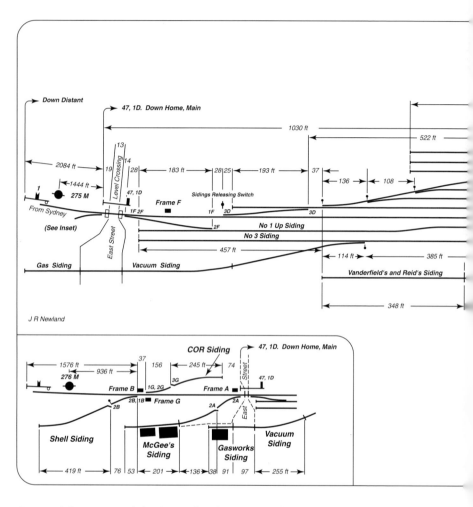

these and demonstrated the day and night time signals, he said to me,

"Now repeat them" which I did without error. He then said to me,

"Gawd, you're sharp!"

From that moment on I was known as 'Cactus'. I doubt that many of the staff at Parkes knew what my Christian name was.

The shunting staff at Parkes consisted of two head shunters, Sid Hobson and 'Matey' Blackett, three senior shunters, one reducing time shunter (me) and six shunters. One head shunter signed on at 4.30am Tuesday to Friday and 12.30am on Mondays, the other signed on duty at 3.00pm on Mondays to Fridays. They were both characters in their own right; Sid Hobson stuttered like no other person I had known. He was a very competent head shunter. Working as his senior shunter was a pleasure.

PARKES

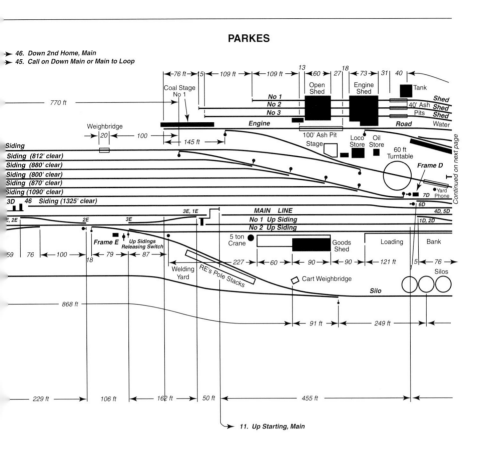

He would work out his moves and plan where he would form his trains. If you paid careful attention, because it was painful to see him trying to get out what he wanted to say, he made the job easy, no matter how busy it was. 'Matey' Blackett was a nice fellow but a panic merchant, who planned his moves as he went along. As a result, no one knew what he had next in mind, which made working with him difficult. On Tuesday stock nights, he 'dropped his bundle' when he put his foot inside the yard. The responsibilities got to him so much he later became a guard, and a very good one too.

When the head or senior shunters signed on duty, they received the shunter's list from the station master or assistant station master. This list contained instructions and information for the next 10 hours. It detailed the incoming and outgoing trains with the approximate arrival times and the scheduled departure times. Each incoming train was

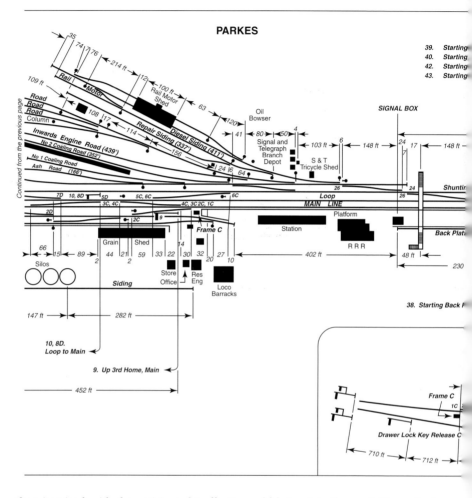

then itemised with the anticipated traffic it would bring into the yard. The outgoing trains were itemised, the type of locomotive to be employed, which of course dictated the load that the train could convey and itemised the traffic that each train was to convey. The stock wagon and other wagon book-outs were also listed.

Two Western depot stations are probably entitled to think of their depots as being the hub of the West. Dubbo is the station to which the title was generally given. In terms of tonnage through their yards, Parkes handled more trains and traffic than Dubbo. This was even so in the 1950s before the standard gauge line was extended beyond Broken Hill. Dubbo handled more stock trains than Parkes and was a far more difficult yard to shunt in than Parkes.

Trains arrived in Parkes from the south, particularly from Cootamundra and Forbes;

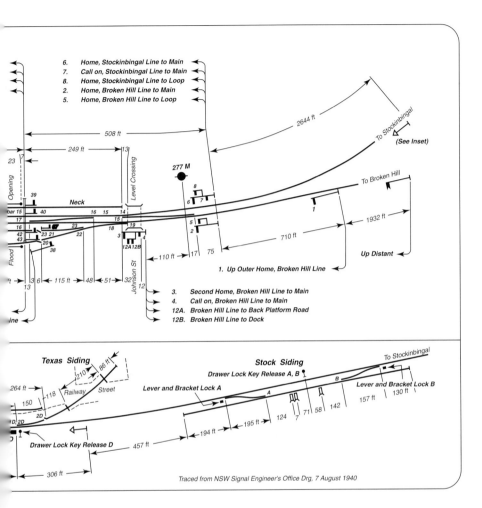

6. Home, Stockinbingal Line to Main
7. Call on, Stockinbingal Line to Main
8. Home, Stockinbingal Line to Loop
2. Home, Broken Hill Line to Main
5. Home, Broken Hill Line to Loop

1. Up Outer Home, Broken Hill Line
3. Second Home, Broken Hill Line to Main
4. Call on, Broken Hill Line to Main
12A. Broken Hill Line to Back Platform Road
12B. Broken Hill Line to Dock

Traced from NSW Signal Engineer's Office Drg, 7 August 1940

the West from Broken Hill, Condobolin and Tottenham; the North from Dubbo, and the East from Orange. Departing from Parkes, pick-up trains conveying Darling Harbour wagons ran to Forbes daily; then to Dubbo, serving especially Peak Hill twice weekly; to Condobolin twice weekly; and to Tottenham, serving Bogan Gate, Trundle, Tullamore, Albert and Tottenham. The heavy shunting shifts were the backshifts, especially on Sunday nights/Monday mornings, Tuesday nights/Wednesday mornings and Thursday nights/ Friday mornings. Afternoon shifts were busiest on Tuesdays, Thursdays, Fridays and Saturdays. The daywork shifts were the same every day.

On at least two days each week, and sometimes more, an additional shunting engine and shunter known as 'the extra shunter' were rostered to assist placement of sidings on the daywork. A quite significant portion of eastbound traffic leaving Parkes emanated from Parkes itself. The extra shunter was a non-rostered job; if the guards were light for time, the roster clerk would roster a guard, and if there was shortage of guards, the shunters received a day's overtime. I spent many rostered days off working as the extra shunter.

While I might not remember all the sidings in Parkes, some of them were: Baker's Brickworks and the stockyards on the Forbes side, McGee's flour mill, Vanderbilt and Reid's building and timber suppliers, the wheat silo, Shell, AMP oil siding (now Ampol), Caltex, Esso, AOR (Australian Oil Refineries), Golden Fleece and COR (Commonwealth Oil refinery, now BP), the goods shed, old loco sidings (which were the repair sidings), Per Way sidings, the *Silver City Comet* and railmotor servicing roads, and the bulk wheat terminal situated in the Parkes—Cookamidgera section.

The goods shed at Parkes was a nightmare for shunters. The head porter in the goods shed (the shunter's No 1 enemy) marked on each wagon, at the close of the day, where the wagon was required in the shed the next day. The positions on the shed road were dump, off dump, crane, under crane, (meaning first required for the next day), shed stage and below stage. The shed road held about thirty wagons, and it was not uncommon for that many to be placed for unloading, and indeed, not uncommon for wagons to be placed in the goods shed loop because the shed was full. The shed was shunted on afternoon shift and traffic for outgoing trains shunted out and the goods shed road traffic marshalled as requested.

The below stage traffic was placed and the balance placed in the goods shed loop leaving open the shed stage for the placement of Darling Harbour traffic arriving on No 11 Goods. The shunting and placing of the Darling Harbour traffic was completed on the backshift. Parkes goods shed loaded out-of wagons daily for Forbes and Orange, tri-weekly for Peak Hill and Dubbo, Tottenham Branch and Condobolin and bi-weekly for Broken Hill. Nearly every day, the head porter would want an additional shunt or shunts and on nearly every day, the shunters told him what he could do with his shunts.

Some of us realised his predicament and did what we could to assist him, nevertheless it made keeping up with the yard shunting difficult if too much time was spent re-shunting the shed. While I have said the head porter was the number one enemy, the enmity did not go beyond his work. He was a likable, single-minded person performing a difficult job, which under the circumstances, were far from conducive to the good working of the goods shed.

He was transferred to Orange on promotion some years later, but unfortunately he developed abdominal cancer soon after. I visited him each Sunday for some months in Orange Base Hospital before he died. He had no family other than his wife, who appreciated the visits. I have seen no other person with cancer suffer like he suffered.

I found the first month or so of working the senior shunter's part of my roster very difficult, and I have to say that I received much appreciated advice and assistance, which

I was more than willing to take from the older experienced shunters. The head shunters were allowed 30 minutes to obtain their lists and inspect the yard. The senior shunters on backshift from Mondays were also allowed this time. I put this time to good use and walked each road in the yard and memorised what each one contained.

Earlier, I named the roads in which the bulk of the shunting took place. Generally speaking, the roads were kept for specific purposes, which made for some degree of uniformity. The weighbridge, new, middle and back roads were all connected to the main line from the eastern or Orange end of the yard. These roads were used to admit Down trains and to form Up trains. A frame worked with a key release, obtained from the signal box by a shunter governed the eastern end working. The closeness of the arriving Up trains and also the time factor decided whether they were left on the main line or loop to shunt as time permitted or admitted direct into the yard.

When Up trains were admitted direct to the yard the engines were released and were returned via an empty road, or if there were none, the engines were taken out onto the main line and sent direct to Loco. Care had to be taken to see that trains were not left for too long awaiting admittance to the yard, one of the reasons being that often crews were on long hours and the locomotives had to be returned to the locomotive depot to avoid crews exceeding shift limits.

The dead-end sidings in the main shunting yard were Nos 4, 5 and 6. No 4 road was used as the Darling Harbour and the Darling Harbour out-of trucks* road for all the Down trains departing, No 5 held the local traffic, for example oil and other sidings traffic. No 6 was used to stow ashes from loco, in loaded traffic for the Per Way Branch, and repair traffic. Traffic for the Broken Hill line was gravitated across the main line down into the long and short roads. There was also a Down turnout, on the eastern end, into the long road from the main line, worked by a key release frame.

Occasionally when a Broken Hill train had departed and the long road was empty, Down trains from Orange were stowed. It was a practice avoided if possible, because generally the shunting engines had great difficulty lifting a train from the long road. The entrance into the long and short roads was also by a frame with a key release. All the releases for keys had to be given by the signalman from the signal box.

It follows from what I have said that, when gravitational shunting of a train took place, the head or senior or both doing the cutting-out signalled to a shunter patrolling the throw-over points which road that he wanted the shunts to go into. Generally he gave the shunter three shunts or sets of road signals that were repeated one for one. It was the shunter's duty to set the right roads as the shunts came to him and to put a light

---

* These trucks contained the Darling Harbour traffic for stations that did not have sufficient goods to warrant a full truck. The Darling Harbour out-of truck for No N3 the pick-up to Dubbo would have contained traffic for Alectown West, Nelungaloo, Mickibri, Tomingley West, and Fairview.

handbrake on two or three of the leading trucks. The shunter 'catching' the shunts in the roads was then able to apply the handbrakes to steady the shunts so they would not come into heavy contact with the traffic already in the roads.

There were of course the occasional mis-shunts (sometimes known as 'Chinese shunts', with an implication that may make my readers blush if published!). Some head or senior shunters accepted that there would always be mis-shunts and when the train was shunted, they would gather up the mis-shunt and put it in the road that it was intended for. Others swore and carried on as though the world was ending.

All trains arriving from the branches were shunted similarly to the Down trains, the Up through traffic going into one of the through roads and the goods shed traffic being set aside into a road and later be picked up and placed into the goods shed loop. When long down trains were shunted, they were taken either up to the loop or the main line as far as the road crossing if necessary. Fifty five vehicles and the engine could be shunted in the loop, and the air would be leaked out of all but about six or seven wagons. These wagons were used for brake power; but even so, it was usually necessary to pull ahead two or three times to clear the points and to have sufficient gravitation for the wagons to run. To the uninitiated, the leaking of the air from the auxiliary reservoirs left the wagons with mechanical handbrakes only.

Parkes Railway Station, situated in the Central West of New South Wales, in May 1985.
John R Newland.

I vividly recall shunting No 11 one afternoon, which arrived as a double-header and 55 vehicles in length. Believe it or not there were 55 shunts on the train, there were not even two vehicles together for the one destination. We left air in about 20 vehicles. To this day I find it hard to believe that we did not pull the train ahead once to have sufficient room for wagons to gravitate. This was mainly due to the good shunting driver who watched the shunter for his signals like a hawk and acted immediately on them. Shunting drivers made or broke a shunter's day.

There were drivers who hated working the shunting engine, mainly because it demanded that the head or senior shunter be kept continually under close surveillance. From a shunter's point of view, there was nothing worse than to signal a driver to go either forwards or backwards and to have no response from him. The good drivers were aware of this and worked in with the shunter, making the task easier in the long run for both. The extra good drivers were the ones who were able to anticipate the shunter's next move and have the locomotive in the gear that would take him in the direction that the shunter wanted. There were only two drivers in this category at Parkes. They could save anything up to an hour in a shift. The smart head or senior shunter saw that when crib was taken, some extra time would be allowed when these drivers were operating.

So far we have dealt with the incoming trains and how they were disposed of. The head or senior shunter after getting his list of instructions concerning the outgoing trains that he was to form, decided firstly the roads he was going to form them in. He also had a number of other considerations, especially on Monday mornings, when the stock wagon book-out was heavy. Did he have enough stock wagons in the yard to meet his book-out or did he have to go out to the stockyards for more wagons? That, at least, would be a 30 minute job which cut into the time that was not really available. The disposition of brakevans also counted heavily. Had his predecessors left brakevans behind the traffic in the dead end roads or did he have to find other vans before he started laying the foundation for his trains?

On nearly every occasion when beginning to form the Down trains to the branches and short destinations No 4 road was the first to be shunted because, as you will remember, it had the Darling Harbour and out-of-traffic trucks, which had to be placed as near as possible to the brakevan of the train. The head shunters, and I certainly did when I was on my own as the senior, shunted the traffic onto the outgoing trains without worrying whether it was marshalled in order. In other words, the Tottenham branch line traffic was dropped onto the Tottenham train as it came out of No 4 road. This applied to all the other trains that were being made up.

When all the traffic for a particular train, and I will use the Tottenham as an example, was in that train's road, including all the book-outs for empty wagons or for stock wagons, and all the traffic in the yard was available for the train, the road was again lifted and the traffic was then marshalled in station order, or at the least marshalled together so that the guard, when he arrived at a station, had only one shunt to make to get all the traffic off for that station. He may have had to make shunts to place it where required at the station, of course.

Generally, the Tottenham train was marshalled from the engine with Bogan Gate leading then followed by Trundle, Tullamore, Albert and Tottenham. If there were book-outs for wheat trucks to any of the silos, such as Yethera, they were marshalled together, generally between the Trundle and Tullamore traffic. The method most commonly used was to drop the traffic for each station into a road so that when the train was shunted for the second time, the traffic for it was in a number of roads. Even then it may have been necessary to shunt this traffic again to get it in order, and this applied especially to stock wagons, so that when they were placed at station stockyards, they were in the right order of loading. The traffic for the train, which by now was in at least four or five roads, was picked up in order and placed back into the road the train was originally formed on, which by this time was marshalled in their proper order. The first question invariably asked of a person doing the shunter's examination was,

"How should traffic be marshalled on trains?"

The answer was, "In station and district order."

That basically is how trains were marshalled, especially for pick-up trains and those required to be shunted en-route to their destination.

The most difficult train of all to marshal was No 21 pick-up from Parkes to Broken Hill. This train had to be marshalled in station order from Condobolin to Broken Hill. The regular guards who worked the train were sticklers for it being correctly marshalled. It conveyed a load in the vicinity of 600 tons and often was up to 50 vehicles long. One can understand the difficulty of working a train of this length. At some of the smaller sidings, having to walk the length of the train in the dark to detach a wagon into a siding with a hand lamp as the only means of illumination, was a difficult enough assignment. If the wagon was marshalled, say, in the middle of the train, it was even more difficult.

One of the biggest problems encountered by head and senior shunters at Parkes was the cross country stock trains coming from the north to the south conveying starving stock for agistment and then returning some months later to their original holdings. These trains invariably consisted of 45 stock wagons and a brakevan. They seemed to arrive at the most awkward times, frequently on Tuesday afternoons when an all-out effort was required to maintain on-time departure of the stock trains going east which were being formed off at least four trains arriving, the last about an hour before the departure of the stock train. When they arrived at Parkes from either north or south, the engine faced Orange and either needed two clear roads, or one clear road and the main line, to reverse the van from one end of the train to the other. These trains were always attended by drovers whose gear was in the incoming van, so there was no hope of using another van.

The train had to be brought into one of the through roads. The practice was to pick up the train van with the shunter and drop it down a through road or through 31 down the main line and onto the train engine for it to push up onto the Orange end of the train. If there were foreign or other depot drivers coming in, almost without exception they refused to push the van back onto the train. The shunters used to be aware of this and watched the train coming in to see who the driver was. If it was a 'foreigner' the bottom end shunter used to cut the engine off and head it into the through road safety dead end or out onto the main line and then have the top shunter drop the van down onto the incoming engine. The drivers used to go mad and refused to move their engines. The reply was,

"You are hemmed in and the only way out is to push that van up."

All the time I was there it worked, but we did not gain many friends among 'foreign' drivers I can assure you.

Other problems that shunters statewide had were the marshalling of hook wagons and bufferless wagons and the safe marshalling of timber trucks which had timber protruding over the ends of the wagons and which fouled fully loaded wagons such as wool, loads of hay and louvred vans. Again, for the uninitiated, when I was shunting, hook wagons were usually 'D' trucks, bogie 'Ds', some bogie flats and about half of the stock wagon fleet. Probably about 25 per cent of automatic wagons were bufferless. Bufferless wagons and hook wagons were not compatible and difficulties arose when wagons of each type were the only wagons consigned to a station. The head or senior shunter would have to find an empty automatic* vehicle with buffers to put between the two wagons.

A similar thing would occur, especially on No 21 pick-up, with single louvre vans and trucks of timber from the North Coast going onto the Broken Hill line. If a suitable Broken Hill wagon could be found to separate the two, it was used, otherwise an empty wagon had to be placed between them. When wagon demand was far greater than that which could be met, this was almost criminal waste of wagons.

One of the tests of skill for a head or senior shunter was remembering in which roads the various types of wagons were leading. On more than one occasion I saw a louvre van dropped onto a 'tailer' (as we called them) truck with results that are not in the text books.

One of the unpublished things that occur in any organisation that relies very heavily on the human element, occurred early one morning when No 86, an Up goods train had departed Parkes in sufficient time to cross the *Forbes Mail* at Bumberry. The train had

---

* Automatic vehicle with buffers and coupling jaws that automatically closed when two automatic wagons came together; they were held in position by a locking pin. A lever extending from the side of the wagon to a point over the automatic coupling had a chain attached. The shunter raised the lever to release the pin when he wanted to uncouple the vehicles. These wagons also had a two link coupling with a "D" link and pin, which was attached to the top of the automatic jaw, to enable them to be coupled to hook vehicles. Hence the three types were referred to as 'hooks', 'bufferless', or 'automatics' or 'autos'.

been formed in the new road. During the early morning the senior shunter had placed an MLV van of perishable traffic on top of the new road. The shunter, knowing it would not be there long, had not applied the handbrake, but relied on the air brake to hold it until it was required. The crew went for crib and one of the shunters set No 86 out of the bottom end of the yard and also came in for crib, without waiting for the train to depart.

About 25 minutes was had for crib and the senior said the first thing is to pick that van off the new road and drop it into the goods shed. Imagine the consternation when they went to get it to find that it was not there! The senior had the presence of mind to tell the assistant station master who straightaway took out the staff for the section, No 86 having cleared Cookamidgera. The shunting engine with a shunter went out into the section and found the wagon near the wheat silo at Parkes. It was still moving in the hollow, but it did not have sufficient momentum to get over the small grade there and was running up and down in the hollow when they arrived. Before they got back into the yard, the *Forbes Mail* was at Cookamidgera trying to get a staff. Fortunately, the *Forbes Mail* was only delayed for a couple of minutes which was not shown anywhere; or in railway parlance, the delay was 'squared'. I am not prepared to admit who the senior shunter was!

Each shunter, of course, was issued with a traffic branch hand lamp. The lamps exhibited three indications—red, green and white. The required indication was obtained by turning a swivel at the top of the barrel of the lamp. These lamps were of the large type and were quite difficult to hold between the legs when standing in between the buffers to couple up hook wagons to automatic couplings. It was the aim of almost every shunter to purloin a Mechanical Branch lamp that, besides being lighter, was much smaller in the barrel and easier to handle. If you could get hold of one without trading your issue lamp, so much the better, but if you could not, well it was worth the risk of getting caught without an issue lamp. Most of the shunters filled and cleaned their lamps, especially the reflectors and trimmed the wicks before commencing each shift.

After I had been shunting about 18 months, the head shunter, Sid Hobson, had a severe medical problem and was off duty for three months. The providing of relief for him became a problem when the three appointed senior shunters all refused to relieve him. The station master approached me one day when I was signing on and said to me,

"Put your hand up."

Not knowing what he was on about, I did so. While I had it up he said to me,

"You have just put your hand up for the head shunter's job for the next three months."

I look back on that experience with some satisfaction; there have not been in the history of the Railways, many men appointed as acting head shunters at 22 years of age. I achieved much of my success from my attitude to the job.

On the first stock night that I was head shunter, the driver of the shunter was one who was always looking for an early crib. At 7.30pm when there were trains everywhere, either waiting admittance or to be shunted, I stopped work for the 15 minutes crib time. The reaction from both the shunters and the driver was amazing. After we had our crib, the effort put in by the driver far surpassed anything I had previously seen from him. The shunters, seeing this, also seemed to pick up their efforts, and the result was at the end of the shift all the outgoing trains had departed on time. I felt at the end of the three months that I had at least done as well as anyone else would have done.

I had somewhat of a rude awakening at Parkes; my lifestyle did not match that of any of my shunting colleagues. A railwayman who did not drink in those days was something of an oddity, or a religious crank. I found once again that I became a 'loner' so far as my workplace mates were concerned. It has to be said that in Parkes, and in fact in every depot in the State, there were far too many addicted to alcohol and that too often, the running staff consisting of drivers, fireman and guards found a release in alcohol.

Some of the conditions that running staff endured at Parkes were horrendous. As an example, a crew would work all night from Parkes to Euabalong West, where they would book off for 10 hours in barracks built of corrugated iron in temperatures that often hovered between 90 and 100 degrees Fahrenheit. Sleep or proper rest under these conditions was impossible. They would sign on again and work all night to Ivanhoe. If they were lucky they would arrive Ivanhoe about 4.00am and get some rest. It happened on so many occasions that, around 10.00am or so, they would go into Ivanhoe to the pub and get a 'skin full' and then back to the barracks and try to sleep it off before their next sign-on.

When they did so, many of these crews would today have blown the top off the breathalyser. They would work back to Euabalong West, book off and then work back to Parkes, having signed on four times in three days to work under conditions that would not be tolerated today. They lived from a tucker box which, after the first meal of fresh meat, contained bread, runny butter, and tinned food. There were one or two enginemen at Parkes who would regularly sign on duty and take charge of an engine when they were affected by alcohol. On these occasions the fireman would have to carry the driver for the whole journey.

One of the very noticeable things to me was the fact that drivers never appeared to be affected when they signed on to work on the main line towards Orange or Broken Hill; it was always on special wheat trains or empty stock specials to the branch lines. I suspect that on occasions, the roster clerks made quick changes. The culture in those days was that you never 'dobbed' in a fellow worker. I have to say I followed this culture; the thing was of course by using Nelson's eye you did not see them. There was one particular driver being discussed at crib one morning and it was said of him what a good bloke he was when he was sober. I responded by saying what a good bloke he had to be when he was sober!

I write this comment not as criticism of the Parkes drivers and guards, for firstly, there were the majority who controlled their alcohol intake and were responsible railwaymen. The criticism I am offering is of a Department which allowed these conditions to exist at Euabalong West, Ivanhoe and Menindee. Certainly, air-conditioning prior to the 1960s was uncommon. However, in these areas, where there was no electricity, no effort was made to provide any amenity for the safekeeping of foodstuffs or to reduce the temperature in the barracks by means of electrically-operated fans by using generating plants charging wet batteries, such as those found on the many outback and rural holdings in this period of our history.

There was, of course, no such excuse for those operating out of Parkes, on the shunting engine and on round trip working, who were affected by alcohol. Heavy overtime also contributed to the problem. It not only provided the money, but it also reduced the time that should have been available for leisure and pleasure. Thirteen-shift fortnights were more often the rule than not. The roustabout guards at Parkes were no better than the enginemen, and the same can be said of them. There were the majority who were sober and responsible; those who had a problem and those who were alcoholics.

The culture of not 'dobbing in' workmates caused me some very considerable discomfort and fear. The topic of conversation at crib got around to thieving from trucks, especially of cartons of beer and smallgoods. I foolishly (or perhaps wisely) said that if ever I saw anyone taking goods from a truck that I would report them to the station master, and would not care who it was. There was deathly silence. Conversation had not started again when I (as acting senior) said,

"Time to work again."

The first job we did was to lift a train from the east and to shunt it out. Before we started, I went alongside the loco to speak to the driver and as I did the fireman leant over the side and hooked his thumbs under my jaw and partially lifted me off the ground. While he had me in this position, he threatened if ever I 'dobbed' anyone he would personally see that I was never able to do it again. It was not until the driver intervened that he let me go.

The answer to whether I was wise or foolish may be found in the fact that the December before I left Parkes, the departmental detectives raided the homes of 15 of the 16 shunters. Two of them were dealt with in the Court of Petty Sessions and were sacked and two more resigned in return for charges not being laid. It was said later that in getting caught, they were the unlucky ones, which I think was probably true. Fortunately I was not accused of having anything to do, which I did not, with the raid by the detectives.

The alcohol problem was also manifested among the shunters. There were 16 shunters at Parkes of whom probably 10 had no problem but about four had the beginnings of a major problem and two were alcoholics at a very young age. Payday was on alternate Wednesdays. On this day my roster called for me to work a half shift from around 8.30pm until 11.55pm. That was, of course, when the roster operated, which was less than half the time. I doubt there was one Wednesday pay day in Parkes that I was not called out to do a full shift in the place of a shunter who had either failed to report for duty, or had reported sick. I was always good for a loan about two days before payday. There were a number of shunters over a period that borrowed from me, but without fail I was repaid on payday.

Safety First was an issue that management regularly brought to the fore, especially through the Weekly Notices and by exhibiting posters. Shunting is in itself an occupation that can be very hazardous if care is not taken by each individual to ensure that he does nothing that may injure himself or his workmates. One of the common hazards, especially at night at Parkes, were the large lumps of coke that fell from the coke consignments for Broken Hill, which fell onto the walkways between the roads. Just prior to my going there, a delegation of shunters had met the station master and chief inspector, with the backing of a weak-kneed union delegate, to complain of the continuing danger from the hazards on the walkways. A promise was made to clean up the roads. Some 14 days later this had not been done. This time the shunters threatened industrial action if the yard was not made safe to work in.

A promise was again made by the Per Way engineer to replace the yardman who had left some considerable time before. Another 14 days and the situation was worse. The shunters did take action and walked off the job midway through a shift. The next turn of shunters refused to come out early, although they did sign on at their normal time. The result was that the assistant superintendent and the chief inspector took statements from those shunters involved in the walk-off before they signed on next day, and from their statements formulated 'defence against punishment charges'* to be answered immediately.

When this happened the shunters collectively told the assistant superintendent that they would not work until the yard was cleaned nor would they reply to the charges. Sanity prevailed when he reluctantly agreed to examine the yard; his information from the Per Way engineer was that the shunters were being unreasonable. Despite the fact that he agreed with the shunters that it was unsafe and assuring them he would have the engineer commit a full gang for a day to clean up the yard, each of the shunters was fined £1 for engaging in a stop-work procedure. This finally brought action from the head office of the union, who had ignored the shunters' problem from the beginning, mainly because of the failure of the local delegate to keep them advised.

* From its beginning the NSW Department of Railways issued under Section 82 of the Railways Act, what was referred to as 'defence against punishment charges'. This was a disciplinary tool. The assumption was the person was guilty as charged; he/she had to convince the Departmental Head concerned that they were not. A difficult thing to do. It was possible to put forward a good defence of your actions. However, it rarely resulted in any action not being taken. The percentage of staff being punished in some form would be in the nineties.

The finale was that the fines were not enforced and each offender was seen and spoken to. Still a form of punishment. Shortly after I went there, a full time yardman was again employed, but even then on Monday mornings, the roads where coke had been shunted were treacherous. This whole issue brought to light the gulf in those times between management and staff, especially wages staff. The superintendent at Orange was not prepared to accept the word of anyone except the engineer who, despite there being a safety issue involved, obviously was not going to say, until forced, that there was a problem for which he was responsible. Much was made of the personalities involved at the time and their lack of understanding of the problems that the shunters faced. To my mind, the whole responsibility lay with the chief inspector who mostly did not rate a mention. If he had been doing his job properly, he would have known the condition of the yard. Even though the shunters had appealed to him twice, he did not bother to see for himself. Can you imagine anyone being fined for engaging in industrial procedures in the last twenty years or more? I cannot.

Toward the end of November 1951, advertisements appeared in the Weekly Notices for fifth class assistant station masters. One of the ploys being used to get the positions filled was that appointments would be made without the applicants being qualified in goods and coaching accounts. The only qualifications required were for the safeworking systems applicable and station management. I made application for Borenore and was duly appointed.

I had some health problems at Parkes, mainly in the form of an *anal fistular*, a most uncomfortable complaint. Around the end of November 1951, I had an operation in Parkes hospital. I will not go into detail, except to say that six days after, with stitches still intact and having eaten only light foods, I felt a bowel movement coming on. I will never forget what followed before the movement was complete. Talk about excruciating!

After about 21 days, I came back to work, on light duties for 14 days. As I walked onto the platform, the chief inspector asked me how I was feeling and before I could answer, asked me would I like to go to Conoble as officer-in-charge for the 1951-52 gypsum lift? His concern was not my answer as to how I was feeling but to whether I would agree to go to Conoble. In thinking about my reply, I took into consideration that the one thing I did not want to be was a shunter for too many years. While I enjoyed it, it certainly was not a career path. This opportunity I thought I might be sensible to accept, so I agreed. The offer for the Fifth Class ASMs had appeared the week before this, while I was in hospital.

I was assured that there would be a bed, blankets, bed linen, cooking equipment and a portable shower, at Conoble when I got there. I left Parkes on the first Monday of the 1951 Christmas school holidays on the *Silver City Comet*. Conoble in those days consisted of seven fettler's houses, a tiny shop and precious little else. The station building was a single building consisting of a waiting room, which could be shut, a signal box room and two toilets. Water was obtained from a line side tank replenished from the water tank attached to No 16 pick-up twice weekly. On the Monday evening I made up my bed; the sheets were brand new and felt like stiff cardboard. All the things promised were there.

As we passed Matakana on the *Comet*, I noticed a train load of empty wagons standing in the loop. These arrived in Conoble for the commencement of the annual gypsum lift, the gypsum mainly going to the Kandos cement works; the balance to Camellia. As there were no bogie wagons in service at that time, the wagons supplied were either 15-ton capacity 'S' or 24-ton 'U' or 'K' trucks. On the Up side were the loop, the dump and a storage road, while the Down side had two storage sidings. Two train loads of empties arrived from Parkes on most days and two engines and vans arrived from Ivanhoe to lift the loaded wagons.

Conoble was simply a hive of industry; a flotilla of motor lorries being ferried constantly between the gypsum open cut mine and the siding. While I made as much use of the train engines as I could to place empties and clear loaded wagons from the dump, this did not keep up the supply of empties. The gypsum company had a tractor that we used to use for shunting. I very clearly remember one day, that will always remain with me as the nearest incident (another is reported further on), that I was involved in a major collision. I was using the shunting tractor to transfer loaded wagons onto the Down side and to bring empties off the Down onto the Up side dump. Both home signals were in the stop position and fortunately I had not gone outside the Up home signal. A train from Ivanhoe due to pick up a full load at Conoble appeared on the horizon and was visible for some 15 minutes before it came past the landmark.

I still had loaded wagons on the main line as it approached. Because the home signal was at stop I did not worry as it approached; all the train crews knew I was there. However the train appeared not to be slowing down at all as it neared the home signal. Something told me things were not right on the engine and with that I ran as fast as I could towards the train and as the engine passed me I yelled out at the top of my voice to the crew. As I did the fireman looked out, made a full brake application and put the engine into reverse. He still hit the wagons with some force but not enough to cause any damage; the guard and the driver being thrown around in the brakevan without injury. The first thing the fireman did was to get off the engine and start abusing me; I said nothing and pointed to the home signal. It was the same fireman who had given me the treatment at Parkes.

I next said, "Where is the driver?"

He by this time had staggered from the van and was approaching the engine. He stopped half way to vomit. The only thing that stopped me from reporting the incident was that this particular driver who was a good engineman and a sober responsible railwayman. He told me he had a few drinks the night before, but thought he must have food poisoning of some sort. He was not only vomiting but had diarrhoea. The train eventually left Conoble with a full load with the fireman and guard on the engine. The only stipulation I made was that there be two men on the engine when the train left Conoble.

The conditions I lived under at Conoble were unbelievable. The temperature was around 85-90 degrees Fahrenheit every day except for a couple of times when it got over the century mark. I could not get fresh food, although I sometimes arranged for the guards to buy some meat in Ivanhoe for me, which I had to cook straight away. I had kippers for breakfast one morning; I have not eaten them since! It was so hot the oil in them had become runny and they were warm. Ugh!

The place was closing down over Christmas Day and Boxing Day, so I decided it was home for Christmas for this bloke. It was the off day for the *Comet*, so how to get home? I checked the goods train programme with the station master at Ivanhoe who told me a goods train was running to Condobolin where the crews were to book off for eight hours then proceed onto Parkes; this to avoid their being on duty for long hours. With that, I found a guy who lived in Condobolin and who was driving home for Christmas. I hitched a ride with him, knowing that I would have about four hours to wait in Condobolin. Imagine my dismay when I got to Condobolin and there was no train there. The crew decided they did not want to book off and went straight through to Parkes. It was Christmas Eve in the lively town of Condobolin. What to do? I had little money, my pay was in the safe at Parkes, (I hoped). I approached a taxi driver on the rank and told him my predicament, told him I had no money on me and I wanted to get to Parkes. He said,

"Get in."

When we got to Parkes, my pay was there and from it I gave him £12. I then got into the Ford Anglia and drove home to Burdett, the second marathon effort I had made to be home for Christmas. My father, being the man he was, later on pushed £12 into my pocket. When I protested he said,

"You could not buy what having you home means to us. Please let me share some of the expenses as part of my contribution towards you being here."

I took the money.

I went back to Conoble and stayed there until the coalminers went back to work, at which point all the empty wagons returned to the coal and allied trades which was the beginning of the third week in January 1952.

The experience gained while shunting at Parkes stood me in good stead later in my career, and the rudimentary knowledge gained of depot station working at grass roots level was used in many positions later in life. I will return to the value of this experience further on in this autobiography.

Thus came to an end my wages staff career after six years and nine months of employment. I believe the time spent in each of the positions that I held in the wages staff was invaluable training that made me, when I came to the salaried staff, a sound grassroots railwayman. One of the great pities of today's railway is that the opportunities for this experience no longer exist. Which is a pity for individuals, but more so I believe for the future administration of the railways at depot station level. I should not and will not name names here. However some of the outstanding special class station masters with whom I worked towards the end of my career, received their education in railway working as I had. I think particularly of the man who was the station master at Campbelltown, at Rozelle and finally at Sydney. Men of his depth of understanding, not only of railways but also of railwaymen, are lost to future generations because of the lack of basic training. Unfortunately, this type of railwayman and railway is now dead. Long live the railways!

My personal life changed direction quite markedly during my time at Parkes. Earlier on I mentioned the brunette who was capturing my thoughts. This capturing of thoughts continued. At the time, dances and annual balls were held in many of the localities within close proximity of Eugowra and especially Toogong from where the subject of the thought lived on a farm with her parents and sisters. We met and danced (or she did and I followed) at many of these dances. Then an invitation to a 21st birthday party, issued to my sister and me, arrived at my home. To my disgust, I was working, and sent my apologies. It did not enter my head to take a 'sickie' so I could go. To me that was not done.

After this, I asked 'the brunette' to accompany me to a dance. I forget where it was, and from then on we went out regularly together. I went home every second weekend and spent more time with her than at home. Being appointed to Borenore suited me very well, because I was off every weekend and would be only about 25 miles from Toogong. The brunette's name was Mamie Peggy Balcombe.

Parkes was also the depot for the SILVER CITY COMET, *a diesel-hydraulic passenger train that served passenger needs between Parkes and Broken Hill in the far west of New South Wales. Services commenced in 1937 and operated for 52 years. This photo taken in May 1985, shows* THE COMET *at Parkes Depot in candy livery.*   *John R Newland.*

Borenore railway station situated west of Orange in the Central West of New South Wales. Although this view was taken in May 1985, very little would have changed since the author's appointment as Fifth Class Assistant Station Master. Borenore was closed in 1989.

John R Newland.

FIFTH CLASS ASSISTANT STATION MASTER, BORENORE

A
S I arrive at Borenore, a new facet of my career opens up, one that did not change my attitude nor me. I am now a Fifth Class Assistant Station Master, a salaried officer referred to in correspondence as Mister. My uniform has gold braid on it. I am in receipt of an annual salary and I am issued with a first class holiday pass. Big deal, I am back to doing signal lights at Borenore!

I often pondered while I was idle at Borenore, how it could be that coming from a shunter at Parkes, where there was rarely a shift the shunting engine was not utilised 85-90 per cent of the time, to Borenore, where about five or six trains per shift passed through, could have been a promotion. There were some crossings, although the loop held only 36 four-wheeled vehicles and a brakevan, the length of a stock train. There was absolutely no comparison with the amount of work involved, or indeed with the amount of responsibility involved.

There of course had to be a starting point for fifth class ASMs, and Borenore was one of them. There was very little in the way of goods or coaching accounts. Borenore employed two assistant station masters, one on afternoon shift and the other a fourth class ASM on backshift. To this day I do not understand why the difference, although certainly there was more traffic on backshift. However, the signalmen at Nashdale and Gamboola, on

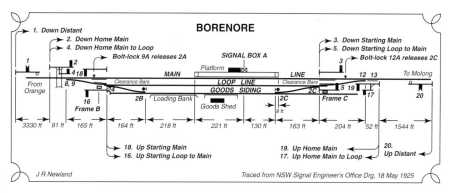

either side, were all seventh class signalmen. To me, this was one of life's little mysteries. I suspect however, that years earlier a position had to be found for someone who was 'owed' by the district administration. When he retired the tradition continued. A sixth class station master was employed, the incumbent being one of the ASMs from my Newbridge days. No better sixth class SM's job existed in New South Wales.

Within a week of my taking up at Borenore, No 31 *Central West Express* pulled into Borenore. The Orange salaried driver, whom I knew because he worked the shunter on arrival at Parkes as part of his roster, stepped off the engine, came to me and took me by the shoulders and pointed me toward the Down Distant signal. He told me it was the most important signal to a driver between Orange and Parkes. He said if a driver of a through train had two greens in that signal and something went wrong and the indication was changed close to it, the train could not be stopped without running into the next section. He also said the signal was inclined 'to hang off' and to take care this did not happen. (Many years later the driver of *Silver City Comet* cars working from Orange to Parkes lost control and collided with an Up train and was killed.) When I told the SM next day, he said,

" Did you tell him to mind his own business?"

"No, I did not. I appreciated what he said to me and thanked him," I replied.

The grades on either side of Borenore were 1 in 40, and these grades prevailed nearly all the way from Gamboola on the Molong side to Nashdale. Borenore itself was on a level portion which extended about 200 yards (yards! Try metres!), which enabled the through trains to gather speed for the 1 in 40 stretch to Nashdale which was nearly two miles, before it evened out. It was this falling grade towards Borenore that prompted the little talk from the driver of No 31. The fact that I record it here is proof of the impression he left. I certainly exercised a good deal of care with the Down Distant.

That there was not a lot to do at Borenore worked well for me, because it was compulsory that I pass, at least, the modified Goods and Coaching Exam to retain my position. If I wished to progress further as an ASM, I had to qualify in 'A' Goods and Coaching plus the male clerical which consisted of maths and English. I took the Goods and Coaching correspondence courses with the Railways Institute, then situated in Castlereagh Street, and which coincidentally is the same location, but different building, where today our son has chambers as the Deputy Director of Public Prosecutions. I passed the annual 'A' standard goods and coaching and the clerical examinations held in Orange in November of 1952. It was not permissible in those days to sit for the 'B' standard without having first passed the 'A' standard.

My becoming qualified led to me being offered a long list of fourth class assistant station master positions. From these positions I accepted positions on the North Coast, Illawarra and South lines. I was appointed to Linden on a reducing time roster that worked Linden only.

WEDDING BELLS

THE romance that began with going to dances blossomed into something with a far greater meaning for both of us. In March 1952, I asked the question men have been asking since time immemorial and was accepted, without hesitation I might add. It was customary, not obligatory, in that era to ask the prospective father-in-law for the hand of his daughter in marriage. This daunting task completed and permission gained, we became unofficially engaged, and the secret remaining with our families until the all important ring was bought.

In April I took two days' leave and we journeyed to Mamie's sister at Granville in the Anglia, the longest trip it had taken. It is difficult to imagine the car journey to Sydney from Orange, the Anglia eight horsepower motor, the road all bitumen, but still the original road, which from Bathurst to Lithgow seemed never ending; I think it had more bends and twists than the railway line still does. The old 'forty bends' between Lithgow and Hartley were all negotiated with a maximum speed of 35 miles per hour—when on the level or going down hill!

The buying of the ring was the great moment of our time together so far. We looked around the jewellers of Pitt and George Streets and finished up in Angus and Coote. We found a lady assistant who at one time had lived in Canowindra. A particular ring that was taking our fancy and Mamie's in particular, was just in the range of being too expensive. Seeing our desire for the ring, the lady said if we bought it she would include the wedding ring in the price, this was an offer not to be refused. Mamie still has the receipt that shows I paid £50 cash for an engagement and wedding ring on 20 April 1952. The announcement of our engagement appeared in the Saturday 21 April edition of the *Sydney Morning Herald*.

After we returned to our respective homes and had family consultations, mainly with the bride's family of course, we set Saturday 21 February 1953 as our wedding day, that day being my parents' Silver Wedding and my sister's first wedding anniversaries and my Mother's birthday.

I had further health problems with the *anal fistula* while I was at Borenore, which resulted in further surgery in Calare private hospital in Orange. While the surgery on this occasion was more extensive than previously and more debilitating in the short term, it was what was required for I have had no problem since.

I had applied for holidays in December of 1952 to commence from Saturday 21 February, stating that I was to be married that day. This was just after I had been appointed to Linden. I also requested that I be transferred to Linden on the completion of my leave, the idea being to obtain accommodation in Springwood and start our lives together there. The answer came back swiftly, no leave would be granted, this despite not having had any in 1952. It also said the transfer would not be effected until the staff position had improved. The salaried staff clerk had signed the memo advising this.

I was not about to take this lying down, so I went to Orange to see the staff clerk and if necessary to seek an interview with Mr J L Russell, who was the District Superintendent. When I saw the staff clerk, he reiterated the answer he had already given. I then suggested to the staff clerk, I was going to see Mr Russell, (the same one who was Chief Traffic Manager for many years), surely I was entitled to the consideration that I had asked for. As I said this, for some reason Mr Russell came into the staff office. Having been the chief inspector at Parkes while I was acting head shunter there, he remembered me. He was also aware that I had been at Conoble. He came over and spoke to me and asked me when was I going to Linden, which to some degree floored the staff clerk, who then, before I could reply, told him that I was going in February after the wedding. Mission complete!

We were to be married in the Cranbury Methodist Church, which was the church Mamie and her parents and her father's parents before them had attended. Cranbury is a district that bordered my home district of Burdett, both places being about 20km from Canowindra. Methodism flourished in the Cranbury area. At the beginning of the century, three sisters married three brothers; from these unions begat the congregation that was at Cranbury. I mentioned earlier my association with Cranbury before joining the railways and while I was in Canowindra, I had attended the Young People's Club at Cranbury.

All the arrangements were going along fine. Mamie had made her frock and those of her matron of honour and the bridesmaid who were her sisters. I had a new suit tailor-made in Orange. My best man was to be Ralph Robinson, a schoolteacher I met and became friends with in Eugowra, and my brother was my groomsman.

In the fortnight before the wedding, Mamie's mother took ill and was taken to Orange for medical treatment. Her condition was such that she was admitted to hospital and operated on for a large abdominal cyst on the Tuesday before we were to be married. This of course ruled out any chance of her being at the wedding. Arrangements were so far advanced that it was too late to postpone the wedding. It was not only sad for Mamie's mother, but also for Mamie and her father. We have a photo of him sitting on his own and looking pensive, and no doubt wondering what might have been. We made arrangements to visit her in Dudley Private Hospital after the reception.

We left the reception somewhere around 8.30pm, after having been married at 5.00pm, and headed for Orange and Dudley Hospital in the Anglia. I thought I heard a strange noise when we left but there so much noise and frivolity I did not take much notice. We went non-stop to Dudley Hospital, and as we were coming into the drive the noise started again, much louder than when we left. Someone had taken the hub caps off and put coins in them. The slower I went, the more noise they made, so our entrance at Dudley was certainly well announced. In addition to the coins, written in lipstick on the rear window was 'Just Married'. Ever tried getting lipstick off?

We left Orange on the Sunday morning and headed for Jenolan Caves, where we spent two days, then to Granville, where we parked the car and thence into Sydney overnight. The next morning, we caught the *Intercapital Daylight* to Albury for an overnight stay. The next day to Melbourne for three days and then on *The Overland* to Adelaide for two more days. I went to Adelaide railway station to confirm our return booking and was told the carriage we were booked in had been taken off the train and we had no seats. The next question was when would there be seats, which brought the curt reply:

"Booked out for a week."

We then booked on a flight from Adelaide to Melbourne, so we could maintain our homeward connections. It was the first time either of us had flown in a commercial aircraft. We had to book into a hotel in Melbourne and finally found one in St Kilda. I still remember the lady, when she booked us in, telling us there were two double beds in the room and only to use one of them! We arrived back home after a trip we would never forget. It was an adventure, as neither of us had been any further than Sydney and to have spent time in two other capital cities was really something. The fact that we arrived home with ten shillings to our name (the flight and extra night in Melbourne saw to that), until I collected my pay at Borenore, seemed to add to the excitement.

So the time came to leave home in the Anglia which was piled to the roof with wedding presents and clothes. There were not a few tears shed. Mamie was leaving home, as I had done earlier, where she had been lovingly nurtured by parents who held inviolate the ethics of the christian church, and who had given her love and support from infancy to womanhood, which she still cherishes today. Knowing how she was feeling, I was able to lovingly sympathise with her and to promise we would come home whenever possible, which we did right to the time her parents died.

Her father was widely known and respected in a wide range of areas. He was a director of Molong Pastures Protection Board for 27 years, a member of the executive of the United Wool Growers and Farmers Association, a member of the Country Party and in later years a patron of it, president of the Cudal Show Society for many years, a member of the original rural electricity scheme board, a member of Lodge Mandagery (I wear his apron with pride still) and treasurer for 30 years of the Cranbury Church Trust. For his services to primary industry, he was awarded the British Empire Medal in the year he died. His greatest achievement in my book was that he was a loving father who cared for his family and set before them an example of good living, of which Mamie at least is proud. His rewards as a father were not always those that they should have been. To me he showed nothing but courteousness, kindness and consideration.

Mamie's mother was a reserved woman who lived to be 96 years of age. She did not go out much, preferring to spend her time as a homemaker caring for a husband and five daughters, of whom Mamie is the youngest. She was a gifted artist and pianist. Her seascapes and landscapes painted prior to her marriage in 1915 still hang in her daughters' homes. To me she showed affection and consideration. When I look back, I am pleased I made the effort to be a good son-in-law; I received many rewards from them both for having done so.

FOURTH CLASS ASSISTANT STATION MASTER, LINDEN

W E arrived at Springwood to a flat, or more correctly a shared house, which had been obtained for us by the lady with whom I had boarded at Blaxland. They had moved to Springwood not long after I had left the Mountains. We soon made friends in the Methodist Church at Springwood, where the congregation was a mixture of young marrieds, young people and those who had retired. The house itself was quite presentable. We had a bedroom, sole use of the lounge and shared the bathroom and laundry facilities. The sharing of a kitchen was the biggest drawback for Mamie. The old landlady had some funny ideas when it came to cooking that conflicted with the cooking a country girl was used to. Although there was a perfectly good laundry with space for a copper, she would not have it in the laundry. The result was that on washdays I had to light this copper in the yard and then carry the clothes from it into the tubs in the laundry. No washing machines in those days.

Very soon after our arrival, we visited the Hodgsons in Penrith and had many good times with them. I remember one day in particular, going to Penrith in the Anglia, picking up Mrs Hodgson and Margaret, returning to Springwood, picking up Mamie and then driving to Katoomba to see the Queen and Prince Philip when they visited Katoomba during the Royal Visit of 1954. We had a very good vantage point close to where they drove past. To this day Mamie says Prince Philip smiled directly at her and waved. I do not know! The Hodgsons featured in our lives many years later, a fact that I will recall much further on in this writing.

Linden had a very small population. The surrounding terrain did not, and still today has not allowed any great building expansion and therefore, there was very little in the line of goods and coaching accounts. Occasionally an older man named Beames would consign timber-cases of copper head gaskets to the Victorian Transport Department in Melbourne. He had the contract to supply a certain number of gaskets each year and used to send them 'to-pay'. Because we held no interstate freight rate books, it was necessary to telegraph the commercial section in Sydney to obtain the rates which were necessary for inclusion in the interstate invoices. This man's real interest was astronomy.

He had a huge revolving telescope that he had made himself except, of course, for the lens. On clear nights, the view at this altitude of the skies from his telescope was superb. He was very much a loner. He lived on his own in a presentable house, but which obviously suffered from the want of some tender loving care.

Linden, like many of the stations between Valley Heights and Katoomba, is situated on a flat area, coming off a 1 in 33 grade on the Down and a 1 in 40 falling on the Up Katoomba side. The purpose, of course, of designing the perway in this fashion was for two reasons. Firstly to allow the through trains to regain momentum before attacking the next grade and secondly, to allow stopping trains an easier take off.

Safeworking-wise it was essentially a through working station; there was not a Down Refuge, but a crossover from the Down to the Up was provided on the Katoomba end of the station. This crossover could be used to go onto the Up Main or into the Up Refuge that held equal to 17 vehicles in the clear. An extension off the refuge would hold another 10 vehicles. No 17B, the pick-up that ran from Penrith on weekdays to Lithgow, was regularly refuged to allow Nos 23 *Caves Express* and 25 the Orange Passenger to pass.

The system of safeworking on the Down Springwood–Linden–Woodford–Lawson was NSW Standard Block Telegraph, which had starting signal control. On the Up, Lawson–Woodford–Linden was also Standard Block, while Linden–Springwood was track block and automatic. The section was effectively divided in two by Springwood's Accept Signal (Signal No 52.0), situated about half a kilometre on the Linden side of Faulconbridge. One of the things which made Linden busier, along with the other safeworking stations Valley Heights to Katoomba, were the returning light engines which

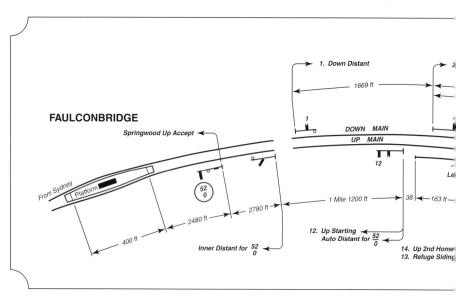

had assisted Down trains from Valley Heights to Katoomba. Quite often, but depending on the urgency of the locomotive requirement at Valley Heights, the train controller would direct these engines be refuged to permit either goods or passenger trains to pass.

I remember one occasion, when there was no direction from the train controller, I let an engine run ahead of a passenger with sufficient running time to clear signal No 52.0 without delay to the passenger. I found, when it was too late to change the route, that the engine was running tender first and, of course, running much slower. The delay to the passenger train was sent to the assistant station master at Linden to answer. An explanation for despatching the engine with insufficient running time was required. This assistant station master was not going to wear this delay and accordingly wrote back that I had no information that the engine was running tender first, and that I was well aware of the maximum speed for an engine tender first.

Had I known, I would have sought direction from the train controller when it was approaching my signal box, who in any case should have advised me of his requirements for the engine. I also said in my answer to the correspondence that when I gave the train controller the time the engine passed Linden, I told him that the engine was tender first. He said,

"You are the first station to have given me a time for it since it left Katoomba!"

He obviously did not know where his trains were and I said so. I also pointed out that in the six months I had been at Linden, this was the first occasion when I was on duty that an engine had run tender first. The reply was not well received in the District Superintendent's office. A reply came back, couched in strong terms, that I should have

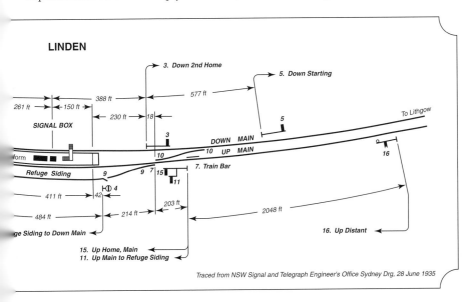

Traced from NSW Signal and Telegraph Engineer's Office Sydney Drg, 28 June 1935

sought a direction from the train controller and that I was considered responsible. I replied that under the regulations governing Train Control Operations on page 201 of the General Appendix Part Two, that it was the train controller's responsibility to instruct signalling staff with respect to the working of trains in his area, and that I did not consider I was responsible. Next move: the Chief Traffic Inspector arrived at Linden to get a statement from this upstart assistant station master who had the temerity to quote the General Appendix to the superintendent. I made a statement containing all the foregoing and heard no more of it. The inspector was none other than Big Jim Hartigan, who was very much in my corner.

I had a couple of interesting experiences at Linden. The first I shall relate concerned a Down single load of empties being hauled by a 57 Class locomotive. On arrival at Linden the driver stopped and said that his engine was a total failure. The mechanical stoker was not working and the fireman could not maintain steam. Not much wonder was my first thought; the second was to ask him to pull ahead and get the brakevan in clear of the home signal. The next move was to advise the train controller of the failure. When I spoke to him, I made a special point that I would require the trailing relief engine to have

Between their introduction in 1929 and the completion of the Western Line electrification in the late 1950s, much of the heavy freight was handled by 57 Class Mountain type locomotives. Here 5704 thunders past Emu Plains railway station in May 1954 with an assortment of goods wagons prior to its ascent of the Blue Mountains. John R Newland.

an automatic drawgear tender because the leading 15 empty wagons were all 'U' and 'Ks' and were bufferless. The position was that the fireman could maintain sufficient steam in the 57 Class to work the Westinghouse airbrake, but would only be able to give minimal assistance in moving the train.

I had intended to use the relief engines to give sufficient assistance in the rear to clear the crossover points and to back the train onto the Up Main with the 57 Class. I was able to do this because of the falling grade toward Springwood, leaving the relief engines on the Down Main. I was then to secure the train and place the 57 Class in the refuge and place the relief engines on the train and depart from the Up Main. By using 'section clear but station or junction blocked' regulation (which I think was clause 21 in the old block telegraph regulations), I was able to accept the two 50 Class engines from Springwood. I took the precaution however, of asking the train controller to have the engines warned the section was clear to the Home Signal only. I obtained line clear from Woodford, cleared the starting signal and then went to the Home Signal to pilot the engines past it. Before I got up onto the lead engine, I had a look at the tender of the trailing engine and discovered it was a hook!

What now? While I was with these engines, I told one of the firemen to uncouple them and still assist with both engines clear of the crossover. I then had to go the train driver and tell him what had happened, and that I would place engine 'A' in the refuge and still leave 'B' on the Down main line. On the way I spoke to the train controller and told him he had brought upon himself another 30 minute delay. He nearly came through the phone; he already had a passenger train standing at Springwood. He could not see how I was to get out of trouble. I suggested to him to leave me alone and I would do my best. When I had engine 'A' in the refuge I backed the 57 Class onto the Up Main (it still had sufficient steam to operate the Westinghouse airbrake compressor). I then took engine 'B' off the Down Main and attached it to the front of the 57 Class now on the Up Main, and lifted all the bufferless wagons onto the Down Main, clear of the crossover, which the 50 Class was able to do. I then took engine 'A' from the refuge and picked up a buffered 'S' truck off the train and placed it and the engine back in the refuge. The 57 Class with engine 'B' backed onto the train with the bufferless wagons. I then detached the two engines and put them on the Down Main. Then engine 'A' with the automatic 'S' truck from the refuge was attached to the train, and the 57 Class was detached from engine 'B' and placed in the refuge siding. Engine 'B' coupled up to its mate and the train departed from the Up Main.

The train controller had wanted to send the passenger from Springwood but I could not legally accept it while I was shunting about. Traffic on the Up was also blocking back at Woodford and Lawson, I forget the actual delay but it was somewhere around 90 minutes from the time the goods train stopped until it departed again. I had to do all the work myself as obviously, the guard had to stay with the brakevan. A light engine returning from Katoomba attached to the 57 Class and hauled it to Valley Heights.

The safeworking regulations for the section between Valley Heights and Katoomba were unique in New South Wales in that they specifically prohibited propelling* trains between these two points and categorically stated that sections had to be cleared by the relief engine coming onto the rear of the disabled train and, with the authority of a signalman's** wrong line order, to return to the station in the rear. I raised this point with the train controller, who I think was not aware of it. There was silence for a time after I had raised it, and from what I now know I am sure he was not on his own. I suggested that, while the movements to be made would be confined to station limits and that as I would be fouling the Up Main with necessary shunt movements, it was not possible for me to accept an Up train from Woodford and I would not accept a train from Springwood until I had the disabled train complete and moving from my station. These movements were agreed to and I think it was probably the train control superintendent who did so. Despite this, the train controller still pressured me to accept that passenger. The remarkable thing about this episode was that no correspondence had resulted. After this incident I sent the first *genl*** telegram I had ever sent.

The second incident was one that was very scary. At the time there were a number of storms about. Although it was only around 10.30am, No 23 *Caves Express* had passed and I had given Springwood line clear for No 25 Passenger. Suddenly there was a most vivid flash of lightning that seemed to run around the signal box, followed by huge clap of thunder. The lightning had struck the earth pole adjacent to the end of the signal box, and there was so much dust in the signal box that I had to get out onto the platform. When I did, I saw that one of the 1500 volt overhead wires which crossed over the line above the fettlers' trolley shed on the Springwood end of the platform had broken and was dancing like a snake striking at a victim. Every time it hit the Up rail of the Down Main sparks flew and a hole appeared on top of the rail.

I went straight back into the signal box and sent 'obstruction danger to Springwood' (the only time in my life I used it). Springwood, upon hearing it, placed the signals against No 25 that was coming into the platform. I could not raise the train controller, so I contacted the Assistant District Superintendent at Lithgow and told him what had happened. He had a direct line to the Electrical Superintendent at Lawson. This man assured the ADS that the overhead wiring was now dead and that I could safely move it,

---

* In railway language or parlance the words 'propel, propelling, or propelled' always referred to an engine being at the rear of the train for the purpose of propelling it forward. This term was only used when there was no engine, or the engine had failed, on the front of the train or vehicles to be propelled.

** When an engine was despatched into a section to retrieve a train whose engine had failed, the driver's authority to return to the station in the wrong running direction was 'A Signalman's Wrong Line Order'. If a starting signal was at the entrance to the section he was authorised to return to that signal. From there he acted under the instructions from the signalman, usually by hand signal.

*** *genl* was the telegraphic code address for all Heads of Branches and many of their Senior Staff, the telegram was confined to serious mainline incidents.

Linden railway station situated in the Lower Blue Mountains of New South Wales taken in May 1985. Despite the rather substantial type of station building, Linden has a very small population and the surrounding terrain cannot allow for any great residential and commercial development. The station's location also suffers from the very restrictive access from the adjoining Great Western Highway.   *John R Newland.*

using a stick. Before I put the receiver back I asked the ADS if he had heard the conversation. He had. I went to shift it before accepting No 25 for two reasons; firstly to get an assurance from the ganger that the line was OK and secondly, to see how they had fared. The ganger and his men were all as white as ghosts.

The wire, when it fell, landed across the trolley shed. To this day I do not know why they were not electrocuted. The ganger said every time it hit the rail, it hit the roof of the trolley shed sending blue sparks around the roof; obviously the shed was well earthed. After the ganger certified that the track was OK, I went back to the signal box and gave Springwood one bell on the block instrument (which was universal for 'speak on telephone') and received no reply. I then rang on the railway circuit telephone and was able to speak to him. His instrument was still showing line clear and he was able to let No 25 depart. The lightning, when it struck, blew every fuse in Linden signal box, placing all the instruments out of order. It was then that we resorted to telephone block working between Linden, Woodford and Springwood. I went back to the trolley shed to get the fettlers to act as flagmen at the two starting signals for me. I was told they were all going home sick for the day. They did not say they were going for a change of underwear; they well may have been.

The electrician arrived on the next Up passenger and was there for nearly a week repairing and rewiring the signal box. I sent my second *genl* telegram. I was able to get fettlers on the next Down passenger from Springwood, and the two signals were manned by flagmen for 24 hours a day before they were restored to use. The same conditions applied to Springwood's starting signal which also had to be flagged for the next 24 hours. Not one supervising traffic officer came near Linden during the time that the signals were out of order, and I remember thinking at the time they must have had a peculiar set of priorities.

One legendary happening at Linden, which occurred some years earlier, had happened once again between officers who apparently did not speak to one another. During the day, No 78 pick-up had detached a truck of sleepers for Linden into the Up Refuge, and there it stayed. The daywork officer detaching it failed to gravitate it into the goods siding which, as I have already mentioned, was an extension of the refuge. Not only did he not do this, he made no recording anywhere of the fact that the truck was on hand. The afternoon officer, who must have known the wagon was there, because he signed on in daylight as the wagon would have been almost opposite the signal box, also made no attempt to place the wagon in the siding. His greatest sin, however, was in not telling the backshift officer that the wagon was in the refuge. Somewhere around 3.30am the train controller directed the officer to refuge a returning light engine for No 46 Mail.

After the Mail departed and he had the road, the officer cleared the refuge signals for the engine to depart. The driver of the engine stopped after hitting something that appeared to be a wagon and came back to the signal box. He told the officer that he had hit a wagon and it had taken off. The officer did not believe the driver and spent some time trying to establish if indeed there had been any train shunted which might have left a wagon. When he found that No 78 had on the previous day shunted, he finally told the train controller that a truck was running away from his refuge. The train controller also apparently took some persuading that the officer was serious. The train controller rang Springwood to tell him of it.

By this time Springwood's track had been occupied for minutes. The officer thought it was the light engine, but also thought it must have been in a hurry to get home at the speed it was travelling. A goods train was in the refuge at Springwood. The train controller directed Springwood to let the wagon run toward Penrith, which was the next point where the wagon could be run into a dead end. The wagon however was travelling at such speed it caught up with No 46 *Dubbo Mail*, which by this time was travelling toward Penrith, on the Lapstone side of the Glenbrook tunnel. It is said, and I have no verification of this, that it hit the brakevan of No 46 with such force that a sleeper dislodged from the wagon and was found on the buffers of the brakevan at Penrith.

It is a fact, however, that it hit the van a number of times around the horseshoe bend between Lapstone and Emu Plains. These bumps or hits steadied it down to the extent that it barely had sufficient speed left to take it over the rise from Emu Plains and over the

Nepean River bridge, but it picked up speed again before entering Penrith yard where it was let run into a rake of trucks without any further damage. The daywork and afternoon officers were both regressed a grade for 12 months. I do not know if the backshift officer suffered any punishment. The two officers concerned were working on the mountains when I first went to Glenbrook.

One evening when I was on afternoon shift, Springwood tapped me (one bell on the Block Telegraph instrument) to say he had a lady there in some distress because she thought she had left a parcel of opera tickets on No 85. He named the carriage she was in. I found them and advised him. He said the lady would drive up and pick them up. I did not think greatly about this and I made the required entry in the lost property book and put them in the safe. Not long after, the lady arrived for her tickets and while signing for them, she said there were a thousand tickets in the parcel and they were worth £15 each, a very considerable sum of money. I do not know how she came to have this number of tickets. They apparently were registered to her and as such, she was responsible for any loss. After she told me this and saying how grateful she was, she scratched around in her handbag and came up with 2 shillings and 6 pence to give me. I declined the offer with thanks. The amazing thing to me was, that if she was going to offer something, and I certainly did not look for anything, that it should be such an amount after telling me the ticket's value. Candidly, I felt insulted but did not say so.

Another of the features of many afternoon shifts was the presence of detectives from the Railway Investigation Branch. Pilfering in those days was enjoying probably what could be described as a successful high point in its nefarious history. It was down to a fine art by a number of gangs, who used to get gang members into a number of wagons on a train from Darling Harbour. Between Springwood and Lawson they used to toss goods out onto the side of the line and their cohorts used to drive beside the line and gather up their plunder and drive off into the night with it. The detectives used to get up on the high cutting coming into Linden and could see if they were in wagons or if the louvre van doors were open and if they were, the detectives would high tail it to Woodford and search the train there. They were successful on a number of occasions, although I think more escaped in the dark than they caught.

One of the assistant station masters at Linden, who will remain nameless although he has long left this earthly abode, featured very prominently in a scandal which became widely known through its reaching the metropolitan press and *The Truth*, in particular. This officer was returning home one evening when he was attacked viciously as he was going to the side path leading to the rear door of his home in Hazelbrook. He was left unconscious and remained so for days. The milkman found him early in the morning. The police and ambulance were called and he was taken to the Blue Mountains District Hospital.

It seemed he had been attacked for no reason at all. However, the police, after some time investigating the brutal incident, arrested a man and the ASM's wife for the attempted murder. It appeared they had been having an affair for some time and conspired to get rid of the ASM by attacking him with the barrel of a shotgun, and leaving him to die where he fell. He carried a large long scar from above his right eye into his hairline for the rest of his life. The man and woman were tried and found guilty of the lesser charge of malicious wounding—why, I have never fathomed. The most cruel and subhuman behaviour, I thought, came from his wife, a woman who had borne him a daughter, who at that time was about five years old. The woman had gone to bed and apparently slept, leaving him to die. The man was given a substantially longer sentence than her, he being responsible for the actual wounding. She received five years and after serving around two years and six months, became eligible for parole. The parole board tried very hard to get the husband to be responsible for her and have her in the house again. Not surprisingly, he refused.

He and I had long talks about the whole business; he apparently saw me as a good listener. He had no inkling that his wife was having an affair and in the beginning was very supportive of her. It was not until she finally confessed her guilt and implicated the man that he realised the enormity of what she had done. With the help of his own mother, he was left to rear a five year old daughter, who had been deprived of a mother. The older lady found that rearing a five year old, who was desperately missing her own mother, quite difficult. She tried to apply those rules to her granddaughter that she used when raising a large family of her own many years earlier. The wife was released on parole after members of her own family agreed to look after her welfare. It was a very sad happening that really ruined the lives of all the participants.

One of the early morning joys was to watch the sunrise (one way of keeping awake!) across the valley that was northeast from the Up side of the platform. On many mornings there would be a fog or mist in the valley that would appear to rise up and greet the sunrise; a magnificent spectacle.

It was in April of 1954 Mamie discovered that she was going to be a mother. We were both thoroughly delighted. It was expected that early December would see the arrival of our son or daughter. The hope was very much for a son, as Mamie had no brothers, being the youngest of five daughters. In about August, I was offered a long list of Third Class Assistant Station Master positions; among them was Orange East Fork, which I took as number one preference. I took the job knowing full well that its reputation preceded it all over New South Wales. I was told by all and sundry that I was mad, that the job was a man killer and that I should have my transfer papers made out before I left Linden. As far as I was concerned that, by getting the position, I jumped about 200 fourth class ASMs. Had I not taken the job, I would not have got any of the positions on that list. I was confident that if I could do a head shunter's job at Parkes, I could do Orange East Fork. Because of the impending birth, Mamie left Springwood in early October and went home, I finally left Linden in the beginning of November of 1954.

THIRD CLASS ASSISTANT STATION MASTER, ORANGE EAST FORK

O NE of the first concerns on arriving at Orange was to find suitable accommodation. Any type of rented accommodation was extremely difficult to get. For the time I was on my own, I had rented a small room with a kitchenette and little else, entirely unsuitable for the needs of a small family. After much searching, I was taken by an agent to see one of the wartime duration houses for sale in the Glenroi suburb of Orange. These houses had two bedrooms, a lounge/dining area, a kitchenette and bathroom complete with tin bath and chip heater. The drawback was the laundry which was built half on our property and half on the next door neighbour's, meaning we had to share the laundry. The asking price was £450. When one went into a bank in those days and asked for finance to buy a house, you were treated as though you were some lowly creature just arrived on the planet.

I finally convinced the Bank of New South Wales that I was a good credit risk; they agreed even more so when my father-in-law guaranteed me. All excitement, we at last had a place of our own. On Sunday 5 December 1954, our son Roy David arrived. Roy was named after his maternal grandfather and David after a good Methodist minister friend of mine.

When I first walked into the signal box at Orange East Fork and saw the row of levers stretching almost to eternity, I was tempted to walk out again! When I accepted Orange East Fork, one of the attractions was that it was three shifts around, meaning each officer had a turn

of daywork. Imagine my absolute disappointment when, in the first week I was learning, the daywork, it was elevated to a Sixth Class Station Master. This of course put the remaining officers on afternoon and backshift. It was a real blow; it was a decision not easily understood in hindsight. The daywork, except for a two hour period in the afternoon, was no busier than any other normal shift. In fact, it was nowhere near as busy as stock nights from about 2.00am in the morning until the daywork shift signed on duty. The hours of duty for the assistants were Sunday 7.55pm to 11.55pm, and Monday to Saturday 3.55pm to 11.55pm. The afternoon shift, when the roster worked, had the first Thursday, Friday and Saturday off. The backshift was 11.55pm from the first Thursday through to the last Saturday in the period. This meant 10 straight backshifts on alternate fortnights; it was not much wonder that there was disappointment at the changing of the staff.

In the 1950s, the shortage of staff state wide was chronic. The Orange District, because of its size and geographical area, failed to attract officers to its general relief staff, with the result that the staff position in *oran* (code for District Superintendent Orange) was worse than any other country superintendent's district. The upshot of this was that the reducing time roster at East Fork was cancelled for probably 30 per cent of the time I was there. The working of 14 backshifts straight at East Fork was intolerable, especially so in the summer months. The afternoon shifts were 13 in the fortnight, by virtue of the fact that the four

Orange East Fork Signal Box taken in January 1988 viewed from the east. The lines to the left beyond the signal box include the beginning of the Parkes and Broken Hill line. The points in the foreground comprise the beginning of the double line to Spring Hill.   John R Newland.

hour shifts on Sunday were regarded as half days. I recall once having worked 54 days out of 56 and then going down with a heavy dose of influenza and going off sick for a day. An hour had not passed when the traffic inspector came to my home to see if I was really ill. I was in bed. The anger I felt at the staff clerk doubting my veracity must have shown in my face when he was saying why he was there, because he was apologising for being there before he finished saying why he was there.

I went for two years without holidays and in the third year we were limited to a three-week holiday. Another imposition was the frequent rostering of 12-hour shifts. It would not have been so bad to work from 4.00pm to 4.00am, however the station master refused to work from 4.00am to 4.00pm which meant I worked from 8.00pm to 8.00am. On another occasion, the backshift officer failed to report for duty. Thinking I was being considerate, I waited until 4.00am and then went to call the station master, but despite all the noise I made outside his window, I got no response.

There was not another soul in the area who knew how to work the signal box; I worked 16 hours (fool that I was) and booked for only 12 hours. The SM swore he did not hear me at his window, but he still signed on duty at 4.00am. I had told the ASM at Orange that I wanted the traffic inspector in attendance after 4.00am, but when his movements were checked with Orange Control, it was found that he was in Parkes. After the event, and the next time I saw him, I spoke to the assistant superintendent, who to my way of thinking, was not only an excellent administrator but also a gentleman. I told him what had happened and that if it happened again, I would not breach the award. His response was that he knew I had worked the 16 hours and that he had made his displeasure known very strongly to the station master.

East Fork was and still is the pivotal centre of the Orange rail network. It stood on the Down Main Western Line at the point where the double line between East Fork and

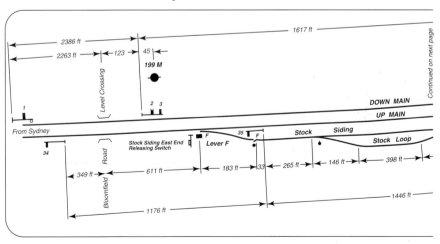

ORANGE EAST FORK JUNCTION SIGNAL BOX

1 Down Outer Distant
2 Down Inner Distant
3 Down Outer Home
4 Home Main
5 Home Main, Main to East Fork
6 Spare
7 Up Main to East Fork
8 Up Main to Main
9 Up Main to Stock Siding
10 Down Starting, Main (6)
11 Down 2nd Home, East Fork
12 East Fork to Loop Siding
13 East Fork to Loco Siding
14 East Fork to Traffic Sidings
15 Spare
16 Spare
17 Trap Points in Up Main
18 Points to Main — Down Main & Catch Point in Stock Siding
19 Points to Main — East Fork
20 FPL 8 and 19 points
21 FPL 8 points
22 Spare
23 FPL 24 points
24 Points, East Fork Jct — Loco or Traffic Sidings
25 Points, East Fork — Traffic Sidings
26 Points, East Fork — Loco Sidings
27 FPL 28 points
28 Points, East Fork — Loop Siding

29 FPL 28 points
30 Up Accept (30 or 63)
31 Call on, Up Main
32 Release for F
33 Release for G
34 Up Starting Main
35 Up 3rd Home, Main
36 Stock Siding to Up Main
37 Up 2nd Home, Main
38 Up Home, Main
39 Up Distant, Main
40 Call on, East Fork to Up Main
41 Key for Duplex Lock, 48 points
42 Up 3rd Home, East Fork to Up Main
43 East Fork to Dead End
44 Traffic Sidings to East Fork
45 Loco Sidings to East Fork
46 Loop Siding to East Fork
47 Up 2nd Home, East Fork
48 Points, East Fork — Loop Siding
49 Key for Duplex Lock, 50 points
50 Points, Branch — East Fork
51 (A) East Fork or (B) West Fork to Branch
52 Starting (A) East or (B) West Fork to Branch
53 Down Distant, Branch
54 Up Home, Branch to East Fork
55 Up Home, Branch to Loop Siding
56 Up Home, Branch to West Fork (1)

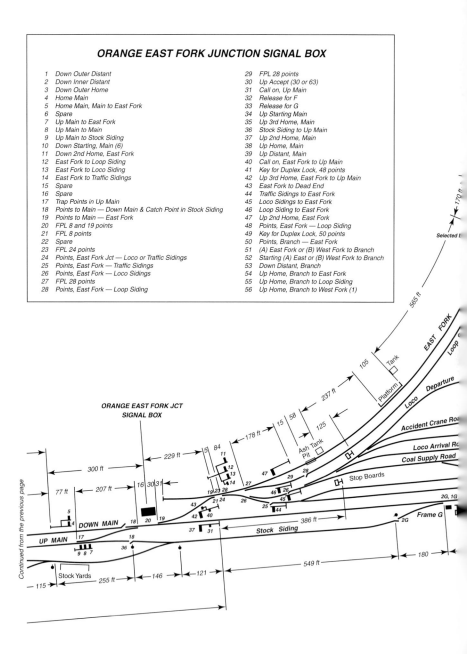

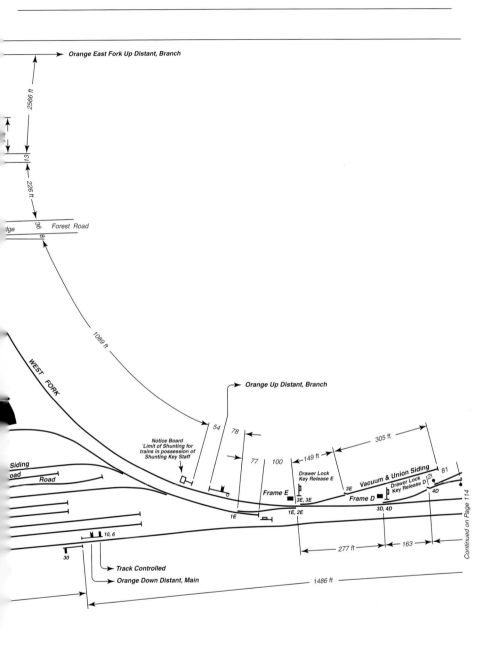

Orange East Fork Up Distant, Branch

2566 ft

131

226 ft

36
|8|

Idge   Forest Road

1089 ft

WEST FORK

Orange Up Distant, Branch

54   78

Notice Board
'Limit of Shunting for
trains in possession of
Shunting Key Staff

77   100   149 ft

305 ft

81

Siding
oad
Road

Drawer Lock
Key Release E

Vacuum & Union Siding

Drawor Lock
Key Release D |2|

Frame E

3E

3E, 3E

Frame D

3D, 4D

4D

1E, 2E

1E

277 ft   163

10, 6

30

Track Controlled

Orange Down Distant, Main

1486 ft

Continued on Page 114

Spring Hill began. At the western end of the signal box was the East Fork that carried traffic to Molong and all points west. The locomotive depot stood inside the three points of the triangle. The Orange stockyards were opposite the signal box. Access to them was by a key release on the Up Main some 100 metres from the Up Starting signal. Emmco siding was situated between East Fork and Orange and was worked from a key release in East Fork box. In the shunting yard (so called) were three roads; one of which held about 54 vehicles, the second about 50 and the third about 12. A loop or refuge was attached to the East Fork. This held 45 vehicles and an engine.

The stockyards had two roads, each of which held about 30 wagons. When stock was loading, wagons from these roads were gravitated to the stock race. Generally sheep vans were placed in one road and cattle wagons in the other. A long lead-in before the roads separated, was on the Spring Hill side. The release for the stockyards was near the Up Starting signal. On the Orange end of the yards, a holding road for unloaded empties or loaded wagons held some 25 wagons. This road was also used to store Orange traffic from Up trains and stock for Rodgers Siding at Orange.

At the entrance to the locomotive depot and worked by a Thompson lever was the coal siding, which ran parallel to the roads in the yard, with about 20 metres separating them. As with all coal roads, it ran up the coal stage from where the coal was released into the coal bins. Beside this road, the locomotive depot had an engine arrival and departure road. An emergency exit road for engines was provided onto the South Fork; this was used when derailments or other emergencies prevented engines from travelling via East Fork Signal Box. At the Orange end of the stock siding storage road was Emmco Siding that was worked by a release from Orange East Fork Signal Box. This siding was shunted at least once a day by the shunters and shunting engine from Orange. At this time, the traffic in the stock storage siding was also cleared to Orange.

The systems of safeworking were on the Down and Up double line between Spring Hill and Orange East Fork NSW Standard Block Telegraph; the worst feature of this being that there was no starting signal control. Between Orange East Fork and Orange single line track block safeworking was controlled by an accepting lever in each of the signal boxes. Between Orange–Orange East Fork and Nashdale, miniature electric staff was used. Orange East Fork was classified as an intermediate staff station. If No 54 motor points failed, which were the points directing trains either into East Fork or Down to Orange, pilot working had to be instituted between Orange and No 54 points, East Fork of course having to sign the pilot working forms to complete them.

The pilot man worked between No 54 points and Orange. For trains destined for Orange from Nashdale, he wound the motor points across and accompanied the train to Orange. There were no pilotman's caution tickets. If the points failed and there were no trains destined for Orange, pilot working was not required. The points were clipped and locked and the signal passed by authority of a flagman under the provisions of Rule 95. It was the only section that I know of in this State where a driver was allowed to enter a section in possession of the staff for the section and to find that when he came to a signal worked by Orange East Fork, and not Orange, at stop, he had to surrender the staff to the pilotman and be accompanied by a pilotman to Orange Box. Two tokens for one section?

The job at Orange East Fork was certainly not for the faint hearted nor for the weak in the back. Some of the signals, but more especially the points and lockbars*, required a good deal of strength to manipulate. There was a certain art, of course, in using the heavy levers especially the facing point lockbars. The art was to hit the lever hard so that the lockbar rose up to rail level and would almost then fall into position. Sundays and Mondays were the easiest days. Tuesday evenings and Wednesday mornings, together with Saturday evenings and Sunday mornings, were absolute bedlam, especially when there were heavy stock movements. Thursdays and Fridays were busy but were manageable without being sinecures. The staff besides the officers were two shunters, who signed on duty at 2.00am and 10.30am.

All Down freight passed through East Fork and was worked through Orange; they formed the Down trains west to Dubbo and to Parkes. All Up freight worked through Orange East Fork. All locomotives, whether working Down trains from Orange or going light engine to Molong to assist, departed from Loco via Orange East Fork. All incoming engines, whether working Down trains into Orange or Up trains into East Fork, went into loco via the arrival road. This also applied to the mail trains that changed engines at Orange.

The only regular Up Goods through Orange was No 34 express goods, which started daily from Dubbo running via Wellington. There were occasions when No 34 picked up stock or LCL containers from East Fork, which meant tying the train up on the main line. Because of the pressure that was always on not to delay No 34, an engine was usually standing on the traffic to be attached at East Fork. No 34's engine was cut off and run onto the Up Main while the engine with the traffic came out of the yard behind and placed (dropped, is a better word) onto the train on the main line.

I remember being a bit snaky one afternoon and threatening to back the train into the yard to do the shunt. Traffic was arriving on a train to East Fork due at the same time that No 34 was tabled to leave Orange. In addition, the traffic was in two places on the arriving train, the driver of which had sent a *zona*** saying the crew wanted relief on arrival,

---

* The term refers to the facing point lock bar associated with the facing point lock that locks the points into position after they had been set for a movement. The lock bar is located alongside, and on the inner side of a rail at points, and prevents the facing point lock being manipulated when the wheels of a vehicle are standing on the lock bar.

**Code word for on duty over 10 hours and consequently *requires relief on arrival.*

which meant that another five minutes was lost while he was relieved by another crew. Less than a minute after I had made the threat, the assistant superintendent, for whom (as I have already said) I would have done almost anything, rang and asked me if I would please do my best. He had obviously been in the Train Control Office!

No 8 goods, which ran from Molong, was timetabled into Orange but on most occasions, it ran into East Fork. In the original scheme, No 8 was to provide the loading for the build up of No 34 at Orange, but more often than not, there was sufficient loading for No 34 available at Orange.

The train that I had the most difficulty with was No 140 pickup that ran Mondays, Wednesdays, Thursdays and Fridays. On Mondays, Wednesdays and Fridays a rostered guard, from Bathurst worked it. The train commenced from Orange and was built up to a load allowing for the pick-ups en-route. It could be guaranteed it would be at least 15 minutes late from Orange every night, the guard finding some reason to be late away. When he arrived at East Fork, it was impossible to get him to move, even though it was due out of East Fork at 12.40am. During the whole time that I had spent there, I doubt if I ever got the train away on time with this guard more than a dozen times. When he came into the signal box for his instructions, he would boil the 'billy' and take his 'billy' of tea down to his van, then go back to where he had to detach the locomotive to attach his loading. If it were one shunt only, he would find a truck with a loose tarpaulin and book time re-tying it. If you got exasperated and walked down the shunting yard to see what he was doing, he would walk away from the truck that he was supposed to be working on when you were about 20 paces away.

Another trick was to lift a couple of Alliance auto-coupling levers as he walked back to the van, so that when he picked up his traffic it would part, thus taking time to re-couple. He got away with these antics for years, mainly because he used to show on his journal the actual time he left a station as being the on-time time for his train, so his journal never showed late running. I have often been critical of chargemen and others for not exercising stronger supervision, but in this case I was just as guilty as anyone else. I will say, however, that in later years, as I became more experienced in the ways of 'bludgers', he would not have got away with what he did.

The Up trains working into East Fork from Dubbo and Parkes were mostly worked by two 50 Classes with a load of 680 tons. The single 50 Class load from Orange East Fork to Bathurst was 640 tons. Leaving aside stock nights for the moment, No 26 which ran from Parkes, conveyed, about 90 per cent of the times it ran, traffic for either Rogers Siding (Rogers Meatworks and siding were situated in the Orange–Mullion Creek section), Orange Stock, short traffic for Blayney or the Cowra line and Orange traffic, which had to be detached at East Fork. The loading off No 26 was the basis for No 266 which, when I first arrived East Fork, was a Bathurst train (1954 and still depot hopping?). This, however, changed with the introduction of 40 Class diesels. The 40 Classes worked No 465 West from Darling Harbour, with an engine change at Orange, and effected the next day delivery to Wellington and Dubbo.

No 466 was scheduled to convey a 600-ton Enfield load, but the great problem that we had at East Fork was that the shunters at Parkes would build No 26 Up with Clyde area traffic and, with the other short traffic on the train, it made life difficult at East Fork. Generally speaking, an hour's shunting was required to form No 466 which was due away at 4.40am. To ensure the availability of the Westinghouse air brake certificate issued by the train examiner to the driver, an auxiliary compressor, known as a ground plant, was placed in between Nos 1 and 2 roads. This enabled the train examiner to properly adjust the brake piston travel without the necessity of having an engine attached. He was allowed two hours for that task and with No 26 arriving East Fork about 2.00am, it was always difficult to get the train formed on time. On most occasions, No 465 with the 40 Class diesel arrived around 4.00am.

The 40 Class, which had a single driving point situated toward one end of the locomotive, had to be driven with the short end leading because of the fumes which permeated the driving cabin when the long end was leading. The engine had to run via the East Fork triangle from Orange, this being necessary to turn the engine. Finding a gap when an electric staff was available on stock nights was difficult. Often Orange Control would not allow the engine to travel via the triangle, which meant that it had to return direct to East Fork and go into the locomotive depot to turn on the turntable. The staff in the depot resisted this course of action; they invariably delayed the engine in the depot.

Whether the train departed on time depended on which examiner was on duty. There were three examiners who examined this train, two of whom did no more than they were required to, especially when the weather conditions were unkind, which they often were. With these two, the train would be ready at 4.40am. The third examiner, whom I was not critical of then although I frequently cursed him, was a perfectionist. While not being critical of his 'perfectionism', he often took more than 60 minutes over the brake allowance time.

To my knowledge, the Mechanical Branch, although they were being constantly debited with delays, took no action against him. He adjusted the piston travel on every vehicle if they were overdue. He inspected the triple valves and adjusted those. The train drivers vouched for his work. They would, and did, all state that any train he examined had handled better brake-wise than that those of other examiners in the West.

Stock night at East Fork on Tuesday nights/Wednesday mornings would see the following movements. The times I am quoting will be approximate, for each light engine that ran an *akru* (code for timetable) was prepared by *oran* that varied from day to day. The Down freight trains of course never ran to the same time on successive days, No 465 being the most reliable. A perusal of the timetable (as set out below on this page) for that period may reveal a variation in the times shown, because I am relying on my memory, for one of my aims in this writing this is to write my autobiography while I have recall of the events at the time.

From about 3.00am until 7.00am this officer did not stop pulling levers on these mornings. On many occasions the assistant superintendent, who used to be on duty either in Dubbo or Orange Control until around 10.00pm on Tuesday evenings, would arrange for Richards siding stock or meat for the private sidings in the Sydney area to come off Nos 50 and 372 and go onto No 62.

While there was not a lot of shunting in these movements, there was so much else moving that getting the margins to shunt was the problem. This was especially so with No 372, because the Down Mails were coming through during this time. Once the through

Train	Time Arrival	Time Departure	From	Destination
L372/62	12.30am		East Fork	Molong
50FS	1.30am	2.30am	Parkes	Flemington
50FS.LE	1.30am	1.40am	East Fork	Loco Depot
155	1.50am		Bathurst	Orange
155LE	2.10am	2.15am	Orange	Loco Depot
465 Goods	3.20am		Darling Harbour	Orange
465E	4.10am via S & E Fork		Orange	Work No 466
L236/238	3.20am	3.25am	East Fork	Molong
372 FS	3.50am	4.40am	Coonamble	Flemington
372FS.LE	3.50am	4.00am	East Fork	Loco Depot
45 Mail	3.45am		Sydney	Dubbo
59 Mail	4.05am		Sydney	Bourke
49LE	4.09am	4.14am	East Fork	Orange
49 Mail	4.12am		Sydney	Forbes
466 Exp Goods	4.40am		East Fork	Enfield
49 Mail via S Fork	4.42am		Orange	Forbes
49E	4.42am	4.47am	Orange	Loco Depot
L65	4.25am	4.30am	East Fork	Orange
62FS	5.10am	6.00am	Dubbo	Flemington
62FS LE	5.10am	5.25am	East Fork	Loco Depot
99 Goods	5.15am		Darling Harbour	Dubbo
99E	5.40am	5.45am	Orange	Loco Depot
L99	5.50am	5.55am	East Fork	Orange
L247	6.10am	6.15am	East Fork	Orange
L107	6.20am	6.25am	East Fork	Orange
91 Pick-up	7.30am		Bathurst	Orange
107 Via South Fork	7.10am		Orange	Parkes
91E	7.55am	8.00am	Orange	Loco Depot
236FS	8.10am	9.00am	Dubbo	Flemington
236FS.LE	8.10am	8.20am	East Fork	Loco Depot

road was given to a Down train, the dead end, which held two engines clear of the points, was available for the purposes of either despatching engines to Molong from Loco, or off a train which had arrived on East Fork into Loco. So effectively, every time the through road was cleared, seven or eight minutes of the available shunting time was lost. Of the time allowed at Orange East Fork for each stock train, 30 minutes was allowed to recondition the locomotive; water was taken, the fire de-ashed and the coal shovelled forward by the fuelman. I always tried to clear the signal near the pit when stock trains arrived so that the second engine was placed for servicing before the lead engine was detached. This was an important time saver, because generally only 20 minutes were available for shunting and for the examiner to do the brakes on the traffic attached.

Many of these trains had train drovers travelling with them, whose job it was to see that the stock arrived at the destination point in as good condition as possible. This particularly applied to cattle coming from the Far West. More often than not, the train was No 62. The stock on this train originated from stations as far afield as Byrock and Bourke. By the time they arrived at East Fork, they had already been in the wagons upwards of 24 hours. Also on many occasions, drovers accompanied stock on Nos 372 and 236. It was a nightmare when the drover wanted to take his stock to the yards to attend to them, which generally meant unloading and reloading the wagon or wagons. Time was of no great significance to the drovers; their concern being, and quite rightly, to get their stock back on their feet and in fit condition to travel the remainder of the journey to Flemington. However, I must confess they frustrated me when I was trying to get some sort of a forecast to give Lithgow Control (*lico*), who would ring every 15 minutes or so.

Some of the train controllers there could get quite nasty, one especially with whom in later years I crossed swords as an equal. So far as we were concerned, No 62 was the best train to have stock go to the yards, mainly because there was nothing close behind it and the balance of the train could safely be left on the main line. But if the train was No 372, we were in trouble because it meant that No 62 was brought into the loop and left there until No 372 had departed. When I was on duty and because there was no pit on the loop, I used to try and get a fresh engine for No 62. I failed to get a fresh engine more often than I got one. However, I recall at least two occasions where I did and actually despatched No 62 ahead of No 372, to the chagrin of my favourite train controller in *lico*. Another move was to put the engine into Loco for servicing; a move fraught with danger, because the shed staff resented having extra work in the depot and made sure the loco was well and truly delayed every time we tried it. I used to think the chargeman lacked supervisory skills and nothing has since changed my mind!

It will be generally well known that today and for sometime past, livestock has not been carried in New South Wales. In fact, the only stockwagons in this state are now exhibits in museums. Whilst there is a case for deploring the loss of revenue, I am firmly of the opinion that it was a good move. I believed during the time I was at East Fork, that the carriage of livestock long distances by rail, cattle especially, was cruelty to dumb animals. The amazing thing to me was that the RSPCA seemed to condone this form of cruelty. It has, of course, to be said there was little alternative other than to transport stock to the metropolitan abattoirs by rail, when no, or few at best, country abattoirs existed. Therein, I suspect, lay the reason for the inactivity of the RSPCA.

The Saturday night/Sunday morning stock nights provided just as much work with the stock. However, the volume of Down trains and engines arriving and departing Loco was greatly reduced. But the work for this officer changed somewhat because no shunter was employed on Sunday mornings, and he subsequently had to work the signal frame and do the shunting. Although it was the duty of the outgoing guard to assist, getting them to do so was difficult, especially the Lithgow guards who claimed they did not know the yard.

The favourite ploy of one guard was not to refuse to shunt, but when the train arrived he would say that his handover was not satisfactory, or he could not read the X2010 Form, and he was going to retake the wagon numbers. The officer never got to see the handover, of course, and did not know if he was being truthful. What the officer did know was who the incoming guard was, which told him the type of handover he would get.

In my first week, I had my only derailment at East Fork. I had taken the road off the engine of No 264 shunting in the yard. It was stopped some distance from the signal and I thought I was safe and altered the road. When the shunter waved him ahead, the driver did not look again and passed the signal and he came off the road. I had to accept responsibility.

I have mentioned that the instruments were not starter controlled between East Fork and Spring Hill. On one occasion No 59 *Bourke Mail*, for which train Spring Hill had obtained line clear, was a few minutes late when train departure was received from Spring Hill. I was shunting No 372 and got back in clear just as No 59 rounded the bend approaching the home signal. I cleared the two homes and starter and probably delayed No 59, which did not stop, a minute with the distant being at caution. (A distant signal has two aspects, caution and clear. If the signal is at caution it tells the driver the home signal may be at stop). As the train was passing the signal box, I heard a distant whistle and looked up to see No 49 coming round the bend and approaching the home signal. Fortunately, I had put the signal back as soon as No 59 passed it. (I was anxious to get another shunt in before No 49 was due.)

I tried to get onto to Spring Hill to see what was going on because he had not asked for line clear for No 49, but I was not able to raise him. About five minutes later he came on the telephone to me and wanted to know if No 49 had passed; it had just done so. I had held it because Orange could not accept it being so close to No 59 and that I had trains to shunt. He admitted he had gone to sleep and had not put the signals back behind No 59, (remember no starter control) and when No 49 passed Spring Hill, the fireman threw the Millthorpe-Spring Hill staff onto the platform, he hoped, because at that stage he did not have it.

That was the first and only time I was involved, albeit innocently, when two trains were in the one section. To use the great railway word, without which many sins would have come to light, it was 'squared' up. I do not know what times Spring Hill gave *lico*; I did not report either train. If the driver of No 49 knew what had happened, he did not say so. When I signed him into Loco, he said,

"Did that make you uncomfortable?"

And with that he opened the regulator and took off. The true answer, if I had been able to answer him was,

"Yes, it did, and it frightened the life out of me when I saw No 49 approaching the Home."

Another frightening episode: I expect, that if anything had happened, I would have been held responsible, although to this day I believe I was a victim of circumstances.

Although No 49 was running about 15 minutes late into Orange, the new engine worked by a Parkes driver, whistled out of Loco on time to work No 49 from Orange to Parkes. Orange Box agreed to take the engine ahead of No 49. The engine came out of Loco and left for Orange without incident. I took no further notice of it and worked signals off the branch. When I had done this, some 10 minutes later, I looked toward Orange and saw that there was green light in Orange's accept. I looked at the track diagram and saw all white, and assumed that Orange had 'dropped' me the road for No 49. It was another safe working anomaly that meant he could do this without East Fork having any control over it.

When I saw the all white on my diagram I cleared the full road for No 49. This train by now was in sight and as it came toward the home signal, I heard a click from the diagram and, as I did I saw the accept signal go to stop. The driver of No 49 made a heavy brake application as he passed the signal box and came to stand without too much discomfort at the accept. It transpired that the outgoing driver of No 49 had left his tucker box in the chargeman's office and remembered as he started to go to Orange. He stopped the engine on the main line, ambled over to the chargeman's office and returned to his engine with his tucker box. This took about 10 minutes. Orange had not, as I assumed, 'dropped' me the road.

The thing that concerned me was that the diagram was not showing a red ball, or so I thought. I discovered that from the point where I had been standing, reflection from the overhead lights on the glass on the diagram obscured the indicator and gave the appearance of all white. It was a serious occurrence and could have ended tragically had the engine not moved when it did. No 49 had the full road and was entitled to be travelling at full speed. When the driver got back to East Fork he wanted to know what had happened. Naturally, for not only did it leave me shaking for some time after, it frightened him too. I held nothing from him and even took him into the box to show how Orange could 'drop' the road and also stood him where I had been standing when I thought the diagram was showing track clear. He was a good driver and a very pleasant older man, I asked him did he want it reported and he said,

"No, but until you were so honest with me I wanted somebody's hide."

I did not blame him for that. I had been at East Fork a long time when that happened and other than my first derailment, I had had no safeworking mistakes and was very meticulous regarding safeworking.

I was the only officer at East Fork who used lever sleeves for the purpose that they were intended. I never had a train standing in the loop or main line on the East Fork without having a lever sleeve protecting, not only the main line signals approaching East Fork from Nashdale, but also the signals at the East Fork end. This was to stop me from despatching a light engine to Molong on a line that was already occupied, which happened at least four times with other officers while I was there. These instances did not result in any collisions because on each occasion the driver saw the wagons and stopped.

A story I was told after I left East Fork concerned the senior inspector at Orange, who, conscientious as he was, made an inspection at East Fork during stock night, or more precisely, morning. About 4.00am he contacted East Fork to find out who the guard was on No 372, because he found a sheep van with the top deck open. He closed it and was going to have the guard for not seeing it and closing and reporting it, in case there was a claim for lost sheep. When the train reached Blayney and made a crossing, the drover stormed into the ASM's Office and reported that some idiot had shut and secured a sheep van door while he was attending sheep in the top deck of the truck. When he went to get out he could not and had been unable to release the door before the train started, not easy to do from inside the van. The poor bloke had ridden from East Fork to Blayney in the sheep van. The inspector copped the rap for this, but still had the guard castigated for not ensuring that the drover was in the brakevan passenger apartment before allowing the train to start. I cannot personally vouch for this but, as they say, my authority for the story is impeccable.

I was involved with two other derailments: each caused by a driver passing a signal at stop. The first occurred when the driver of 6029 whistled out of Loco. I was shunting in the yard forming his train, and could not give him the signal straight away, but for whatever reason, he moved off as soon as he had whistled, running past the signal and straight into the dirt with the leading pony and all driving wheels derailed. I forget the number of the train he was to work; it was, however early in the morning when there was a lot of steam and fog around the locomotive departure road. It caused absolute chaos. All engines had to enter and depart the loco depot from the emergency road. The train concerned was cancelled, that being the only locomotive available.

There was locomotive coal in Orange required for outgoing engines that could not be placed at the coal bin because of the derailment. For this reason, two Down trains from

Orange were cancelled. The time from the derailment until the engine was re-railed and the perway and interlocking restored to use, was 10 hours. An argument then began as to responsibility. The Bathurst driver said he had the signal and I must have taken it off him. The Mechanical Branch representative then wanted to know if I could see the back light in the signal. The answer at that particular time was 'No', because of the steam and fog. This really had no bearing on the issue but he tried to prove that, if I could not see the back light, then the driver could not be expected to see the signal. He next asked how did I know that the driver did not have the signal.

The obvious answer was that the back light was irrelevant because the road was set out of the yard and that the signal was clear for that movement and it was impossible to set the road from Loco with this movement in operation. This still did not satisfy him and the telegram sent *divn* (code address for irregularities not affecting the main line) showed the Mechanical Branch representative dissenting from the traffic inspector, the Per Way inspector and signal engineer who were satisfied the driver was responsible.

The second incident concerned a 36 Class, whistling out of Loco. On this occasion, the Parkes driver working No 49 whistled out of Loco on time. As No 49 was approaching and had the full through road, I gave the driver the first signal from Loco which should have bought him to a stand at the bracket of signals controlling the entrances from East Fork, loop, yard and Loco. The locomotive did not stop at this signal and continued into the dead end and up into the ash drag, derailing the front pony wheels of 3616 (No 49's allocated engine. This locomotive had a Giesl ejector and a narrow funnel fitted; the purpose being to make the locomotive steam better; it was the only 36 Class so fitted). Once again this was the only locomotive immediately available and the engine was re-railed in about one hour and thirty minutes.

With a bit of swift work, the train left Orange about 75 minutes late. The train controller set all the connections out of Parkes back an hour. The driver of No 49, well known for his eccentricities, lived up to his reputation and arrived in Parkes only 30 minutes late. The result was that the train controller could not get all the crews lifted back up again and two of the services sat at Parkes waiting for crews. This episode had two consequences for the driver; firstly, he was charged with running past a signal at stop to which he admitted, and secondly, he was charged with driving his train at speeds in excess of the speed boards. This he denied but it was proved that he must have exceeded the speeds because of the sectional times he ran. He was reduced to a fireman for six months, most of which I believe he spent on the shunter at Parkes. He was not a young man.

In this period a return submitted by the district superintendent to the Goods Trains Superintendent, Sydney, was known as the *Too Early Return*. A *Too Early* case occurred when a train was more than 30 minutes late and the crews had not been re-set for a later departure by train control. The ADS Orange and the District Locomotive Superintendent Bathurst were jointly responsible for the examination of each *Too Early* and for fixing responsibility either to the Traffic or Mechanical branches. There were many ways of overcoming *Too Early* cases that I am sure that the administration knew of, but did nothing because it reflected on the management of the district if there were too many cases.

The most common, if the train was just over, for example 35 minutes late, was to get the guard to book 28-29 minutes late. Most guards would do this and were able to adjust their times at crossing points before arrival at destination. The most effective way was to 'kid' the guard into making it an OK special, making whatever his times at all points the *On Time* time. The Orange guards would generally do this, for two reasons: firstly, the officers at East Fork were able to make life easy for them with respect to train numbers, and secondly, the guards booked 25 minutes to walk to Orange. About five times out of ten, they got a ride to Orange on an engine and still booked 25 minutes walk. The Bathurst guards were generally co-operative, but the Lithgow guards almost never, as they generally worked stock trains for which delays were recorded by train control.

I had my share of *Too Earlys*. From the time I first started at East Fork, I kept a notebook in which I recorded how every train on each shift departed and I was able to answer correspondence accurately and not have to rely on memory. If a train was late, I would make brief notes showing the work I had to do, the time it was completed, and the time the train engine went on. This book was very valuable to me over the years. There were numerous occasions when the assistant district superintendent would ring to ask me what I had recorded against a particular train.

One *Too Early* that I was concerned with was the late loading of stock at Orange Stockyards from the *Open Destination* sales*. I had placed the wagons some two hours prior to the due departure time of the train and put the delay down to waiting stock loading ex-sales. Some time later I received a very strongly worded letter from the train delay clerk (whom I think, from the tone of his correspondence, hated all ASMs!) stating that the stock wagons had not been placed in time and that the agents claimed they waited for wagons to load stock into. This, to begin with was not true because there were no stock in the yards when I placed the wagons.

I did not answer this paper straight away, but decided to do some research and find out what the laid down times were for the loading of a stock wagon. I could not find it in the appendices, including the local one, but I did find it, of all places, in the Western Working Timetable. The time per wagon? Nine minutes. I took great glee in writing back, quoting page and paragraph, saying that as they had loaded nine wagons, their allowed

---

* Local Stock and Station agents would order a number of sheep or cattle wagons to convey livestock sold at sales. As they were not aware of who would purchase the livestock or to where it was to be conveyed, the wagons would be ordered to 'Open Destinations'. The railway officers then had the task of arranging suitable transit when the sales were over.

time was 81 minutes and, on their own admission, they had taken longer than that. They had been levied train detention charges, which was their reason for making the claims that they did. The real cause for the delay was the late finishing of the sale at the yards.

The only constant clerical work that we had was a return called the *Shunting Mileage Return*, which was a daily record of the movements of all engines departing and arriving Loco. It showed the time spent shunting by incoming and outgoing engines on goods trains. The return also showed the train or light engine number, the number of each locomotive, the time it arrived into traffic at East Fork and the time it departed for Loco. The allowance for a light engine was five minutes from Loco departure time until it was despatched from the signal box. The same time was allowed for an engine arriving off a train from either Orange or Molong.

When Up goods trains arrived with two engines, the second engine was required, at the minimum, to stow the train if it was not working through. Generally, the drivers on this engine were Orange men who had worked light to Molong and were happy to shunt to build up their working time. This was all recorded in the shunting time column of the return.

In cases where the train was a single or both crews had worked through from Parkes or Dubbo, it was difficult to get them to do more than to stow the train, which was fair enough, but sometimes when Orange traffic was on the train, it made things difficult if this traffic was stowed in the yard with the East traffic. A shed fireman and mate were employed in the loco depot. This crew often relieved incoming crews, which helped our cause.

The shunting mileage for these trains recorded the locomotive standing time as a regular five minutes to detach the lead engine, and five minutes to the traffic branch for the engine to run to Loco; the second engine had recorded all the time spent shunting as well as the time spent crossing other movements. On outgoing trains, the Westinghouse air brake examination time was shown against Loco and the shunting time required forming the train to traffic. The only comment I have is that I am pleased that reconciliation was never made between the driver's sheets and the shunting mileage return.

Pilfering at East Fork was fairly minimal, although one guard was said not to have bought any timber when he built his house. I do not know if this was so, for I did not see him, although there were times when I saw car headlights in places that one would not expect to see. I remember walking through the stockyards on my way to work on backshift one night and kicking an empty beer bottle. I picked it up and took it into the signal box with me and sat it on the bench near the control phone. During the course of the morning, the shed fireman was in the signal box and asked what the bottle was doing there. I said where I had found it and was going to give the identification number on the bottle to the Railway detectives who were in town. When I said this he turned as white as a sheet. No more was said, it did not have to be, as I had no idea where the detectives were. It was an 'off the cuff' remark that hit home.

In 1956, the Anglia clapped out and I bought a 1956 Hillman Minx Mark 8A. This was a good car and we had it for ten years. Also, and more importantly, in October that year our daughter Faye Narelle was born.

After I had been at East Fork for about 3 years or a bit more, I decided that I wanted to be in Train Control. At this time, I had not completed my B standard Goods and Coaching, having still to get the first section of Goods, which I was having trouble with, and the second section of Coaching, which was also troublesome. The fact that I had not passed these had no influence on my decision to concentrate on Safeworking with a view to passing the train control examination. I actually passed both sections in 1959, obtaining 100 per cent in the coaching paper. In those days, a minimum age of 28 years had to be attained before being allowed to sit for the examination. About October 1956, a Train Controller's examination was advertised in the Weekly Notices, this being about two months before my 28th birthday.

There was not another one held until late 1958. During this time there were two vacancies in Orange Control. I tried to get one of the acting positions, but because of the shortage of salaried staff, I was not given one—both going to guards. When applications were called, I applied and duly presented myself back to the Devonshire Street Institute for another examination. I was staggered at the number attending the examination, there being some 150 aspiring train controllers who were attempting their first hurdle. I was not confident when I saw this number. I felt that I had done reasonably well in the exam, but that there were many others in the same position. I did not make the grade that year, nor did the two acting men at Orange.

In July of 1959, applications were again called, and this time I passed the examination. There were two sections to the examination: the first was on safeworking, safeworking irregularities and derailments, etc., and was of four hours' duration; the second was on general knowledge, and the correct answers really told the examiner if the candidate had any knowledge of such things as drawgear capacity of various types of passenger rolling stock, how to calculate the load of an engine working on one side, the calculation of an engine load when the boiler pressure had been reduced, and a series of questions on Westinghouse airbrake including the setting of grade control valves, the explanation of the IP and HP grade control settings and an explanation of how these valves had different release times and how much air they retained in the brake cylinders. Finally a description was required of an auxiliary air reservoir including triple valves. In the examination I did were also a series of questions on diesel locomotives including calculation of loads for a varying combination of engines.

In the section outside of questions that related to train control and depot working, there were a couple of questions which I think were designed to test the analytical thinking of the candidate. Questions in this section, which was of three hours' duration, were designed to test the depth of a candidate's general knowledge. The next hurdle after passing the examination was the interview by a board, which consisted of the Assistant Chief Traffic Manager, the Assistant Goods Train Superintendent, the Assistant Passenger Trains Superintendent and the Staff Superintendent. I was very nervous at this but despite that, I felt that I had answered their questions without too many serious blunders. A week after the interview, the three of us, the two acting men and myself, were advised we had been accepted and were to attend a train control school to begin in early August.

And so, after almost five difficult years, I finished on a Saturday afternoon shift at East Fork. I say difficult years, not so much because of the job, but because of the constant working of overtime, which I have already mentioned. This in the finish became a real drag, although I must say there was an improvement from about mid-1958. The constant working of 14 straight backshifts placed a strain on the individual working it, and it also affected his family and family life. I must pay tribute here to Mamie, who showed much understanding of the tiredness I used to feel toward the end of 14 backshifts and she had often 'bitten' her tongue, when she had reason to object to my irritatibility.

At Christmas time in 1958 Mamie discovered that she was pregnant again, to the surprise of us both; the medically prescribed safeworking we had carefully followed failed and we were to be parents again.

Orange East Fork platform taken in January 1988 viewed in the direction towards Parkes and Broken Hill. *John R Newland.*

THE 1959 TRAIN CONTROL SCHOOL

HAVING no relatives in Sydney with whom I could stay at this time, I was forced to stay at the Department's Macdonaldtown Hostel for the duration of the Train Control School. It has long since been demolished. It was a great barn of a place if ever there was one. Each room was a cubicle with a space of about 12 inches between floor level and commencement of the wall and with probably 15 feet above the top of wall to ceiling level. The rooms would have been more suitable for stabling horses than humans. The meals were reasonable and expenses at least covered costs. The concern to me was that Mamie would give birth while I was in the school. Fortunately, it was not until the school had finished on 28 August that Cathy Lynne arrived.

The school was an interesting experience. It consisted of clerks, assistant station masters and guards. The senior man in the school was Kevin Gill, who eventually retired as deputy chief executive. Of the 13 in the school, I was the fifth in order of seniority. I was also among the youngest at thirty. You will recall I mentioned Alec Gillies as being a Morse operator at Cowra when I was there. Alec was in the school. I say it was interesting because of the range of the men who comprised it. There were those who, even in the school, betrayed irritation when pressure was put on them. Then there were the other types, the obviously too laid back 'she'll be right mate' types. In between those groups, there were those not used to making decisions, which came out particularly amongst the guards. Finally, there were those who would make decisions but had no confidence in them and accordingly, displayed reluctance which in hindsight, should have been obvious to the instructor.

The Instructor was Max Gates, who was a Chief Train Controller, Programme Sydney (the definition of this position is explained further on) and had conducted many train control schools. We learned about diagramming on train control graphs on single and double line. We had lecturers in safeworking who, although we were all countrymen and would certainly go back to country destinations, concentrated on accidents and irregularities in the metropolitan area. We had lectures in the industrial awards, in rostering engines, guards and loco enginemen. We were taught the importance of keeping running tonnage balances. We were instructed in the art of formulating timetables for special important trains to run in sections already heavily trafficked. We were reminded of the timetable's importance in selecting trains to put aside or cancel, and to get any special train through sections where there was not really a timetable path. We received lectures from the Passenger Train, Goods Train, Staff, Safeworking, Metropolitan Passenger Train and Train Control Superintendents, some of whom I thought were extremely able men but two whom I thought held their positions under false pretences, one particularly so. Whether he was a better operator than he was a speaker I do not know. I should think he must have been, for he exemplified the wooden Indian to perfection.

We had a number of excursions, one to Enfield Marshalling Yards, one to Sydney Station Signal Box and several to the Train Control Section. The highlight was a visit to the Commissioner's Office where Neil McCusker addressed us and impressed upon us that the art of good train controlling was not to have too many horizontal lines on your diagram, they representing standing time. He also spoke of the diesel age that was just beginning to become a potent force in the more efficient utilisation of engine power and

The class of the 1959 Train Control School. The author is standing at the extreme left.

revolutionising of the running of through freight trains. His instruction to all staff was that diesel engines not only should be rostered 23 hours in a day, they should be productive in that period. I was to discover much later the vagaries of the metropolitan area played havoc with this direction.

The school finished with a dinner which was billed 'The Dinner of the 19th Train Control School'. The attendance of many of the senior administration, including the Chief Traffic Manager and many of the middle management officers of the time, was a tribute firstly, I thought, to Max Gates and secondly, was an indication of the importance that was given to the train control system. The dinner was held in the same room as the junior porters' dinner some 15 years earlier. This dinner was important to all of us because at it, we were to receive our appointments. I desperately hoped I would get Orange but was not all that confident, believing that the two acting train controllers would get those positions and that, although I believed a third and possibly fourth vacancy would shortly occur because of the vacancies in the first class positions at Dubbo and Werris Creek. There was no guarantee and I could well finish at Werris Creek. I was therefore greatly relieved when I heard that I was appointed to Orange, but that for the first six months, I would relieve the senior inspector at Orange. There were four appointments made to Orange, one being the holiday relief position for Dubbo/Orange.

In about June of 1959 we sold our first home for twice the amount we paid for it and bought a very nice two-bedroom weatherboard home in Spring Street in East Orange. Although it had only two bedrooms it had the easy capacity to extend. We did not require that. We moved into this home before I left East Fork. Having recently purchased the Spring Street house was another of the reasons I was most anxious not to leave Orange. In hindsight, it was probably not a wise move to have bought the house. However, when we first entered negotiations, the applications had not been called for the train control school. The first house was crowded with two children, but the most important consideration was that the offer we received, was just too good to refuse.

ACTING SENIOR INSPECTOR, ORANGE

I ARRIVED back in Orange from Sydney on the *Central West Express* on the Saturday after the completion of the Train Control School and was handed a letter from the District Superintendent advising me to be prepared to stay in Dubbo overnight on the Monday. I was to commence as Acting Senior Traffic Inspector Orange. This direction did not fill me with glee, because by this time Mamie was within a week of the expected arrival of the third child. Although her sister who was expecting twins and her husband lived in Orange, they would have been available in an emergency but I was anxious to be on hand. The District Superintendent, though quite difficult to work for, was quite a considerate person but he was not aware of my position.

On the Monday morning early, I duly fronted and found that the District Superintendent (DS), the Assistant District Superintendent (ADS) and myself were to go to Dubbo by car and inspect private level crossing gates, especially those between Wellington and Dubbo. It transpired that the Commissioner had been to Nyngan the previous week on a private visit and found, as he drove along, that not one of the private level crossing gates between Geurie and Dubbo was closed. We were to close them and seek out the property owners and remind them of their obligations in respect to the gates, namely, that they were to be kept closed and only opened to permit access to or from their properties. We had to make sure that the penalty notices advising this were on the gates and readable. The District Superintendent left us at Dubbo and, with the Assistant District Superintendent, I spent the next two days interviewing farmers and advising them of the requirements. Some farmers would close the gate adjacent to their property to prevent their stock from getting onto the railway line and leave the gate from the road open. It was an experience in public relations, an area I was largely ignorant of. When we drove back on the Tuesday afternoon the gates were all closed. I went back to Dubbo by train about a fortnight later and found every gate was open again. Silence was golden!

After returning to Orange on the Tuesday evening, I had just arrived home and was called to my first derailment, a minor one, in Orange yard when two trucks had been derailed at a set of throwover points. It did not take long to see, especially after the flange

1 Control, OrangeEast Fork Jct Up Home, Branch to West Fork
2 Up Home, Branch
3 Up Call-on, Branch to Main or Branch orWeighbridge Road
4 Up 2nd Home, Branch to Back Platform Road
5 Up Home, Branch to Main
6 Down Accept, Main (10)
7 Down Home, Main
8 Down Call-on, Main or Main to Branch or Weighbridge Road
9 Down 2nd Home, Main
10 Up 2nd Home, Branch to Main
11 Down Starting, Main
12 Up Home, Branch to Extended Loop or Up Sidings
13 Down Home, Main to Extended Loop or Up Sidings
14 Down Call-on, Main
15 Down 2nd Home, Main to Loop
16 —
17 —
18 Up Shunting Neck to Extended Loop or Up Sidings
19 Down Shunt on Extended Loop
20 Extended Loop to Up Sidings

21 Extended Loop to Main
22 FPL 23 points
23 Points, Main — Branch Crossing East
24 Points, Main — Extended Loop
25 FPL 23 and 24 points
26 Catch Point in Shunting Neck
27 Points, Extended Loop — Nos 2 to 7 Up Sidings
28 Points, Extended Loop — Nos 1 Up Siding
29 Extended Loop to Loop
30 Up Starting, Main (30)
31 Starting, Extended Loop to Branch
32 Extended Loop to Main
33 Extended Loop to Up Shunting Neck
34 (A) No 1 Up Siding to Extended Loop (B) Nos 2 to
35 Up Shunt on Extended Loop   (to Ex
36 —
37 —
38 —
39 FPL 40 points
40 Points, Main – Branch Crossing Middle

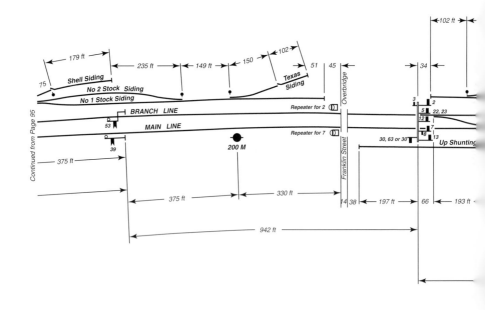

NGE SIGNAL BOX

ts, Branch – Weighbridge Road	61 Loop to Extended Loop
40 and 41 points	62 Release for Main Releasing Switch
44 points	63 Up Starting, Main (30)
ts, Main — Loop	64 Branch to Main
44 and 53 points	65 Up 3rd Home, Main
ch point in Extended Loop	66 Starting, Main to Branch
Down Shunting Neck to Weighbridge Road, (A) to	67 Up 2nd Home, Main
re (Back Platform Rd or Main	68 Loop to Main
ts, Branch — Down Shunting Neck	69 Down Starting, Branch
ts, Main — Branch Crossing West	70 Down Shunt Ahead, Branch
49 and 50 points	71 (A) Weighbridge Road to Main or Branch, (B) to Shunting Neck
50 points	72 Starting from Back Platform Road
ts, Main — Extended Loop	73 Main to Branch
50 points	74 —
re	75 —
re	76 Release for Loop Releasing Switch
Platform Road to Down Shunting Neck	77 Up Home, Main to Loop (6 Frame B)
re	78 Up Home, Main
to Down Shunting Neck	79 Up Outer Home
to Extended Loop	80 Up Inner Distant

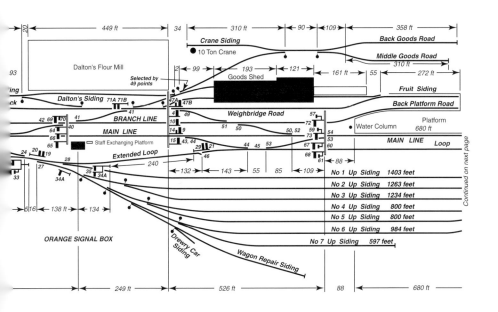

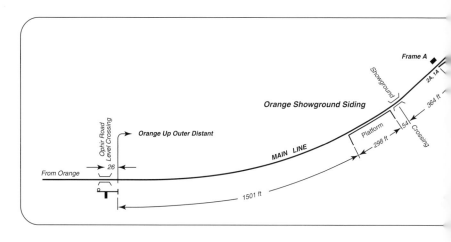

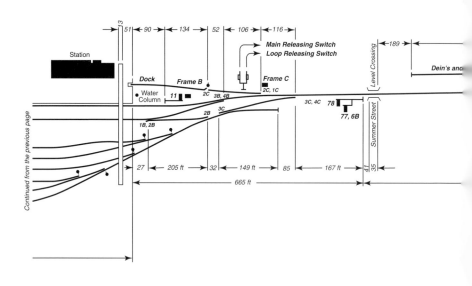

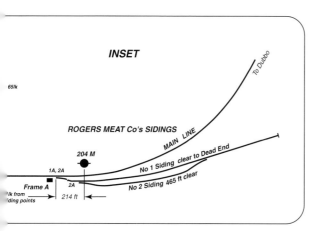

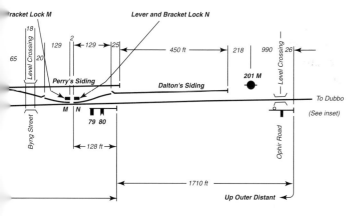

gauge showed that the wheel flanges on the lead truck were hardly worn and to deduce that the points must have been incorrectly set. The shunter, who swore he had examined them prior to the shunt, vigorously denied this. When I agreed with the Mechanical and Per Way Branches that it was a Traffic responsibility, the shunters thought I was the worst in the world. They thought or hoped, because I had worked with them from East Fork, I would side with them. Blind Freddie could see what had happened. That was the first *divn* wire I sent. I had a moment of temporary pride when I put my name to it as the acting senior inspector.

On the Wednesday, when I arrived for the morning meeting with the DS and ADS, I was told that I would have to go to Parkes and be the supervising inspector while the staff instruments were changed between Gidgeera and Forbes. This time I spoke out and told them of the impending birth, which by this time was two days away from the expected date. The ADS who was also acting, and was in fact the chief inspector at Parkes, volunteered to do the job. On 28 August, which was the Friday after, Cathy Lynne our second daughter arrived. Mamie was put into the same ward as her sister who had twin boys on 19 August.

One of the most difficult things I had to learn in a hurry, was to type the correspondence sent from the Traffic Inspector's Office. The statements taken from staff and the answering of correspondence from the District Superintendent's Office were all expected to be typewritten. I spent a good deal of my own time practising and after a short time, I was able to laboriously meet requirements, even if there were plenty of 'Xs' crossing out mistakes. There was no whiteout ink then, nor word processors!

Another interesting episode concerning level crossings involved the gates at Margaret Street at Orange, otherwise known as the Showground Gates. These gates were unattended and classified as private gates, meaning they were to be kept closed and only opened by members of the public and stock drovers, when they needed to cross the line. They were in fact manned for the three days of the Orange Show. A complaint was made to the Orange Police by a member of the public living nearby, who stated that one day someone would get killed at these gates. The Traffic Sergeant suggested that he and I should go to the gates and stop the first person that went over the crossing and did not shut the gates. We were there about five minutes when our first victim crossed the line from East to West. The Sergeant duly stopped the car. I accompanied him to the offending car. As I approached I recognised the driver who had worked on the railway at Orange but had resigned and joined the Police Force! I said two things, the first to the sergeant who was asking for driver's licence,

"You had better give that back to him; he is one of yours," and the second to the driver,

"You had better 'piss' off while the going's good".

Both things happened. We were there for about two hours and probably warned a dozen people. As far as I was concerned no one was going to get 'booked' after we had let the policeman off the hook! As a part of our wider investigation we recommended that the gates be permanently closed, because people were able to cross over the line closer to Orange in two places, both of which were protected. This was accepted and as far as I am aware, still applies.

The traffic inspector had traditionally been the person to qualify staff in safeworking in his area and who wished to qualify for higher duty, as had been done for me in earlier years with Big Jim Hartigan. My first request was from a porter at Wellington, who wished to qualify in electric staff and tablet. I had to go to Wellington and sit in on an inquest in which a male person had been fatally run over and advised the SM Wellington that I would examine this porter while I was in Wellington for the inquest. The first question I asked him was,

"What are the bell signals for a stopping passenger train?"

He did not know. I thought what have I here? Someone thinking I was a soft touch or someone who had not learned the bell codes. So I asked what was the purpose of the electric staff system. He had no idea. I then told him that he had failed and I would recommend that he not be re-examined for twelve months. I also had plenty to say to the station master, for the system was that, the applicant only needed to apply to the station master to be examined in a subject, who then recommended to the superintendent that the person be examined. His only verbal defence was,

"I wanted to get rid of the lazy bastard".

I have to say I did not blame him for that but the porter was still at Wellington when I left the district five years later.

The inquest was an eye-opener to me. The man, who lived at Farnham, which used to be a siding between Stuart Town and Euchareena, was run over by No 46 *Coonamble Mail*. He had been drinking at the Iron Bark Hotel at Stuart Town all afternoon and apparently decided to walk home a distance of some five or six miles. He was run over while apparently asleep in the 'four foot' (to the uninitiated, the space between the rails). He left a widow and a large family, who were in very poor circumstances before and after he died. The driver of No 46, did not see him until he was too close to stop. The main reason for this was that he was lying just over a rise and the engine headlights did not shine on him until the engine had topped the rise and started down the incline. It was then too late to stop, although the driver applied the emergency brakes, tossing sleeping passengers about in their bunks and jolting the sitting passengers from their seats.

At the inquest the family was represented by a very able local solicitor and the Department by a solicitor from the Legal Branch. He had only just joined the Railways and knew nothing of the workings of a railway. It soon became evident that the local solicitor was running rings around him. The coroner who was the local Clerk of Petty Sessions was full of his own importance and, to my inexperienced mind, was biased toward the family of the deceased. Despite the fact that it was summer with the temperature in the high nineties, he declined to allow anyone into the Court without a coat. The counsel for the family was trying to prove the driver negligent by claiming he should have seen the deceased sooner and been able to stop. The driver estimated he was travelling about 25 miles per hour when he topped the rise.

At the lunch adjournment, I spoke to the Departmental solicitor to try and get him to rebut the obvious conclusion that counsel was coming to. In fact I thought there was a possibility of the driver being charged with negligence causing death or manslaughter, the way he was heading. It was not until I drew a diagram on paper that I was able to convince the Department's solicitor that it was impossible for the driver on a dark night to have seen the deceased sooner than he did. I also pointed out that he was not going to look for people sleeping on the line over every rise he topped. This aspect of the events was virtually ignored by the solicitor in his summing up.

The Coroner in his verdict was very critical of the driver. To my mind he was grossly unfair to him, however he stopped short of any recommendation concerning the driver, but the verdict he bought down was virtually an open finding, leaving the way open for the family to claim compensation from the Department. I was really nonplussed over the whole affair. I felt a great sympathy for the driver and told him so. I thought his union had let him down by not having legal representation for him. I finally thought the Department had been badly represented from a legal viewpoint. The summing up from the Department's solicitor gave the Coroner no lead at all as to what the Department's attitude or its responsibilities were. He made no rebuttal of the strong case the family counsel gave regarding duty of care.

While in my acting capacity I did not do general and annual station inspections but I was authorised to do the annual inspections of sidings. I was doing this, travelling by car, between Dubbo and Molong, on the line otherwise known as 'the scenic'. When I arrived at Cumnock, I introduced myself to the ASM in charge and asked for his SPA (Sundry Persons Accounts) and his Ledger Book. As I had driven into the station, I noticed that a Darling Harbour truck had been unloaded and that the goods shed, which was open, was empty. A quick look at the SPA, showed that the local general storekeeper had a credit account, which was considerably short of covering the freight on the just unloaded Darling Harbour truck. Unauthorised credit was regarded very seriously and if brought to notice, attracted strong Departmental action.

I said to the ASM,

"I am going to inspect the Up Home Signal."

There were complaints about it being difficult to see (which was true, and one which

I was going to have to inspect at night from an engine). I had not gone twenty yards towards the signal when I saw the ASM hotfooting it across the road to the store, which, of course, I had given him the opportunity to do. When I returned from the signal, the SPA was open and showing a credit to the storekeeper. As I looked at the SPA the first time, my mind went back to Canowindra and Bill Boag. He would have said to the storekeeper,

"Take your goods and drop in the cheque after."

In this case, I suspect the wagon had arrived late the previous day and the store had his goods before the ASM started work. Neither the ASM nor myself said anything about it. We of course talked on other subjects. I understood the camaraderie and trust that existed between the locals and the railway staff in these bush towns. Had I gone to a major station and found the same thing, my reaction would have been different. The same ASM later retired as a chief inspector. My devious mind often wondered whether he would have extended the same understanding. He was well liked, so the answer is probably in the affirmative.

I was sent to investigate why No 31 *Central West Express* had on two occasions, booked time lost to signals at Millthorpe, there being no other train involved that would cause less than a through road to be cleared for the passage of No 31. When I asked the station master why this was so, he denied that the train was delayed there and that on each occasion, he had cleared the through road for the train. Something about his manner made me think that he was uncomfortable and was not telling the truth. I did not say any more to him, but went back to Orange and told the District Superintendent that I thought he was being less than frank. He suggested I go out in the car the next day and station myself near the distant (the line ran parallel with the road) and watch the passage of No 31. Sure enough, the distant signal was not cleared for the train.

When I turned up at his station about three minutes after No 31 had passed, he turned a bad colour! When I questioned him he said he had been in the toilet when the train left Polona and returned in time to clear the home signal without delaying the train. I told him he was lying because I had watched the home signal clear some minutes before No 31 came into view. He finished up being severely reprimanded. I found it difficult to understand why, when he was clearly caught out, that he continued to prevaricate. He was the only person I pursued during my acting time with any venom, recommending that he be fined £5, the maximum penalty in that era, not so much for not clearing the signals, but for deliberately lying in his response to me and later in his defence against punishment.

I quite enjoyed the experience for six months. It was certainly different from anything else I had previously done and gave me a different perspective of administration. In the latter part of my writing, I have refrained from mentioning names, partly because some of those with whom I associated in the 1950s may still be alive and partly because I have been able to effectively cover the things I wish to say without doing so. I wish, however, to make an exception with the Assistant District Superintendent at Orange, the late Robert (Bob) Kitchener Goldberg who, during my time, proved himself a most able administrator and a thorough gentleman. I respected him greatly from the time he first came to East Fork before I took up duty there until he retired shortly before I left Orange. He was approachable, diligent and caring. I have no doubt that had I stepped out of line he would have treated me no differently to anyone else. During my acting time, he relieved the District Superintendent for holidays and because he did not like driving, took me to Dubbo with him on a couple of occasions. I still remember the first time we pulled out of the Departmental garage at Orange.

"I want", he said, "to enjoy this trip to Dubbo."

I got the message. Having driven an Anglia for seven years, I was not a speedster in any case!

Every year during the first part of December, the Broken Hill miners celebrated their Picnic Day at the Darling River at Menindee. To get everyone to the picnic, they hired three passenger trains of about eight or nine carriages each and carrying around 500 passengers. Invariably the carriages were the light drawgear suburban type sets, e.g., LUB, LOB, SIB and DUB type sets etc. The carriages were worked by special trains from Sydney to Broken Hill, drawgear capacity demanding they be sent as three trains from Sydney to Parkes. Then two sets were joined for the flat country running from Parkes to Broken Hill. Along with the Chief Inspector Parkes, I was sent to Broken Hill to supervise the running of these trains.

Everything went according to plan on the day. The three trains were on time arriving at Menindee between 11.00 and 11.50am. It seemed a million children were on the trains enjoying every minute of the day. They were stuffed all day with lollies, drinks and ice creams (before they melted). At Menindee, they had races on the river banks. At about midday, in what shade there was, they lined for their lunches of half warm sausage rolls (it was a hot day, so half warm was probably about right!), small cakes and a bottle of soft drink.

A virtual banquet was turned on for the adults. Delicious ham and salmon salads, in polystyrene boxes, which had been packed in ice, for mains and fruit salads for desserts. There was so much beer and wine loaded on the train at Broken Hill that I thought that we must have been going for a week. At lunchtime, they sent down to the pub at Menindee for more beer! My colleague and I were treated right royally, the problem was convincing the picnic committee that I did not want to drink alcohol—I thought it best to say not "while I was working" rather than that I did not drink. In Broken Hill, it was taken for granted everyone did, including many women. Certainly the women on that day consumed their fair share and then some.

On the return journey the bulk of the children with their parents were on the first train which left about 4.30pm. I should say, lest I give the wrong impression, that the family groups of mum, dad and children, in the main, drank very little and made it truly a children's day. The second train was due to depart about 5.00pm and the last about 6.00pm. The first train departed on time packed with tired and happy children.

The second train was about to leave, but before doing so the guard made a continuity test of the airbrake. As the driver was recharging the trainline with air, a trainline pipe burst about three carriages from the engine. Examination of the pipe showed it was completely rusted through, and that there was no chance of repairing it. We held a conference with the chief locomotive inspector as to what course of action should be taken. Obviously we could not let the train run with air to only three carriages. Being the junior partner in this team, I did not have much to say. The locomotive inspector, however, realised when delays were being apportioned, this one sat squarely with his Mechanical Branch.

He suggested that we try and get the people for the third train up a bit early and combine the two trains, having the third train marshalled in front of the second train so that the airbrake was operative on the first 12 carriages. The suggestion then was that the three of us and the two guards would act as brakesmen on the five trailing carriages that did not have air, so that in the unlikely event of a breakage of drawgear, we could apply the interior handbrakes and stop the carriages from moving. It was highly irregular however, but safe enough on the flat country we were travelling on, the only gradient being an ascending grade of about 1 in 100 from Wahratta to Broken Hill, so we all agreed. As we were breaking up from our little discussion, my colleague and the two guards had moved off, I said to the Loco inspector,

"I think those train sets only have interior handbrakes in the end guard's compartment."

He said to me, " Shut up!"

I did. The drivers went like the 'clappers' and we arrived in Broken Hill without incident, almost on the scheduled arrival time of the second train. Believe me, there were some 'cot cases' among the men and women of the third train's carriages, which were adults only, when we did arrive.

About late January of 1960, I began to learn Orange Control, a position I had worked hard for a long time to get, and one which at that time I thought would see me in a few years sit for the Traffic Inspector's examinations and be my path to bigger and better things. Alas, as you will see, it was not to be.

SECOND CLASS TRAIN CONTROLLER, ORANGE

THE first day I commenced learning Orange Control, I realised that a whole new world of endeavour lay ahead of me, one that I had striven to attain for the previous three years and one that I had attained, finally. There were subtle changes. For instance, uniforms were a thing of the past; it was a collar and tie, at least during daylight shifts. Yes, train controllers wore collars and ties in those days and were pleased to do so. The standard of dress of today's controllers reflects not only on them, but on a department that has let the too rigid standards of the pre and post war years decline to a pathetic standard that seemed to me in my final years, to indicate a lack of respect for the position by both the controllers themselves and the administration. There was also a change in the demeanour of the District Superintendent, the Assistant District Superintendent, the senior inspector and office staff towards new controllers, especially those who had worked in the district prior to their appointments.

The DS at Orange during this time, as I said earlier, was a caring person, but he was also difficult to approach and very difficult to work with. He had an abrupt manner that frightened many people and led to his not being overly popular. I have often thought since, especially after seeing him in action in Sydney in later years, that this abruptness was a defence mechanism. The ADS was responsible for the train running and operation in the district and it was with him that we had most of our dealings. The train control areas were all known by a code name, which was their telegraphic name also. Orange Control was *orco*, Lithgow was *lico*, Dubbo was *doco*, Werris Creek was *weco*, South Grafton was *soco*, Goulburn was *goco*, Junee was *juco*, Newcastle was *neco* and Sydney Control Areas were *syco*, followed by the name of the area, for example, South Control was *syco south*.

It was usual for train controllers before they took up duties in their areas of responsibility, to have a tour of it. Having been over the whole of the Orange district on numerous occasions, and having worked in the two most important points, I thought it unnecessary and concentrated on learning the duties for which 12 days was allowed.

The Orange Control area commenced at East Fork on the eastern end and extended to Wellington inclusive on the Main Western line and from Orange/Orange East Fork to Broken Hill, including responsibility for the Bogan Gate/Tottenham Branch. The systems of safeworking were: electric staff Orange to Wellington and Parkes; the section Manildra to Molong, (on the Up only), was a divisible electric staff section. Pinecliffe was the station, at which the first train reported with the ticket portion of the staff and the second train then with the staff portion departed Manildra. This working was especially adopted to enable W44 ore train Broken Hill to Sulphide Junction to make a crossing at Molong with W27 passenger Orange to Parkes.

It was also used when a goods train departed from Parkes about 9.00am. This was not a regular train, running probably once or twice a week on average, the exception being the wheat season when it ran daily. W44, running at a faster speed with 60 Class Garratt locomotives, was waiting line clear at Manildra before the goods train cleared Pinecliffe. From Parkes to Goobang Junction was single line automatic and from Goobang to Broken Hill was staff and ticket.

Two train control diagrams (graphs) were supplied for each 24 hours commencing 6.00am, one for the section Orange to Wellington and the other from Orange to Broken Hill. There was very little work on the Wellington graph, so it was the bottom one on the controller's desk. Train control diagrams are virtually foolproof, but not necessarily mistake proof. The stations or signal boxes in the area are shown on both ends; in addition the

Orange railway station and the pedestrian footbridge taken in January 1988. Some of the siding roads in the station's vicinity have since been taken up. *John R Newland.*

names are abbreviated at the 1200 hours position. Time is broken into 10-minute segments with a heavy blue line, then further reduced to five 2-minute light lines. All country diagrams begin with the station nearest Sydney at the top, so that in effect, all Down trains start at the top and go down and across it.

The station furthest from Sydney on the graph is where Up trains commence, so Up trains go up and across the diagram. Hence, on a single line, if an Up and Down train depart at the same time at the opposite ends of the train control area, there comes a point at which they must cross. In staff and ticket sections it is the train controller's duty to 'set' the staff so that whenever a train arrives at a station, irrespective of the token it is to take in the advance section, a staff is available. This must necessarily be so, because the staff is required to open the ticket box, if the ticket is to be the authority for the driver to enter the section ahead.

Early in my learning, I realised the importance of the correct setting of the staff and for a long time after I took up, marked on the graph lightly in pencil either an 'S' for staff or a 'T' for ticket in the space between stations. In essence, time is depicted across the graph from left to right, and motion goes from the top of the graph toward the bottom, and vice versa, from the bottom of the graph. The distance from Sydney is shown against each station or siding.

On single lines, it was the policy to free hand in the anticipated running and crossing places of trains on the following day's diagram. When controllers took a new diagram at 6.00am with this information, they, if they were good controllers, adjusted these freehand times so that if a train was late or out of course, the new path and times it would take could readily be seen and the consequent alteration to crossing stations became obvious. It was at this point that the setting of the staff became critical. If a train ran so late its crossings were affected and the staff settings could not be amended, it was necessary to get the ganger to transfer the staff so that it was correctly set to allow the amended crossing to take place. It did not matter whether it was day or night time so far as staff transfers were concerned. It was not uncommon to have gangers transferring staffs by motor trike at midnight.

A train clerk was employed to prepare diagrams for each day, and also to make out the *akrus* (timetables) for any special trains or light engines required to run. Mostly diagrams were printed as Monday to Friday and then Saturday/Sunday. All passenger trains were printed on the diagram. Trains that ran on Mondays, Wednesdays and Fridays only were included as were the trains that ran on Tuesdays and Thursdays. The train clerk deleted the appropriate trains each day with an ether compound that left a white line when drawn over the path of a train. When I took up as a train controller, it was the strict policy that only black lead pencil was to be used on diagrams. The most sought after pencil was the 'Staedtler F'.

The entrance door to every train control room in the State had 'Silence' emblazoned on it in some form or another. Most doors had a glass top portion and the word inscribed into the glass. To the majority of rail staff it did not mean much, but was impressive when groups came on tours of inspection. The desk was on an angle, similar to any school desk, and was approximately eight feet long and three feet wide. In the console in front of the controller, was a microphone that was hidden behind a cut out square covered by a coarse material and framed by a fancy plywood design.

When stations called, the sound came over a speaker, which was also hidden. In order to speak, the controller was obliged to work a foot pedal, which was pressed when he replied. The co-ordinating of the voice and the foot pedal did not take long to learn but was difficult for the first few days, it later became second nature. Mamie swore there were times at home I used to subconsciously do it in conversation and that I often did it in my sleep. In every station, signal box or locomotive depot telephone in the controller's area, a magnetic ratchet key ringer was fitted, each one having a different series of gaps, based on the long and short formula. In front of the controller was a console that had a key for every telephone in his area. To ring a station, the controller turned the key to its full extent, about three parts of a circle. As it returned to normal, a magnetic spring-loaded field passed over the gaps. As it did, it selected the control telephone to which that series of longs and shorts was dedicated and gave one long ring. The controller was aware if the required telephone rang because of a ring back that came back over the speakers. He was equally aware if it did not ring from the lack of ring back.

The Senior Train Controller's Office was behind the Control Room, entrance being gained through the 'Silence' door. The senior train controller was responsible for the setting of a daily train programme that would clear the available tonnage from Parkes, Dubbo and Wellington on the Up and from Orange to Parkes and Dubbo on the Down. He was also responsible for the economic balancing of engines. This summary of duties does not seem much, but entailed a lot of organising. He spoke daily with Station Master Parkes, Senior Train Controller Dubbo, Chief Train Controller Lithgow, Station Master Orange, Locomotive Senior Chargeman Orange and Parkes. Obviously, the train controllers answered to him. The incumbent while I was in Orange was a good hand, a good fellow who sometimes took the edge off his goodness with sudden bouts of ill temper, this especially so if he had over indulged the previous evening. In fairness, I must say that was not often and add that the man's nature had given him a short fuse. The train clerk, while he spent time in the control office, spent far more time assisting the senior train controller.

A Wheat Officer was employed to liaise with the Wheat Officer in Sydney (telegraphic code *Mana Wheat*) and to arrange for trains from Parkes and Dubbo to shift the wheat that had been ordered by the Grain Elevator Board to meet the following week's export shipment and domestic mill wheat requirements. A telegram was received each Friday from *Manna Wheat* stating the tonnage required, the type of wheat and the silo it was to come from. In the harvest time, he was also responsible for the clearance of wheat from district silos to the bulkhead at Parkes. The timetables for the special trains required to run were the responsibility of the train clerk.

Train control hours at the inauguration of the system in New South Wales were based on a 6 hours 30 minutes shift 12 days a fortnight—this was when the working week was 44 hours. The high-pressure nature of the position was the reason for the hours. Certainly there were times when the job was high pressure, but like many other jobs, it had its moments of relative tranquility. Personally I do not think the high pressure times at Orange Control were any more high pressure than for an ASM at Orange East Fork on heavy stock nights.

I, in fact, said this to one of the 'newly out of the district' appointees from my school. He laughed at me. He had been a guard and found the transition from being told everything he had to do, to being the one doing the telling, was very difficult. He was finding the pressure as a train controller difficult to handle. He had the attitude that everything that happened or went wrong had happened to him personally. In later years, as senior train controller in Sydney, he regressed back to his former position. I have recorded this not as a criticism of the man, but to show that personality and temperament played a formidable part in the success of a train controller. While some of the questions in the control examination were designed to test the thinking capacity of the examinee, there were no attempts at assessing the suitability of the individual to work under pressure in sustained 'pressure cooker' situations. Had there been, some of the train controllers of later years would not have made the grade.

I will try to deal with the duties of each of the shifts, taking as my criteria the steam era at Orange, with the daywork shift commencing at 6.00am for a 30 minute handover and taking charge of the Train Control Board at 6.30am.

Commencing about 6.50am, the gangers from all the unattended stations on the Broken Hill line came on for their train running for the day. I recall very vividly the ganger from Gunningbland. At 6.56am precisely on every weekday morning and announcing himself, irrespective of whether anyone was speaking to the controller and taking no notice of the direction on every train control telephone, 'to listen before speaking', he would say,

"*Gunninnnnnnnngbland*, Ganger Carter speaking, may I have the train *runninnnng* please."

After a couple of attempts to get him to wait until the line was not busy, like all the other train controllers, I gave up. If I was talking or listening to someone else, I used to ignore him until I was not busy. One of the funny things was that every one seemed to know him and when he spoke, people just stopped and Ganger Carter got his running. I never met the man but would like to have done so. What I did find out about him was that he had the best-maintained length on the Broken Hill line. The giving out of the running took until about 7.30am. Manildra, Condobolin and Bogan Gate stations had no backshift officer and therefore did not get a backshift programme and took the running from control for their respective gangers.

The train movements in the area at this hour were trains departing from Parkes off No 49 Mail, which continued to Forbes, with the Condobolin, Tottenham and *Silver City Comet* trains in one direction, and from Orange to Wellington with Nos 65, 99 and 247. From Wellington No 34 which attached perishable and container loading at Orange and ran through to the metropolitan area. From Orange, No 107 ran to Parkes; No 86 from Parkes; No 32 from Dubbo via Molong and No 8 from Molong to Orange East Fork; L32 and L8 light engines from Orange East Fork to Molong to assist Up trains over the steep grades back to Orange. There were at least three goods train running between Parkes and Broken Hill. These trains, combined with the other duties, made for a reasonably busy time.

From about 8.00am onward the train running programmes with Ivanhoe, Menindee and Broken Hill were ratified for the next 24 hours an anticipated programme was set for the following 24 hours. It was the responsibility of the train controller, each day, to see that there was sufficient water at Ivanhoe for the next 48 hours. At that time, all Ivanhoe's water requirements, including the town supply was supplied from the overhead tanks in Loco Ivanhoe. The water was supplied from the Darling River at Menindee in 7,000 gallon water tanks (commonly known as 'water gins'), fourteen to a train, hence 98,000 gallons to a train. The controller was responsible, with the Station Master Ivanhoe, for maintaining the supply and programming the trains required.

A daily return of water on hand at Ivanhoe and expected consumption for the next 48 hours, together with the train programme was prepared for the ADS. On the occasions when goods trains from Parkes were lightly loaded, empty water gins were sent to Menindee. When making these arrangements, the controller had to be sure that a similarly lightly loaded train was available from Broken Hill to lift them from Menindee. The programme on the Broken Hill Line was basically stable but each day's programme was slightly different, the main reason being to suit crew rosters and availability.

Locomotive crews and guards were located at Ivanhoe and Broken Hill. The train crews on the *Silver City Comet* and the once-weekly night passenger from Parkes to Broken Hill, which ran Wednesdays and returned Fridays, worked to Ivanhoe and were relieved by a crew who worked to Broken Hill. The guard and corridor attendant on the *Comet* worked to Broken Hill. A goods train bound from Parkes to Broken Hill had crew changes at Euabalong West, Ivanhoe and Menindee. The crews who signed on at Ivanhoe usually worked to Menindee and changed over with a crew from Broken Hill who had worked an Up train.

The Broken Hill line, from its opening, was serviced exclusively by 32 or P Class locomotives. These utitility locomotives served the department admirably and to my mind, were the locomotives which best served the NSWGR in any sphere.

They conveyed a variety of tonnage loads at different section running times. The load most used however, was a 600-ton load known as a *saru* load. (I have no idea where the term originated). The running times for the load were a bit slower than fast stock speed. The maximum speed for four-wheeled vehicles which every train conveyed was 35mph. The advantages in using this load were mostly crew related. The faster than full goods time eliminated many of the long hour cases of the late 1940s. The *saru* loads were mainly retained when I was at Orange.

As a general rule, the engines worked from Parkes to Ivanhoe, where they relayed on to the next train. They were serviced at Eubalong West where the outgoing driver was allowed time to give a normal preparation. The fire was cleaned and the coal shovelled forward by the fireman. At Ivanhoe they were prepared for traffic at the locomotive depot, and whistled out of Loco as fresh engines. On the occasions when no engine was available at Ivanhoe and the train engine had to work through, it was detached and serviced at Loco. If this happened the time allowed was 90 minutes.

The line was originally formed as an ash ballast track. It was improved as time went by with metal ballasting, it was however, still a very rough ride. The *Comet* which was timetabled at 60mph in places often lost between 15 and 30 minutes due to temporary speed restrictions. In the summer a cloud of dust miles long trailed the train.

When the line was upgraded for the standard gauge to Perth, it was rebuilt completely with metal ballast. The drainage problems of earlier years were rectified. The line became a main line similar in standard to statewide main lines. During the floods of the 1950 and 1954 particularly, the line was closed for long periods because of back up flooding from the Lachlan River in the Eubalong West to Roto sections. During my time in *orco* the work of upgrading the line began. A metal ballast plant was established at Mellelea Siding, which became a full staff station with crossing facilities and siding space in the former Eubalong West—Gunebang sections. With the advent of the first of seventeen 49 Class diesel locomotives, especially designed for the Broken Hill line conditions, dieselisation of the line began in about 1956. In 1960 when I took up, there was a mixture of steam and diesel with diesel being predominant beyond Condobolin. No 21, the Pick Up from Parkes to Broken Hill was still worked by steam. This train was timetabled to take 24 hours to Broken Hill. It left Parkes at 10.30pm on Tuesdays and Thursdays. No 16, the Up Pick Up left Broken Hill on the same days and about the same time. The amount of Out-of traffic between Ivanhoe and Menindee from No 21 regularly occupied up to two hours, the traffic being mainly for Darnick and Kaleentha. The train was a scourge of the ADS whose every effort to get it to run somewhere near the time met with failure.

The duties of the train controllers with dieselisation varied slightly. Water for instance was still critical at Ivanhoe but it was not necessary to programme special water trains. There became an excess of water gins which were stored at Menindee. Engines no longer changed at Ivanhoe, the 49 Class working through to Broken Hill refuelled at Ivanhoe on the main line. The setting of the programme arrangements did not change, the controller conferring with Ivanhoe, Menindee and Broken Hill daily.

The work of setting the Broken Hill line programme was generally completed by 9.00am at which time this controller had a cup of tea. Between 9.30am and 10.00am, the senior train controller completed the following day's programme. When this was received, it was entered into an *amba* book ready for the issuing of the 10.00am *amba*. For the uninitiated, *amba* is the code word for the train running programme for the following 24 hours. To get every station to the telephone for the sectional *ambas* an 'all stations key' was provided on the control console. On the Parkes leg, stations connected were Orange East Fork, Orange Box, Nashdale, Borenore, Gamboola, Molong, Manildra, Parkes and Parkes Signal Box. When reading out the *amba*, the controller gave the number of every train running for the following 24 hours. In addition, he gave the times for the light engines running between Orange East Fork and Molong. For any special trains running, he gave the Special Train Notice number. At the conclusion of the *amba*, he obtained an acknowledgement from each station. On the Main West leg the stations were Orange Signal Box, Station Master Orange, Mullion Creek, Euchareena, Stuart Town, Mumbil, Dripstone and Wellington.

From the time the *ambas* were completed until midday, the time was occupied with the general duties of a Train Control board. One of the very important duties of a controller on any board was the giving of running information to Per Way staff, electricians and other people authorised to use motor trikes. In Orange Control the information was often sought from unattended staff stations. Once a motor trike had been given train running information and entered a section, it was the responsibility of the controller to see that the information given was maintained.

If a train arrived at a station more than 10 minutes ahead of scheduled time, the regulations called for the driver to be issued with a T6 300 form. This form advised the driver of the time the fettling staff were advised that he would depart from the station he was at. The same form was used if a train had been scheduled to run at such short notice and it did not appear on the original running given to gangers at 7.00am. In each case, provision was made on the T6 300 to either advise the driver he was running ahead of the times given, or the fettling staff had received no notice of the running of his train. In effect, it put the onus on the driver to be especially on the look out, a point which many drivers had objected to, probably with some justification. If a driver objected too strongly, I would hold the train until within 10 minutes of the advised time of departure, especially if the area was similar to that between Cookamidgera and Molong where there were many sweeping bends and cuttings that limited the driver's vision.

Station Masters or signalmen who had issued train running to persons in charge of tricycles, either manual or motor, using the information from the morning *ambas*, were responsible for advising the controller when a train was running to a different time or running earlier than advised. It was then the duty of the controller to direct the issue of a T6 300 form. This form was an advice to a driver of the times that the fettling staff had in respect to his train. It was equally the controller's responsibility when a guard reported ahead of time from an unattended signal box or crossing loop, to see that the train was either held to time or issued with the warning notice. I objected strongly when a station would let a train go after warning the driver without first speaking to me. Often when trikes went into a section they would stop at a take off and advise the controller they were off the running line and would report to him again before putting the trike on. To do this they used portable telephones by attaching long poles, made up of short rods screwed together, to the wires that carried the control telephone network. (The control telephone lines were distinguished by the larger insulators on the crossbars of the telephone posts.) While it was still necessary to warn the driver with respect to fettling staff, a warning to the driver regarding the trike was not necessary. I applied this stand on all the Train Control Boards that I later worked. It must also be said that stations in the Sydney control area invariably spoke first to the controller.

The morning shift was completed with the finalising of the passenger and blue ribbon freight train delays. I do not intend to go into great detail about the train delays at this point. They are something I wish to write more fully about when detailing my experiences as a Senior Train Controller in Sydney. Suffice to say, that every passenger train that incurred delays, had them recorded from its originating point to its destination. This also applied to the blue ribbon freight services. As an example, if No 45 Mail passed Orange East Fork on time and was say 10 minutes late into Dubbo, the Orange Controller would be responsible for the correct compilation of the delays from East Fork to Wellington inclusive, the Dubbo Controller being responsible between Mary Vale to Dubbo.

There were many things that could delay a passenger train, for example, in holiday times with heavy brakevan traffic. When recording brakevan traffic delays, the number of suitcases and parcels unloaded had to be shown. There were speed restrictions, which were recorded in the Weekly Speed Notices (a train controller's bible!). Permissive losses also often caused delays; these occurred when trains ran with a permissive tonnage over the fixed load. The permitted loss of time was shown in the timetable, and such delays would be recorded as say, five minutes permissive loss Orange to Wellington, load 380 tons fixed 354 tons. After completing his own delays, the controller contacted Dubbo Control for the delays in his area. This information, together with Orange Control area delays, was relayed to the train controller at Lithgow. Orange Control was responsible also for passing on to him the delays occasioned to Up passenger trains between Dubbo/

Parkes and Blayney. Each Orange controller completed his own delays, generally toward the end of his shift.

The midday shift was one where all the *ecces* (the code word *ecce* means the tonnage which will be available from a station at the close of day) from every station and siding in the area were collected and collated for the senior train controller for the following morning. The telegraph operator at Parkes connected the stations on the Tottenham line direct to the Control Board. While I was at Orange, a new assistant station master had taken up at Albert (on the Tottenham line). He knew nothing about *ecces*, apparently not having been instructed in his duties by the outgoing officer. The result was that empty wagons lay at Albert for more than a week before the traffic inspector had gone there to see the new officer, more or less on a courtesy visit.

I think before the visit had finished, some of the courtesy had vanished. He had not given Control an *ecce* all the time he had been there. Obviously, the controller concerned was equally as culpable as he was for not asking for the *ecce*. The result was that the guards of the tri-weekly pick-up were not aware of the empties that were not required, especially in view of the fact the officer gave them no indication otherwise. The truck clerk in *oran* also had a finger in the pie because he had not been getting a truck report from Albert. By the time the correspondence finished, the officer, the controllers concerned and the truck clerk were all seen and spoken to. I thought the controllers and the clerk were fortunate; as far as the officer was concerned, he knew no better having been a porter in the metropolitan area, who had spent most of his time at Parramatta on barrier duty. The inspector spent some time nurturing him and before he left Albert, he became a proficient officer.

An important facet of the railway operations in the Orange control area was the supply of water. On the Broken Hill line especially, there were many fettler's trolley sheds with water tanks, and wayside water tanks were generally to be found in every ganger's length. (The area of track a ganger was responsible for was referred to as his 'length'.) A number of unattended stations had groups of fettler's residences, generally four or five houses, which in the summer time, especially, were dependent on the water tank attached to the pick-up for their water supply. The information regarding water requirements came from different sources. Station masters at the attended stations sent telegrams to Parkes and *orco* with their requirements.

These stations were also responsible for obtaining information from gangers at unattended stations for inclusion in their telegrams. The telegrams quoted the mileages and numbers of tanks to be filled. It was the responsibility of the officers at Parkes to issue guards with the water mileages and the numbers of tanks that were to be watered at each mileage. Mostly the water tanks were of the four-wheeled square type that was set in 'U' truck frames. It was sometimes necessary at Parkes to use a 7000-gallon water gin on No 21 between Condobolin and Broken Hill. The time taken to supply water to these tanks in the summer was significant. The time taken could affect the Working Timetable crossings. The controller when he received all the information redrew the forecast train running on the graph. It was not often that a staff setting was affected, but when the controller setting the programme received the water requirements, he would have an idea of the time required in a section.

On the midday shift, the office clerks would often want to use the control telephone, if they could not get through on the circuit telephones. The truck clerk was responsible for the supply of goods wagons to meet orders and for directing the movement of wagons not required at stations after unloading. The *dyak* clerk (*dyak* was the code word for empty stock wagons on hand) was responsible for the distribution of empty stock wagons to meet livestock orders in the *oran* district. The livestock clerk was responsible for receiving all livestock orders from stations in the district, and for allocating the loaded wagons onto stock trains and for formulating the timetables required. These timetables were printed in the Special Train Notices issued from the Superintendent's office. These clerks were the ones who mostly made the requests and I had no difficulty with this. However, two of the other controllers, and one in particular, would tell them where to go in no uncertain terms, saying the board was not for their convenience. Perhaps this was so, but it did me no harm in co-operating with them.

The *Silver City Comet*, by the late 1950s, was more than 20 years old and was beginning to behave like a train of its age. It became quite unreliable and often ran late in both directions because of engine shut downs. Each power car had two Gardner diesel engines. An engine shutdown left one engine to run the train and to supply power for the air-conditioning and buffet car. It was not uncommon for a relief power van to head out from Parkes to meet the train, generally at Condobolin, although if given early enough, advice was given and if the travelling fitter thought it necessary, it would go to Euabalong West. The problem then, of course, was the staff setting. Because the staffs were set in the Up for the passage of No 46 *Silver City Comet*, gangers would have to transfer staffs towards the relief van running on the Down.

If the *Silver City Comet* was more than 60 minutes late, the practice was to split the *Forbes Mail* and run two divisions from Parkes to Orange. To avoid having to run both divisions to Sydney, there were times when the Passenger Train Superintendent would authorise the attaching of the second division to No 58 at Orange. Only one sleeping car was attached to No 60, meaning that sleeping car passengers from the *Silver City Comet* had no beds from Parkes. Mostly they were able to be accommodated in No 58 at Orange, thus avoiding most of the wrath of sleeping berth passengers.

The *Silver City Comet* fleet of four power vans were known as DPs. When the decision was taken to run the *Central West Express* to Orange and return Sydney daily, the *Comet* cars were used to service the Orange-Dubbo-Parkes legs formerly served by No 31 running on alternate days to these points. The demand that this running had placed on the *Comet* vans was obviously greatly increased. The diligence of the Parkes fitters and travelling fitters were all that saved the department from many delays and avoided the need to run buses on the Orange leg. While there were four DPs, generally only three were available the other being at Chullora undergoing overhaul. To allow the *Silver City Comet* to maintain timetable time on the long climbs between Parkes and Dubbo to Orange, only two passenger cars were attached.

A parcels van-cum-brakevan, known as a DEH, ran from Sydney attached to No 49 *Forbes Mail* to Parkes where it was attached to the *Comet*. These vans were converted from the original *Silver City Comet* brakevans and were light drawgear (30 tons). They were always attached to the rear of the train hauling them. They were reversed at Orange. In the fruit and melon seasons at Menindee, they would be stacked full with fruit for the Sydney fruit markets.

Because of the regulations mentioned earlier about the guard riding the last vehicle between Valley Heights and Katoomba, a brakesman was provided from Sydney to Lithgow. The *Silver City Comet* had electro-pneumatic braking. When they converted the DEHs, the Westinghouse air brake system was also fitted to enable them to be compatible with ordinary passenger rolling stock. It was always my hope that nothing would happen to Nos 49 or 60, which called for clearing the section from the rear, it would have meant two bites of the cherry to clear the section, it being necessary, to lift the DEH with the 30-ton drawgear capacity, and then return for the balance of the train. This was very time consuming.

No 60 was recognised as a very difficult train to run on time and, as a result, it mostly had a dedicated locomotive. For some time the locomotive was 3616, which had the specially fitted Austrian-designed Giesl Oblong ejector equipment, to make the loco steam well, its narrow funnel distinguishing the engine. Orange salaried drivers worked the train every day except Saturday when the Parkes men had the pleasure. I remember from my shunting days how they hated working the train; it was somewhat different negotiating the 1 in 40 grades from Molong to Orange than working a 32 Class on the flat country! (In altitude Orange is a 1,000 feet higher than Molong.)

The 6.00pm shift was mainly basic control work; the maintaining of engine balances; dealing with engine failures when they occurred and re-rostering engines or, in extreme cases, cancelling trains for want of an engine; keeping tonnage balances and seeing that each goods train run had sufficient loading. The tonnage balance at Molong was important, because on occasions trains such as No 26 from Parkes conveying livestock and would leave Parkes with perhaps 100 tons under the single load, which meant that if L26 was running, there had to be additional tonnage at Molong to make the 680 tons from Molong. The train controller had to make a forward tonnage balance, taking into account No 32 from Dubbo and the fact No 8 was a starter from Molong. On the basis of this balance, a decision had to be made whether L26 should run or whether L8 and No 8 should be cancelled. If L26 was cancelled, the controller had to be sure that he had sufficient loading at Orange East Fork to make No 466 a full load.

The Special Train Notices (STNs) were available from the office despatch room about 5.30pm and were delivered to control around 6.30pm. Special trains that were shown to run, together with the stock trains programmed on Tuesdays and Saturdays were all pencilled onto the forward diagrams by the afternoon controller. Each day's STNs had a listing of all stock and perishable traffic movements. Controllers made good use of this information, checking the actual loadings and recording alterations to it on the Control Diagram and amending the list left by the livestock clerk. Occasionally the ADS would ring from home wanting to know what stock or what perishables had been loaded for a certain train. It was always a comfortable feeling to be able to answer straight off.

No 11 goods from Orange to Parkes was one of the key trains on the afternoon shift. This train which often conveyed stock wagon book outs for the trains running to Forbes, Condobolin, Tottenham and Peak Hill lines, was tabled to cross No 26 goods or No 50 fast stock at Bumberry. Its punctual running was important, especially after the advent of the 40 Class diesels working Nos 465 and 466 goods. The section running time between Manildra and Bumberry on the Down was something like 50 minutes and on the Up 30 minutes. No 11 was tabled into Bumberry before No 26/50. If the train was either late from Orange or delayed otherwise for more than about 30 minutes, the controller was in a quandary. He knew that generally the crews worked No 11 and changed with No 26/50, the Parkes crews would be working to see that they did not go past Bumberry and if No 11 was late, the Orange crew would do their damnedest to see they did not pass Manildra. It was really a balancing act, but my habit was to force the crossing at Bumberry, if at all possible. The other side of the coin was that there was more lee time at Parkes to shunt No 11 than there was to shunt No 26 at East Fork.

The office cleaners used to come in about 6.30pm to clean the control and senior's rooms. The lady cleaner, who was quite deaf, would turn the vacuum cleaner on regardless of what was happening in the line of conversation on the board. One day, in particular, the vacuum cleaner was turned on behind the Board, causing the controller, well known for his forthright foul language, to let go calling the cleaner and the vacuum cleaner all the names he could think of. When he had finished, a young face appeared from behind the board and said,

"We are not all deaf!"

Apparently the mother was ill and her daughter had taken her place. Profuse apologies and much embarrassment followed; he had not seen the cleaner come into the room.

The afternoon shift rounded off with the completion of the delays. While controllers worked on their own and each to his particular method, there was an unwritten law that each controller helped his mate on the next shift as much as possible, by heading the forms to be used in the next shift. This particularly applied to the backshift, where tonnage balance forms used when taking figures from the ASM Parkes or the Dubbo Train Controller and the engine balance forms were made ready. The delay sheets for the following day were also collated and dated with the trains not running, which were shown as being deleted on the seven-day sheets. Provided there were no engine failures or other happenings out of the ordinary, the afternoon shift was a comfortable one, just enough work to fully occupy the controller but not enough to place any undue strain on him.

The ADS, every Tuesday evening was either in Dubbo or Orange Controls watching the progress of the stock trains coming in from Nyngan and Coonamble. He would check the stock listing for each train against that which had loaded and made alterations to the listings of the trains as the evening progressed. I have recorded in my experiences at East Fork how stock and meat, especially, used to be detached from one train and attached to another. There was very little shunting done at Troy Junction with the Coonamble trains so far as listed traffic was concerned.

In most cases where amendments to listings were made, the stock or meat was taken off a Coonamble line train and put onto a far west train as these trains did not go near Troy Junction. Obviously East Fork was where the transfers had to take place. On most Saturday evenings, the ADS would be in Orange Control arriving generally around 8.30pm. He would expect the Senior Inspector at Dubbo to have all the particulars of loading and the changes to listings available for him. There were, as a rule, less changes on Saturdays because there was no stock loaded from open sales. He had very little regard for one inspector whose actions and words irked the gentleman in him. The only time I ever saw him say anything that was sarcastic or derogatory to anyone was to this man. He annoyed him so much one evening that he demanded he be in the Superintendent's office on the Monday morning prepared to give a statement. To this day I do not know if that happened.

The backshift commencing at midnight was probably the critical shift in terms of train working and preparation. The information gathered formed the basis for the senior controller to set the following day's programme. Sunday and Monday nights were reasonable shifts for which I was grateful, the Sunday night being the shift I took up on, early in 1960. As I sat in the chair for the first time, I was very nervous, but at the same time I felt not a little pride in my achievement. I have never been one to share those feelings with anyone other than Mamie, who knew me well enough to know without being told.

Stock nights in control were challenges, just as they were in the other positions I had worked in the district, from Acting Senior and Head Shunter at Parkes to ASM Orange East Fork, the difference being a different perspective when working each job. At Parkes and East Fork, the aim was to form the trains and get them 'out of your hair', so to speak, on time and not have to worry about the departed, but concentrate on the next arrival. Your duties were confined to the limits of the place of employment, which was as far as your vision extended.

It took me probably about a fortnight to realise my vision had to be greatly expanded to encompass the whole Control area from Orange to Broken Hill and Wellington. That each station and signal box would not make a move train-working-wise without reference to control or 'the man on the wall', a term I had on many occasions used. Now I was the 'man on the wall' and had to perform accordingly. The threading of the light engines from Orange East Fork to Molong for the Up stock trains was an important factor in keeping the trains on time, but there was not much of a problem when the whole program was running to time. However, when one of the stock trains or the light engines got off course, decisions often had to be made whether to delay the engine(s) heading to Molong and hope the time could be regained at Molong in the turn around. I invariably gave preference to the stock train.

The only time I did not was if the stock train was so late it would miss its crossing with No 49 Mail and it would have to stand and wait for No 49, then I would advance the engines a section. Generally engines went coupled. For example L372 and L62 ran coupled, and L62 obviously had time to spare at Molong. Engine failures in Loco often meant that the second of two engines was not ready on time. On these occasions, I invariably accepted the one engine, even though it made an additional crossing somewhere when the second engine appeared. I reasoned it was better to have one engine on time for its train than to have the two of them late. I have to say that my time at East Fork taught me that some of my predecessors did not think that way; it was once again the easy way out and some times sheer perversity, the controller not having to answer for the delays because they were Mechanical Branch's.

Orange railway station taken in January 1988. The station, which opened in 1877, featured a second storey, being the Station Master's residence. *John R Newland.*

I have earlier in my writing commented on the detrimental effects of alcohol. At one time, one controller in particular, and another to a much lesser degree, were victims of alcoholism. I am not suggesting that the Department suffered or that a controller under the influence was ever on the Control Board. I do suggest however, that this was so because the controller to be relieved did not hand over until the relief was fit to take over or the controller for the next shift arrived. The story is told of the morning the DS, alighted from No 45 Mail and was walking towards the departmental garage when a bottle was thrown from the window and landed in the ash bin narrowly missing him. He kept walking and went home. What he said to the people involved later had a salutary effect for a long time. The controller left Orange while I was at East Fork, his problem plagued him all his working life, in many respects I felt sorry for him.

At around 4.00am each morning, the ASM at Parkes would come on with his tonnage figures. These figures included Up traffic to East, Down traffic to Broken Hill, Forbes traffic and traffic beyond to Cootamundra, traffic for Tottenham, Condobolin, Narromine, plus traffic for West of Dubbo and across country to Binnaway. To me this was home territory, but the Controller who had been appointed from outside the area initially found some difficulty getting the various tonnages onto their correct forms because he did not know the locations of all the stations. The engine balances were completed with the chargeman at Parkes. Similar information came via *doco* from Dubbo. The tonnages we were concerned with were the Up tonnage from Dubbo and the cross-country tonnage from Dubbo to Parkes and beyond.

To Dubbo we gave the Down tonnages from Orange with emphasis on the traffic for west of Dubbo. When the wheat harvest was in full swing, the number of bulk wheat trucks, the trains they were set on and the silos to which they were to load, had to be available to the Senior and to the Wheat Officer. The previous day's delays were finalised with *doco* and together with *orco's* delays, would be passed onto *lico* by 4.30am. *Lico* in turn had to pass onto *syco west* the delays in the *oran* and *esk* districts by 5.00am for the Train Delay Clerk in *syco*. The time on the backshift from about 3.30am seemed to fly, I remember and am still grateful to the senior train controller on the first stock morning I worked. When he came into the Control Room, he gathered everything that was on the desk and disappeared into his own office. While I was reasonably up to date, I appreciated that I had not given him a perfect set of sheets from which to work. He, for his part, knew I would be 'uphill'. Before I went home, I thanked him for his consideration. He said nothing, but gave me a look I have not yet fathomed.

It took me about three months to feel completely at home. After that I enjoyed the job and was very contented. The change in the working hours made a huge difference. The 50 per cent daytime working made home life much easier for us both and gave me time with the children that I had not had before. The stint of daywork as the acting inspector set me on a rest pattern that I had not enjoyed for five years. This time together with the control hours saw me lose the fatigue that I was suffering when I left East Fork. I had not realised how much the constancy of East Fork, together with the overtime hours, had taken from me, until I was about six months into the new working conditions and feeling every inch a new man. I suffered a short-term financial loss, which was not sufficient to worry us. In the long term the financial gain from the additional salary was its own reward.

In January of 1962 I was offered the position of First Class Train Controller Lithgow and Dubbo. I accepted both, giving preference to Lithgow. Something like a month later, the staff clerk called me into his office and informed me I had been appointed to Lithgow Control. He then went on to say that Allen Tobin who was working on the Second Class Board in Lithgow and who had been in our Control school, had been appointed to Dubbo. The question of course, was would I accept an appointment to Dubbo in lieu of Lithgow. My reply was that first I would talk to Mamie and get her reaction. She did not really want to leave Orange, but was quite prepared to go wherever I was employed, so the decision came back to me and I agreed to accept the Dubbo appointment.

I put the house on the market and found great difficulty in selling it. At that time a recession had just begun, which made it almost impossible to get home loans, hence no finance, no sale. We finally rented the house to a doctor, whose treatment of our pride and joy still leaves me annoyed, perhaps the blame for its condition when they left may have better been attributed to his wife.

I went to Dubbo in May of 1962. Mamie and the family followed sometime in June when I had found a house to rent. It was not really what we wanted. It was an old style brick home that was as filthy as our home was later left. We stayed there for less than two months and moved into a much more attractive home in Macquarie Street in Dubbo. We left Orange with some regret. We had been close to family, both Mamie's and mine, our three children had been born there and we were established in the Church and in the community. I had been Superintendent of the Intermediate Department of the Sunday School and active in the Men's Brotherhood. In this capacity I had visited the Orange Base Hospital nearly every Sunday afternoon in search of men who had no visitors, or whose families lived in other regions.

I made a number of friends and was able to help some of them in a practical way. In the hospital, I found the head porter who had been in charge of the goods shed at Parkes. He had transferred to Orange and shortly after was diagnosed with abdominal cancer. He lived for about three months after admission; it was one of the most tragic illnesses. The poor man suffered an agonising death. His only visitor was his wife, who found difficulty coping.

I was given a send off by the office staff at Orange and jointly we were farewelled from the Church.

CATHY, THE BEGINNING OF A LIFELONG STRUGGLE

A S a family unit we had enjoyed good health. The two older children on a couple of occasions had croup which, though frightening, did not cause concern for the attacks were brief and neither of them suffered any effects from it. Mamie had suffered a severe bout of quinsy before she was pregnant with Cathy; shortly after her recovery from it, she had her tonsils removed, which were infected, being the cause of the quinsy. I had been in Control about nine months when I went to work one morning on the 6.00am shift with a pain in my stomach. The longer the shift wore on, the more severe it became. I saw the shift out went home and from there to the doctor. I arrived in the surgery around 2.00pm and at 4.30pm was in the Orange Base Hospital having an emergency appendectomy. I soon recovered and was back at work three weeks later.

We had some concerns about Cathy. She was very slow crawling and walking. We had taken her to the doctor a number of times, but there was nothing

Cathy at age 16.

obviously amiss and his opinion was that the ligaments in her legs were slow to firm up, which was the cause of her not walking until she was two years and two months old. She was a very pretty and lively baby.

One Friday afternoon of late October 1961, Mamie found her in the hallway, lying on her back and staring blankly at the ceiling. We took her to the doctor, who admitted her to the Base Hospital with suspected meningitis. They rested her on the Friday night and ran tests, including a lumbar puncture (the taking of fluid from the spine) on the Saturday morning. I had previously arranged to be part of a group of men from the church who formed a working bee in the Methodist portion of the cemetery on the Saturday afternoon. We had seen Cathy in the morning and although she was somewhat lethargic, she appeared to be herself again. As I arrived home from the working bee, the doctor turned into our drive.

I instinctively knew that something serious had brought the doctor to us. It had. The tests detected blood in the spinal cord which indicated that Cathy had some brain related problem, but what that was he did not know. Before he came to us, he had spoken to the head neurosurgeon of the Children's Hospital at Camperdown. He advised us to leave Orange that evening and take Cathy to the hospital, where she would be admitted. His final words to us were,

"Your case is not hopeless."

Those words will forever be entrenched in my mind because, 'He knew not what he said'.

While we had a vehicle capable of the journey, it needed two new front tyres before setting out on a miserable night to drive to Sydney. There being no automatic teller machines in those days, we had available only the week's housekeeping money. I went to the garage where I had dealt for years and told him my problem. He put two tyres on, filled it with petrol and told me to pay him when I had the money. I then went to see one of the ASMs at Orange station at his home. I told him my problem, and without question, he loaned me £20, which was what he had in cash. After leaving Roy and Faye with Mamie's sister, we left for Sydney around 8.00pm. Cathy had been sedated; we placed her in blankets on the back seat of the Hillman.

The Great Western Highway (a misnomer I am sure!) was vastly different to what it is today. The journey from Bathurst to Lithgow seemed never ending, but having finally passed Lithgow we were faced with the 'Forty Bends', which I am sure some will remember. It had rained lightly from the time we had left Orange. After we left the 'Forty Bends' and headed for River Lett, intermittent fog was sent to try us, but once we reached the top of Victoria Pass the fog lifted and we had a good run until we came into Church Street at Parramatta at around 1.30am.

A sports car passed me at the rate of knots and pulled in front of me. He was making a good path so I followed him at a far greater speed than I would have had he not been there. It was not long before the inevitable; the police siren and then both of us directed to pull over. As soon as we stopped, I got out of the car and told the policeman we urgently needed to get to the Children's Hospital with Cathy, who by this time was stirring and starting to cry, he took a look into the car and waved us on. I do not know what happened to the other driver. It was good to have had the support of so many people in our trouble on that evening. I had no idea where Bridge Road, Camperdown was and started looking for it about five miles before we found it. It was well sign-posted and we arrived at the hospital around 2.15am, having stopped only the once to talk to the policeman. I was exhausted and worried.

We had admitted Cathy and were having a cup of tea when the lift door opened and a small insignificant-looking man in his pyjama top and a pair of slacks approached us and asked if we were the parents. With our acknowledgement he said,

"I will examine the child".

The way in which he spoke made me confident that here was someone who knew what he was about. Insignificant in stature though he certainly was, he was a giant among his colleagues and revered by the nursing staff. We had many dealings over many years with Dr Marcel Sofer Schrieber, who passed away in 1996. To us, he was a man of understanding, compassion and professional etiquette. After the examination, he returned to us and said he could not immediately diagnose her condition, but he suspected something was causing abnormal pressure on the brain. Tests were to be arranged for the Monday, and in the meantime he would keep her under mild sedation. We then left the hospital and drove out to Granville and knocked on the door of Mamie's sister's home at around 5.30am, totally exhausted from what had been a traumatic night. We went back to the hospital on the Sunday afternoon to find Cathy very drowsy and drifting in and out of sleep. We also took the opportunity and each napped with her.

On the Monday morning, we were at the hospital in time to see her before her pre-med treatment prior to her being wheeled off to the theatre. She was to have another lumbar puncture, an encephalogram and have fluid drawn from the brain through a small-bore hole in her skull. What to expect? Would it be something easily treatable, which of course was our hope and fervent prayer, or would it be something more sinister requiring major treatment? These thoughts were going through my mind, and also of course, through her mother's. The doctor finally emerged mid-afternoon and took us into his rooms which were in Wade House where Cathy had been admitted. He came straight to the point. Cathy had a brain tumour in the front lobal portion of her brain. It was in a most difficult position and while surgery was the only possible treatment, the prognosis was that she had only a 50 per cent chance of surviving it. I felt devastated, and we automatically reached for each other's hand for support. I asked Dr Schrieber what would be Cathy's chances of survival without an operation, his reply short and succinct, "Nil". We had to make the decision then whether to proceed with the operation or leave Cathy to her fate. There really was no decision. We gave permission for the operation to take place.

The operation took place on Wednesday, 2 November 1961. We were advised by Dr Schrieber to be at the hospital early, but said that we would be unable see her and that he did not believe the operation would be complete until 6.00pm. When I asked why if we could not see her that we should have to be there early, the reply was,

"I think you should be available all day."

I did not pursue the question. It was the longest day I have ever spent. I could not concentrate to read the paper. We talked to one another in desultory fashion. The room where we waited was filled with parents waiting for their children having day surgery or treatment, each one as anxious about their child as we were about ours. About lunchtime, one father asked me why was I waiting. When I replied, he said,

"My daughter is having a cast removed from her broken leg and I thought I had trouble."

We bought some lunch in the canteen and sat in the garden for most of the afternoon.

It was closer to 7.00pm when Dr Schrieber came to see us, still in his theatre dress. He said he removed about nine tenths of a benign tumour, the balance being in such a position he was not able to remove it. He said she had survived the operation quite well, but she would be in intensive care for some days and that it would be some time before she regained consciousness. I asked about the balance of the tumour and he said that he was going to treat it with cobalt radiation that he thought would shrink and kill the balance. When I also asked about the probability of the tumour growing again, the question was effectively evaded.

It was a great relief to know that she had survived the operation and that she was in as good a condition as such major surgery would permit and I felt that the prayers offered on her behalf had in part been answered. I also had a premonition that this was not the end of Cathy's problems. How right I was! The conveying of the news of the operation to our respective families was not only an ordeal but expensive from public telephones.

We were at Granville the following morning when the next door neighbour, who had a telephone, came to the door saying that I was wanted on the phone by the sister from Wade House. She told me in effect that if we wanted to see our daughter alive we should get to the hospital as quickly as possible. While I did not tell Mamie the exact words the sister had used, I said we should get to the hospital quickly. I was driving along Parramatta Road when the lights went to amber. With more city driving experience I may have kept going. I did not and came to a stand at the lights. Before I had stopped, I was hit in the rear by a taxi, the driver of which got out screaming about my driving ability and parentage.

There was not much damage. When he calmed down I reminded him that it was he who was the idiot and that if he persisted I would call the police and most likely he would be charged with negligent driving. I was too concerned about Cathy to spend time there arguing, so I told him to forget the matter and kept driving. When I sold the car many years later, it still had the little crinkle in the bumper bar where he hit me. We went straight to the intensive care unit to find that she had rallied and was again breathing without life support.

We went back to Orange and work on the Saturday after the operation. The following weekend we took Roy and Faye to see Cathy. Although it was now nine days after the operation and she was back in the ward, she still had made no effort to sit up but lay permanently on her back. When her brother and sister came to her bedside, she made a Herculean effort and almost sat up to greet them. It was one of the few times I found it difficult to keep my emotions under control. Men did not cry, especially so in that era. My reason for wanting to not show too much emotion was for the sake of the family. I wanted them to be able to look to dad when they were upset and find him in control of himself and perhaps the situation.

Although we were covered for intermediate ward, which Wade House was, with the Railway and Tramway Hospital Fund (as it was then), the hospital insisted on money up front. Mamie's father came to our aid and paid the bills as they came. I, in turn, gave him the cheques from the fund as I received them. The fund covered about 90 per cent of the hospital costs. At that time we were in the Grand United Order of Oddfellows Medical Fund; this Fund paid about 75 per cent of the bills. I was a long way out of pocket with these bills, and while we did not consider the cost of travel and the expenses associated when we went to see Cathy, it was all a drain on the finances.

The time came for the commencement of the cobalt ray treatment at Royal Prince Alfred Hospital, and with it came another blow; a special sister had to accompany Cathy on each visit. This accompaniment, known as 'specialling', was not covered in any Fund. The treatment was over a fortnight on alternate weekdays. Mamie went down during the second week and took her. This money, also to be found up front, was a real blow.

About three weeks after the cobalt ray treatment we went down with Mamie's mother and father to bring her home. This was in mid-January 1962. We had planned to take the children down on the train at Christmas time to see her, but they both got the chicken pox, which put a stop to that.

After she came home, Cathy very gradually picked up and it seemed she would recover normal health, from her diagnosed *cystic haemangioma* of the *Cavernous Corpus Callosum*.

FIRST CLASS TRAIN CONTROLLER, DUBBO

DUBBO CONTROL, *doco*, was unique among train control boards in New South Wales, mainly because of its size. It covered the area from Wellington to Dubbo, Molong to Dubbo, Parkes to Dubbo, Dubbo to Binnaway-Werris Creek, Binnaway to Gwabegar, Dubbo to Coonamble and Dubbo to Nyngan. It was not a particularly busy board, but on occasions, when failures occurred in two or three areas, it was one that was difficult to work. My readers may recall my comments about the grading of Borenore; the analogy could also be applied to Dubbo and Orange controls. There is no doubt that Orange Control was by far the busier board and, in terms of the duties of

The view of the railway approaches to Dubbo taken in January 1951 viewed from top of the Harmon coal loader. The lines from Coonamble and Binnaway are at the left, the original line from Sydney is in the centre, and the line from Molong and the deviated line from Sydney (known as the 'long mile') are at the right. The 'triangle' linking the Coonamble and Molong lines is in the centre. The Fitzroy Street level crossing, Frame 'B' and the 287 mile post are at the right of the photograph. John R Newland.

each board, deserved to be a first class board if Dubbo did. My opinion is that Dubbo should have been the second class board and Orange first class. I believe, however, that Dubbo was the first class board because when Train Control was originally commenced in the State, the Broken Hill line would not have been as busy as it was in the 1940s, 1950s and 1960s and that the Dubbo area would have been busier. It certainly could be a handful on stock nights.

By the time I arrived in Dubbo the controllers had voted for 8 hour 30 minute shifts with a 9 day fortnight which, with the blessing of the Australasian Transport Officers Association, had been proposed by the Department. The controllers in Orange had voted against the proposal on the grounds that 8 hour 30 minute shifts were too long and would take too much out of a Controller and render him likely to make poor decisions because of fatigue toward the end of a shift. I went along with the majority in Orange, although I was not totally convinced eight hours on Orange Control Board would have been any more arduous than eight hours at Orange East Fork. I found the long shifts tiresome to begin with, but the end result of having eight days off together was a welcome reward. As events unfolded in Dubbo the days off were a great blessing to us.

The systems of safeworking were electric staff on Wellington to Dubbo-Narromine-Goobang Junction (the junction for Broken Hill and Narromine lines, about three kilometres west of Parkes) and Troy Junction to Werris Creek and Dubbo East Junction to Molong. The balance were staff and ticket, the train programmes being such that with some exceptions on stock nights, the staff settings seldom varied. As a matter of interest, when the line from Dubbo East Junction was opened to Molong, it was provided with single line automatic signalling to facilitate the working of stock trains. During my time it was divisible electric staff.

I found *doco* to be a fragmented board to work. The train working on the day shift was quite busy, but was such that the set crossings rarely varied unless something ran drastically late, hence not many train working decisions had to be made. The short sections between Merrygoen and Binnaway were the only places where crossings were often changed. I recall on the Tuesday morning after I had taken up on the Monday, the ADS rang me and asked me were the stock train crews camped at Coonamble available for their return journey jobs. I hesitated because I was not sure and he, sensing my hesitation, said to me,

" I would have thought that a good train controller would have checked."

He would never catch me out again. In fact, he never again rang me with that question. On the Saturday morning I asked my predecessor the same question; his response was,

" I ... hope so."

A point I made after that gentle reminder was to check with the guards on arrival at Coonamble and see whether the stock wagons they placed at the various loading points

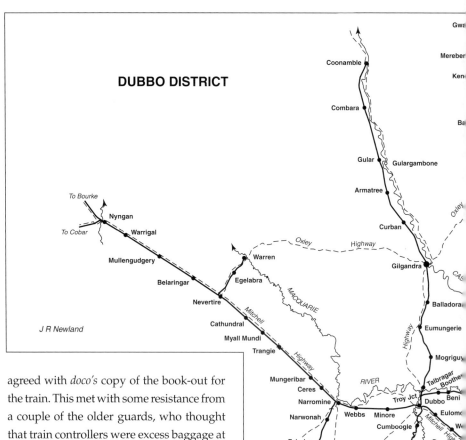

DUBBO DISTRICT

J R Newland

agreed with *doco's* copy of the book-out for the train. This met with some resistance from a couple of the older guards, who thought that train controllers were excess baggage at the best of times. When one of the guards did not provide confirmation of the book-out, I put pressure on him by requesting the Station Master Dubbo to direct on the book-out and that he confer with Control from Coonamble before signing off. I became an entry in his little black book; someone to be 'set up' at a future date. I was aware of this and with two guards, in particular, I acted by the book.

The daywork collected the *ecces* from the stations and sidings as had been done in *orco*. The train delays were finalised with Orange. These delays, which were for trains leaving

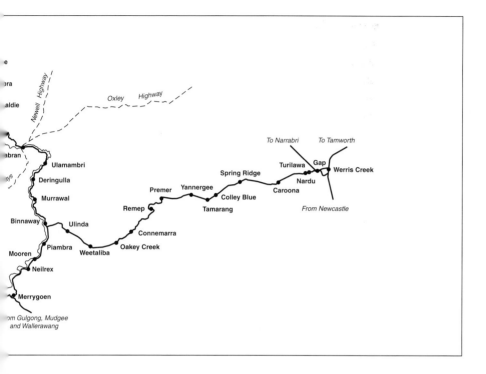

Sydney the previous day, became known as 'finalisers' because they were actually printed in Sydney separately as the finalising delays for long distance passenger trains and were perused by Administration the day after the train journeys had been completed. There were constant requests for train running information from Per Way staff. Once again, it was information quickly and easily given. For example, someone ringing from stations Narromine to Parkes would on most days have only one train to watch for. The train running was not given to gangers; they had to ring the nearest manned station for their information.

The following day's programme came from the senior train controller around 9.30am. *Ambas* were given for stations Dubbo to Wellington, Dubbo to Nyngan and Dubbo to Molong. Peak Hill, being the only manned station Narromine to Parkes, used to ring on the railway circuit telephone for his train running programme. The day work seemed to consist of a multiplicity of small duties that did not really pressure the controller, but kept him occupied most of the time.

The afternoon shift saw the origination of some of the trains I mentioned earlier as in running through Orange East Fork. No 32 from Nyngan commenced early in the day from Bourke and conveyed wool and general goods, empty returns for Cooks River, together with oil tanks and often TRCs of meat from Tancreds Meatworks at Bourke.

No 32 was built to the full 680 ton load from Dubbo, Mondays to Saturdays. Because of the type of traffic offering, the train was quite often a length load, (a term used when the number of vehicles on the train reached the maximum number shown in the Working Timetable for the section concerned, which was mostly 55 vehicles).

On weekdays, Nos 65 and 99 ran from Dubbo to Nyngan, No 65 conveying a full through load to Nyngan from where it was shunted for the Nyngan and Cobar traffic, and then continued to Bourke with the Darling Harbour traffic for second day delivery. No 99 shunted the road and supplied the book-out and general goods for Narromine, Trangie, Nevertire and intermediate sidings, the traffic for these trains having mainly arrived from Orange by trains of the same number.

Mullengudgery, an unattended station between Trangie and Nyngan, was a heavy stock loading point, with cattle outnumbering sheep loading. Because the controller had no confirmation until the arrival of the stock train, which was generally No 236, whether loading was completed and whether the ordered wagons had been loaded, he relied on the guard to appraise him of the situation before he started to shunt.

It was often the case that wagons would fail to load, and also the case that the stock would be late loading, causing delay to the train. On occasions, the failure to load meant that there was insufficient stock to run Nos 236 and 238 as stock trains. On these occasions Nos 236 and 238 were amalgamated at Dubbo and run as No 238 conveying stock from both trains. The minimum number of stock wagons a train could convey and still be

A panoramic view of Dubbo railway station and yards viewed from the top of the Harmon coal loader taken in 1951. The loco shed is in the middle foreground.   John R Newland.

classified as a stock train, was 19 stock wagons. Below this number of wagons offering for a listed stock train, it was permissible to build the train to a full goods load, renumber it and run it to a full goods train timetable.

The Orange ADS was very careful about this, for the slower running of the train could well have caused it to miss the livestock sales at the Flemington or Homebush sales, when the latter closed. Thus, on numerous occasions, trains conveying less than 19 stock wagons were treated as stock trains, being built up to 500 tons with goods traffic. The other point he considered also was the additional time cattle would be in transit, something I had made comment on earlier.

On most afternoons, a goods train left Dubbo with cross-country goods for Binnaway and then to Werris Creek. These trains were always worked by 32 Class locomotives and were timetabled at goods speed. Any 'U', 'K' or similar type wagon loaded in excess of 32 tons was not permitted to run at a speed exceeding 20 miles per hour. (Vehicles over 32 tons were restricted to 20 mph because of the condition of the permanent way).

There was a considerable time difference between goods running at the maximum speed of 35 miles per hour and of 20 miles per hour. There was never any thought given by anyone from the senior train controller down to shunters whether a train should convey at 20 miles per hour traffic. The exception to this was when a train was conveying livestock, the senior train controller would give a direction for there to be no 20 mph traffic.

Generally, the first the train controller knew he had a 20 mph train was when he

either received the train load message or the guard reported at the first staff station after departure, whether it was from Dubbo, Binnaway or Werris Creek. It was a difficult area to police, for there was just sufficient 20 mph traffic to be a nuisance. It consisted mainly of coal from the Hunter Valley coalfields, superphosphate and timber, which came unheralded and unsung from Werris Creek. In most cases there would only be one or two trucks on a 650 ton load. I tried (not very forcefully I must admit) unsuccessfully to have 20 mph traffic kept for certain trains.

The time saved in train hours and crew payments would have been significant. I am pointing out the 20 mph traffic problem because, to me, it was symptomatic of the failure of administration and senior train controllers, responsible for programme setting; and for station masters (and their assistants) and train controllers to pay attention to detail. My effort to make specified trains 20 mph was mainly with the ADS, whose attitude was that, it was ever thus and all too difficult. It should not have been. One could list stock and perishable traffic onto certain trains and be sure it would be on those trains. I could see no reason why the same philosophy could not have been maintained with 20 mph traffic. I was a voice in the wilderness.

It was also something I sometimes felt that had been abused by guards showing 35 tons for a wagon on their X2010s, when in fact it was under 32 tons. An instance of this occurred with a train departing Dubbo for Binnaway. The X2010 for a train load taken by the junior at Dubbo showed all wagons less than 32 tons. On arrival at the first staff station, which was Barbigal, the guard announced his times. I challenged him, saying he was conveying only 35 mph traffic. He was adamant that one of the wagons was a 35 ton wagon. I did not believe him, but there was nothing I could do about it.

Some passenger services from Dubbo to Bourke, Cobar and Coonamble were worked by 900* Class DEB sets which, though fairly rough riding, provided a good fast service on Mondays, Wednesdays and Fridays, connecting off No 45 *Coonamble Mail*, (No 59 *Bourke Mail* having been deleted from the passenger services just prior to my going to Dubbo). These returned to connect with No 46 departing Dubbo on the same days. A railmotor formed the service to Binnaway three days a week off No 45. The motor returned from Binnaway to connect with No 46. Another railmotor ran from Molong to Dubbo and return conveying high school students to Dubbo and passengers from and to the *Forbes Mail*.

Two 600 Class* served Coonamble, Brewarrina and Bourke on other days. However,

---

* The air-conditioned self propelled sets which worked Dubbo to Bourke were known as 'DEB' sets or 900 Classes because all the carriages including the power units had serial numbers beginning with 9. They consisted of two power and two trailer cars. With a power car at each end they could be driven from either end. The 600 classes, which ran to Coonamble, were similar in type, the exception being they were non air-conditioned.

Sydney often called these in to augment the metropolitan area fleet. When this happened, a railmotor was used. At holidays times, a train was formed using a First and Second Class carriage with a brakevan off No 45. A 30 Class hauled the train on these occasions. The cross-country railmotor from Narromine to Cootamundra ran three times a week in each direction. The only time I had any difficulty with the running of the passenger trains was due to train failure; the 900 Class working from Bourke once failed some 30km from Nyngan. Although these trains carried an emergency coupling that allowed for the connection of a locomotive, there was not a locomotive within two hours of the train. The passengers were put onto coaches, which conveyed them to Dubbo, while No 46 was held for 45 minutes awaiting their arrival. The crew stayed with the train, the corridor attendant travelling with the passengers. A fitter travelled by Departmental car to the failed train. He repaired it and it was available next morning to run the Bourke service.

The backshift in Dubbo on most nights was a drag, the train working virtually looking after itself. The occasions on which the controller had to make decisions affecting crossings were the exception rather than the rule. Even on stock nights, the trains running towards Molong were unopposed. No K3 from Parkes was the only train between Parkes and Narromine. If there was a cross country stock running from Dubbo and either train ran out of its course, the sections were short and, with electric staff, crossings could be made to suit. Nos 65 and 99 running toward Nyngan were unopposed. Between Dubbo and Werris Creek there would be a maximum of four trains in an electric staff area.

From about 3.30am, when tonnage figures were being obtained from Nyngan, Dubbo, Binnaway, *weco* and Parkes for the information of the senior train controllers at Dubbo and Orange, it became busier but never frenetic. Programmes were checked with Binnaway and Nyngan and engine balances made out which, unless there had been a failure, was the same as the senior train controller had formulated the previous day. It was not good grounding for a Senior Train Controller's position in Sydney.

The pick-up from Dubbo to Coonamble on Sundays, Tuesdays and Thursdays was a very difficult train. We never knew how much 'out-of traffic' for the various stations, all of which were unattended, was on the train and the times, therefore, given by the guards had to be accepted as being factual. I am reasonably sure they were not always so. I believed, but could never prove it, that on some occasions, the guard called Curban and gave times for that station when in fact they were already in Coonamble. On the return journey, they stretched the work out, especially the shunting of Gilgandra yard, to a point where they arrived into Dubbo just under long hours.

('Long hours' was a term used throughout the system to indicate a crew was approaching shift limits. The exceeding of these was a breach of the Industrial Award for the staff concerned).

These trains were worked by guards whose roster was the Coonamble trains and the

Binnaway motor. When guards not on the roster worked the trains, the difference in the arrival times at both Coonamble on the Down and at Dubbo on the return home were significantly different. I pointed this out to the retiring senior train controller and to the incoming senior who had been a guard in Dubbo and was told on both occasions not to rock the boat. It was a sore point with me at the time and even more so later when one of the guards became a train controller and boasted to me how they got away with 'murder' as guards on the Coonamble line.

The train clerk in Orange seemed to be aware of what was happening. However, instead of writing to the guards for an explanation of the time spent at various locations, he wrote to the train controller asking him to explain how the time at unattended stations was occupied. To add insult, he invariably asked what action had we taken to expedite the train. It was impossible to provide satisfactory answers and, from a controller's point of view, it was an exasperating situation that could only be righted by the traffic inspector riding with the guard on a couple of occasions. When this was suggested to him, the reply was,

" You don't think I'm going to spend all night going to Coonamble, do you? "

He should have done so.

The district superintendent very jealously guarded his authority with respect to Rule 307. (Rule 307 granted the right to suspend safeworking regulations and make special arrangements for working trains affected by emergency situations. This authority was issued to District Superintendents, the Train Control Superintendent, Safeworking Superintendent and the Passenger Train Superintendent).

I recall being in *orco* when the staff instrument between Parkes and Gidgeera failed. I was told by Parkes Box first, then very shortly after *juco* came on saying he wanted a '307'. I told him that the DS was very particular, and that I would explain the situation to him before saying "I want ". I then buzzed on the intercom and told him *juco* had a staff failure. He said to tell *juco* to ring him on the side phone, which I did. Some 10 minutes later the DS came into the Control Room and said *juco* had not rung him. With this I latched onto *juco* and vacated the chair. When the DS announced himself the Controller said,

"I want a 307 for this staff failure."

The blast he got was worth listening to if you were not on the end of it. In no uncertain terms, the DS said the issuing of a '307' was his prerogative and that he would decide whether there was to be one issued. The next voice was that of the DS at Junee who, while not apologising for his train controller, agreed with what he had said about the issue of a Rule '307'. Finally it was issued. I learned from that.

One Saturday afternoon, the staff instrument between Narromine and Wyanga failed for the railmotor going to Parkes. Before I rang the DS, I asked Narromine did he have persons available for pilot working. He said,

"No, but he could arrange to get them."

I then rang the DS and told him of the staff instrument failure. His response, as always, to this was,

"What do you want me to do about it? "

I said to him,

"I am advising you that a passenger train is being delayed."

He then asked me what had I done about it. I told him of the position for relief staff at Narromine. He still refused to give a '307 ' and, despite the fact there was not a train between Narromine and Parkes, pilot working was introduced. The cost in wages and salary at time and a half on Saturday and for a pilotman and staff to man Wyanga seemed not to be a concern to him. I suspect it was debited to the Signals Branch. The motor was delayed for about two hours, but as it did not appear on the Sydney delays, the DS was prepared to take the delay rather than issue a '307'.

On another occasion at about 4.00am, the guard of a stock train at Elong Elong advised me that he could not get an electric staff for the Caratel Loop section and that the instrument was dead. A goods train had left Merrygoen, heading for Dubbo, at about 3.30am and was to lift bulk wheat from Mendooran and cross the stock train at Caratel Loop. With some trepidation, I rang the DS and advised him of the staff instrument failure. He knew as well as I did that Elong Elong and Caratel Loop were unattended and that it would take hours to get pilot working in operation. To my mind, the only sensible thing was the issue of a '307', at least for the stock train. He agreed after I had outlined the train position between Dubbo and Merrygoen, which of course, he had to know. It was then necessary to wait for the guard of the goods train to report at Caratel Loop before any further move could be made. The DS gave me the '307', which I wrote down and repeated back to him, assuring him that I would not make a move until I had heard from the guard at Caratel Loop. He then went back to bed. While I waited for the guard, I called the District Signals Engineer. He gathered his linesman and the electrician and headed for Caratel by road.

Fortunately, the guard of the goods reported on arrival at Caratel. Caratel Loop, for some reason which I cannot recall, was one of the few places where the first train to arrive for a crossing took the main line and worked the opposing train through the loop then departed from the main line. I asked him to see if the staff instrument was showing staff in or out. He came back and said the instrument was dead. I then relayed the '307' to the guards at Elong Elong and Caratel Loop. The '307' authorised the stock train to depart from Elong Elong without being in possession of the electric staff for the section Elong Elong to Caratel Loop. It also directed the driver and guard of the goods train at Caratel Loop not to move until directed to do so. The way this DS wrote '307s' was like writing a short novel. I almost filled a sheet of paper with the wording. Imagine the guards trying to see by the light of a handlamp and resting their pads on the telephone receptacles, which were made to hold telegram forms about six inches long and about 4 inches wide, writing the wording of a '307'. It was difficult and slow, and usually took 30 to 40 minutes to issue under these circumstances.

I went about my work, which had been severely disrupted by these events, until the circuit telephone rang about 5.45am. When I answered it, I found the guard of the stock train ringing from Boomley, an unattended siding midway between Elong Elong and Caratel. His message was that the engine of his train had leaking boiler tubes and was a total failure. This news really deflated me. Before ringing the DS again, which would be done with even more trepidation, I sat and thought out the situation. There was an engine available in Dubbo that could go to the rescue of the train but there was no crew available until about 10.00am, without cancelling a regular service.

The engine at Caratel Loop was a 32 Class. These engines, when used tender first, had a load reduction of 40 per cent because they had no trailing sands. 32 Classes were not provided with sand pipes that would sand the line to prevent slipping when travelling tender first. Given this, the train was conveying a load of 450 tons, plus 90 tons for the dead 32 Class fast stock load and the full goods load was 640 tons. The driver said he was confident that his engine could convey the load tender first.

I was not so confident, because the gradient from Boomley to Caratel Loop in one place was 1 in 100. This was not all that daunting, however it was a cold frosty morning. I thought about this and then rang Caratel Loop again and spoke to the driver, suggesting that he lay sand on the track as he went along. He told me he was one jump ahead of me and had intended to do that. The other concern I had was whether the engine would have sufficient water. The Caratel driver said he had a hose connection on his engine and could, if needed, take water from the dead engine. What he did make even more clear was that he had come out of barracks and there was no way he was going to go to Boomley and work from there back toward Binnaway. To have done so would have breached the Enginemen's Award.

Armed with this information, I again rang the DS who gave me the usual characteristic greeting. When I told him of the trouble, he went off his head, abusing me and asking,

"What the bloody hell do you want me to do about it?"

I was somewhat ready for him and reminded him, gently, that the train was already on a '307' and while it was, he was responsible for the safeworking. He calmed down then and apologised for his outburst. I gave him all the information I had gathered from the drivers and we then had quite a long amicable discussion on what would be the best way to tackle the problem. I had already advised Binnaway to call the outgoing crew, who fortunately were Binnaway men, and to send the outgoing engine toward Merrygoen as soon as possible. I also contacted the Merrygoen SM by the public telephone and got him to go over to the station.

The DS decided to issue another '307'. He addressed it to Merrygoen, as well as to those who had already received the previous '307'. In it he cancelled that '307' and issued one that authorised the driver of the goods at Caratel Loop to proceed with his engine only to Boomley and return to Caratel Loop without being in possession of the train staff for the section. Under the provisions of the Rule '307', the Station Masters at Dubbo and Merrygoen were not to allow any train to proceed from their stations towards Elong Elong or Caratel Loop until the complete arrival of the stock train at Caratel Loop. The driver of the failed engine was directed to ensure the fireman protected the train with detonators in accordance with the provisions of Rule 243. The fireman was further directed that he was to wait where he set down the last detonator. From there he was directed to pilot the relief engine onto the failed train. This great epistle was also laboriously written down by the guards of the stock train at Boomley, the goods train at Caratel Loop and by the Station Masters at Merrygoen and Dubbo.

When I finished my shift, the engine had gone from Caratel Loop, the relief engine was about to leave Binnaway for Merrygoen, and the chargeman at Dubbo had 'leaned on' a driver on 'book-off' day to agree to travel with a fireman on the railmotor to Caratel Loop to relieve the goods train driver. After the arrival at Caratel Loop of the stock train, the relief engine left Merrygoen tender first to work the stock train, and the dead engine was placed in the siding at Caratel Loop. The signals engineer advised from Elong Elong that the problem had been rectified. The relief crew who had travelled by the railmotor worked the goods train to Dubbo. The bush fire brigade from Mendooran was contacted and they supplied a thousand gallons of water to the engine at Caratel Loop while waiting for the railmotor. The driver and fireman had been on duty over 10 hours before the motor arrived.

A joint investigation was held into the incident. The Mechanical Branch admitted the engine had been 'booked' on its previous run with leaking tubes, and the only reason it had been used was because of a compressor failure of the engine originally rostered. Having admitted this before the investigation, I could not understand the reason for continuing with it. A relief traffic inspector from Sydney, who had just come from a school for inspectors, asked me the next morning why, if I was frightened the engine would not lift the load tender first to Caratel Loop, I did not place the engine in the siding at Boomley. His face went beetroot red when I suggested I had never seen a piece of paper operate a ground frame! (The key on the electric staff was required to operate the ground frame).

The biggest and most frustrating problem I had in Dubbo occurred one Saturday evening and began in the vicinity of 6.00pm. The train concerned was No 63, the so-called *Mudgee Mail*, which on certain days of the week, had Coonabarabran as its final destination. The return No 54 left Binnaway without problem on time, the ASM Binnaway telling me at the time that there were thunderstorms in the area and one was about to hit Binnaway. He said,

"Say a prayer over your staff instruments".

The man must have been psychic. The guard of No 54 reported at Piambra that he could not get staff from the Neilrex instrument. I could hardly hear him, but he seemed to be saying that there was a heavy storm with gale force winds blowing. Once again to the DS. I was not, of course, going to ask for a '307' but I was duty bound to appraise him of the situation at Piambra; by not doing so, I would be putting my job in jeopardy.

When I was connected to Orange telegraph, the operator told me he was at the Golf Club, which of course he had every right to be on a Saturday night after a round of golf. He finally came onto the telephone. The reception was as I expected,

"What do you want me to do about it?"

My careful reply,

"I am acquainting you of the situation, sir."

This brought even more vitriol. I am sure he had an audience, as he referred to me as being incompetent. I did not take that too kindly and told him that a passenger train was standing at Piambra and I was seeking a direction from him. I had the guard of No 54 standing by on the telephone at Piambra because the Control telephone was not ringing. Finally the DS came back to me with the decision he would issue a '307'. It was addressed to the driver and guard of No 54, ASM Binnaway and ASM Merrygoen. There were no trains in the area. After about 45 minutes the Mail left Piambra, the driver in possession of a '307' as his authority to traverse the section.

The events that followed were nothing short of pathetic. I answered the side phone around 8.15pm. Having not heard from No 54, I was starting to get anxious. It was the guard from a farmhouse near Mooren to say the line was washed away on the Dubbo end of Mooren platform. I could not raise Binnaway on any telephone. What do I do now? I thought for a while and rang the ADS and advised him of what had happened, and of the reception I had had from the DS. He simply said,

"It is Saturday night."

I had told *orco* who had told *lico* of the delay. When news got to *syco west*, he advised Traffic Trouble who apparently advised the passenger train manager. I finally got through via Sydney to Binnaway. The only engine was one required on the Monday and was not in steam, which of course meant it would not be available for 4 hours, even if it was lit up immediately. I had asked Binnaway to call the ganger and his men. In the meantime the ADS had gone to his office and rang me from there. I was able to tell him that the ganger, who lived close to Binnaway station, had gone out about 30 minutes after the report from the guard at Mooren. He had rung the DS and although he did not say so, I think he (the ADS) was displeased. There was no provision in the Rules and Regulations for propelling a passenger train. The old Rule 202 specifically prohibited propelling of trains, although in my view the DS, if he chose, could override this with a '307'.

The ADS advised the passenger train manager of the situation. It was decided to wait until we heard from the ganger who was riding to the scene on a motor trike. The guard again rang to say that the storm had eased but that he thought the line was scoured to the extent that it would need ballasting. This information left the situation even more up in the air. When the ganger arrived he agreed with the guard, who again rang from the farmhouse to say the ganger had closed the road toward Merrygoen. The decision was then made, I think between the passenger train manager and the ADS, to issue another '307' (which did override Rule 202) authorising the propelling of the train to Piambra at a speed not exceeding 10 miles per hour and there, to reverse the engine and run tender first into Binnaway. The '307' was duly issued and very shortly after I lost the telephone line to Binnaway. There was such a roar on the board that I had to close that leg off.

Just after this, the DS came on the phone wanting to know how No 54 had gone. When I told him what had happened, he really went on. He was home by this time but could not be located for some time because he apparently went elsewhere after leaving the Golf Club. I rang the ADS and told him of the conversation and that I was to be taken off safeworking and was to report to the Senior Inspector's office at 9.00am on the Monday morning. The ADS said,

"Do not worry about it".

In the meantime, there was more trouble between Mooren and Piambra. The ganger decided, in his wisdom, that he would ride his trike in front of the train. Fortunately he did, because he came on another washaway and was able to stop the train.

By this time, a decision had been made to obtain a crew and use the 600 Class at Mudgee to take passengers to Wallerawang, to connect with No 60 *Forbes Mail*.

Torrential rain after the storms in the Piambra area had flooded every little causeway and in this case the water could not get through the culverts and simply ran over the line. After about an hour the water subsided and the ganger allowed the train to pass. While this was happening, no one knew where the train was. The only thing certain was that it had not arrived at Piambra. There was no means of communication in working order from Dubbo, including the public telephone. I was able to get *weco* through Sydney. He told me the train was lost and thought it a huge joke. There were no Per Way vehicles or Departmental vehicles of any kind that could be used to send out a search party. The ASM Binnaway refused to even consider taking his vehicle out in the conditions that had prevailed. There was relief all around when No 54 rang Binnaway on the circuit telephone from Piambra. There was less, however, when he said he had been trying to get a staff without success! This information came to me via *weco, neco, syco north* and *west, lico* and *orco*. The ADS rang me and told me that the passenger train manager was personally issuing a '307' to Binnaway and the crew, using the Departmental lines, via Werris Creek to Binnaway. No 54 eventually ran via Werris Creek to Sydney. What a night!

Around 11.30pm, the DS rang me on the side phone. He asked me if I had advised the local signal engineer, which I had, of course. I was then wished a pleasant good night I took it to be a form of saying forget what happened earlier. Despite the difficulty everyone had with him over '307s', I liked the man. He had a short fuse by nature, but I think he had a mortal dread of '307s' to the point where he became paranoid about them. He was a good superintendent, who later rose to the rank of passenger train manager and who will feature again in my writing.

My official history declared that when I retired, I had been fined twice in my 43 years of employment; once for getting off the road at Parkes and the other as a train controller at Dubbo, an incident over which about 6 people were fined sums ranging from £2 (my fine) to £5. The first task I performed when I took over the Board on afternoon shift one Thursday, after having eight days off, was to take the load of a stock train from the station master at Coonamble, whose words to complete the message were,

"The stock has loaded as listed, 36 sheep vans a load of 490 tons."

Accepting that at face value was my mistake: I ticked off the stock listing as being loaded OK.

On the Sunday morning, when I came out of church, the traffic inspector was waiting for me. He told me that the train load of stock from Coonamble on Thursday had almost gone to the wrong destination, namely to Corowa instead of Tocumwal. It was intercepted, as it was about to leave Culcairn. The STNs issued in *oran* and *juco* showed the stock was for Tocumwal, a fact which I should have checked, but was not given the stock destination on the load message. The mistake started in Coonamble, when for some reason, the stock was ticketed for Corowa. The load message from Dubbo showed the stock was for Corowa, yet no one picked it up, including the controller who took over from me in Dubbo. The ASM at Parkes did not pick it up and actually sent a telegram to *Stock, Oran, Jun* and *Juco*, showing the stock was for Tocumwal, despite the train load message from Dubbo and the incoming X2010 showing Corowa. The junior at Parkes sent the train load message as Corowa.

When the Station Master Junee got the train load message showing Corowa, he spoke to the controller at Junee and *they cancelled* the train to Narrandera/Tocumwal with the stock and put up one to Corowa. It was not until Tocumwal enquired from the controller on the Junee No 2 Board how the train load of stock from Coonamble was running, that alarm bells started ringing. The controller answered the question with a question,

"What stock train?"

Unfortunately for all concerned, the owner was present at Tocumwal when it was established that the train now in Culcairn was the train with his stock. His sense of humour departed him and he rang the Livestock Superintendent in Sydney. That was when it hit the fan! Hence the traffic inspector waiting for me to come out of church. In the statement I made, I was very careful not to gloss over my responsibility, because I felt that had I followed my usual course of taking nothing as read and checked the listing and destination with the Station Master Coonamble, it would not have happened.

In my defence, which I did not try to use departmentally, I had problems which had manifested themselves again with Cathy and which were to plague her for many years. At this stage, I had not come to terms with what was happening to her and as a result, my work performance was not what it should have been. Those who were fined were the Station Master Coonamble £5, the backshift controller at Dubbo, the Assistant Station Masters Dubbo, Parkes and Junee, the controller on the No 2 Board at Junee (who failed to check the listing when the train left Parkes), the controller on the Main Line Board Junee, who cancelled the train to Narrandera and Tocumwal. Several others were reprimanded for accepting the cancellation of the train and for failing to check the stock listing against the load message. It was a comedy of errors really, and something that reflected very badly on the Department and its officers, me included. A better way to describe it would be to say 'incredible!'

The way that wages and salaries have increased with the progression of time make interesting reading. When I was appointed as a train controller, the salary was around £550 per annum, with annual increments spreading over five years. I was not on top Second Class money when I went to Dubbo on around £720. Just prior to my leaving Dubbo, the salaries increased to a £1000 a year. I found this amount of money staggering, but I realised of course, that it was all relative and that at the end of the day, the cost of living increases demanded these salaries. The escalation of salaries from this time meant that after taking nearly twenty years to reach the first £1000, the second thousand came in the next five years.

CATHY, THE CONTINUING SAGA

WE had been in Dubbo for about six months when Cathy developed a soft spongy lump above her eyebrows which extended to her hairline. Mamie was not well at the time and I took Cathy to the local doctor. I went into his surgery concerned but not overly so about this lump. I came out deflated. He would not come out and say directly what he thought the problem was, although I was confident he knew, but instead said,

"You have to take her back to Dr Schrieber."

We made the appointment for when I had my days off and left Roy and Faye at Orange. When we left Dubbo, we were prepared for the worst and took Cathy's pyjamas and clothes with us. It did not take Dr Schreiber long, after we got to see him (for which we waited two hours after having left Dubbo at 4.00am), to say that she had *cranial osteomyelitis*, which would need investigation under an anaesthetic. It was with heavy hearts we left her in the hospital and drove back to Orange that evening, arriving there dog tired.

It would not be exaggerating to say that the next year, prior to my transfer to Sydney, was the most difficult of our lives to that time. In all, Mamie went to Sydney on 11 occasions to see Cathy, to be with her before and after surgery that occurred no less than nine times before the osteomyelitis was cleared up. Each time she was taken for surgery, a little more bone was scraped away, until a small area of bone about 10 millimetres above her eyebrows was all that was left of the bone in her forehead. All the bone from the point of the original incision, which went over her head from just above each ear to ear to the back of her head, was clear. The affected bone was only from the incision forward. A cosmetic plate to give her the appearance of having a forehead was rejected by her body and had to be removed because it was causing further infection. For the rest of her life, her forehead just inside the sparse hairline could be seen to pulsating, similar to that of a baby in the first few months of life. A *perpetual fontanelle* approximately half an inch deep, where the gristle that remained joined the bone of the top of her head was visible.

In 1963, she spent 11 months in the Children's Hospital. I drove down with the family a couple of times, once on her birthday. We gave her a little party on the lawns between Wade House and the main hospital building. On another occasion, we all drove down expecting to bring her home. It was not to be, another infected area manifested itself and she had to stay for treatment, and more surgery. I vividly recall leaving the hospital with Mamie and Faye crying, with Roy because he was a boy, desperately trying not to. My own eyes were wet with tears and as I made a left hand turn from Johnston Street at Balmain and faced the west I was almost completely blinded. I had no idea where the road was and tried to stop, much to the annoyance of other motorists. As a result of all the travelling and expenses associated with having Mamie in Sydney, staying at the mother's quarters, we were suffering severely financially.

On one occasion, Mamie and I left Dubbo in July at 3.00am. I had come off afternoon shift and tried unsuccessfully to sleep before leaving. As we approached Wellington, the windscreen became frozen with frost on the outside and fogged on the inside and I had to drive with my head out the window. The car had no heating. Despite being rugged up, it was cold inside even without putting my head out the window. I had to drive like this until we got away from the Wellington valley and up onto the higher country, a distance of about 20 kilometres. We had to keep going because we had an appointment with Dr Schreiber at 11.00am. Once again, it was with some hope of bringing Cathy home. We also had an appointment with a dermatologist. We arrived at the hospital, to find once again, that the Doctor's waiting room was full, he having been called to attend emergency surgery for a child accident victim. We finally saw him and the dermatologist at 5.00pm. We were told they considered that in a home environment, no matter how careful we were, the risk of further infection was too great and that she should stay in the hospital. We had a light lunch in the cafeteria with the only money, beside petrol money, we had. When we found Cathy was not coming home we had bought some things for her. We left the hospital at about 5.30pm and drove to Orange arriving there at about 10.45pm—cold, tired, dispirited and hungry.

During this period Mamie was not well, having bleeding haemorrhoids, which got to the state that surgery was the only answer for a cure. This was performed in Orange, once again the children being farmed out to our friends in Dubbo. It was just before Mamie went to hospital that Faye, playing on a slippery dip in the park opposite where we lived, was pushed off and suffered severe concussion. I took her to the doctor who admitted her to Dubbo Base Hospital. In the meantime, Roy, working on his bike, caught his thumb between the sprocket wheel and the chain while attempting to get the chain on again. A trip to the doctor was all he required.

After Cathy had been 11 months in hospital, we brought her home. The osteomyelitis still had not cleared. We had to dress the area twice a day. The infection used to run continuously from a small hole, about half an inch above her right eyebrow. We used to bathe it with a saline solution and apply cicatrin powder to it.

During all this, we were active in the South Dubbo Methodist Church. Mamie was in the choir, and I was the Sunday School Superintendent and also a member of the Men's Group which embraced the Dubbo main church and South Dubbo. On one occasion, Mr W R Lawrence, who had been an Assistant Commissioner of Police and who held offices in the Methodist Church Conference, was to be the guest speaker at the Men's dinner. I was to meet him off the plane and we were to give him lunch. While he was at our home, it was necessary to dress Cathy's forehead. While he did not say anything at the time, he was so moved by what he saw on her forehead, that before he left the next day, he arranged to have delivered an arrangement of flowers for Mamie and a large box of assorted goodies for Cathy. One of the ladies told us when he was telling a group of them what he had seen, that he became quite emotional.

While Dubbo for us was a most trying time, it was made easier by the many people in our church who assisted us by looking after Roy and Faye, and who all gave us love and encouragement. Another who showed great care was the ADS—he never failed to ask after her.

In hindsight, going to Dubbo instead of Lithgow proved one of the most expensive decisions I ever made. Had we been able to commute to the Children's Hospital from Lithgow, our circumstances would have been dramatically different in all facets. The continual dividing of our family would not have been necessary. It would have been a simple matter to visit daily by train from Lithgow, and our financial situation would not have suffered like it did, nor would the Hillman have run up the mileage it did. I think I would have had more job satisfaction; Lithgow was more of a challenge than Dubbo, of that I am sure. Dubbo was only occasionally a challenge; Lithgow was often so. Although he knew of the troubles we had, the late Allan Tobin, a colleague and friend, never realised how much I regretted the decision that left him in Lithgow.

On one of our trips to Sydney for checkups, I went to the staff office, then on the second floor at Central. The purpose was to see where I was on the seniority list and how long it would be before I could expect to be offered a senior train controller's position in Sydney. We had been to see Dr Schreiber, so I had Mamie and Cathy with me. Generally I was not one to play on sympathy, but on this occasion, I took Cathy in with me to see the Chief Clerk, who agreed readily to see me when I explained at the front desk what I wanted. Cathy had a very small bandage on her forehead, which revealed the horror of what was left of her forehead. I have forgotten the Chief Clerk's name; otherwise I would use it. He showed so much concern for us both, bringing Mamie into his office and getting from us the detail of some of the ordeal we had been through in the past 12 months. He was anxious to know how we coped with Cathy's illness, how her siblings reacted to her continuing ill health, and what support did we have. The answer to that was, that in 1963/64 there was no such thing as official support for parents. We had the support of family and friends—nothing else. His concern for Cathy left a lasting impression on me.

At this time, I was the second in line for a Sydney position. The Chief Clerk told me to go back to Dubbo and speak to my superintendent, who by this time, had just been appointed to Orange in place of the previous incumbent who had been appointed Metropolitan Goods Superintendent, Darling Harbour. The Chief Clerk told me he would ring my superintendent that day and discuss my problem with him.

I went back to Dubbo, feeling it would not be long before something good happened for us, for a change.

It did. The next, day Tom Hetherington who was my friend and the District Superintendent Orange, saw me in Dubbo and said that I should apply for a transfer in the grade on the grounds of Cathy's continuing need for specialist treatment, which was only available in Sydney. I made the application and one month afterwards, almost to the day we left Dubbo on that last trip, I was transferred as a First Class Train Controller to a temporary extra position in Sydney Train Control. Before I left Dubbo, however, two sudden vacancies occurred in Sydney and I was appointed to one of these and I actually took up as a Senior Train Controller in Sydney.

Nevertheless, the Department through, I am sure, the Staff Superintendent's Chief Clerk, was compassionate in the way he moved to ensure that we did get to Sydney. I have long appreciated what was done for us at this time, and I am pleased to be able to record here my feelings for those officers who made it possible. I hope that some day Tom Hetherington reads this.

THE TRIALS AND TRIBLATIONS OF BUILDING A NEW HOME

WE arrived in Sydney sometime in mid-May of 1964. We were fortunate in finding a partially furnished, double brick house in reasonable condition inside and out at Lindfield. We found this house, signed the lease and were installed in it about four days after we arrived in Sydney. It was about 15 minutes walk from the station, shops, schools and church. Cathy at this stage was still in the Children's Hospital. She finally came home late June of 1964.

Roy and Faye went to Lindfield Public School, but they found it something of a culture shock. Although they were doing well in the Dubbo School, they were both placed in the lowest classes, because the school considered their standards were much higher than a country school's. Faye set about showing them this was not necessarily so, but despite the fact at the end of the year she had the second highest aggregate in the combined classes of her year, she was snubbed on the prize giving night, despite being beaten by half a percentage point by the School Inspector's daughter who was given a 100 per cent to Faye's 99.5 per cent. Faye received no recognition of her effort. All the second place getters in all the other classes received prizes and recognition.

I asked the question of the deputy headmistress, "Why?"

The answer was that the second prizes were given by the parents for presentation. When I asked why someone had not given me the courtesy of explaining the custom, she had no reply. The final insult, to my mind, came the following year when she was still left in the class recognised as the weakest of the classes. She was happy enough and was at the top of the class, so I said nothing further. Roy found a male teacher to whom he could relate and was quite happy. The important thing was that we were united as a family. There was no possibility of them having to be shunted off to other families while we visited Cathy again in hospital.

After we had been in Lindfield for about three months and paying £14 per week rent, we started to look around for a block of land with a view to building. Had I known what I now know, I would not have been in such a hurry, but I did not know what the pitfalls could be in building, so we went forward in good faith. We looked at land at Pennant

Hills, Beecroft, Frenchs Forest and Turramurra. We did not particularly like the first two, because there appeared to be considerable work to be done before building could commence. The French's Forest was a good block that appealed, except that it was too far from the railway line. There were Government buses, but their timetables did not suit shift work. We were very taken with the block at Turramurra, which was closer to North Turramurra and fronted Little Cowan Creek, a part of Ku-ring-gai Chase National Park. The street was built on one side only.

The drawback was that there was a right of way over the drive that was shared with the next block, and had a sheer rock wall of approximately 4 metres. The entrance to our block was via the shared right of way with next door. We thought about this for some time, despite the pressure that was being put on us by the salesman. The block was priced at £1,850 and had a sufficiently flat area at the top of the rock wall to allow building without excavation. The only cost was for the removal of a huge old gum tree that was 75 per cent dead and to which the Council did not object.

We finally decided to purchase the land from Young Constructions, who were the vendors and builders. We thought it was a good arrangement because we shared the same solicitor, which eased the expenses. I partly paid for the land from the proceeds of the Spring Street home at Orange. I had put this money on a fixed deposit for two years, so that no matter how tight we were for money for medical expenses, it could not be got at. Young Constructions had advertised in the *Sydney Morning Herald* for some years, and I used to read their advertisements with interest when we were in Dubbo. This was the reason we approached them in the first instance and they had offices at Milsons Point.

We purchased the land in late August 1964. One-day while we were looking at the block, an enterprising tree and stump remover approached and offered his services to cut down the tree and cart it away for the princely sum of £150. I was not having that on so I asked him if he would cut the tree down and cart away that portion which fell onto the street. He quoted £40, to which I agreed.

He said to me, "What are you going to do with the trunk?"

I then suggested to him that he cut the tree down and leave it for a week before he came back to cut up the branches on the street. If the trunk was still there, he could take it too and I would pay him the full price. When this huge old gum tree fell, the only portion of it on the top level was the trunk. I cleared some of the pith from the centre of the tree that, apart from soft pith, was hollow and set a fire in it. When it was alight, I covered it up with dirt and completely sealed it off. When I came back about four days later, all that was left of the trunk was a very fine ash. A perfect outline of the tree was in ash from the stump to the edge of the rock face. I had not spent my early years in the bush without gaining some knowledge! My friend the tree remover was amazed. He told me he thought I was 'nuts' when I suggested I would look after the trunk.

Young Constructions had a basic brick veneer house design of three bedrooms, a lounge room, kitchen/dining room, bathroom and laundry. A patio measuring about two metres by four metres was located at the entrance and extended from the front door to the edge of the lounge room. The addition of a planter box at the front was meant to conceal the lounge from the view of visitors. A breakfast bar and a built-in wardrobe in the master bedroom were also included. The house was quite small which, because of three growing children, concerned me. Mamie, however, was satisfied we would be able to manage. We did, but there were certainly times when a little more room would have been useful.

In late 1963, there was an economic recession which caused obtaining of finance to be very difficult, and no money was to be had from the banks. Finally, the solicitor came up with a building society loan with a difference. The loan was with the Australian Holy Catholic Guild Building Society, and it certainly was a loan like nothing today. The maximum amount that I could borrow was limited to the building erection cost, which was £4,500. The method of financing was by the paying of interest only on the loan for 12 years. In addition, I had to take out an insurance policy for the amount of the loan. At the end of 12 years, the policy paid off the loan and I was to receive whatever bonuses the policy had accrued.

Originally, the total repayment was £44 per month, which was manageable. The drawback was that I had to take out a second mortgage to have sufficient money to pay the balance due on the block, which was about £1,000. Before taking out the second mortgage, we had to take bridging finance to cover the cost of the land, because the credit union would not allow building to commence until the land was vested in our names. Then, the finance company providing the second mortgage, would not lend on it until the building was complete. This bridging loan was costing about £30 per month. We repaid the second mortgage off at about £26 per month over two years and six months. The additional amount was also manageable, had all things been equal. Unfortunately they proved not to be.

After the financial arrangements had been set in place, we signed a contract with Young Constructions in late November of 1964. The cost of the house we selected to erect was £4,450. I did not expect too much progress until the New Year, which proved to be the case. With no movement in February, I started to make enquiries and was assured that the foundations would be laid the first week in March. It was late March before the bricks for the foundations were on the block.

By this time, I had a sense of unease concerning Young Constructions and spoke to the solicitor about the delays and asked him if were they in financial trouble. I was assured the building would be completed within the six months of the contract time. I remember reminding him they had better 'get their fingers out' because four months had gone. In

April, the foundations were completed. The bricks arrived in May and within days the place was a hive of activity. The brickwork was completed in late May. Then things stopped again. June came and went with no more activity; another visit to the solicitor, because I could get nothing from the builders; another assurance every thing would work out satisfactorily was forthcoming. I told him that the payment of rent and the bridging loan under these circumstances of continuing delay by the builder was less than acceptable. He agreed. But that was all he did.

In mid July, we received a letter from the solicitor to the effect that Young Constructions had gone into liquidation and that we should make arrangements to see him at our earliest convenience. In the meantime, I received a letter of demand from the receivers of Young Constructions for the money so far spent, demanding payment within seven days, or they would take the appropriate action with the Sheriff's Department to sell my land to satisfy the debt. This also went with us to the solicitor. The comment of the solicitor was that it was unfortunate that this should have occurred. I retorted that, it was not unfortunate, it was bad management and probably I should get another solicitor. He replied,

"You had better stay with me, because if you do not, you will be up for more legal expenses than you can imagine."

The final outcome would have been that I would lose the land and the deposit on it and be required to pay for the work done by Young's. I must have been going red in the face when he was saying this, because he told me to calm down and that he had made arrangements that would see the house completed by another builder. When he had said this, I asked him did he not think that I had every right to be angry and frustrated. Once again he agreed.

When I showed him the letter from the receivers, it was his turn to explode. He said they had not paid for the bricks nor had they paid the subcontracting bricklayers. What happened after that I do not know, but we heard no more. The second builders, a firm known as Knights Timbers, who in addition to owning a timber yard at Merrylands, were builders themselves, and took over the contract. This firm did not start work until late October.

They were spasmodic; they would do some work and disappear for a month, then come back and do a bit more. The way they were behaving led me to believe that all was not well with them either. Another telephone call to the solicitor bought the same platitudes, everything will be OK. But it was not. In April of 1966, Knights Timbers went to the wall, with the house about 80 per cent completed. We were desperate by this time. In the week they went into receivership, I received a bill for £180 from the solicitor. At the time, it seemed the final straw.

Once again we went Parramatta to see the solicitor. He at last had some sympathy for us and told us not worry too much about his account, saying, which I thought was as close to a compliment he could give,

" I know you are honourable and that you will meet your obligations".

I replied that I would have appreciated the obligation being less than it was. There was no comment, but the next bill substantially reduced the original figure. A subcontractor carpenter who had built the house, and who had not been paid by Knights Timbers for his labours, agreed to complete the project, provided the solicitor guaranteed he would be paid for all the work that he had done. The house was completed in November of 1966 and we moved in on the 26th of November—two years and three months after buying the land.

We were in a desperate financial position, although Cathy was home and seemed to be progressing favourably, we were still receiving bills from doctors that we had not heard of, many of the accounts being way over the amount covered by the GUIOOF, which was our medical fund. I had determined, not to fall back on Mamie's father for assistance. I know it would have been forthcoming, but we however were suffering from lack of funds and lived from pay day to pay day.

There was a good deal of overtime available. Every time I was offered a shift, I took it, which helped and probably was the only reason we survived financially. The Hillman, after giving years of sterling service running between Orange/Dubbo and Sydney, reached the point where it needed either new piston rings, or a new motor and differential. Before we ran into all the trouble with the building, we thought it best to get rid of it and buy a reasonable second-hand car. We bought a 1963 Falcon in early 1965. It proved to be a lemon. The odometer, it was obvious after the car was driven for a while, had been wound back. I had to put a new motor in it. There was no redress for a buyer in those days, who bought on the principle, 'buyer beware'.

CATHY'S EDUCATION

CATHY started school in the first term of 1965 at Lindfield, going with her brother and sister in the morning. Either Mamie or I met her after school, the kindergarten finishing half an hour earlier than primary classes. We had never pushed Cathy at all, nor had we for Roy and Faye for that matter. She could count to ten, but beyond that we knew little of her abilities. Apart from the obvious lack of bone from just above her eyebrows and reaching about three inches into her hairline, she was a normal looking child, whose speech was good, who was alert and who was quite perceptive.

We had an interview with the headmistress before she started school, in which we outlined all the problems that had befallen her. I made it clear to her that we did not know how much her learning had been affected. We knew that if she went shopping with her mother, she knew all the things that she bought and of their brands. I had always thought she knew these things more by recognition than by reading. Unfortunately, I was proved right.

It was evident, very early in her school life, that she would have problems, not only with her learning, but also coping with the taunts from the other children about her forehead. This was another reason that we were apprehensive about her going to school. The children were no different from any other. They were just children, who delighted in tormenting her, as children from time immemorial have been wont to do. There was mostly nothing personal; it was just that her forehead was a target too good to miss.

The most significant early problem was one that we had not recognised. We knew she was left-handed (which she, we thought, took from me) but there was more to it than that. Everything she did was mirror reversed; she started to write from the right hand side of the page and progress toward the left. Her natural inclination was to try and read this way also. This was a trait for which the school had no method of remedial teaching, or indeed much inclination to do so. It was hinted that perhaps she was too young for school, a hint I did not hear. At that time, there was nothing that the Education Department was able, or perhaps prepared is a better way of putting it, to assist Cathy. I was determined that she should have the same opportunities as any other child to learn.

The headmistress finally agreed that she could stay at the school until the end of the year, when we expected to move anyway. I felt some sympathy for her, because I felt she had an understanding of what Cathy had been through in her short life. I also understood that Cathy could be disruptive, more through boredom than anything else. I saw her as a challenge to the school; the school saw her as a problem that they wanted shifted. I was appreciative, nevertheless, of her being allowed to stay and expressed that gratitude to the headmistress. It was important for Cathy's sake that she did the things the other children did and going to school was one of them.

For some reason best known to herself, on one Sunday afternoon, Cathy took herself up to the public tennis courts at Lindfield, which was about two blocks from where we lived. She wandered around there for a while and apparently caught the eye of, or started talking, more likely, to a lady there. What she said to the lady we do not know. What we do know was that the lady contacted the police. We, by this time had missed her and were ringing the friend where Faye had gone to play to see if she was there. Mamie happened to look out the window and here was Cathy with two policemen holding each hand and bringing them to the back door. They had enjoyed Cathy, she told them her mother was Mamie Peggy Ellis and she lived at 36 Chelmsford Ave, Lindfield. I told the police that, while we were a little embarrassed at them having to bring her home, that we were pleased she knew her address and was prepared to tell them.

Roy completed his final year in Primary School at Lindfield with the exception of the final three weeks, which he spent at North Turramurra. He turned twelve while he was there. In 1967, he commenced High School at Ku-ring-gai High, which was then four years old, when he was 12 years and one month old.

Faye also commenced at North Turramurra Public School going into Year 5 at the commencement of the new term in 1967. Cathy also was enrolled and started at North Turramurra. We had seen the headmaster, who had previously been in Canowindra and had taught the children of my brother and sister. He had a report from the school at Lindfield concerning Cathy. He was prepared to enrol her to get her back into the system and start her at the school. He contacted the school counsellor (something which had been started at Lindfield). It was not very long before she was accepted into an OA class (a class for children with learning and developmental disabilities). One of the few things for helping that we ever got for Cathy, came from the Education Department; they picked her up each morning, along with the other children in the class from various places. A lady contracted to the Department for the purpose did this. So, Cathy now had her own school, her own school uniform and her own transport. These things made her feel a part of the system and built up her self esteem.

This was a period when we were living as a normal family, or as close as a family can be to normal when, one member, by virtue of ill fortune, requires an unequal portion of her parents' time (especially her mother's). The siblings in our case were as understanding and loving, as it would be possible to get. Neither Mamie nor I will ever forget our very great appreciation of the love and understanding that was invariably extended to her by her brother and sister. On many occasions, they could have been forgiven for not exhibiting the understanding they did.

Financially we struggled on; it took us a long time to get a decent washing machine after the Wilkins Servis that we bought in Orange 'threw in the towel'. (The pun was accidental!) We gradually got carpet in the lounge and bedrooms and long life linoleum in the kitchen/dining room.

SENIOR TRAIN CONTROLLER, SYDNEY SOUTH CONTROL

TO SAY I was apprehensive the day I reported to the Train Control Superintendent would be a fair description of my feelings. I was duly taken around the various Control Boards, being the South, West, North, Goods, Illawarra and Traffic Trouble. I was introduced by the Assistant Train Control Superintendent, taken to the Assistant Freight Trains Superintendent and finally to the Freight Trains Superintendent (known, for those with long memories, as the 'Great White Father').

He surveyed me with the steely-eyed look he was known for and said,

"I have heard nothing of you."

I received a lecture about punctuality, was reminded of the importance of the position and of the responsibilities attached to it. I said nothing other than,

"Pleased to meet you Mr ...."

After shaking hands with him. I thought if he had not heard of me, he was not going to hear much that day either.

The third floor at Central Station was home to the Goods Train (as it was known then) Section. The only access to it was gained by a stairway from the second floor. This was so until years later, when fire escapes were provided. Those who occupied the floor were the Goods Train Superintendent, the Assistant Goods Train Superintendent, the Rolling Stock Superintendent, the Train Control Superintendent, the Assistant Train Control Superintendent and *Mets*, as the Office of the Rolling Stock Superintendent was known, employed a staff of about ten clerks.

The Train Control Superintendent was responsible for the train control and engine control sections. Apart from the train control sections, which each had their own control rooms, the Chief Train Controller and Engine Clerks were housed in another area next to *Mets*.

Not long after I came to Sydney, the Centralised Motive Power Control (CMPC) room was constructed. It took over the area formerly occupied by the Chief Train Controller and others. It was an air-conditioned office and was totally enclosed, the reason being to maintain a constant temperature for the computers. This enclosed room housed the first computers that were installed to control the rostering of locomotives.

The staff who occupied that room were the CMPC Supervisor, the Chief Clerk in CMPC Chief Train Controllers Programme, the Main Line Diesel Clerk, the Electric Engine Clerk, the 48 Class Engine Clerk, and clerks for the North, West and South sections of CMPC. A liaison District Locomotive Engineer also was provided.

When we returned to the Control Superintendent's Office, I was advised that I was to learn South Control and that I was entitled to 12 working days for that.

South Control was responsible for the area commencing at Liverpool and finishing at Goulburn North Signal Box. Safeworking was double-line automatic signalling from Liverpool to Mittagong, NSW standard block telegraph from Mittagong to Moss Vale, automatic signalling Up and Down from Moss Vale to Exeter, NSW standard block telegraph Exeter to Marulan and double-line automatic signalling from Marulan to Goulburn. The Picton-Mittagong loop line and the limestone line from Medway to Medway Quarry were staff and ticket, while the cement line from Berrima to the Blue Circle cement works was electric staff. The key points from a controller's train working standpoint were Cabramatta Signal Box, Campbelltown Signal Box and Moss Vale Box. I travelled the section from Campbelltown to Moss Vale on No 401 pick-up. I spent time with the Station Master Moss Vale before going to Goulburn on a goods train and returning home on No 38 *Canberra-Monaro Express* worked by a 900 Class DEB set.

The attended safeworking stations and/or signal boxes were Cabramatta, Liverpool, Ingleburn, Campbelltown, Glenlee, Menangle, Douglas Park, Picton, Bargo, Yerrinbool, Mittagong, Bowral, Berrima Junction, Moss Vale, Exeter, Bundanoon, Penrose, Wingello, Tallong, Medway, Marulan, Towrang and Goulburn North Signal Box. Liverpool Signal Box rarely spoke to South Control. With the suburban electric services terminating at that point, his main contact was Traffic Trouble. Cabramatta Box was important, because it reported the Down trains as they came onto South Control's area of responsibility and the Up trains as they departed it. Ingleburn had an Up Refuge that was often used, but he rarely spoke to the Controller unless the Controller directed him to refuge an Up train. Ingleburn station was attended 24 hours for safeworking purposes.

Campbelltown signal box reported all trains as they passed. Douglas Park was another station with an Up Refuge Loop, which was used only in emergencies. I sometimes, if the ASM was on duty, advanced Up trains that were required to shunt Menangle, to give them a greater shunting time margin. Picton Signal Box reported all trains; a water column was available on the Down Refuge Siding; the Up loop was on the Sydney end of the station which held some 75 vehicles. Bargo had a Down Refuge with a water column between it and the main line. Ash pits were available on the main line and loop. Every freight train worked by a steam engine took water and de-ashed the firebox at Bargo.

A local regulation was in force that 60 Class Garratts were not allowed to use the loop ashpit. Yerrinbool was attended in daylight hours only and had Up and Down Refuges,

SOUTH CONTROL BOARD MONDAY TO FRIDAY

DOWN TRAINS
- ††† ELECTRIC TRAIN STAFF
- † ORDINARY TRAIN STAFF
- ‡‡ SINGLE LINE TRACK CONTROL
- ‡ SINGLE TRACK BLOCK
- A AUTOMATIC SIGNALLING
- BT BLOCK TELEGRAPH
- BDI BIDIRECTIONAL

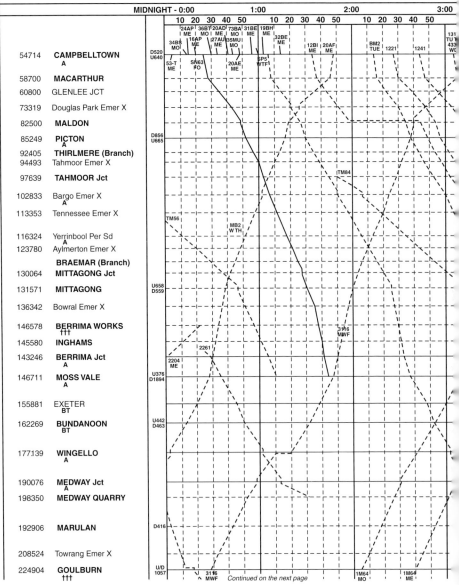

54714	**CAMPBELLTOWN** A	D520 U640
58700	**MACARTHUR**	
60800	GLENLEE JCT	
73319	Douglas Park Emer X	
82500	**MALDON**	
85249	**PICTON** A	D856 U665
92405	**THIRLMERE (Branch)**	
94493	Tahmoor Emer X	
97639	**TAHMOOR Jct**	
102833	Bargo Emer X A	
113353	Tennessee Emer X	
116324	Yerrinbool Per Sd A	
123780	Aylmerton Emer X	
130064	**BRAEMAR (Branch)** **MITTAGONG Jct**	
131571	**MITTAGONG**	U658 D559
136342	Bowral Emer X	
146578	**BERRIMA WORKS** †††	
145580	**INGHAMS**	
143246	**BERRIMA Jct** A	
146711	**MOSS VALE** A	U376 D1894
155881	**EXETER** BT	
162269	**BUNDANOON** BT	U442 D463
177139	**WINGELLO** A	
190076	**MEDWAY Jct** A	
198350	**MEDWAY QUARRY**	
192906	**MARULAN**	D416
208524	Towrang Emer X	
224904	**GOULBURN** †††	U/D 1057

Continued on the next page

CAMPBELLTOWN - CANBERRA - UNANDERRA - MOSS VALE

NOTE: *This train control graph shown on these and the next two pages is of a much later period than is covered in the text. The Unanderra—Moss Vale line was under the control of the Illawarra Controller during the period of the text.*

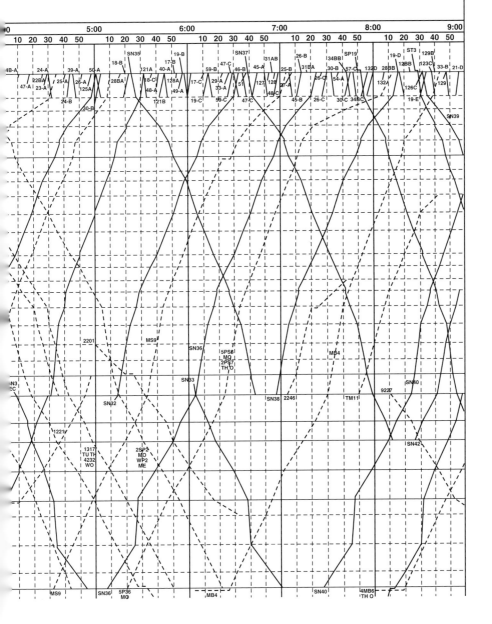

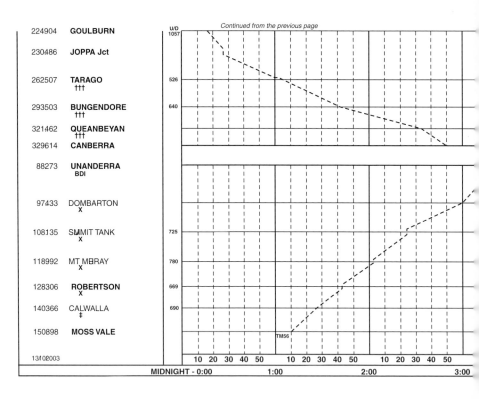

| 224904 | GOULBURN | U/D 1057 | | | | | | | | | | | | | | | | Continued from the previous page | | | | | | | | | | |

which were both back-in sidings holding 55 vehicles. Mittagong had Up and Down Refuges both were back-in sidings holding 70 vehicles. Mittagong reported all trains. Bowral had Up and Down Refuge Sidings, used mainly for trains that shunted there. Unless a train stopped at Bowral; they were not reported as the station was in automatic working more often than not.

Berrima Junction and Moss Vale were very busy locations. I will deal more fully with them. Exeter was the proud possessor of a goods siding and nothing else; it reported all trains. Bundanoon had back-in Up and Down Refuges, which were regularly used and reported all trains. Penrose had a goods siding. This station regularly cut in and out, the times it was cut out were supposed to coincide with the published timetable running of trains. It rarely did. Wingello had back-in Up and Down Refuge Sidings and reported all trains. (I later found this a key station). Tallong had a water column and ash pits on the main lines. Sidings were not provided.

All 50 Class standard goods engines working on the Down took water and did the fire at Tallong. Garratts, 36 and 38 Classes working Up and Down goods and stock trains did not. Medway Junction was provided with a crossover from the yard to the Up Main and a three-road shunting yard for forming limestone trains. Marulan had an Up Refuge

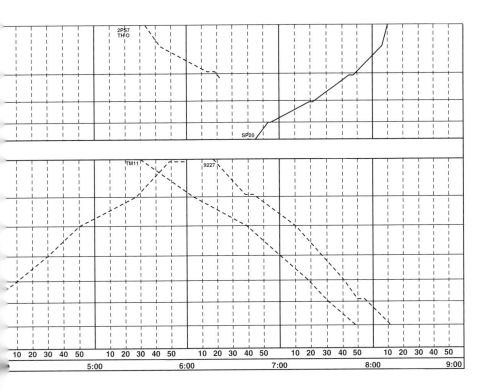

Loop and a back-in Down Refuge. Marulan reported all trains. Towrang was unattended, but had a Down and Up back-in Refuge Sidings that could be used in emergency. The Station Master Goulburn had to provide the staff to operate the signal box.

Many signal boxes were equipped with what was known as 'the blue lever'. When it was desired to switch out the signal box, it was first necessary to have the block instruments for all lines correctly set. The instruments could then be switched out. Main line signals in both directions would then be cleared. The 'blue', or closing lever(s) would then be pulled over and the key removed for safe storage.

In the case of manual block working, the closing lever(s) simply locked the signal levers. In the case of semi-automatic signalling, pulling the closing lever over generally allowed the signals to function fully automatically.

When the signalman wished to cut-in again, he made contact with the signal box on either side of him to make sure that there were no trains in the section. When he had established this, he reversed 'the blue lever' and exchanged the required bell signals to resume ordinary working.

As I began to learn the Board, I found the attitude and manner of addressing the staff at the various points was nothing short of appalling, by two controllers in particular, one more so than the other. Every time the slightest delay occurred or someone did not immediately answer the control telephone, this controller was abusive beyond my belief. He would swear and literally scream down the telephone. On one occasion, No 66, the *Intercapital Daylight Express,* had failed between Campbelltown and Ingleburn, the signalman at Campbelltown objected to the manner that he was being spoken to. The controller then became personal. Shortly afterwards, the Traffic Trouble Officer came to the room, complaining that the Assistant Station Master and the signalman had contacted him saying that they would not answer the control telephone again until they received an apology from the controller and an assurance from the Trouble Officer that there would not be a repetition of his conduct. He really 'blew his top' then.

The Trouble Officer, being an older man, told him quite plainly that he would apologise and that he (the Trouble Officer) would give the assurance that Campbelltown required. He calmed down after that. The other controller, who I came to look upon as the best train-working controller I ever worked with, was very hard to please. While he was generally not abusive, he seemed to be rousing all the time. This method of dealing with your fellow employees was foreign and distasteful to me, and I can truthfully say that I never resorted to it. I hasten to add that the majority of controllers who were inclined to my way of thinking, but there were a surprising number whose attitudes toward their jobs and staff left much to be desired. Generally, these were the people who were less successful as train controllers. My 'favourite' train controller from Lithgow when I was at East Fork who by this time was in Goods Control, had not changed; he was still as difficult as he was in Lithgow.

In 1964, there were still many goods trains worked by steam locomotives. Those that were not were the interstate freights, the fruit expresses, the limestone trains and all trains from the Illawarra. The express passengers and the mail trains were diesel hauled, but the urban passenger services to Moss Vale and Goulburn were steam hauled, mostly by 38 Classes. The goods trains from Enfield, which conveyed general traffic including empty livestock wagons and trains from Rozelle with empty wheat wagons were almost always worked by steam locomotives, which included 50 Class goods engines running at full goods speeds, 36 Class, 38 Class and 60 Class Garratts each running to the sectional times laid down in the working time table.

It took me some time to learn the running times for each type of locomotive, including the running times for the diesel trains running to A, B, C, D and E schedules* together with the 48 Class diesels which were slower than the 50 Class goods engines with full loads. All up, there were about 15 different sets of running times.

---

* These schedules were applicable to bogie vehicles only. They covered a variety of types of loads. 'A' schedule was timetabled at 100km/h and was limited to vehicles with bogies equipped to run at that speed. 'D' schedule was the timetable speed for loads of bogie wheat/coal hoppers and similar wagons. Speed was 70km/h and most trains conveyed 29 wagons and a brakevan.

I adapted fairly quickly to the graphing of trains on the double lines. The pace of the board took some getting used to. The controllers were engaged in conversation on the board for probably 75 per cent of the time. The balance was spent on doing the delays, keeping tonnage balances up to date and continually re-running the trains on the diagram in pencil as they changed from their plotted courses. At the beginning of each shift, a forecast of the arrival times of trains at Cabramatta was given to the Metropolitan Goods Train Controller. Conscientious controllers on all the boards regularly updated these forecast arrivals. Those who did not wore the wrath of the Goods Controller. A pattern soon revealed itself to me, that generally speaking, I found the bulk of Enfield and Rozelle trains left the Metropolitan area from about 11.00am until about 5.00pm. A schedule 'A' or 'B' runner bound for South Dynon from Cooks River departed Cooks about 2.30pm, and the Darling Harbour trains from about 8.00pm. There were a number of bogie interstate trains running mostly at 'C' speed interspersed with the goods train programme.

As was the case with *orco* and *doco*, the *ecces* were an important midday shift duty. The controller gathered them from each station for both Down and Up loading. He was also required to give to the Chief Train Controller Programme by 4.00pm on week days what was known as the *cutas*, *cuta* being the code word for such-and-such a train is required to lift the following traffic at station so-and-so. The Down *cutas* were for 41A and 401 between Campbelltown and Moss Vale or Goulburn, the Up *cutas* being for Nos 256 and 78. The latter were more in the form of loading figures than small *cutas*. The cement traffic from Berrima often amounted to hundreds of tons going north.

The working of the facilities at Bargo became critical, especially in the evening. Most crews wanted to be able to do their fires, take water and have crib at the same time. The time allowed for all three was generally 40 minutes. This was not always possible and on many occasions, it was necessary to direct a driver to have crib at Picton. If I were going to do this, I generally tried to get word to the driver at Campbelltown. The 15 minutes crib time at Picton would mean that a train ahead would get away from Bargo before the second one arrived. On many nights, when stock wagons were heading south, mostly on Tuesdays and Thursdays a locomotive inspector would be stationed at Bargo to supervise the Mechanical Branch working there. One inspector in particular, who became very well known later, would, if a crew was having trouble with the engine or were not maintaining the timetable running, would ride with them to Mittagong. He invariably came on the control telephone and told me when he was doing this. It was remarkable the difference that he made. On many occasions, trains that had lost time, would lose no more when he rode them. I used to be pleased to see him at Bargo.

The pattern for the Up trains was that, before the first fruit express passed Cabramatta at about 2.40am, that sometimes two or three goods trains would have gone to Enfield or Rozelle. On stock nights, stock trains would pass over Cabramatta up to 5.00am bound for, by then, the Homebush Saleyards, and on most nights, there were two trains from the Murrumbidgee Irrigation Areas conveying fruit and meat It was always a battle to get the interstate-next-day delivery train from South Dynon to Cooks River ahead of the peak hour. No 466 was scheduled through Campbelltown about 6.20am, which was supposedly the last margin available ahead of the peak hour services.

Some Trouble Officers would take this train later. If the train was not going to make Campbelltown by 6.20am or by the time nominated by Traffic Trouble, it had to refuge at Picton until after the *Southern Aurora* and the *Spirit of Progress* had passed, making it about three hours late into Cooks River. The 'Great White Father' was never pleased when this happened. (Nor should he have been). I made a point of ensuring that I did not make a train-working decision that would delay this train. When shipment wheat trains were running, they normally crossed Cabramatta between 9.30am and 4.00pm with wheat to tip that day. Any train after that went into the next day's tip at Rozelle. In effect, the bulk of the Down trains ran on the midday shift and afternoon shift, and the bulk of the Up trains on backshift and daywork.

The through trains on South Control provided only a part of the train controller's duty. The running of the limestone trains between Medway Junction to Berrima Junction and the South Coast, from Marulan to Maldon, demanded constant attention, as did the clearing of the cement loaded trains at Berrima and Maldon. The clearing of milk loading at Moss Vale, Bowral and Menangle was performed by either No 78 pick-up or No 256. There were many more passenger trains to contend with than I had previously been used to.

The running of these, coupled with the interstate express freight trains and the intrastate Darling Harbour next day delivery trains, all of which were recorded delay trains, made South Control a very demanding job.

To assist those who may read this in the future, I believe I should attempt to outline the responsibilities the train controller had to each station and each station had in turn not only to the controller, but also to the Department:

Campbelltown: In 1964, this was the outer limit of the suburban passenger services network. There were two passenger trains, worked by 32 Class locomotives, which terminated there each evening and returned the next morning. A regular service between Campbelltown and Liverpool was formed by 600 Class diesel cars that ran in the off-peak periods in multiples of two, that is a driving car and a trailer car, and in peak hour periods with four cars. These services, as a rule, were self-regulating and did not require much input from the controller, whose main duty was to see they were not delayed in running by slow moving goods trains.

On one occasion one of the 32 Classes for the early morning passenger failed. I was not advised by the assistant station master and I did not know until the engine clerk from Engine Control came to tell me he had ordered a crew and engine to Campbelltown to replace it. The first question I asked was,

"What time would it leave Enfield?"

Answer, "I do not know, they have not found a crew yet".

I then rang ASM Campbelltown and said something like,

"A little bird just flew through the window here and told me you have an engine failure for one of your passengers—that is not right is it? Surely you would have told me if it was."

He was quite indignant; he had told Engine Control, what more did I want? He was told quite nicely, but in strong terms, that the train controller was the first and only one he should have told, because the responsibility was then his to arrange for a replacement. I then asked which engine had failed. It was, of course, the engine for the first train. I told him to have the crew prepare the available engine, to use it on first train out and get it on time.

In the mean time, I checked again and there was no crew in sight for the second engine. A goods train with a load of wheat was approaching Picton at this stage. I told the engine clerk to get an engine and send it out for the goods train. I then told Campbelltown to stow the wheat train and to use the diesel engine to work the second passenger. He objected to stowing the train, which was not a very long one, in his yard. He claimed that he had nowhere to put it. When I asked him what about where the carriages off the first train had been stowed, he had no answer. I relate this happening, not for my part in it but more in an endeavour to highlight the lack of experience of the staff emerging as very young officers, in places such as Campbelltown.

This ASM, I found out during a conversation from him on the side phone, was in his second week as a relief ASM after having completed a training school for Fourth Class ASMs. He had no real appreciation of his responsibilities, having been virtually thrown in the 'deep end'. I felt somewhat guilty for having been so sarcastic with him; his training to that point had not prepared him for a station with the responsibilities of Campbelltown. The staffing position was still such, that the people in Staff Branch, were left with not any alternative but to use these young officers, for they were all that were available.

The Station Master at Campbelltown and his assistants were responsible for the running of the station; the supervision of the passenger services and rostering of staff for the passenger services. There were guards attached to Campbelltown depot. They managed the balancing of rolling stock in conjunction with Traffic Trouble, to ensure that they were able to meet the morning peak hour traffic. Campbelltown was not classed as a depot, the ASM's therefore were not required to despatch the 6.00am reports that depots stations were required to do. The positions, which could be quite busy, did not require the supervision and responsibilities of many other Second Class ASMs in depot stations. The station master was responsible for advising the train controller of the *ecces* for Menangle, including the milk for Nos 78 or 256 pick-ups.

In 1964, Glenlee coal mine, controlled by Campbelltown, loaded coal for shipment on a fairly regular pattern. The coal trains were hauled by 60 Class Garratts and conveyed 29 BCHs (bogie coal hoppers) and a brakevan which, when fully loaded, made the 60 Class haul 1760 tons. The station master was responsible for setting the coal programmes at the direction of the Yardmaster at Rozelle and the Coal Officer in the Rolling Stock Superintendent's Office.

Apart from the few trains which loaded at Campbelltown off the dump, it was impossible to supervise the running of these trains, they disappeared out to Glenlee where there was no communication, not be heard of again until they approached the main line looking for a margin to run to Rozelle. The set up was that usually there was an empty train sent to Glenlee, to commence the coal lift, this engine leaving the empties and returning light engine. Each following train was supposed to place their empties and pick up the loaded on hand.

At least 60 per cent of the time, the wagons were not loaded when the next rake of empties arrived, and it was commonplace to have a train at Glenlee waiting for three hours for completion of loading. On occasions they would be waiting for so long that the Garratts would have to come into Campbelltown to get water. By this time, of course, the next train of empties would be at Campbelltown waiting to go out, with yet another due from Rozelle. I found it almost impossible to get any of the Chief Train Controllers, responsible for setting the programme, to cancel a run to allow the coal programme to get back on schedule.

This form of working continued until there was a new Station Master at Campbelltown. He would not tolerate the gross amount of unproductive standing time. He had difficulty getting the Yardmaster Rozelle to listen. This officer had been 'King of Rozelle' and no one argued with him, including the Coal Officer.

Enter a new Assistant Goods Train Superintendent, who had once been a Traffic Inspector at Darling Harbour: the Station Master approached this officer and achieved remarkable results. The programmes were made more flexible, and more time was allowed at Glenlee to load the wagons. A new arrangement was brought into being. The Station Master at Campbelltown became responsible for the setting of the Glenlee and Campbelltown coal programmes, the Yardmaster at Rozelle and the Coal Officer supplied trains and wagons as he ordered, and at the times he ordered.

This arrangement did not completely reduce the standing time, but the delays that occurred were because the mine could not fulfil their obligations. Under the new arrangement, they were charged so much an hour waiting time. This charging had two effects: firstly it made the mine management come to the party by advising Campbelltown if there was the likelihood of delays; and secondly, enabled the train controller to advise the Chief Train Controller, who then was obliged, by direction from the Assistant Goods Train Superintendent, to reorganise the programme.

I strongly suspect that the mine management was never charged for delays. The threat, however, achieved the result of reducing standing time. The working of Glenlee had been the area in South Control where I felt that I was ineffective and had been able to do nothing about it. The reference to the Station Master Campbelltown will be the first of many to follow as he and I later both moved to different positions.

Menangle had Up and Down passenger platforms, and several sidings in the yard. These sidings were chiefly for the use of the dairy company, three and sometimes four bogie milk vans being loaded daily for Darling Harbour or Pippita. The empties were placed in by No 41A pick-up to Moss Vale and lifted by Nos 78/256 pick-ups weekdays and No 256 on Saturday and Sundays. In the middle 1960s, there was still some fodder being loaded in the area around Cowra and branches for Menangle, which went South from Cowra and was generally placed by No 78, which started from Goulburn.

The sidings were worked by a release which, when operated, enabled a key to be obtained to work the frame. The porter was required to advise Station Master Picton of the milk traffic he had offering.

Menangle railway station in December 1985 showing the small yard and some of the sidings still then remaining. *John R Newland.*

Douglas Park railway station in May 1986 showing the Up Refuge Loop at the right of the photo.   *John R Newland.*

Douglas Park had Up and Down platforms, a small goods siding, which occasionally received fodder and an Up Refuge Loop. The ASM on daywork only, was required to give his *ecce* to the controller. I often thought it would be the best job in the State. To me, it was another of the mysteries of staffing. Why it should have been staffed with an Assistant Station Master when Menangle was not, I could not fathom.

Maldon was the home of the Commonwealth Portland Cement Company and was situated on the Down side of the line. Access off the Up line was by way of a crossover to the Down Main, then by shunting into the siding. This siding was worked by a ground frame. Obviously, the releasing key could not be obtained if a train was approaching on the Down main line. After the train was in clear, the guard restored the key to allow main line working.

Limestone for the cement was obtained from the Medway limestone quarry, but was despatched from Marulan. Mostly two 14-wagon trains each with a tonnage of 900 tons, supplied the limestone daily. The trains ran to schedule 'C' conditions and were tabled at 50 miles per hour (80km/h). The incoming trains would deposit their load and pick up the empties from the previous train and depart from the siding onto the Down main line.

It was the guard's responsibility to confer with Picton before taking the main line key. The signalman in turn would advise the controller that the train was ready to depart from Maldon for Marulan. The controller in turn would advise Picton the margin he wished the train to take. The guard, after being advised when to take the release, restored the key after his train was completely on the main line. By 1964, much of the manufactured product was despatched by road. That which was not was picked up, was usually conveyed by No 256 pick-up.

Picton was the once busy depot of the 1890s had by now none of that glory. Only the visible signs of a past locomotive depot remains to show what it had once been. It had a Down back-in refuge and an Up run-in refuge loop, both holding in excess of 75 vehicles. There were some unused sidings from yesteryear together with a couple that were still used. A small amount of freight, mainly fodder, was consigned to local dairy farmers. It was the junction for the Picton—Mittagong Loop Line. On day shift, a station master and signalman were employed, the signal box being an elevated one apart from the main station building. On afternoon and backshift, the signal box was worked by the ASMs, the platform and booking offices being attended to by portering staff. So far as the train controllers were concerned, it was just another safeworking station.

A passenger service formed by an empty railmotor from Campbelltown conveyed the early commuters from Picton to Campbelltown. This service stopped at all stations allowing the Moss Vale passenger to run nonstop from Picton to Campbelltown. A daily

Some of Picton railway station and signal box in November 1983 showing some of the sidings in the vicinity of the station.   *John R Newland.*

railmotor service starting from Moss Vale ran between Mittagong and Picton and returned on the Loop Line. This motor was timed to connect with the main line services, both on arrival at Picton and at Mittagong on the return.

A Down water column and de-ashing pit was available at Picton. They were, however, only used when there were trains ahead requiring to use Bargo's facilities. Generally speaking, if a driver on a 50 Class was forced into having crib and doing his fire at Picton, he would stop at Bargo for a water top up. On weekends, when Bargo was unattended, a goods train hauled by a 50 Class steam or 48 Class diesel engine required an hour and thirty minutes start on the *Southern Aurora* and the *Spirit of Progress*. This would give the required 10 minutes clearance into Mittagong. On the 1 in 75 rising grades with 600 ton loads, the goods train got down to seven miles per hour for the some of the way, and it was not until they topped the rise near Aylmerton and ran into Mittagong, that they had any respite from the continuous grade.

The station master gave the *ecces* in the afternoon. On most occasions, there was little traffic loaded at Picton, but his *ecce* of course, included the milk lifts from Menangle.

Bargo had ashpits and watering facilities available from the Down Refuge Loop and main line. It was not common to use both facilities at the same time, although there were occasions when I arranged for 60 Class Garratts running behind a goods train to use the

Bargo railway station in November 1983 showing some of the sidings in the distance.
John R Newland.

main line facility and keep going ahead of the goods train. Bargo was purely a safeworking station from control's point of view. A daywork Sixth Class Station Master (goodness knows why) and afternoon and backshift ASMs were the staff complement. Bargo was a key station in the steam days, but even in my time was losing its significance.

I found, for some inexplicable reason, the ASMs were reluctant to report their trains. It became irritating to have to continually ring them. After a while, I came to the suspicion that it was a deliberate ploy to stir up the controllers. The SM was a shunter at Cowra when I was there. I had no trouble with him. Little goods traffic moved into or out of Bargo. The *ecce* given in the afternoon, if it consisted of anything, were empty wagons from inwards loaded, usually Departmental sleepers.

Yerrinbool was an unattended safeworking station with Down and Up back-in refuge. A female station attendant looked after the public. The universal SL (standard lock) key locked the signal box. Rarely used, although I did use it once, which will be recorded later my recollections of South Control.

Mittagong Junction Box is situated about two kilometres from the main station, was worked by a track circuit release. The guard taking a key and admitting his train to the Loop Line would, when it was clear, restore the main line, return the key to the Annett

8113 and 8133 speed past with a container freight past the former site of the Mittagong refuge yards in May 1986.   *John R Newland.*

lock, and take the staff for the Mittagong Junction—Picton section of the Loop Line. In my time the only train to use the section was the daily railmotor. Very occasionally, 41A the Down pick-up, would convey sleepers or some such traffic for Buxton. 41A generally took traffic to Thirlmere from Picton and then returned to Picton.

Mittagong was another station which held a much higher profile in the early history of the Great Southern Railway. The buildings on the Up platform originally housed a refreshment room and hotel type accommodation, but these facilities were phased out in the late 1890s. The advent of the 'P' or 32 Class engines were responsible for the facilities being made redundant. Some use of the ground floor buildings was still being made by the Chief Civil Engineer's branch.

One of the brewing companies had a malt extracting plant at Mittagong, which, when I came to South Control, still operated; truck loads of bagged barley being regularly consigned there. At the end of the barley harvest for most years, large numbers of trucks were unloaded in the malt siding. In those times, there was not any farm storage facilities for barley, the farmers loading it directly in bags onto rail wagons, as it was harvested. The malt siding closed down around 1968.

Up and Down back-in refuges were provided. Mittagong could not accept a following Down train until the train being refuged was in clear of the main line. When deciding whether to despatch a slower running train ahead of a passenger, the controller not only had to allow for a ten minute running margin ahead of the following train, but he also had to allow at least five minutes to stow the train. If I had Bowral in manual working, I generally kept the train going on to Moss Vale. The running time for 50 Class steam or a 48 Class diesel was 14 minutes to Bowral and 10 minutes to Berrima Junction and two minutes to Moss Vale, another safeworking station, albeit an important one from the controller's viewpoint.

While I was in South Control, the Chief Civil Engineer's Branch spent months and many thousands of pounds reconditioning the track between Mittagong Junction and Thirlmere. To this day I do not know why. I thought then and still do that it was a criminal waste of money. Especially so, when the Commissioner of the time, probably upholding Government policy, would not spend any money on building maintenance. The policy was that unless money spent was toward something that would make a return, it was not to be spent. Then came this wastage on upgrading track that was rarely run over! But who was I, a mere train controller to question the reason? As I have said, the line was never used other than for the railmotor (which was replaced by a bus in the late 1970s). The only exception being once, when a main line derailment occurred between Mittagong and Picton, the Up *Southern Aurora* and *Spirit of Progress* were routed this way. There, of course, was an alternate route via Wollongong for these trains.

An ASM retired from Mittagong in 1965 at the age 69 years and 364 days. He had worked the 56 years of his working life in the Southern Highlands, the last 30 of them at Mittagong. The sad fact was that he died six months after he retired. He retired off backshift, so he was 70 years of age, five minutes after signing on duty. After ringing the all stations key for the 4.00am *amba*, and before I started giving it out, I made sure every station between Campbelltown and Goulburn was listening. I did something rarely, if ever, done. I made a short farewell speech to him over the control board. He greatly appreciated it. The response to me from the staff was one of appreciation for recognising someone who was a legend on the South.

The *ecces* were given in the afternoon, and consisted mainly of empties from inwards loaded, especially from the malt siding. Little outward goods was handled.

Bowral was probably the busiest commercial station on the Southern Highlands after Moss Vale, in terms of passenger revenue, parcels traffic and milk despatched. In 1964, a Darling Harbour truck was received twice weekly. It was also a station to which fodder for the local dairies was often consigned. It was a difficult place to shunt especially on the Up. Down and Up back-in refuge sidings were provided. As a general rule, No 78 picked up the milk, shunting from the Up Main. The controller, when allowing the train to

Bowral railway station in May 1984 showing the siding in the distance.

John R Newland.

depart from Berrima, had to be sure that he not only had a margin on the Up, but also one on the Down as well.

The station had to be cut into manual working for these movements. The SM daily gave the *ecces*, consisting mostly of milk traffic for Pippita or Darling Harbour. They reported only trains that they had dealt with, including the passengers.

Berrima Junction was so called because it was the junction for Blue Circle Cement Works at Berrima and employed a Sixth Class Station Master and Third Class Assistants. It was a very busy and important station. On the Down, Nos 401 and 41A shunted, detaching the empty bulk cement wagons and any inwards traffic destined for the cement works or Berrima Junction itself. On most week days, six or seven limestone trains from Medway went directly to Berrima cement works. These trains were programmed by a senior train controller, who was known as the Illawarra—Goulburn Programme Officer.

The limestone trains when I started in South Control, were worked by single 44 Class diesels and conveyed 14 bogie lime hoppers (BLHs) and a brakevan with a total tonnage of 980 tons. The cement works limestone trains detached the loaded wagons and picked up the empties from the previous train. This system of relaying the wagons worked well, and it was only occasionally that a rake of empties was not ready. The controller, when it did happen, had to decide, if none were available at Berrima Junction or Moss Vale,

Looking south towards Moss Vale in December 1985. The turnout in the foreground is for the Down Inspection Road which leads to the triangle for the Moss Vale—Unanderra Line. Moss Vale station is in the far distance.   John R Newland.

whether to wait for the empties or to run with what was available. If there were only three or four short, I generally ran with them because by so doing, I could keep the whole programme running close to schedule.

Berrima Junction usually received one limestone train a day. This material was used for the manufacture of fertiliser. On most days Berrima Cement Works and Berrima Junction loaded between 1200 and 1500 tons of cement for Nos 78 and 256. The loading originating from the cement works was generally worked into Berrima Junction by the works shunter. This train did not appear on the Control Diagram, it coming and going without the controller being aware. The only time he would know it was there was if Berrima Junction delayed a limestone train shunting it.

The *ecces*, or in this case the loading figures both actual and forecast were given in the afternoon. No 78 commenced from Goulburn and was the return of No 401. Enfield rostered guards worked them and like many rostered guards on pick-ups, they knew all the tricks and were masters at missing margins by a few minutes (refer to my paragraphs about No 140 at Orange East Fork and to the pick-up from Coonamble to Dubbo). No 78 built to a full load and No 256 commencing from Moss Vale off No 41A, cleared the cement from Berrima each day.

Approximately every six months, a ship loaded with gypsum from South Australia for Berrima Cement Works would berth at Port Kembla and disgorge about 8000 to 9000 tons into about 170 bogie wagons. Always on a weekend and commencing on a Friday night, the Gypsum Programme, as it became known, started arriving at Berrima Junction. Each train conveyed 17 wagons, a brakevan and was hauled by two diesel engines. Mostly, the first train's engines ran as light engines from Berrima after leaving their load at the cement works. These engines would go to Moss Vale and be attached to services either bound for Enfield or Port Kembla.

Occasionally the locomotives went light engine to Port Kembla. On these occasions it was necessary that the dynamic brake system was working on the lead unit. If it was not the units were not permitted to run as light engines. After the first train, the trains detached their loaded wagons and attached empties, sometimes depending on the position for empties running back to the Coast with them. The Truck Clerk in Sydney made every effort to supply the empties from Enfield to Port Kembla, because every time a train took empties from Berrima, it had to go to Moss Vale for a two-hour brake examination due to the steep grade down to the Coast. This process tied up Moss Vale and led to delays on the Up traffic from the deep South and the limestone traffic to the Coast from Medway, which ran as normal. There were generally around 10 trains over the weekend from Port Kembla to Berrima.

Berrima Junction was a key station from the controller's viewpoint, so I made it my business to get to know the voices of the ASM's and to put a name to them when I heard them. Having worked for so long at Orange East Fork, I had an appreciation of how busy they could get. In essence, I did not make frivolous use of the control telephone and tried to work in with them. It paid dividends, because they would plan with me the movements they intended to make, and unless something came unstuck, neither would speak until they reported back to me, when the train had left, or that the movement was complete.

Moss Vale: Until I went to South Control, I had no idea of the importance of, or of the amount of operational work that was performed at Moss Vale. It was manned by a Second Class Station Master, First Class Assistant Station Masters, a Third Class Assistant Station Master, on daywork, was the roster clerk and assistant to the SM. Third class signalmen, guards, senior shunters, shunters, booking office clerks, station assistants and junior station assistants were employed. The Mechanical Branch employed locomotive crews and examiners. Examiners were especially important at Moss Vale, because every train that ran on the branch to Port Kembla had to have the brakes fully examined to grade-control standard.

The grade controls were set in the intermediate position, prior to leaving Moss Vale, for the 1 in 33 descending grades between Summit Tank and Unanderra. This regulation

The platform at Moss Vale railway station in March 1984 showing the Up Refuge Siding and signal box. The station comprises a rather large area island layout, the Down Main line being on the other side of the building complex. The station once had accommodation for visitors which was located in the second storey.　　　　　　　　　　　　*John R Newland.*

applied to trains conveying limestone and trains carrying fully loaded bogie wagons on interstate services. On trains with return empty steel wagons and bogie flat trucks or opens, the grade control was left in the normal position. One of the factors that caused delays at Moss Vale was that every train examined at Moss Vale to go down the 'mountain', was allowed 120 minutes brake time at Moss Vale. Limestone trains, as a rule, ran pretty much to their timetables. The trains that caused the delays were the interstate trains that ran anywhere within hours of timetable and seemed invariably to follow a coast limestone train in from Medway, which inevitably created delays at Moss Vale.

The areas of Mittagong, Bowral, Burradoo and Moss Vale were quite heavily populated, with people who worked in transport, the mining industry, some local manufacturing, and local shops. In the rural industry, dairying and beef cattle were the main farming activities. A passenger train service that provided for this population saw No 50 passenger, the 6.12am from Moss Vale as a commuter service to the city. No 20 passenger from Goulburn, which served as a sweeper for the *Spirit of Progress*, departed around 7.15am picked up at Moss Vale about 8.15am and served as a shopper train to Campbelltown and the city. No 9 mixed paper train carried school children from Exeter to Goulburn High and primary schools. No 34 in the afternoon provided the return for the school children.

A 30 Class locomotive and carriages provided a connecting service to Wollongong off the *Spirit of Progress* and, in addition, took school children from Calwalla and Burrawang to Robertson. In February 1967, these steam-hauled passenger trains were replaced by CPH railmotors with brakes modified to deal with steep grades. The railmotor that provided a service on the Mittagong—Picton Loop Line also departed from Moss Vale. In the afternoon No 49 departed from Sydney around 5.10pm terminating at Moss Vale around 7.00pm. No 19 departed from Sydney around 5.40pm and arrived Moss Vale around 7.30pm bound for Goulburn. In the morning, No 4 *Spirit of Progress* and No 2 *Southern Aurora* were timetabled around 7.00 and 7.15am respectively.

The Down *Intercapital Daylight* No 65 and the *Canberra Monaro Express* No 37 stopped at 9.50am and 10.10am. No 1 *Southern Aurora* and No 3 *Spirit of Progress* in the evening were at Moss Vale around 10.05pm and 10.15pm. No 66 *Intercapital Daylight Express* and No 38 *Canberra Monaro Express* were at Moss Vale about 6.50pm and 7.15pm. In addition, No 11 *South West Mail* and No 13 *Cooma Mail* on the Down and Nos 12 and 14 of their return stopped at Moss Vale.

There was never a shift when at least one passenger or mail train ran did not run. On back shift, the early morning mail trains arriving from Temora and Cooma, were sources of annoyance, more than anything else, when they tangled with the 'high-wheeled' interstate freights. On the one hand, we were expected to give priority to the fruit expresses and the recorded delay interstate trains, but on the other we were expected to give priority to the passenger services, if for no other reason than that the General Appendix Part One* told us to do so. On most backshifts there was no problem but on stock mornings, with the additional stock trains, it became difficult, especially on the block sections between Marulan and Exeter. A General Order was in existence that gave us permission to delay the mail trains for 10 minutes to ensure a fruit/perishable or next day delivery train from interstate arrived into the metropolitan area in time to meet consumer/client demands.

On Saturdays and Sundays, a tourist passenger train ran from Sydney via Unanderra to Moss Vale and return. Because of the magnificent scenery between Unanderra and Moss Vale, they were popular trains. People were able to alight at Ranelagh House platform, which was about ten feet long (three metres) and also at Robertson there were craft shops, a rain forest and eating establishments. Ranelagh House, a beautiful guesthouse, served meals from solid silver cutlery and table accoutrements. It was full of 'old world' charm, and is still so today.

On more than one occasion, I took one of the mail trains 'on' for 10 or 15 minutes to keep a freighter on target to get into the metropolitan ahead of the peak. Although this was generally recorded on the delays, it was rare for correspondence to follow provided the delay report was worded correctly to indicate that the train given preference and the time saving to the prioritised train was shown. I have related this under the heading Moss Vale deliberately because it was in this area that I would delay one of the mail trains to advance a delay-recorded or 'blue ribbon' freight service.

Although I have said that the limestone trains ran reasonably close to their timetable times as a general rule, they nevertheless required constant supervision. They were worked by Moss Vale crews, which was one of the reasons they ran on time, because it was to their advantage to be at the appointed change-over point on time. By the same token, if for some reason they were off the scheduled path, it was very difficult to get them to head toward Medway if they were within an hour of getting relief. At this time, Moss Vale did not have a 'call truck' to ferry crews around as they do today. It was common sense to hold the train for its new crew.

Another problem that often occurred was the failure of Medway quarry to load the trains to schedule. In most cases, it was bought about by insufficient production from the quarry to load a train without delay. They did not work from a stockpile, but loaded directly from production line into the wagons from the overhead bins that the wagons passed under. One of the most difficult things from a controller's viewpoint was getting accurate information, especially at night time from the quarry foreman. There was, of course, no point in sending another train out to Medway Junction to stand for hours if the delay in loading was to be considerable.

* There were two general Appendices, Part One and Part Two. Part One contained general regulations, including a section on Train Control. Part Two was the safeworking appendix.

The sensible thing to do was to cancel a run and let them catch up with their production and at the same time, save excessive unproductive standing time. By holding a train at Moss Vale until a fresh crew was available, it was possible to delete a train and still keep the programme running near to schedule. Delays at Medway of any substantial period were uncommon, the delays being mostly in the order of an hour to two hours. It depended on the positions of the limestone trains, and importantly, the amount of stone (if the information was available) at the cement works as to whether I cancelled a train or let them run late.

The Port Kembla Branch was very busy between Moss Vale and Unanderra. As it was a part of Illawarra Control, I shall leave any comment until I come to my time in that area. Suffice to say there was an oil train daily, at least one goods train with traffic emanating from the industrial areas, and mostly three and sometimes up to five steel trains daily. Couple these with the coast limestone trains and the interstate trains returning with empties to Port Kembla, on an average day there were 16 or so goods train movements, through which the passenger train each way had to be threaded on the single line.

These trains occupied the Up side of Moss Vale Yard. Any shunting required was done with the train engines and the completed trains were examined by the train examiners in the Up yard, or as it was sometimes known, as the 'Coast' yard. It was not uncommon to have two and, on occasions, even three trains at Moss Vale either shunting, having their brakes done or waiting on a staff from an arriving Down train. In the very busy periods trains, would often spend three hours at Moss Vale while they shunted, had the brakes done and waited for a path after the arrival of a Down train.

The Assistant Train Control Superintendent (known as 'Old Fred') used to take a fiendish delight in issuing correspondence, commonly referred to as 'bungs', over the graphing of trains at Moss Vale. For example, if a train was there for, say 180 minutes, the signalman would give the arrival and departure times and break up the time occupied into shunting time, brake time, standing time and finally crossing time. If those times did not add up 'Old Fred' took to the graph in red ink and issued a paper to be answered by the controller responsible for recording incorrect times. He seemed to me to be more interested in the nit-picking things than in the train working.

There were often questionable train working decisions made, by me as often as anyone else, around the Moss Vale area. They were based mainly on incorrect forecast information regarding the anticipated departure of a train or the anticipated arrival of a coast train that did not make its forecast arrival time. Adding to the Moss Vale problems were the slow loading at Medway Quarry or slow releases from Berrima Junction and the cement works. In most cases these were explainable, the question being rarely asked. I thought he would have been better off pursuing this aspect of the train working, with Moss Vale, Berrima Junction, Medway and the controllers, rather than worrying about a few minutes difference in the total times, especially as mostly the train could not have left earlier because of a crossing. Then sometimes, having a slight unkind streak in me, I wondered if that was the limit to what he could see.

There was (and is) a triangle at Moss Vale with the Engine Run Round Road forming the base of the triangle. The line from Unanderra splits at the point of the triangle with each line branching to join the main line. The points from the yard were worked from Moss Vale Junction Box, operated by the shunters. This triangle was used for turning locomotives, the 38 Classes for No 50 in particular, the diesel engine for 41A, if it was a 48 Class or a 45 Class.

Exeter was distinguished more by the beautiful Southern Highland country surrounding it than anything else. Fourth Class Assistant Station Masters worked around the clock. So far as train working was concerned, it was a 'through' signal box, having no refuge sidings. Once a train left Bundanoon it had to go through to Moss Vale. On backshift, they gave the road to Bundanoon for the next train as one passed their starting signal and cleared the home signal, and on the Down they took the road from Bundanoon as it was available and cleared the 'accept' and 'through' signals.

This may not have met the safeworking regulations, but it ensured they never delayed a train through falling asleep in an overheated signal box on a cold winter's night. There was no goods traffic and very little passenger traffic. No wonder it was high on the priority list of people wanting to transfer from country areas. A small siding on the Down side was used mainly by Per Way for the receival of sleepers. Per Way was becoming much more mechanised and used to load the sleepers on motor lorries and take them to the point where they were required.

From an engineman's point of view, one of the most difficult sections to work between Cabramatta and Goulburn was the 1 in 75 gradient from Werai platform (which no longer exists) to Exeter, a distance of about six kilometres which had long sweeping transverse curves. Trains conveying loads of empty stock wagons and other empties got into difficulty regularly when it was frosty or wet, especially when worked by 50, 36, 38 or 59 Classes. The 50 Classes lost time more often than they ran the running times laid down in the Working Timetable. Shorter trains that did not get on two curves did not have nearly as much trouble.

I did not have any failures, but on one occasion sent an engine from Moss Vale to assist in the rear of a train into Exeter. By sending an engine in to push the train from the section, I had to hold Up traffic at the Home Signal at Exeter until the propelling movement had been completed. Fortunately, the point where they usually pulled to a stand had an automatic signal fitted with a telephone. Another occasion on a Sunday morning when the Up programme was light, I instructed the driver to take half the train forward and stow it on the Up main line at Exeter, while he went back for the rest, on the authority of

Exeter railway station and signal box in May 1984.   *John R Newland.*

a guard's 'wrong line order'. The train was worked on this occasion by a 48 Class diesel which had slipped to a stand on the frosty rails.

Bundanoon was the holiday destination prewar and for a long time afterwards. However, it was starting to look 'tatty' and the tourist trade had fallen off with the advent of the motor vehicle. Vacant shops were dotted along the street. The beautiful old Bundanoon Hotel had been allowed to deteriorate. I have to say I have been back there in recent times and was glad to see there has been a transformation, especially with the Hotel; maybe it will yet recapture some of its former glory.

There was some commercial activity, both passenger and freight, which certainly would not have paid the wages of the staff. Its importance was the fact that it had back-in refuges, both Down and Up, which held 50 vehicles.

To keep Moss Vale flowing, I would often send a train to Bundanoon ahead of a priority train with five minutes or so less clearance running time and chance delaying the priority train. I did get delays doing it but never got caught being unable to justify my working. In the steam era it was another station whose refuges were used more regularly than they were in the 1960s when diesel was half king. I often found it necessary to refuge Up steam trains, Garratts excepted, to wait a margin at Moss Vale for admittance into the yard and the steam facilities. Garratts requiring to take water only, could be accommodated on the main line at Moss Vale.

Bundanoon railway station in May 1986 viewed from the overbridge.   *John R Newland.*

Penrose railway station in May 1986.   *John R Newland.*

The Station Master was the Assistant Station Master at Springwood when I had the problem with the COD parcel. Third Class ASMs completed the staffing. No wages staff were employed, the ASM's being responsible for the signal lights that were not electrically operated.

Penrose could only be described as a village, there only being a general store serving scattered housing. Penrose was a safeworking station only, which was cut out every weekend from about midday Saturday until around 6.00am Monday morning. During the day, meal breaks were provided between certain hours when the signal box cut out.

It was the Controller's duty to decide whether the train working required the signal box to be cut in. He could vary the ASM's break by thirty minutes one way or the other to suit the train running. The ASMs generally were keen to work through their meal breaks, for overtime at Penrose was scarce. I tried to be fair both to the staff and the Department, if I thought the train working justified them staying on and that I would advance trains by avoiding standing time at Bundanoon or Wingello waiting line clear, which standing time in some cases delayed trains also at Exeter and Tallong, I kept them on duty. We often had to justify to the District Superintendent Goulburn the action we took. Fourth Class ASM's worked around the clock.

Wingello was the key safeworking station between Moss Vale and Goulburn, with back-in Down and Up Refuge, which held 75 vehicles. The surrounding area was heavily timbered and is on the border of Morton National Park. Wingello could also only be described as a village. The Sixth Class Station Master was the best and most co-operative operator of a small signal box that it was my pleasure to work with. He reported every train the moment they passed, he answered the control, almost before it had finished ringing and if a train was approaching for which he had not had a direction and he thought it would be required to be refuged, he would come on and quietly say,

"Would you like me to put so and so away."

It was a certainty if he asked that question, the train did need to be put away. One of my regrets was I never met the man. His hobby from which he apparently was quite commercially successful was lapidary. A power operated Up Outer Home signal was provided. This meant that the clearing point for Up trains was the Home signal and a train could be accepted from Tallong while the previous train was backing into the refuge siding. Ten minutes was required to back a train of 50 vehicles long in clear. It was a key station because Goulburn Control would regularly let goods trains go from the Goulburn 'wheat yard' sidings with just sufficient clearance to get to Wingello. Any train over the length for Bundanoon, if it did not have clearance to Moss Vale, was refuged. The staffing was completed by two Third Class ASMs. Wingello in my time was not provided with cut-out facilities, so it was manned 365 days of the year full time.

Wingello railway station in May 1986.   *John R Newland.*

Tallong railway station in May 1986 showing the locomotive watering facilities.
John R Newland.

Tallong employed Fourth Class ASMs around the clock, but was really a signal box with a platform in the wilderness. It could best be described as a geographical area. Watering facilities were available, as were ashpits. The only engines to use them were 50 Classes which, even in the time I was in South Control, became a rarity.

Medway was the junction off the main line to Marulan limestone quarries. In its original planning Medway was a small shunting yard, with three sidings situated on the Down side, which made up loaded limestone trains brought in from the quarries situated some five kilometres from Medway by the company shunt engine. Empties were deposited from the trains returning from the cement works at Berrima and were transported to the quarry also by the company engine.

With the advent of total dieselisation in the late 1950s and bottom discharge bogie wagons, block trains were introduced which ran direct to the quarry and were loaded under the limestone bins as the train slowly passed under them. This completely transformed Medway from being a busy shunting point to no more than another signal box in the wilderness. The only important duty that they had other than keeping in touch with the quarry regarding the running of the limestone trains, was to invoice the wagons and keep a wagon book.

From a controller's point of view, the important function was keeping in touch with the quarry. It was difficult at times getting trains onto the main line. Before a train from the quarry branch could be despatched the Down line from Tallong to Medway had to be clear, with the block telegraph instruments showing 'line closed'. Obviously the block instruments on the Up had to be showing 'line closed' before the signalman gave the 'is line clear bell' signals to Tallong. When Tallong was cut out, due to staffing shortage or being on a meal break, it was much more difficult having to work with Wingello. The same rules applied to Medway getting the train away, except that the 'line clear' was now extended to Wingello.

Marulan is a small town on the Hume Highway. Marulan was a significant railway station, not so much for its passenger revenue, but for its limestone trade. An Up Refuge which held 50 vehicles, was not often used, unless it was for a train worked either by a 50 Class steam engine or a branch line diesel. It was the case with trains worked by other than these locomotives that, if they had clearance from Goulburn over a following train in the automatic signalling section, they would invariably make Wingello. Once again, this logic did not apply when Tallong was cut out.

Marulan loaded two 14 BLH trains a day to Maldon. Two rakes of wagons were in use. The limestone was actually quarried from the Marulan limestone quarries and transported by road to Marulan where it was dumped by hydraulic lift dump trucks into the wagons from an embankment. If there were no wagons available, it was dumped on the embankment for loading into the wagons by front end loaders. The loading for these trains was very reliable, much more so than at Medway. The two trains daily took loaded wagons from Marulan and returned with empties. The first train usually started engine and van from Goulburn around 9.00am, picked a rake of 14 loaded wagons and ran at 'C' schedule to Maldon.

After stowing the loaded wagons and doing any necessary shunting, usually not much, the train returned to Marulan, generally engine and van, although on occasions it took bogie cement wagons for Canberra and Moss Vale, and then proceeded engine and van to Marulan. As the second train, it normally departed Marulan around 4.00pm. On arrival at Maldon, it shunted out the empties and waited for the loaded rake it brought in to be unloaded. The normal departure usually about 7.30-8.00pm, the train running direct to Marulan at 'D' schedule with the 28 empties. On most occasions the engine returned light with the brakevan to Goulburn. The Station Master at Marulan while I was in South Control (and for a long time after) was the afternoon parcel porter at Cowra when I was there.

One of the most important and demanding tasks was the sending of the *ambas* at 4.00am, 7.00am and 11.00am. The first *amba* for the day was received around 4.00am when the backshift Chief Train Controller put out his programme for the next 36 hours. An Up *amba* was also obtained from *goco*. On receipt of these *ambas* the programme was

Marulan railway station in January 1986 viewed from the Hume Highway overbridge.
John R Newland.

written in a book which was ruled up with station or signal box names on one side of a double page while the *amba* or programme was written into the other. The 4.00am *amba* was fairly straight forward, the train controller calling all stations on his all stations key and giving out the trains to run for the next 36 hours.

The time the *amba* was given and those stations that acknowledged, were recorded in the *amba* book. The 7.00am *amba* consisted of train running information; I was always very meticulous with it. It was the responsibility of the train controller to forecast every train that would run while the fettlers were out on the track. He drew the trains onto the diagram in pencil. At 7.00am he rang all stations and read the times each train would pass every station. He had to include the Down express goods, the goods from Enfield, the Up express goods, the goods trains from Goulburn plus the limestone trains between Marulan/Medway and Berrima. The whole operation from starting until he completed reading the times for every train to every station from Marulan to Picton, usually took about 30 minutes. With the ever-present train working to contend with as well as getting the finalising delays from *goco* and *juco* for the delay clerk, the time from 6.00am to 8.00am was always very busy.

At around 10.00am the daywork chief train controller issued amendments to the 4.00am *amba*. These amendments were incorporated in the *amba* sent at 11.00am to all stations for the following 36 hours. During the time I was in South Control, it was the duty of the back up Trouble Officer to come and enter the times for each train at Cabramatta on the Down and at Goulburn North box on the Up on the following day's diagrams. This information was obtained from the *amba*. Some of the Trouble Officers were very diligent in this regard, while others did not bother. I found myself doing it in my own time if they did not do it.

I spent almost two years in South Control and during that time, I managed to keep my 'nose clean' although I had a number of failures, irregularities and derailments. The first irregularity, which led to an enquiry being conducted by the Safeworking Superintendent, was that of a driver of a Glenlee coal train who passed a signal at stop in Campbelltown Up yard. The signalman informed me of the fact, I told him to get the ASM to speak to me. Before that happened, the driver came on the telephone and asking me could I 'square it up', I told him unfortunately, "No" it had been officially reported by the signalman and that there were witnesses to the signalman reporting it to me. I told the ASM when he came on to send the appropriate telegrams to *Divn* and *Safe*.

I also advised the Trouble Officer who arranged for a locomotive inspector to meet the driver at Rozelle. I thought nothing more of it. About a week later I was advised to attend the enquiry into the incident. I was a bit surprised about there being an enquiry. After all, there was no derailment, the driver had admitted responsibility, or he had until he found the inspector waiting for him at Rozelle. After the usual beginnings of a witness at an enquiry, I was told the train concerned was not recorded on the train control diagram. I was, to say the least, taken aback with this statement from the chairman. I said nothing for probably thirty seconds thinking about it, I then said,

"Can I see the diagram, please."

The locomotive representative started to object, I think he could see the Traffic Branch being involved in this too, from his viewpoint, the more the merrier, or better for his Branch. The Chairman overruled him and said "yes." When I examined the diagram the first thing I saw was the train which was not supposed to be on the diagram. What I had failed to do was to put the train number in the little circle that we all drew for that purpose. I pointed it out to the Chairman and said,

"There it is," he said. "Come back all I said."

This episode staggered me, although the train was certainly not numbered, it was on the time that the signalman had said in his statement, it was on the time the guard's journal showed leaving Campbelltown, it was reported through Cabramatta and shown on the diagram at the time the Cabramatta train register book recorded, still the Safeworking Superintendent could not pick it. He obviously could not read a train control diagram properly, either that or he had not examined it but had taken the word of his clerk. I would like to think that that was the case, but either way, it was sloppy. He said to me at the time and handed me a biro to do so,

"Put the number in the circle."

I did not hear anymore about it. I was not asked if the driver rang me and I did not volunteer the information. He was reduced to a fireman for three months, after being found responsible.

The first Christmas Eve I spent in Sydney was on the 5.30pm shift. The driver of a goods conveying bulk wheat trucks from Rozelle with a 50 Class rang me from that point and asked me if would I give him a 'go' ahead of the 'cats', the universal nicknames given to No 1 *Southern Aurora* and No 3 *Spirit of Progress*. I told him it was up to him; if he got to Picton with sufficient clearance to get to Mittagong without delaying them, I would let him go. I would have, in fact, 'touched' them for a few minutes for him, but did not tell him so. By this time I had been around long enough not to trust 50 Classes. I was surprised that a goods engine would be used on Christmas Eve when there were diesels available, I checked with engine control and he said the locomotive was working to Cootamundra for the wheat lift commencing on Boxing Day. When he passed Campbell-town he had to take about two minutes off the running time. I told Picton he wanted a run ahead of Nos 1 and 3 and to tell me when he came on his track. When Picton came on, he had lost two minutes and had not regained them, so I told Picton to refuge him and to let him follow the 'cats'.

When he left Picton, he had about 30 minutes margin over No 9 *South West Mail*.

Because it was Christmas Eve there was no one on at Bargo. When Picton gave me Nos 1 and 3 and his departure, he made the remark,

" That bloke took a long time to get off the track."

I was having a fairly easy night and was watching the time fairly closely, when he should have been on Mittagong's track, so I rang him out of curiosity. No sign of him. Time went on and No 9 passed Picton on time. Time dragged on and still there was no word from the driver or guard of the train.

All I could do was sit and wait until he either appeared on Mittagong's track, or he, or No 9 rang Mittagong. No 9 rang Mittagong from a signal on the Mittagong side of Bargo just as he came onto Mittagong's track. I put the train away at Mittagong. When he came out of the refuge, he stopped and spoke to Mittagong and said they had run short of steam and had to stop three times to raise it. He also said he would not take the locomotive past Moss Vale. He lost a total of 50 minutes in the section. How fortunate was I that I refuged him at Picton? Engine control had engines returning home light attached to a train from Goulburn and one of these was used to work the train to Goulburn. I expect the driver was late for Santa Claus, because that was the reason the poor fellow wanted to get home, I felt sorry for him. The engine was still at Moss Vale on Boxing Day when I came to work. It was sent light engine to Cootamundra, during my shift.

On another occasion, I had two goods trains between Bargo and Mittagong, both worked by 50 Class engines. The first I knew of any problem was when Mittagong advised me he had the fireman of the first train on the telephone from the signal box at Yerrinbool. The fireman told him the compressor had failed. The train brakes were on. The engine, of course, became a failure. The only way to move the train was to leak the air out of the wagons and move it non-air. I declined to do this. I told Mittagong to get the guard on the telephone and when the fireman of the following train rang, to direct him to pass the signal. The Guard was instructed to cut the signal box in and make sure his train was inside the home signal. He was then directed to go the home signal and to wait for the arrival of the following train. The total train was to be attached to the rear of his train and the engine then detached and used to provide air to pump the brakes off. They were directed to place the train in the Down Refuge and to secure it with handbrakes. The engine was to stay on the train until clear of the refuge points.

After the train stopped, the rear engine was to pump the brakes off, detach and stand clear on the main line while the failed engine pushed its train into the refuge. I hoped the brakes would stay off long enough to allow this. While this was happening, I examined the loads of the two trains and found the failed train conveyed two trucks of stud bulls and a louvre van shown perishable. Fortunately they were both less than 10 vehicles from the engine. The second train conveyed 45 vehicles and consisted of a mixture of loaded wagons. I told the guard, who by this time, had realised there was a control telephone in the signal box, that when the train was in clear in the refuge, he was to attach the engine standing on the main line to the failed engine in the refuge. Then he was to bring the first 10 wagons out with him and to place them on his train on the main line and depart with the engine with the compressor failure as the second engine. The whole episode took about 60 minutes.

In mid winter of 1969, I received a panic call from the SM Mittagong. He had been advised by the guard of No 4 *Spirit of Progress* from a farmhouse that his train was derailed with three carriages badly derailed. There were people injured. The ambulance had been called from the farmhouse before the guard spoke to Mittagong. I told Mittagong to ask the guard if the Down main line was clear and when he got the answer, to tell him to go back to his train and protect it. He was not sure if the Down main line was clear. He had gone straight to the farmhouse to ring for assistance, which was fair enough. I asked the SM Mittagong to speak to the farmer to see if road access was available to the derailment. It was. I told him to advise the police. I then told Traffic Trouble Officer who ordered the breakdown gang from Sydney.

Next I told *goco* to tell his District Superintendent, whose area the derailment was in. I told Moss Vale to call the Chief Inspector. The senior officers from the Passenger Train Section were arriving and were in the control room within 10 minutes of the derailment occurring. The Chief Inspector rang from his home, wanting to know what I knew, which was not very much, I asked him to get a taxi to the scene immediately and to let us know what the situation was regarding passenger injuries and whether the Down Main was clear.

While I was speaking to the Inspector, the Chief Traffic Manager walked in, he realised who I was talking to and took the telephone off me and reiterated almost word for word what I had asked him to do. It now became an order. I told the SMs Bowral and Mittagong to get their fettling gangers to the scene. Whenever there was a major emergency, it was amazing how soon the control room filled up with people, some who needed information for their particular jobs and others out of curiosity. The CTM who was standing looking out the window into Eddy Avenue and seemingly not taking much notice suddenly said after about 15 minutes,

"Any who do not need to be in here leave now."

The place almost emptied immediately. It restored some semblance of sanity in the room. It is extremely difficult to work with about six or seven people all trying to look at the diagram and all talking at once.

Soon after the CTM arrived, the Passenger Trains Superintendent also arrived. I suggested to him that until we found out if the Down Main was clear or not, we should not let No 65 *Intercapital Daylight Express* and No 37 *Canberra Monaro Express* leave Sydney. Obviously if the Down was not clear, they would have to run via Wollongong and Unanderra to Moss Vale. At about 7.50am we had word from the ganger that the Down main line was clear. It was decided at that stage not to introduce single line working until after the passage of these two trains. No 20 *Southern Highlands Express* was terminated at Moss Vale and a bus service was provided from there.

The first indication we had of the position at this time came from the ganger. Three carriages were derailed, the middle one of the three was pointed down the embankment at an angle about 60 degrees with the main line and was leaning away from the track. It had become uncoupled from the derailed carriage next to it, but still facing in the right direction and upright. The third carriage had partly followed the second, but was upright Very soon after the Chief Inspector advised that there appeared to be no life threatening injuries, but that the ambulance had advised that a number of people from the second carriage had sustained serious injuries. Arrangements were made for the train engine to come into Mittagong with the lead portion and for a light engine to come from Berrima and to go into the section on the authority of a wrong line order and return to Bowral with the balance of the train. Coaches were ordered to transport the passengers to their destinations. The Mechanical Branch were not prepared to let the train run until all the carriages had been inspected for possible defects suffered in the accident. Single line working was introduced from Mittagong on No 37 *Canberra-Monaro Express*. About midday, after they had been inspected, the carriages of the rear portion were taken to Mittagong and coupled up with the lead portion and despatched to Sydney. They formed the *Spirit of Progress* that evening supplemented by NSWGR air-conditioned carriages.

A large private crane was hired to lift the second carriage back onto the track. It was placed on pony bogies to enable the section to be cleared. I did not see the results of the Board of Inquiry that was set up, and in fact, I did not appear before it. From the information I had gleaned, it appeared the leading bogie of the second carriage had a hot bearing and screwed off when rounding a right hand curve, which was the reason the carriage headed away from the Up main line. The leading wheels of the bogies on the lead carriage were still on the rails. The second carriage carried the rear away from the rail until the couplings gave way. It took almost 24 hours before the carriages were re-railed and the track restored.

During times of disruption like this was, the control officer is under extreme pressure. Not only does he have to make all the necessary adjustments to crews and order crews for relief purposes for those who will incur long hours unless relieved and to adjust the goods services. For example, I cancelled the first leg from Goulburn of the Marulan limestone train and also, I had to withstand the abuse of the Illawarra-Goulburn programme controller. His argument was that I could have cancelled someone else's train, and as it happened after he went home and while I was still in the room, my successor cancelled the second leg as there was no path for them. In addition, the crews were needed to provide relief for other trains.

The goods programme from Enfield was severely curtailed by the Chief Train Controller Programme. The interstate freight programme was maintained but suffered delays at Mittagong, waiting for paths vacated by passenger services. The 'cats' in the evening were the only trains that did not suffer some delay, they being delayed for only as long as it took to give the driver either a pilotman's caution ticket or for the pilotman to accompany.

The only other major incident I had in South Control also occurred at Mittagong. A wheat train conveying 29 BWH and a van hauled by two main line diesel locomotives came to grief at the Up platform when a vehicle about tenth from the engine derailed and mounted the end of the platform and finished on its side on the platform. A number of wagons behind it were also derailed. The Down main line was not fouled. Traffic Trouble Officer was advised along with District Superintendent Goulburn. The break down units were ordered. Remarkably this derailment did not cause a great deal of delay. The driver requested relief, which I arranged.

While it was coming, I had Mittagong 'sweet talk' the driver into cutting one engine off and crossing onto the Down main line and then onto the Up via the crossover at the Bowral end which was clear and attach to the rear of the train and to put those trucks not derailed onto the Down main line. I then put that engine back onto the Up main line and closed it down. Shortly after the relief crew arrived and took charge of the engine still on the Down Main. They came away with the trucks still remaining upright and lifted the wheat off the Down Main. After the examiner from Moss Vale declared the wagons fit to travel, I let the train continue, with one locomotive, on its journey.

The recording of the delays to the passenger services, blue ribbon freight services from Darling Harbour and the interstate freight expresses was an important part of the duties in South Control, as indeed they were on all Boards. To enable senior officers, when checking train delays, to quickly identify which section they were dealing with, the passenger delay sheets for each board were coloured. South was green, West was yellow, North was pink and Illawarra was blue.

The freight delays sheets were not coloured. The delays to the through passengers and freights were completed firstly with *goco* and then with *juco*. I always used the Control Board to do the delays with *goco*; some used the side telephone and ignored stations as they called. I found if the stations heard you speaking, they would not interrupt unless it was urgent, then they would come on and say 'so and so is urgent'. It was necessary to do the Junee part of the delays using the side telephone. If a station came on while I was doing them, I would put my foot on the pedal so they could hear me speaking.

So my recollections of South Control conclude. I enjoyed my time there and if I were asked which of all the train control boards I had worked that I enjoyed most, I would probably say 'South Control'.

The first Traffic Trouble office on the Third Floor, Sydney Station. Close liasion was maintained with Electrical Trouble and the large map showed where power was cut off in the overhead system in the event of irregularities. State Rail Authority of NSW.

A typical NSW train control installation in 1947. The controller is recording the movement of trains on the 24-hour graph. State Rail Authority of NSW.

SENIOR TRAIN CONTROLLER, NORTH CONTROL, SYDNEY

ABOUT June of 1966, I signed on for the 5.30pm shift in South Control. As it was the second Wednesday in the fortnight, the roster for the following fortnight had been exhibited, and I found to my surprise that I was booked on the roster to learn North Control. I had not been asked if I would like to learn the job, but I had no choice anyway. The thing that irked me was the lack of courtesy, in not giving me some warning. When I said this to the Roster Clerk, he was surprised and said,

"Why would you want prior notice?"

When I said,

"To study the Northern timetable and to prepare myself a set of running times for a walk-up start to the job."

His reply was,

"Being like that will not get you anywhere."

I did not bother to reply. I have to say that the attitude of most senior officers and administrative clerical staff had changed significantly from that of which I wrote when I was at Parkes in 1950. The attitude of this older clerk was a hangover from that period.

The Goods Train Superintendent was a despotic administrator; no one was ever right. However, he was quite approachable on the times he came into the train control boards. The Rolling Stock Superintendent, the Assistant Goods Train Superintendent, the Train Control Superintendent and the Passenger Train Superintendent and his Assistant were men who treated the individual controllers with the respect that they in return received from the controllers. Again, for those with long memories, the Passenger Train Superintendent was known as 'Poison Pen Jack'. He certainly was vituperative in his correspondence with someone who had erred. As an individual, I was always treated well by the Administration, as were the majority of the controllers. This treatment, I probably should say, was earned; those who did not receive it 'reaped as they had sown'.

As I had already learned a Sydney control board, the learning time was only six days, which for North Control was adequate. North Control was a faster job than South Control, the main reason being a greater number of trains running. The area controlled started at

Epping Signal Box and ended at Fassifern. Any subjective comparison would have shown South Control to be a much more difficult board to work. North Control was basically train working. The two areas which demanded the most attention were Gosford, because that was the point where electrification ended, and Hawkesbury River to Cowan on the Up, because about 95 per cent of all goods trains attached a bank engine to assist to Cowan. Any train experiencing delays in running, would have a compounding delay resulting much more quickly than it would on South Control. The only commercial activities between Hornsby and Fassifern that used rail transport were at Wyee and Dora Creek.

North Control was, as I have said, a fast Board in terms of the volume of trains that passed over the section. With the exception of the morning and afternoon peaks, which as far as North Control was concerned, were bounded by Flemington Goods Junction and Cowan in both directions. Goods, interstate and fast fruit trains were continually moving on the section.

Some of the areas were very difficult to get to in times of derailment and other irregularities. Access by road to stations such as Hawkesbury River and Woy Woy were very difficult. It was possible to get to Hawkesbury River by train from Hornsby in about 35 minutes; to do the same journey by road took something like an hour. Similarly, Woy Woy was about 50 minutes by train but at least an hour by road. This, of course, meant that in times of failures on the Cowan Bank, the obtaining of wrong-line working orders was done by walking, a slow process on a section where trains could bank up in almost the twinkling of an eye.

The commercial activity at Wyee was the bulk cement depot, which served the rapidly expanding building industry of the Central Coast. The regular No 269 pick-up placed the loaded cement wagons, generally from Berrima, while No 258 lifted the empty wagons to Enfield. Dora Creek was the loading point for biscuits and cereals manufactured by the Sanatarium Health Food Company at Cooranbong. The siding was on the Down which meant that No 269 placed the empty wagons and lifted the Up loaded to Broadmeadow for No 258 to lift to Enfield for transfer to their final destinations; the Down loaded going to Broadmeadow and thence onto their final destinations.

The method of safeworking from Epping to Fassifern was double line automatic. It was the first and only time that I worked a train control board with only one system of safeworking. As I did with my recollections of South Control, I will name each station on the section with a description of its activities.

Epping was the point where North Control took over goods trains from the metropolitan area. The train controller only spoke with the Epping signalman. The only exception was if there was an irregularity that demanded the attention of the officer-in-charge of the station. Getting the order of running of goods coming from Enfield, Darling Harbour,

Epping railway station in July 1984 viewed in the direction of Hornsby.

John R Newland.

Cooks River and Clyde was nigh impossible. Reliance was placed on the signalman at Epping to try and find out what trains were in what was commonly known as the 'black out area'. (This was before the advent of No 2 Goods Control which is mentioned later on).

The good signalmen at Epping, and to my mind there was only one, would ring the signal boxes at North Strathfield, Flemington Goods Junction and Chullora seeking information. The others were either allegedly 'too busy' (not all the time!) or could not be bothered. Accordingly, it was not uncommon to get a goods train travelling at full goods speed pass through Epping with a 'high-wheeler' interstate freight express right behind it. This used to annoy me because it was a matter of common sense for the signalman at Epping, when he knew the order the trains were coming in, to have the slow train put on the relief road and the fast on the main line to run past the slow one while it was travelling on the relief road. Invariably when challenged, the signalman would say he did not know in time to put the slow train on the relief road. When we got the slow train first, if it was not over 60 wagons long, which they rarely were, they would be refuged in the Down Refuge at Hornsby.

Hornsby was one of the busiest stations in the metropolitan area from a train working viewpoint. With the exception of (then) an hourly service to Cowan, every suburban passenger train either terminated at Hornsby, or went to the carriage sheds at Asquith, or they terminated and formed another service from Hornsby on either the North Shore Line or the main line towards Strathfield. A 15 minute service was provided on the North Shore Line and a 30 minute service on the main line outside peak hour. At the height of the peak hour, a train departed or passed through Hornsby every minute.

Special class signalmen were employed in the signal box and telephone boys assisted them. I have already said a Down Refuge was provided and water columns were still in existence on the Down and Up Mains. It was not uncommon for the mails in either direction to take water for a minute just to top up. This was especially so early in my time when 35-36 Classes occasionally worked through. The steam locomotive depot of the pre-electrification area was gone but there was still a turntable used to turn steam locomotives which worked the trip train on the 'Point Line'. The North Shore Line was referred to as the 'Point Line' by the old hands and seemed to be a carryover from pre-electrification days. Only one chief controller regularly used the expression and that was Max Gates.

A small amount of loaded goods traffic was received which was mainly timber and

Hornsby railway station in December 1984 viewed in the direction towards Newcastle.
John R Newland.

an odd truck of fodder in the form of chaff. Parcels traffic was much heavier, the parcel vans delivering and receiving the bulk of the traffic. Parcels traffic and luggage from North trains was unloaded from the brakevans, often causing delays due to the lengths of the interstate trains, the brakevans being off the platform on the first stop. A significant parcels office which had an entrance from the street, was situated on Platform 4.

Because it was a busy signal box, I was always content to speak, at least in the first instance, to the telephone boy. Generally if I rang the signal box, it was to find out if a train could be handled if it was allowed to keep coming and pass Hornsby at a nominated time. I invariably asked the telephone boy to ask the signalman for an answer. Sometimes the signalmen would come on the phone themselves; other times they would give the telephone boy the answer. I had no difficulty working this way and thought it was matter of courtesy to give a busy signalman the opportunity of speaking or not.

My controller colleagues almost invariably expected the signalman only to answer the control telephone and when the telephone boy did answer it, they would not speak to him other than to say, "put the signalman on". The times when I would ask whether they could handle a train were approaching peak hour or just after it. In the off-peak periods, the goods trains from the metropolitan area were slotted into margins from either North Strathfield or Epping and on the Up, the controllers directed them into paths from Gosford, Hawkesbury River or Cowan. While knowing who the signalman was at any signal box was important to the controller (to this controller anyway), and knowing who the controller was, was also important to the signalmen.

I found with the signalmen at Hornsby that they would assist me if they could. This was especially so on the Down, when they would have a goods train approaching that I had asked to refuge for a passenger train or a fast running interstate train. If they found either train had been delayed, they would come on say,

"I have so-and-so approaching but there is no sign yet of the train you want him in for."

Warning me of this often allowed the goods train to be advanced to Hawkesbury River or even to Gosford ahead of the train for which they were to be refuged.

I have made mention of 'telephone boys': they were employed in major signal boxes. Their function was to attend the telephones, take messages for the signalmen and to record the passing, arrival and departure and terminating times of each train in the Train Register Book. Many of the senior signalmen in the metropolitan area served times as telephone boys.

Cowan was the northern limit of the metropolitan area, and was little more than a village in 1966. It was important as a safeworking station because it was on top of the Cowan Bank. The 1 in 40 gradient which constituted the bank between Hawkesbury River and

Cowan, was one of the most difficult climbs in the State, so much so in fact that the usual latitude of five tons over the fixed load for a section was not permitted. Bank engines were employed on almost every train, the exceptions being the *Brisbane Limited* and the *Gold Coast Overnight Expresses* when worked by two locomotives and often the *North Coast Mail* and the *North West Mail* when they were under 265 tons. An Up Refuge was provided at Cowan, enabling the bank engines to be detached in the refuge if a priority train was running close behind. In foggy and wet weather, trains of all descriptions often lost time due to slipping on the wet rails, and as a result copious amounts of sand were deposited on the rails.

In the early days, a truck called a scrubber truck was locomotive-hauled over the section to remove the sand from the rails on a weekly basis. This practice ceased with the advent of dieselisation and the electrification to Gosford. The notion that this type of engine power would not deposit sand on the rails was ill conceived, because sand is still needed to be used. The caking of sand was a cause for concern as it made steel to steel contact of the wheel on the rail faulty, thus interfering with the electrical track circuits that controlled the signalling.

The bank engines always ran back light engine to Hawkesbury River. In my time they were always 46 Class electric locomotives. In the steam days, it must have been most unpleasant running back tender first in the early hours of the morning. The bank

Cowan railway station in November 1983 viewed in the direction of Hawkesbury River.
John R Newland.

engines were critical to the smooth running of the Up Goods programme, and there were times when it was necessary to hold a goods train back at Cowan to get a bank engine back to Hawkesbury for the next Up train, especially so, around 5.00am when a delay of 10 to 15 minutes to a train would mean missing the last path ahead of the peak hour.

Hawkesbury River Station served the township known as Brooklyn which was situated on the banks of the beautiful Hawkesbury River. This tourist attraction is easily accessible by rail and also by road via a circuitous route from the Pacific Highway. Cruises on the river, together with boating, fishing and other water sports, took crowds there on weekends, especially in the prewar and postwar eras. There was no goods traffic to speak of; anything in the goods line was usually a small consignment from a Darling Harbour louvre van that served all stations to Fassifern, other than Gosford, on No 259 pick-up.

The station was situated at the very beginning of the Cowan Bank. In fact, the Sydney end of the platform was where the climb commenced. While it was not a concern for stopping trains, the 60km/h speed limit on the curve at the Sydney end of the platform stopped drivers of through trains from getting a fast run at the bank. Down and Up Refuge Loops were provided and both were used on a regular basis. The Up Refuge had

Hawkesbury River railway station in November 1983 viewed in the direction of Cowan, which is some 187.8m higher in elevation and at a distance of 8.5km away.   *John R Newland.*

two sets of points off the main line which permitted either two trains being stowed or provided for one exceeding 50 vehicles long.

The refuge held a total of about 100 vehicles; so if two trains were to be stowed, it was the practice to run into the refuge from the set of points nearest the Gosford end with the first train and then set back into the Gosford end of the refuge, which was a dead end, clear of the admittance points. The second train was then run into the refuge in the normal manner. This was not a regular happening and only occurred when emergencies were being encountered on the Cowan Bank.

In the afternoon peak hour during my stay in North Control, a new timetable provided for a fast passenger to run via the refuge to pass an unloading stopping commuter passenger. The stopping train was tabled there for four minutes and with few exceptions, this was the time it was there. If the following train was five minutes late from Hornsby, I would keep the stopping train ahead of it into Gosford, where it terminated. The time actually required to unload the passengers was a minute, which meant I had a nine-minute margin, which would be reduced to six minutes by the fast train running through Hawkesbury River on the main line. The stopping train conveyed passengers by the hundreds for Woy Woy. It was a remarkable thing, but if the train ran ahead of the through train, it seemed that the passengers got off at Woy Woy in much less time than they normally took. I used to think that told me something, that is, they appreciated getting home that bit earlier and they co-operated so that their train would not delay the fast train behind it.

Facing and trailing crossovers were provided at the Gosford end. Two bank engine stabling roads was situated between the two main lines, one at the Sydney end of the platform, the other at the Gosford end of the yard. The dedicated bank engine crews were all Gosford men, who either travelled passenger to Hawkesbury River or were attached to their first bank at Gosford. The ideal was to get four banks out of each set of men per shift.

This was very difficult to do, especially with two of the crews who knew every legitimate trick (and some that were not), which would cause delay. From the time a train to be banked stopped, it was allowed seven minutes to attach the bank and move off. It was rare to get two particular drivers moving in less than 12 minutes. The determination of these two crews was never to work more than three banks. They rarely did. All the controllers issued locomotive debits slips on numerous occasions, without any result. We complained both verbally and by correspondence, the more correspondence one driver got, the more difficult he became.

At certain times in the early morning when the two bank engines were available, I used to send the second bank to Gosford, attaching it there to the train engine. This meant the saving of time at Hawkesbury River, and in some instances, allowed a train into the metropolitan area ahead of the peak hour. The bank engine drivers were loath to return to Gosford for obvious reasons. While I had complaints from drivers, not once did I have one refuse to go. The drivers of trains to which they were attached from Gosford still had control of the train, the units working separately to Cowan, where it was simply a matter of lifting the coupling pin to detach.

Another ploy we used when it was getting close to peak hour, was to confer with the Centralised Motive Power Control (CMPC) engine clerk with a view to sending the bank engine through from Gosford to the metropolitan area. The standing time saved by allowing the train to run into the metropolitan area amounted to about two hours. Not only were savings made in non-productive time, the earlier availability of engine power also had the effect often of allowing the metropolitan freight programme to be met. This was mostly achievable, because as peak hour approached, only one bank was required and that was generally for No 2 *Brisbane Limited* or No 4 *Gold Coast Overnight Express*, if they were worked by a single unit. The Electric Engine Clerk in CMPC often arranged for the bank engine to work through to Sydney on No 2.

I found the staff at Hawkesbury was very difficult to deal with. With the exception of the station master, they all had a reluctance to answer the telephone. They had what would today probably be described as an attitude problem. I had a strong suspicion that amongst them, there was one who drank too much, at least off the job, and who because of tiredness and irritability found performing the normal duties of an assistant station master at Hawkesbury River (which were not particularly onerous, but did demand constant attention) just beyond his reach. My suspicions regarding this officer would be confirmed on the nights he arrived for work on the backshift fully rested. I also discovered in a roundabout way that one of them was having marital problems and this may well have explained his constant surliness. It came as no surprise a number of years later to find the first assistant station master, then at another location, reduced in grade because of his constant failure to sign on duty at the appointed time. I should make it clear that I only had suspicions of him and that his speech was always normal.

In the twelve months I was in North Control, I only had one failure on the Cowan Bank. A train conveying perishable traffic departed from Hawkesbury River around 3.00am after attaching the bank engine. The train moved off the Hawkesbury River track indicator in the normal running time. After it was about ten minutes overdue onto Cowan's track, the ASM Cowan advised me of the fact. I had four goods trains of varying descriptions between Hawkesbury River and Fassifern, one of these having departed Gosford conveying a load of wire for Ashfield.

I advised Hawkesbury River to put this train in the bottom end of his refuge and have the locomotive ready for assistance if it was needed. At that point there was nothing on the Down, a train having passed Hawkesbury River just after the failed train departed. After about 20 minutes, Cowan received a call from a telephone attached to an automatic signal from the observer of the train engine to say that the diesel engine was a total failure, with ground relays (electrical malfunctions which caused an indication to the driver via the driver's control panel that his locomotive had become defective).

He advised that the bank engine had left for Cowan with a driver's wrong line order issued by the driver of the diesel locomotive, for the bank engine to return with an assistant engine. By this time, a Down interstate freight had departed Hornsby. I had no chance of providing assistance from the Cowan end. I was also alarmed that they had left the dead diesel engine on the train, because by my calculations that would have put the train in overload for two engines.

I instructed Cowan to stop the Down train and direct the driver to stop where the guard of the failed train was protecting his train (or should have been in accordance with Rule 243) and to direct the guard to accompany his train to Hawkesbury River. I then instructed Cowan to send the bank engine back to the failed train with the driver's wrong-line order as his authority to proceed in the wrong running direction. The safeworking instructions were that the driver who issued the wrong line order, also cancelled it when it was returned to him. I reminded Cowan to remind the bank engine driver to see this was done. He was also directed to advise Cowan when he was again attached to the failed engine.

Having done this, I directed Hawkesbury River to prepare a signalman's wrong-line order for the driver of the goods train stowed in the refuge, to proceed with his locomotive only to the disabled train, accompanied by the guard of the failed train to pilot him onto the rear of the failed train and return with it to Hawkesbury River. During the time the guard was at Hawkesbury River, I asked the ASM to check the total tonnage of the train. With the diesel locomotive's dead weight, it would have been over the load for two engines from where it was situated on the bank. It was 4.30am when the disabled train finally arrived back.

The dead engine was detached into the engine siding and the train departed at 4.45am. I was not able to get another engine for the wire train, so the train crew went home passenger back to Broadmeadow. The wire train was lifted with another engine and crew during the day. By cancelling the wire train, I was able to maintain the bank engine programmes and still land the trains that had left Broadmeadow when the failure occurred into the metropolitan area ahead of the peak hour.

To the uninitiated among my readers, the then safeworking regulations provided that if a driver on a double line section became disabled and unable to continue and was of the opinion that relief would be available from the signal box ahead, he sent his fireman forward walking with a driver's wrong-line order. That order assured the signalman at the signal box that the train was stationary and that the driver would not allow it to be moved. If relief was available, the fireman with the wrong-line order piloted the driver of the relief engine onto the failed train. If an engine had become a partial failure and was capable of hauling portion of the load to the signal box in advance, stowing the front portion and then returning for the rear portion, he had to obtain a wrong line order from the guard, authorising him to return for the portion of the train remaining.

If, after consultation, the driver and guard agreed relief would be available from the station in the rear, it was the guard's duty to protect his train with detonators placed in accordance with Rule 243. (The same rule applied to the fireman when going forward). The guard was then required to walk to the station in the rear. If relief was available and the decision was made to haul the train back, the signalman would provide the relief driver with a signalman's wrong-line order authorising him to return the train to his station on the authority of the order. The guard returned with the relief engine, acting as a pilot to the driver.

If it was decided to propel the train from the rear out of the section to the advance signal box, no order was required from the signalman, the guard piloting the relief engine to his train. If this happened, no train was permitted to pass the disabled train while it was being propelled from the section to the signal box ahead. It will be obvious that a failure in a long section would cause lengthy delays while the fireman or guard walked, sometimes in the dark for perhaps miles, on rough and uneven permanent way. This was, of course, why I directed the Down train to stop and pick up the guard and take him to Hawkesbury River. The delays to the interstate freight were readily explainable under these circumstances.

In late 1966, the section of track between Hawkesbury River and Cowan on the Up, as was with most track in New South Wales at that time, was in need of urgent maintenance. The Chief Civil Engineer's Way and Works Branch wanted possession of the Up track for 24 hours from 9.00pm on a Saturday night to 9.00pm on a Sunday night. The Electrical Branch decided if this was to be so, that they could also work on the overhead wiring and required the power be switched off for both tracks. Both requests were strongly resisted by the Traffic Branch saying too much disruption would occur to normal services. They were overruled from the Commissioner's Office and possession and power off was authorised.

This was, to my knowledge the first possession issued for an extended period. Previously, Ways and Works had to operate under the 'as traffic permits' theory. With the advent of expensive machinery which could re-condition track, it was folly for the Branch not to have time to work on the track. In the balance of time to my retirement, track possession became a regular feature of weekend working, with possession lasting whole weekends. The regular services were cancelled, and buses used in lieu. I state this here to show the symbolic importance of this possession, a precursor to events that I will deal with more fully, further into my autobiography.

The Passenger Trains Manager instructed his timetabling staff to prepare a timetable for the passage of the normal weekend trains over the Down line between these two stations. He refused even to consider a reduced service or to consider amalgamating some of the Gosford services. The Chief Train Controller's programme in Sydney realised the position and tabled on the backshift only No 409, the perishable interstate freight.

Not so Newcastle. Despite the Special Train Notice specifically stating the programme was to be reduced to perishable trains only, they set up almost a full programme. The track possession was to a point at the Newcastle end of Hawkesbury River platform, including the crossover points. This crossover that allowed Up trains to run directly onto the Down Main was not available, which meant that Up trains had to use the crossover that a Down train would use from the Down to the Up. In short, Up trains had to reach a point on the Up line where the brakevan was clear of the crossover points. The train then backed onto the Down Main.

I signed on duty at 11.30pm on the Saturday night. The first thing I did after taking charge of the Control Board, was to get the Special Train Notice (STN) and pencil the trains onto the diagram. I found that if the trains ran as the STN showed, the section would be continuously occupied from 4.00am to 9.00am. After examination, I believed the STN timetable was unrealistic and that they had not allowed sufficient time at Hawkesbury River for any Up train requiring to crossover. At 12.30am, I formed the opinion that at best the last early morning train, the *North Coast Overnight Express*, would be anything up to an hour late arriving Cowan.

I told Newcastle Control that I would not accept any goods train after 3.00am, irrespective of what it conveyed, for at least 8 hours. This brought a war of words from him. He told me I would get them and that was it. I told that him the three trains that were already between Broadmeadow and Gosford would not get through and that two of them would be stowed at Gosford and the third at Wyong, and that if he wanted to send a train knowing this, I could not stop him. There were, I informed him, two trains between Gosford and Hawkesbury River. I assured him it would stand at Morisset at least until the Up road was restored. He generally reflected on my ability and of anyone who worked in Sydney, so I suggested to him that he obtain a copy of the STN and read it. He put the Up goods programme on hold.

Two goods trains were in the Gosford area when I signed on duty. I found a number of things my predecessor had done, which with the kindest thought, could only be described as diabolical. He had arranged for both the trains at Gosford to be banked with the engines returning to Gosford from Cowan. This was unbelievable. How he thought I was going to work the bank engines back to Hawkesbury River over the single line working, I will never know. I understood then why he was in such a hurry to go home. I actually arrived for work at 11.10pm, when he asked me as I walked in,

"Can I catch the 11.20pm train home?"

Muggins agreed. I dropped onto this pretty well straight away and arranged for the diesel bank engines to work through to Enfield. This gave me two crews available at Gosford if I needed them. I then arranged for the engine roster clerk to send two engines light attached on passenger trains to Gosford to replace them. I was not concerned about engines because I knew I was going to have the engines of the two trains I had ordered stowed at Gosford available in an emergency. I arranged with Metropolitan Goods Control to have the stowed trains depart Gosford after the track had been restored on the Monday morning.

In addition to the two Up trains having to traverse the single line, a Down freight train, which had been timetabled for 9.00pm through Cowan but was nearly three hours late and was still to pass Cowan. Behind this train was the last passenger for the evening. I elected to let the passenger follow the goods although it meant delaying the first of the Up Goods at Hawkesbury River. In hindsight, I was pleased I did. From the time the Down passenger passed Hawkesbury River until the goods train had backed from the Up Main to the Down Main and had taken the authority from the pilotman, was 20 minutes. I knew then I was in for a rough night. The following goods train, which was at Hawkesbury River's Up Accept when the first train departed on the Down Line, was not ready to depart when it arrived at Cowan. I had hoped at least that I could get a train onto the Up Main while another was travelling to Cowan and thus be ready to depart. In each case, all night, up to another 10 minutes was taken.

About 2.00am I checked to see where No 409, Interstate Perishable was. It was due over Epping at 2.15am, but at that time, it had not left Homebush Saleyards from where it was due to depart at 1.45am. The forecast was for at least 90 minutes late. To be able to get it through the single line, I had to have No 409 at Cowan no later than 3.45am. I advised my 'friendly' counterpart in *neco* (Newcastle Control) No 409 was forecast 90 minutes late and, if it maintained 90 minutes, I would get it through and gave him a time at Fassifern. I also told him if it was more than 100 minutes late, it would sit at Hornsby until 9.00am. He told me I was not game to do that. I told him to wait and see for himself.

No 409 passed Epping at 3.30am. When it did, I rang the signalman at Hornsby and told him to refuge the train and tell the driver he would not leave there until No 4 *Gold Coast Overnight Express* left Hawkesbury River in about five hours time. I ordered relief for the crew from the Enfield Loco and guards' roster clerks. I advised *neco* of the fact; he said nothing over the control board, but rang me on the side phone and abused me because he had to re-set the train all the way to Brisbane. I told him,

"Tough!"

And I hung up. This train controller will be mentioned again before I finish with North Control.

As I feared, the time allowed at Hawkesbury River for the passenger trains on the

STN was significantly less than was taken by each train. It was necessary for the points to be clipped in the forward direction on the Down main line. Again, for the uninitiated among my readers, when a passenger train conveying passengers is required to pass over points in any direction that are not protected by a facing point lock, the points must be secured with a point clip, a gadget which passes under the rail and clasps onto the point of the rail and is then screwed up until the movable clasp is tightened onto the stock rail, thus preventing any movement of the points.

Following regulations took 10 minutes each time the points were clipped. The trains thus took 10 minutes for point clipping, at least 10 minutes to back across and five minutes for the pilotman to give the driver the token that he was to take. It was a block section to Cowan, the timetable section stating that a block post would not be provided in the section, it being considered unnecessary. This was probably so, but not for the reasons that the timetable section expounded. It was taking longer to get trains ready at Hawkesbury River than it was for them to run the section to Cowan.

The times varied. The first mail train took 35 minutes to get ready, the driver on arrival getting off his engine to argue with the ASM that he was not going to propel a passenger train for anyone. The ASM contacted me and said the driver refused to propel onto the Down Main. I told the ASM to direct the driver to carry out the instructions issued by the Chief Traffic Manager, and that the STN that had a clause authorising propelling in station limits. The driver then demanded to sight the STN (he should have had one). Something like 10 minutes was wasted which compounded into about 40 minutes before the final passenger left Hawkesbury River, later in the morning. My original estimate of No 4 being up to an hour late was 30 minutes out, it was 90 minutes late through Cowan, although some of that was due to the late running of the train itself.

The proverbial hit 'the fan' on Monday morning when the Passenger Train Manager got his delays. Despite the fact that I had stuck very carefully to running the trains the way STN directed and had taken the precaution of writing this into the delay reports, he called for the diagram to see how many freight trains had been involved. He also wanted the train controller for a statement in his office at 9.00am. I was home in bed. The Assistant Train Control Superintendent, of whom I have been mildly critical, took the diagram to him personally and pointed out to him that No 409 had stood for over 5 hours at Hornsby and that no goods trains had been involved.

It transpired that the Goods Train Superintendent was having apoplexy over No 409 and had called for the diagram first. The Assistant Train Control Superintendent had taken it to him. He too wanted the train controller's blood. They were in his office when the Passenger Train Manager rang. On the Tuesday morning, before I went home, the Assistant Train Control Superintendent, who was in early, saw me and told me the Passenger Trains Manager and the Goods Train Superintendent had had words over the working, but both agreed the train controller had carried out the directions of the STN and was therefore blameless.

I stated this working was symbolic. It turned out to be so in more ways than one. The Timetable Section was hauled over the coals for the STN that they had put out. I do not claim that this track possession was the only one which brought about the changes to the Timetable Section that were made, or that consultation between Heads of Branches had not agreed that total possession was desirable with the advancing technology being used by the Chief Civil Engineer's Branch. Arrangements, however, were made shortly after for a special group to timetable events such as this.

They went to a room of their own with a senior timetables clerk in charge. This room became known as the 'Ballast Room' and, as I indicated, wielded immense power up to and after I retired many years later. They said what trains could run, and nominated those services which had to be cancelled. They also arranged for and timetabled buses that ran in lieu of passenger services.

Wondabyne was an unattended station with very short platforms on the Up and Down sides. It was also an area where sandstone was quarried. To accommodate the loading of wagons, generally 'S' trucks, a Down Siding was situated on the Gosford end of the platform. Blocks of sandstone weighing 5-6 tons were lifted into the trucks with a crane. Very few people used the platforms; those who did had week-enders across the water and went to them by boat. There was only one house, between the line and the water, very close to the line. A somewhat eccentric old lady lived there, waving at every passenger train as it went past.

Gosford was the catchment station in the 1960s for the commuting Central Coast work force. It was not until the extension of the electrification to Wyong and subsequently Newcastle that the pressure eased at Gosford. Even then, the movement by so many people to live in the region, seeking cheaper land, which was served by a fast electric train service to the city, made for a population explosion.

Gosford passengers were the new interurban trains, known as the *Blue Goose* because of the colouring and shape of the fronts of them. In addition to these, three electric loco-hauled non-air conditioned carriage trains departed Gosford each morning. These carriages were reasonably comfortable and were gas heated. The trains consisted of eight carriages and conveyed approximately 500 passengers. With the number of passengers requiring tickets, especially on Monday mornings for weekly ticket sales, Gosford booking office was a very busy place. Only a small amount of goods traffic was dealt with, because by this time, the Darling Harbour traffic came by road directly to the stores. Gosford was under the 50 mile limit and even in the 1950s, most of the wholesale merchandise was transported by road.

Wondabyne railway station in February 1985 viewed in the Gosford direction. This is an isolated platform with no other public access. Its main scenic 'attraction' is that it is situated alongside a tidal tributary of the Hawkesbury River.   *John R Newland.*

Gosford railway station in May 1984 viewed in the direction towards Sydney.
       John R Newland.

A signal box that pre-electrification was reasonably busy, became very busy post-electrification when almost every goods train in both directions changed engines. One or two interstate bogie express freight services which commenced from Cooks River were diesel hauled, these same services returning from Clapham or Acacia Ridge ran through with diesel engines to Cooks River. With the exception of the Up *Newcastle Flyers* (worked by 38 Classes to Gosford), every Newcastle Up passenger terminated at Gosford and the passengers changed to interurbans.

These trains which were worked in the main by 35 Classes with some 36 Classes, returned to Newcastle with passengers off the terminating interurbans. There was a service to Newcastle about every two hours. In the afternoon, when the Newcastle suburban passengers services became less frequent, the 600 Class diesel cars ran a service to Gosford, where they connected with an interurban arriving at Gosford from Sydney around 7.30pm.

Gosford was the key to the northern line working. A CMPC Engine Clerk situated in the Train Control Superintendent's Office, Sydney was responsible for allocating and the rostering of twenty 46 Class electric locomotives. It was the responsibility of the North Engine Clerk to balance the engines arriving into Gosford on the Up Goods services onto the Down services. These engines were a mixture of 35, 36, and 38 Class passenger, and 50, 59 and 60 Class freight steam engines. Mingled with these would be some main line diesels, especially 43 Classes and some 48 Classes. As in South Control, these engines all had different running times and loads. It follows, therefore, that the train controller had to be very careful when 35 and 36 Classes were rostered on to Down goods trains, brought in by 46 Classes, that he did not get over the load for the passenger engines running at what was known as 'three-quarters' speed.

It was my practice, and that of most of my colleagues, to compile an engine balance at the beginning of each shift and to go through that balance with the Mechanical Branch Roster Clerk at Gosford. The main purpose, from my standpoint, was to see that I had an engine or engines to cover each train arriving and departing Gosford in both directions during my shift. The fact that the engine I rostered onto a specific train at the beginning of a shift might not work the train it was set on, did not matter. The late or out-of-course running of the Up trains especially meant that as engines arrived, were turned, re-prepared and became available, they were utilised on the next Down train.

Gosford yard had an Up Refuge Loop and Up Siding from which an engine could be changed; and a Down Refuge Loop, and two Down sidings, one of which was wired for electric engines. The locomotive depot was situated on the northern end of the yard, if it could be called depot. The District Locomotive Engineer (DLE) and roster clerk worked from demountables. A siding, known as the Garratt siding, was provided for 60 Classes and whatever preparation, if any, they required was done in this siding.

The turntable was near the end of the platforms on the Down side on the Newcastle end. Facilities were provided for the overnight stowing of carriages from the terminating locomotive-hauled services in what was known as the 'Race Course' siding, (which from observation should have been known as the water sidings, because they backed right up to the Brisbane Waters). These sidings held three normal passenger trains. The interurbans were stowed on the Up side in the electric sidings, which were fitted with decanting equipment. Three platforms were available, the Up and Down through platforms and Platform No 3 which was one side of the Down platform.

As a general rule, the Newcastle trains starting from Gosford were placed on this platform, so those passengers changing only had to walk across the platform. The Up interurbans from Gosford often departed from the Down platform on which they had arrived, crossing onto the Up Main via a crossover on the Sydney end of the platform.

I recall one evening when the 600 Class diesel cars forming No 141X to Newcastle failed on arrival at Gosford. I made arrangements for the locomotive-hauled cars which were to form 'the all stations to Newcastle' to be made ready as a replacement. The passengers were in the relief train when the signalman advised me that the 600 Classes were now OK. I directed he transfer the passengers back over the platform into them. They no sooner got into them than I was advised that they had again failed, back went the passengers to the relief train. Before they had got over the bridge, the ASM this time came on and said the 600 Classes were going again.

By this time I was getting frustrated. If I was, what about the passengers? Because of the difference in speeds, I decided to give the 600 Classes one more go. It was the wrong decision; they got into the 600 Classes, went about 10 yards and stopped. I told the signalman to get them into the relief carriages and to get rid of it. The passengers were nearly into the carriages when the ASM again came on and said the diesel cars were again running. I told him,

"No way am I going to allow those passengers out of the relief train. Get rid of it."

I told them if the Mechanical Branch was satisfied the cars were running OK, they could use them on the all stations to Newcastle. This happened. Complaints were made by the Mechanical Branch over the working. In my reply, I stated that I was not prepared to see the passengers change trains four times. As it was they were delayed 30 minutes. With a light load, the 43 Class diesel that hauled the carriages ran almost the 600 Class timetable to Newcastle.

At 3.15am on a weekday morning, I was advised by the Gosford signalman that he had the fireman of No 675 Down Goods speaking from a telephone attached to an automatic signal. He advised that the train had pulled the trailing drawhook out of an empty MRC meat wagon about five vehicles from the brakevan on the 1 in 40 grade on Wondabyne bank. The train was worked by an electric locomotive and was 55 vehicles long. I straight away told the signalman to direct the fireman to obtain a guard's wrong-line order and to take the front portion of the train to Gosford. Fortunately, as it transpired for me, I wrote in the remark column of the diagram the time that Gosford rang me and also the time and the fact that I had directed the train come forward with a guard's wrong-line order.

I was very quick to arrange this working, because already in the section between Hawkesbury River and Wondabyne was an empty 600 Class diesel unit and another goods train. The 600 Class diesel was not suitable to propel the brakevan and remaining five vehicles to Gosford. I therefore had little option but to clear the section from the Gosford end. I was also mindful, even at 3.15am, the first commuter passenger was due from Gosford at 5.50am.

After giving the fireman the directions at 3.15am, no word had been heard by 4.00am from the crew nor had the engine appeared on Gosford's track. I directed Gosford to tell the driver of an Up Goods train to stop and tell the crew to get to Gosford with the front portion. At 4.20am another Up train was due to leave Gosford. Having still not heard from the crew of No 675, I directed Gosford to tell the guard and driver of this train to instruct the crew to come into Gosford. Having a suspicious mind, and knowing the guard from earlier experiences in the West, I directed the guard of the Up train to make sure that the guard of 675 had wrong line order forms, and if necessary to supply him with some as I suspected he may not have had any.

I had called the Chief Inspector Hornsby, who did not respond and then the District Locomotive Engineer Gosford, who I wanted to accompany the engine back to the train to assist with the attachment of a tail rope to form a makeshift coupling. The front portion of the train eventually appeared on Gosford's track indicator at 4.40am arriving Gosford 4.50am. After the train had left, the guard spoke to Gosford and said they had spent time trying to attach the tail rope to the MRC, but they had broken it twice. The tonnage a single tail rope could haul on a 1 in 40 grade according to the General Appendix Part I was 120 tons, If tonnage above that, the tail rope was to be doubled. A maximum of 240 tons could then be hauled in this manner. It can be said that both the driver and guard should have known this. However, I would wager no more than 10 per cent of drivers and guards would have known or remembered.

I arranged with the ASM Gosford to send two tail ropes back with the engine. The engine together with the DLE and two tail ropes departed on the Down road back to the train at 5.05am. The next indication that the train was moving came at 5.45am when the Down track indicator lit up. Because tail ropes were being used, I played safe and directed the Up passenger not depart until No 675 had finally arrived complete, delaying it for five minutes.

During the whole of the proceedings, both the Chief Train Controller Programme and the Trouble Officer were either in North Control together or singly and were aware of what was happening. I appreciated the advice of the Trouble Officer, nominally in charge of the floor at this time, because I had not long been in North Control and was somewhat unfamiliar with the area. To have endeavoured to use wrong-line orders from Hawkesbury River to haul the last goods into the section back to Hawkesbury River, with the engine of a Down train refuged in the loop 20 minutes after I was advised of the failure, and then get a wrong line order to the driver of the 600 Class from the signalman and have him change ends and drive back to the home signal and be piloted from the signal into Hawkesbury River, by the ASM would have taken far too much time.

Because of the long delays that occurred, and the time it took to clear the section, the Goods Train Superintendent ordered an inquiry into the working. I was about the last witness called. The first thing the Traffic Inspector conducting the inquiry said to me, as he pointed to my remarks on the diagram,

"This is what saved you."

Before the event came to a conclusion, I had filled the whole remark column on the right side of the diagram. The driver and guard were eventually held responsible for the time taken to clear the section and the Mechanical Branch accepted responsibility for the draw gear breakage, it being nearly rusted through before it left Enfield on that and many other occasions.

Another feature of the morning's proceeding was the number of signal boxes and stations asking this new train controller mundane questions in an endeavour to get him to 'bite', a pastime apparently used quite successfully on previous occasions. Two stations in particular, Wyee and Morisset had not spoken to me on backshift in the time I had been on North. Wyee started and at about 3.45am asked me the time. I told him straight off, giving him no chance to come back at me. Then Morisset asked how the *Brisbane Limited* was running and I told him. Fifteen minutes later he asked how the *Brisbane Express* was running. I told him without comment.

The next morning when things were reasonably quiet, I checked with the adjoining stations and found that Wyee and Morisset signal boxes were both in automatic (switched out). I rang Wyee twice and got no response. I then rang again and hung onto the ring key making it ring continuously. When he finally answered the telephone, I told him the time. Next Morisset, with the same procedure before he answered the phone, I told him that the *Brisbane Limited* was on time. I waited half an hour and rang him again. This time I told him that the *Motorail* was on time. The message was received at all points and during the time I was there, I did not get another frivolous call when I was in trouble.

I found the signalmen at Gosford good to work with. By keeping them well appraised with what was coming towards them and advising them quickly of any amendments to the engine changes, they were able to plan their own work and I felt that at the same time, they were having an input into what was going on. In the normal course of events, we had very little contact with the station officers. On Monday mornings only, the 5.50am from Gosford commenced as empty cars from Newcastle. On one occasion, an engine failure at Newcastle caused it to be about 50 minutes late. As soon as I found out I advised the ASM Gosford to arrange to put the cars on hand for the second locomotive-hauled train onto the platform and use them on the 5.50 am and get it on time. He seemed reluctant to do this. I asked him,

"Why the hesitancy?"

"What about the passengers from Newcastle going through on the 5.50am?" He said.

I said they are advertised as 'empty cars'. He did not believe me, saying,

"I have been here for years and did not know that."

I knew for two reasons; the first staring me in the face on the diagram, for the cars were shown as 120E/C, the second reason was that while I was learning, I wrote in my note book the working of the car sets from Gosford. Being a bit concerned about his saying that it conveyed passengers, I asked him had he ever seen passengers on it. He had to admit he had not. I was not about to alter my decision to despatch the 5.50am on time. The whole exchange with the ASM made me wonder, as it seemed incredible an ASM on his own admittance, had been at Gosford for a long time and did not know the car rostering. The second thing I wondered about was what he thought he could do for passengers on it anyway. They certainly were not going to leave Gosford any earlier than the carriages they were in.

We had to work closely with the Mechanical Branch chargemen, especially when a train on the Up ran out of course and consideration was being given to changing the engine balance to maintain the Down programme. There were occasions when 2 x 46 Class engines worked Down trains to be met at Gosford either by a 60 Class Garratt locomotive or two freight locomotives off separate Up arriving trains. It sometimes meant the 1000 ton load Down train had to be set aside at Gosford to await the 60 Class, this in turn was likely to incur long hours for the locomotive crew.

Another train which was a regular feature of the late afternoon working was the coal loaded from Metropolitan Colliery near Helensburgh. On occasions, this was hauled by 3 x 46 Class with 1800 tons and was met usually by a 60 Class and a freight engine. (Yes, coals to Newcastle!) The provision of relief for the crews was the responsibility of the Mechanical Branch. However, the controller had a responsibility also to ensure excessive hour cases did not occur. The 60 Classes did not require, as much time at Gosford to re-prepare as the conventional engines, because they did not need to turn and, aside from taking water, needed no other preparation. In addition, they were able to travel Broadmeadow to Broadmeadow without de-ashing the fire. I should qualify that by saying, that it depended on what work the locomotive had done before leaving Broadmeadow, because I found if I was tight for engines, mostly they were de-ashed, but if the engines were loose, they seemed not to. Perhaps I am being cynical!

Both Up and Down trains requiring engine changes only, which was mostly the case, as not many trains other than the pick-up shunted at Gosford, were allowed 15 minutes to change engines and for the crews to transfer from the electric engine arriving on the Down to the changeover engine, which at that time were mostly steam. The same applied on the Up, where 15 minutes was allowed to transfer from the Up arriving engine to the 46 Class electric. If the crew had not had crib another 15 minutes was added to the time.

A good working relationship with the controllers in *neco* made the job easier for both parties. The accurate forecasting to them of the Down trains, especially on afternoon shifts with trains that required engine changes at Broadmeadow to head either to Brisbane or the North West with interstate or Darling Harbour next day delivery traffic, enabled them to set their crews, to adjust their engine balances and most importantly, to keep the extremely busy Broadmeadow yards running smoothly. In turn, their forecasting of Up trains at Fassifern was important, for it was from this information that engine balances were made at Gosford.

There was only one person in *neco* who would not forecast. He was the most disliked train controller in the State without a shadow of a doubt. He was disliked by staff in his control area, his colleagues in *neco* and Sydney and finally by the Administration. He was the only other person I met in my entire career who had the same attitude and outlook as the Station Master at Eugowra. He was open to no reason at all and could in fact be described as intractable. He would not forecast trains, but demanded them. If by chance a forecast went bad or was not amended, he would report it.

Because there were more passenger trains and equally as many Blue Ribbon and interstate trains as South Control, the train delay sheets took much more time. Again a good working relationship with the opposite number in *neco* made them easy. I used to work a lot with a controller who liked to do the delays on the side telephone. This was different to the method I had adopted in South Control, where we would ignore the calls on the board unless we knew they demanded attention. I was not so sure, but went along with him, because using this method, we were able to do them more quickly. I never met him even though I worked for twelve months with him, more than any other controller in Newcastle. He was an older man and retired shortly after I left North Control. He was the exact opposite of his colleague.

The formulating of the delays with that 'friend' was purgatory. He was difficult to get to answer when we latched onto *neco*, but if he called us and there was not an immediate response, the fact was recorded on the delay sheets. He demanded 'I's' dotted and 'T's' crossed. But if he was queried on a delay, he ignored the query and continued on or latched off. Sydney controllers regularly wrote him up on their delay sheets to no avail.

Ourimbah in the mid 1960s, had quite a large produce store which received truck loads of hay and chaff into the siding on the Up side. A crossover enabled Down trains to shunt. Up and Down Refuge Loops were provided, but were seldom used. I only recall using them once, when an engine failed on the main line at Gosford, and I could see a bank up at Gosford so I refuged a goods train to allow a passenger to pass. An assistant station master on day work manned the station, weekdays only.

Tuggerah was a very important safeworking station prior to the extension of electrification to Wyong and subsequently Newcastle. At that time very little passenger traffic used Tuggerah. Up and Down Refuge Loops were provided which held 75 vehicles and a level crossing was situated at the northern end of the platform. The turnout into the Down refuge was on the northern or Wyong end of the platform. This meant that when a Down train was refuged at Tuggerah only the brakevan tail lights at night or the brakevan in daylight was visible to the signal box. These refuges were used more than any other between Gosford and Broadmeadow, for the purposes of allowing faster trains, both passenger and interstate goods, to pass slower trains and for crib purposes.

Because of the refuge situation at Tuggerah, when an Up train was required to have crib, the ASM at Wyong was required to show the 'crib board' to the approaching train. This enabled the crew, if they wished, to stop and obtain hot water. It was the controller's duty to advise both Wyong and Tuggerah of his requirements. The running time for a full goods train between the two stations was four minutes. The train crews did not like having crib at Tuggerah as they preferred to go on to Gosford where the change engine and crib time was 30 minutes, which gave them more time to have their meal.

The train controller had to be careful when directing crews to crib at Tuggerah to see that they had been on duty more than three hours. The Enginemen's Award provided that they have their crib between the third and fifth hour. If they had not been on duty the required time at Tuggerah, they would not have crib there. I did not get caught this way, but two of my colleagues continually did. The train load messages, which at that time were sent by teleprinter from Broadmeadow to Sydney Telegraph, were generally received by the time the train had passed Fassifern, so that there was no excuse for not knowing what time the driver signed on.

One morning around 7.00am I was advised by the signalman at Gosford that he had the fireman of the *Gold Coast Motorail* on a signal telephone advising him the engine was a total failure, and that the train was situated between Ourimbah and Lisarow (an unattended platform). Behind the train was a goods train worked by a 60 Class Garratt locomotive conveying 1000 tons, which was approaching Ourimbah but was too long for the Ourimbah refuge. The safeworking regulations of the time frowned on propelling passenger trains with any engine, let alone a 60 Class.

Ourimbah railway station in May 1984 viewed in the direction towards Newcastle.

John R Newland.

Tuggerah railway station in May 1984 viewed in the direction towards Sydney. The level crossing has since been replaced by an overbridge located about 150m away. *John R Newland.*

I told the signalman at Gosford to tell the fireman to hang on; this was to give me breathing space. My immediate reaction to the problem was to propel the *Gold Coast Motorail* into Gosford using the 60 Class but not detaching it from its train. I thought about this for a few minutes and then decided to do just that. I reasoned that the 60 Class hauling its own train would not have the capacity to push the passenger hard enough to do any damage, and that in fact with the additional 500 tons of the passenger, he would be hard put to move it all, especially the last two miles into Gosford.

When the fireman of the 60 Class rang from a signal, he was advised to proceed to the rear of the passenger and to propel it into Gosford, but he was not to exceed 15 miles per hour. I also directed the signalman at Gosford that not under any circumstance was he to allow a Down train to leave his station until the combined trains had come to a stand at his platform. A delay of around 30 minutes was occasioned to the *Motorail* arriving at Gosford. After the necessary engine change, it was 45 minutes late. I had, however, arranged with Engine Control to attach two 46 Class electrics, which saved time at Hawkesbury River and Cowan. The train arrived Sydney 35 minutes late.

News that Ellis had propelled a passenger train with a 60 Class spread like wildfire around the control boards. The general opinion was that he was for the long jump. Around 8.30am the side telephone rang and on it was the Passenger Transportation Manager (as the passenger section head was then called). His first words were,

"I believe you propelled the *Motorail* into Gosford with a 60 Class, and I also believe he was hauling his own train". "That's correct, sir." I answered.

"I am glad to see someone around the third floor has a bit of initiative," he replied.

That was all I heard of the incident.

Wyong was, even before electrification, quite a busy passenger station, nothing of course to what it is today. The only passenger trains between Sydney and Newcastle that did not stop were the Down morning *Newcastle Flyer* and the Up afternoon *Flyer*. The *Northern Tablelands Express*, worked by a 900 Class DEB set and the locomotive-hauled air-conditioned *North Coast Daylight* both stopped there to pick up passengers for stations beyond Muswellbrook and Dungog respectively. They likewise set down on their return journeys. Two goods sidings were provided on the Up side for the small amount of inward goods traffic. An Up Refuge Loop that held about 50 vehicles was provided on the Up, but this siding was not used often. The only time I used it was if I already had a train at Tuggerah and Gosford was 'blocking back'* waiting Down engines. Wyong reported all passenger trains and any goods train that stopped or shunted. A short 'back-in' Refuge Siding was provided on the Down side.

* 'Blocking back' was a term often used by operating staff to indicate that, for some reason, a delay was being experienced. Trains halted at signals because of that delay were said to have blocked back. I suppose in every day speak it would be called queuing up.

*Wyong railway station in May 1984 viewed in the direction towards Sydney. Locomotive 4853
with a freight is refuged in one of the loop lines.*   *John R Newland.*

Wyee hardly rated a mention in those days, in terms of passenger traffic. It was however,
an important station for a large bulk cement depot. Almost daily they received bulk
cement wagons which were detached by No 259 and when empty, were picked up by No
258. Wyee only reported the trains it dealt with and for much of the time was in automatic
working. Small Down and Up Refuge Loops were provided, which I do not recall using
in my time.

What I do recall quite vividly was an experience I had with single line working between
Wyong and Wyee on the Up road, which was scheduled between 9.00am and 4.00pm.
The working was proceeding according to plan, and the morning *Newcastle Flyer* was
delayed only for safeworking purposes. In the afternoon I had the so-called *Midday Flyers*
in each direction which, in the normal course of events, passed between Wyee and
Morisset, and a Down high-speed Brisbane express freight train. The freighter followed
the *Flyer* from Gosford and at Tuggerah, it was only about eight minutes behind the *Flyer*
departing from Wyong. I gambled and let the *Flyer* go on a ticket and brought the freighter
up to Wyong to follow it, with the pilotman, on signal clearance. That was no problem,
the freighter went on its way and should have arrived Wyee about 15 minutes later
allowing for slow running passing the work site.

The working I adopted was supposed to delay the Up *Flyer* for about 10 minutes which I was prepared to wear to save 45 minutes delay on the freighter. When the *Newcastle Flyer* went past the work site, the ganger, in his wisdom, obstructed the Down line with his machinery, for what purpose I did not find out. However when he got it foul of the Down Main, the engine on the whatever machine it was cut out and he could not start it. I had no idea this had happened until the traffic officer in charge advised Wyee. Around an hour later, the freighter arrived Wyee, delaying the *Flyer* 70 minutes.

The subsequent examination of the happenings by a joint investigation team found the traffic officer was jointly responsible with the ganger for the obstruction of the Down main line. They criticised the train controller strongly saying, that had he not allowed the freight train to proceed, the delay to the *Flyer* would have been reduced. This train controller responded to the enquiry by saying that the train working was his responsibility, that he was given one line on which to run the trains normally using two lines. How he did that had nothing to do with the enquiry, which was formed to investigate the events surrounding the track machine fouling the Down track over which the ganger had no jurisdiction. I added any dissatisfaction with the working adopted would be for the Train Control Superintendent to adjudicate on.

I also drew attention to the Special Train Notice and circular for the working that made no mention of the Down line being obstructed. The Per Way representative objected

Wyee railway station in March 1985 viewed in the direction towards Gosford. Up and Down Refuge Loops were provided.   *John R Newland.*

to this, saying surely the ganger on site had some latitude. Obviously he was trying to absolve his Branch. I told him I regarded the STN as my Bible. While it was not admitted, the ganger did not expect a Down train to follow the *Flyer* and, like me when I sent it, took a gamble on being able to obstruct the Down for a period of time and then get clear for the Up *Flyer*. Had the thing not failed, he might have got away with it. I heard no more of it. I was pretty uncomfortable about it for a while, until the Assistant Passenger Transportation Manager was in North Control as I signed on for 11.30am shift the morning after. He said that they had obviously examined the working closely and that they had, with the benefit of hindsight, thought I should not have sent the freight. I certainly agreed with that! Seventy minutes on a *Flyer* — ulcer fodder!

There were a number of features which came out of that. Similar enquiries revealed many irregularities, particularly with respect to safeworking and safety issues. These issues became the subject of amendments to the regulations; in particular, the protection of the 'live' road when it was accidentally or otherwise obstructed. In a separate incident the driver of the freight train complained he had had insufficient warning from the flagmen. There was no question of his not stopping in time but rather, it was a question that the detonators were not placed in accordance with Rule 243. Not long afterwards, it became necessary for flagmen to be given training in their duties. This incident was not the catalyst for the training; a number of incidents involving flagmen at other locations brought the realisation, that with the track possessions being regularly approved, safety of the work site was an important issue.

As the approval for weekend Per Way possessions and for out of peak hour possessions on weekdays became more prevalent, the method of single-line working came under scrutiny. The long time method of using a pilotman was labour intensive and while not inefficient, could not be said to be particularly efficient either. The safety of it properly executed was never in question; finding staff sufficiently well acquainted with the rules of pilotworking was. A system known as Special Staff Working was introduced. It was based on the Staff and Ticket system so widely used on branch lines, the difference being that it was portable. When Per Way possession was granted for a particular section, the Circular authorising the working together with the Special Train Notice for the occasion nominated the working to be under the provisions of Circular No 100, which encompassed the special staff working.

The new system was gazetted as Circular 100 and consisted of some 10 pages of regulations for the new working. A number of specially selected traffic officers were appointed to take charge of sections where working was required. When introducing the working, the traffic officer wrote the station names of the section over which the working applied with the special staff. A receptacle large enough to write the names of two stations on a piece of light cardboard was provided on the staff. Most train controllers welcomed the knowledge that traffic officers who knew their jobs were in charge of the special working. They did not assume any of the controller's duties associated with train running.

Every safeworking employee of the Department was required to become familiar with the regulations. In areas where it could be used, it became a necessary qualification before the employee was appointed. As train controllers, we had to be proficient in it. I do not recall whether it was adopted prior to my leaving North Control or afterwards, but it was introduced around the years 1967 or 1968.

I have made a number of references to circulars. These were the authority by which other Branches took possession of the track or removed power from overhead wiring. The circulars gave precise information as to the work to be performed and the time the track or power was to be restored to normal working. The circulars were printed and distributed by the Timetable Section and issued with the Special Train Notices. They always appeared over the name of the Chief Traffic Manager.

Morisset was a safeworking station that was mostly in automatic (switched out) and reported only the passenger services. A back-in Down Refuge Siding and an Up Refuge Loop each holding about 50 vehicles were seldom used. In earlier times, the refuges along the way that I have mentioned which were not now being regularly used, were used in the early days of steam. Morisset was a watering point for the very early days of steam, so was Wyong. Morisset must have been a railwayman's dream job; the passenger traffic was light, there was little freight and unless control directed they cut-in to manual working, they mostly ran in automatic. Staff were a sixth class station master and two fourth class ASMs.

Awaba was another safeworking station with virtually no commercial traffic of any kind. Down and Up Refuge Loops holding 75 vehicles was regularly used. Once an Up train of more than 50 vehicles long left Awaba, it had to go to Tuggerah if a following priority train was overtaking it. This fact made the forecasts I mentioned earlier from *neco* very important, because the run from Fassifern to Awaba was nine minutes for full goods. Very early in my time in North Control, I made it my business to get to know the assistant station masters who worked around the clock.

Their co-operation, when our unfriendly controller was occupying the chair in *neco* was vital. I had worked with one of them as juniors at Mount Victoria but I had not heard of him again until I came to North Control. They were all good to work with and would ring signal boxes to see how the trains had left Broadmeadow and to keep me posted so sensible train working decisions could be made.

My friend's wife had worked in the refreshment rooms at Mount Victoria and used to get us cups of coffee when we were on backshift.

One evening, Awaba advised he had the fireman of No 3 *Gold Coast Motorail* (again)

The yard layout at Morisset viewed from the railway station in March 1985 in the direction towards Newcastle.   *John R Newland.*

Awaba railway station in August 1984 viewed in the direction towards Sydney.
           John R Newland.

advising that the engine was a total failure on Hawkmount about six miles from Awaba. I told him to tell the fireman to stand by the telephone. The thought of the fireman walking all that distance did not fill me with joy (nor him either I suspect). I asked Awaba where the train was that had been forecast over Fassifern about the time he advised me of the failure. He said it was approaching. I told him to put it in the refuge, instruct the crew to secure it and cut the engine off.

I had decided to do something, once again, that was not generally done, although I could see no safeworking reason why it could not be done. I directed the ASM to issue the driver of the engine with a signalman's wrong-line order and to instruct him to proceed to where the fireman would be protecting his train. I also advised Awaba to tell the fireman to go forward and to protect his train, taking with him a driver's wrong-line order for a relief engine. The relief engine ran to the point were the fireman was on the Up Main, returned to Awaba and then left on the Down Main to attach to No 3. From the time I was advised of the failure and until No 3 arrived Awaba was 30 minutes. I sent the guard of the goods train back to Broadmeadow with the engine crew of the stowed goods train. They were Broadmeadow men so they were made happy. Another engine and crew were ordered for the goods train.

Once again my colleagues thought I had done the wrong thing, in sending an engine into a section to come back on the wrong road. The conservatives thought I was mad. I must have done something right because there was no ensuing correspondence regarding the delay.

Ambas were sent on backshift about 4.30am and on daywork at about 10.00am. The daywork *ambas* were sent when a copy of the Chief Train Controller's 36-hour programme was received. The Chief also put out a programme at around 4.00am. I used to send the full programme on the day work and on the backshift, I used to give the programme until about 8.00pm that evening. The 4.30am *amba* was the basis for stations to set out the train running for the Per Way gangers.

WEST CONTROL, SYDNEY

W EST CONTROL was the only control board in Sydney that I did not learn. However on weekends and public holidays I worked it. When I first went to Sydney, the Control Boards were worked in tandem on weekends, the North and South Boards operated together and the West and Illawarra from midnight on Saturday to midnight on Sunday. This meant that on the night I described at Hawkesbury River with single line working to Cowan, I also had charge of the South Board which, fortunately, did not cause any problem.

It is fair to say that when special working was on either the North or the South, management, when approached by control officers, mostly looked sympathetically at the work required on the Board without special working. If a heavy train programme or any additional work was on, it that would make working the two boards together untenable, additional staff necessary to man each Board was provided, if not for the full time, then for the period where the working was the heaviest.

West Control was generally referred to as the 'Old Men's Home'. It was by far the easiest board in Sydney. Mostly, it was not as difficult to work as either Dubbo or Orange, but when things went wrong, it was just as chaotic as any other board. Those nearing retirement and whose ability demanded they not be placed on any other Board, staffed it. I recall, however, one who had worked in the West for a long period of time with a doctor's certificate stating he was suffering from stress (yes, even in the 1960s!). When his turn for promotion came near, he produced a certificate saying he was not suffering stress any longer and was appointed Chief Train Controller and went straight to Traffic Trouble. He worked for a number of years in this position and was respected for his work.

The safeworking system between Parramatta and Valley Heights was Track Block and Automatic Down and Up. Between Valley Heights and Newnes Junction, it was mainly Block Telegraph, and was automatic signalling between Newnes Junction and Zig Zag in both directions, with a final block section from Zig Zag Box to Lithgow Coal Stage Box.

The General Appendix Part 1 dedicated a half page for the special working that was to apply for trains that failed between Valley Heights and Katoomba. The first important point was that the guard MUST ride in the last vehicle between Valley Heights and Katoomba. In those instances where the train brakevan, especially on the mails, was not the last vehicle, then a brakesman had to be supplied. When No 49 conveyed the light drawgear DEH parcel van for the *Silver City Comet*, a qualified baggage porter was provided. Whenever a *Silver City Comet* car had to return to Parkes after overhaul, they had a brakesman all the way, firstly because of the mountain regulation and secondly because it was not equipped with standard Westinghouse airbrake. The vehicle was attached to the brakevan by means of a special coupling. The air hoses were connected with the air tap on the brakevan being open and the tap on the *Comet* car closed. This meant that if the *Comet* car became detached for some reason, the train would stop. It also meant that the brakesman had to get busy and to apply the handbrake to stop the light car, because there was no other way.

The clearing of a section when a train had failed could only be done from the signal box in advance. It was not permissible to send an engine in from the rear either to haul the train back or to propel it forward. There were, in fact, few failures on the Down; nine out of ten trains used double engines and even if they lost time in a section due to the failure of one engine, they still made the station in advance. During my time in Control in Sydney, I was only aware of one time when one engine failed and the second engine took the first portion and the dead engine to Lawson where the first portion was stowed, the good engine returning for the second portion.

In the days prior to electrification, West Control was a very busy Board, in a train working sense. The area extended from Parramatta to Lithgow Coal Stage Box and from Blacktown to Richmond. The responsibility on the Richmond Line was confined to the stock bound for Riverstone Meatworks or Richards Siding (as it was often known). When the Chief Train Controller wanted to run a stock special to Riverstone with stock arriving from the South or from stock detached at Blacktown from Western trains, he would ask the West Control Officer for a timetable for an 'AA' special, or if there was more than one train in a day, the second was a 'BB' Special. I made many enquiries why they were called this, but no one was ever able to answer. The old hands all said it had ever been thus. Richmond loaded sand and gravel to Wolli Creek, usually one train a day worked by 48 Class diesel-electric locomotives.

A morning passenger worked by a 32 Class steam locomotive and a suburban type set of carriages that arrived at Central around 7.30am was provided for the Richmond Line commuters. The balance of the passenger services were provided by railmotors plying between Richmond and Blacktown. The passenger train returned in the afternoon from Central around 5.00pm. The passenger services between Penrith and Lithgow provided both a good commuter service to the city and time at Penrith or Katoomba for shoppers. On the Down, one of the 'stumpies' I referred to in my Linden and Glenbrook junior days, left Penrith around 7.20am worked by a 32 Class locomotive and became a school train from Glenbrook onwards. It returned in the afternoon with the children from school. No 31 *Central West Express*, No 23 *Caves Express* to Mount Victoria, No 25 *Orange Passenger*, an afternoon *Stumpy*, No 77 passenger to Mount Victoria, No 57 *The Fish* to Mount Victoria, No 47 *The Chips* to Valley Heights and No 85 *Lithgow Passenger* and a 10.00pm *Stumpy* from Central served the Down. A *Stumpy* from Mount Victoria around 5.30am commenced the day's Up passenger services. No 10 *The Fish*, No 14 passenger from Mount Victoria, No 48 *The Chips* from Valley Heights and No 18 from Lithgow were early morning commuter and shopping trains. No 30 *Caves Express*, No 28 *Central West Express*, and No 26 *Orange Passenger* were the afternoon passengers.

The stations between Parramatta and Penrith rarely had contact with West Control, the exceptions being Blacktown and St Marys, which reported goods trains and the country passenger trains. Once a goods train passed Parramatta, there was little that could be done with it until St Marys. This enabled the controller to request St Marys to hold it while the passenger passed if it did not have sufficient running time to Penrith. Additionally, in the peak, some all- station services were on the main while fast trains were timetabled on the suburban to run past them. The signalmen ran the peak hour trains strictly to the timetable.

In the steam days, the 50 Classes mostly took water at Penrith before facing the mountain climb to Valley Heights. If they had had a good uninterrupted run to Penrith from Enfield, they would not have to take water. However, they took water as a precaution when it would be nothing for there to be three trains ahead of them waiting to get pilots at Valley Heights in the early morning .

Penrith was an important outer urban station, the suburban electrics being stowed there for the commencement of the next morning's peak . It was a depot for both the Traffic and Mechanical Branch train staff. The passenger revenue was heavy and goods being the reverse. Very little in the way of goods arrived in to Penrith. Already in my time, the fodder for the local dairies was starting to be transported by road. Dairy Farmers Limited had a big depot at Penrith but they did not use rail. The supply of milk came from the surrounding districts by road tankers.

Emu Plains was, until the electrification arrived, 'sleepy hollow'. It had two main line crossovers. It was always manned, during the day with a sixth class station master and third class assistants. With the commencement of electrification, a number of electrics ran to Emu Plains where they crossed over and returned to the city after the driver changed

Penrith railway station in October 1984 viewed in the direction towards the Blue Mountains.
John R Newland.

Valley Heights railway station in May 1984 viewed in the direction towards Sydney. The sidings at the right lead to the locomotive depot and roundhouse.
John R Newland.

ends. It was a trap for unsuspecting and new train controllers because, while it was clearly shown on the diagram, it was only a small distance between Penrith and Emu Plains. More than one train controller got caught with an Up goods train coming off the mountain at the time the electric was due to cross over. Once the goods, of course, passed a certain point, which was the Emu Plains accept signal, it had to keep going. If the officer at Emu Plains was alert enough, he had his Up Accept at stop before the damage was done.

Glenbrook had a Down Refuge and was manned continually, as I have previously written. In later times, modifications were made to the signal frame to enable the signal box to cut out for automatic working.

Valley Heights was the beginning of the serious climbing (1 in 33 gradients) on the Blue Mountains. It had a small locomotive depot headed by a district locomotive engineer, clerical staff and fitters and their mates who were employed on each shift. About 12 drivers and fireman completed the staff. I should not forget the very beginning, should I? There were, of course, the important callboys attached to the staff. What a difference telephones made in later years! The station staff consisted of a fifth class station master and two third class assistants. To make the jobs of the station staff easier, a signal box complete with sixth class signalmen, attended to the safeworking duties.

The signalmen were the main point of contact for the train controllers. There was no Up Refuge, but on the Down there was a refuge loop and two long sidings from which the assistant engine could be attached to a waiting goods train. Access to the sidings was from the refuge siding, the points being at the entrance to the refuge siding, from where it was possible to admit a train into a siding while the refuge was occupied. The water columns were only available from the main line and refuge.

Every train that arrived Valley Heights on the Down, with the exception of the *Stumpy* passenger trains worked by 32 Class engines, the 17B pick-up and an odd load of empties worked by 57-58 Classes in the steam days and 46 Classes in the electric days, were assisted from Valley Heights. The assists were always 50/53 Class Standard Goods engines, even on the passengers, which meant the maximum speed between Valley Heights and Katoomba was 35 miles per hour, with an average of about 25-28 mph. The economical management of the bank engines was the most important duty the controller had. This was especially so in the days of steam when many more trains were running. It was not uncommon to see three bank engines attached at Katoomba and despatched for their next duty ahead of a goods train which had been held back to let them run back to Valley Heights.

Valley Heights station and locomotive depot was a blotch on the beauty of the Blue

Mountains. Valley Heights station always looked dirty, even when it wasn't; I have to say that! As a Relief Junior, I had cleaned it. The locomotive depot, like all depots, mostly had a pall of smoke and smog hanging over it. The arrival of electric locomotives changed all that, and it did not take long for Valley Heights to change character. The surge of building in the Lower Blue Mountains following the electrification saw Valley Heights have its share of those buildings.

Springwood was the most heavily populated of the Blue Mountains towns between Penrith and Katoomba. A fifth class station master and two assistants, a block porter or safeworking porter, a seventh class clerk and two juniors completed the staff. It had a crossover from the Down to the Up Main and an Up Refuge Loop. The Up Refuge was used by all Up Goods trains to release the hand brakes, take water and to do the fire. It was the guard's duty to release the handbrakes that had been applied at Katoomba while the fireman did the fire and took water. The crew invariably had crib.

The only exception would be if there was another Up train waiting to get into the refuge, when the controller would ask the first to have crib on the main line at Valley Heights. There was an urn provided in the signal box at Springwood. The fireman generally got off before the train stopped and got the hot water for himself and the driver. They did not take too kindly to having to go to Valley Heights for crib and drink tea that had been made for 30 minutes.

Linden has been described at length in a previous chapter.

Woodford was purely and simply a safeworking station. It cut out from about 3.00pm Saturday until early Monday morning. The section became Linden—Lawson.

Lawson was the next largest Blue Mountains town after Katoomba and Springwood. It had Up and Down Refuge Loops, each of which held 60 vehicles. A water column was provided on the Down. Although they were not tabled to take water between Valley Heights and Katoomba, drivers often did so, especially if they were having difficulty maintaining steam or the locomotive was priming.*

For the shrewd driver, it served two purposes. Firstly, it gave him a 'breather' and an opportunity to raise steam and secondly, he could always justify taking water. The *Stumpy*

---

* Priming occurred when some water in the boiler had not been converted to steam. It often occurred when engines were due for a boiler washout. A large amount of smoke, water and steam issued from the exhaust stack and if working hard, the locomotive rapidly lost steam. Mixed in this smoke was a polluted amount of water that stained whatever it came into contact with. The Railways Department paid out many claims over the years to householders whose white sheets were ruined with it. I had more than one shirt that had been primed on.

Lawson railway station in May 1984 viewed in the direction towards Katoomba.
John R Newland.

Wentworth Falls railway station in May 1984 viewed in the direction towards Katoomba.
John R Newland.

passenger trains also often sneaked water. They would put the hose in for about two minutes and get enough to make sure that they got to Katoomba. They often ran a couple of minutes early into Lawson, thus 'the man on the wall' rarely knew when they had taken water. The station was staffed by a fifth class station master, two third class assistant station masters and two junior porters.

Wentworth Falls had an Up Refuge Loop with the entrance near the Katoomba end of the platform, which held 60 vehicles, but it was not often used. The Blue Mountains Grammar School attracted many pupils for the school trains. Otherwise, Wentworth Falls was primarily a safeworking station with its coaching (passenger) revenue coming more from tourism than from commuter passengers.

Leura was a safeworking station, with a Goods Siding only. It had cut-out facilities and did so every weekend.

Katoomba was the hub of the Blue Mountains. Everything in the name of tourism in the Mountains emanated from Katoomba. Readers will recall the famous Paragon Cafe, the Carrington Hotel, the Metropole Hotel, Gearins Hotel and, of course, the Three Sisters.

Katoomba railway station in September 1984 viewed in the direction towards Mount Victoria. The level crossing in the foreground has long since been replaced by an overbridge located west of the station. *John R Newland.*

There were goods sidings on the Down. A Darling Harbour truck was received at least once weekly off No 17B. Timber was unloaded on a regular basis. A third class station master and two second class assistant station masters plus booking clerks and platform porters manned the station. The safeworking was conducted from a signal box toward the Lithgow end of the platform. An Up Refuge Loop was provided, together with several storage sidings. All Down trains detached their pilot or bank engine which turned, took water and returned either attached to another pilot or singly, whichever the train controller decreed, to Valley Heights.

I found difficulty sometimes keeping track of the pilot engines returning, unless the signalman reported their departure, because within a reasonable time, they would be through Lawson before they were reported. Every goods train in the steam days, and all trains conveying four-wheeled vehicles when electrification came in, went into the Up Refuge. The handbrakes were applied the full length of the train, the guard starting at the rear and the fireman from the engine. The brakes were applied sufficiently heavily to severely retard the vehicle while the air brakes were off. This retardation prevented the train from gathering too much speed while the driver was restoring the train line pressure. With the advent of bogie vehicles and the issue of grade control valve certificates, trains still went into the refuge at Katoomba, but only to set the grade controls, which were generally reset to normal or the 'Ex' position at Springwood.

Medlow Bath was a small stop for the Blue Mountains town famous for the Hydro Majestic Hotel, and was a safeworking station only. Fitted with cut-out facilities, it was mostly cut-out. No backshift staff was provided. A Caltex oil depot located on the Down side shortly before Medlow Bath, was shunted with a release taken from an Annett shunting key release. It was one of the many places where a portion of the train always had to be on the main line.

Blackheath was a very popular tourist area. The revenue of Blackheath was predominately coaching. A goods siding and crossover from Up to Down were provided, but by the mid-1960s, very little goods traffic was received or despatched. Another safeworking station only.

Mount Victoria was, in effect, a mini-depot. It was the terminal point for all but one of the interurban passengers from Sydney. It was equipped with Up and Down Storage Sidings, Up and Down Refuges, and main line crossovers. A barracks for enginemen and guards booking off in the evening to return on an early morning train, refreshment rooms on the Up and Down platforms, water columns on Up and Down, a turn table, ashpits and a locomotive crew who worked the *Mudgee Mail* and finally two corridor attendants who worked *The Fish* and the *Lithgow Passenger*, and a signal box.

Medlow Bath railway station in May 1984 viewed in the direction towards Sydney. The Caltex oil depot, which no longer exists, was situated in the distance.   *John R Newland.*

Mount Victoria railway station in December 1984 viewed in the direction towards Lithgow. Beyond the station are situated the stabling and Up Refuge Siding.   *John R Newland.*

It was unusual for a Down or Up goods train to be refuged at Mount Victoria, although occasionally on backshift, a goods would be refuged for No 310 Fruit Express. On occasions, coal trains were loaded by front end loaders from coal deposited on the dump by coal lorries coming from Hartley Colliery.

Bell was unattended in my time as a Senior Train Controller, although in later years, it was manned and Newnes Junction was closed. Today, Bell Signal Box is permanently closed while Newnes Junction is switched in as required for Clarence Colliery trains.

Newnes Junction was a safeworking station only, manned by fourth class ASMs round the clock. An Up Refuge Loop and crossover from Up to Down were provided. Assistant engines on Up goods were often taken off and returned to Lithgow. All goods train guards put out an X2010 train consist at Newnes Junction, and the train load was sent to Sydney Telegraph. The engine numbers and total tonnage of the train and any short of destination (if any and rarely) were given to the train controller. The ASMs also compiled a tonnage return for District Superintendent, Lithgow.

Zig Zag. In the steam days, a bank engine regularly assisted trains in the rear, and then returned to Lithgow from Zig Zag.

Lithgow Coal Stage Signal Box reported the arrival of Down and departure of Up trains. A good working relationship with the signalman was essential to the train controller, especially on stock days. Accurate forecasts from the signalman made West Control almost a breeze. Inaccurate or no forecasts made it more difficult, but was still a very good job.

The delays recorded on yellow sheets in West Control were much less in number than those of the North and South Boards. Whilst I may have seemed a little cynical of West Control when it was compared with the other boards, it served a very useful purpose staff wise. When I arrived in Sydney, there were two men in the shadow of retirement, who had been in *syco* for many years; they both had refused promotion to Chief Train Controller. It was but fair that they should, under these circumstances, see the close of their careers in a comparatively easy job.

Bell railway station in April 1984 viewed in the direction towards Sydney.

John R Newland.

Zig Zag platform and signal box in April 1984 viewed in the direction towards Sydney. This was the place where bank and assistant locomotives were detached. *John R Newland.*

SENIOR TRAIN CONTROLLER, ILLAWARRA CONTROL

A FTER about nine months in North Control, the Assistant Train Control Superintendent called me in as I was signing on at 11.30am one morning late in 1967 and told me the Goods Train Superintendent had approved my learning Illawarra Control. An indication of whether a train controller was considered capable, was made known when he was appointed to learn Illawarra Control. It was the complete Train Control Board. It had everything from single-line working, double-line working, depot working, tonnage balances, engine balances main line and branch line, passenger train working, passenger car balances, diesel car balancing, shipment coal train working, conveyance of metal ballast hoppers from Bombo and Shellharbour, interstate steel trains, superphosphate, boat loads of gypsum for Berrima and arrangements for conveyance of milk traffic from Nowra, Gerringong and Dapto to Darling Harbour.

It is difficult to know where to begin describing Illawarra Control to someone who may read this in years to come. Probably the best way is to start at the beginning of the control area at Sutherland from where it extended to Nowra—Unanderra—Moss Vale and the Port Kembla network complex. Safeworking was a real mixture. Automatic signalling was provided from Sutherland to Helensburgh and Otford to Coalcliff. The remaining double line sections as far as Mt Keira were operated under block telegraph regulations. Electric staff was used between Coalcliff and Scarborough, Unanderra and Nowra, and Unanderra and Moss Vale. The Port Kembla Branch was largely automatically signalled.

Sutherland was equipped with an Up Refuge Loop that was on a 1 in 40 falling grade towards Jannali. More than one train found its way into the dead end over the passage of time; this dead end was cut into the rock face and was some eight to ten feet high. Imprinted into the rock face were the marks of buffers that had come into contact forcibly with it. The Cronulla Line entered the main line on the Waterfall end of the platform. From the controller's viewpoint, the signalmen reported all goods trains. Generally speaking, they knew without being asked, although on occasions they would come on and say they were going to refuge an Up train at the Trouble Officer's direction.

Waterfall was an important cog in the working of the South Coast. The loads for all engines increased 100 per cent from Waterfall to Port Kembla. It was common practice for the Chief Train Controller, Programme Sydney, when he had heavy tonnage for the Coast in Enfield Yard, to send a train to Waterfall and return light engine to Enfield. On many of these occasions, the Mechanical Branch often requested a trial on a locomotive under load to Waterfall and to return light engine.

The loading would be picked up by following trains, which were advised prior to departure from their originating point that they would be attaching at Waterfall. Failure to do this would see some crews refuse to lift any loading. This happened a number of times to me. Every time it did, I issued a Locomotive Debit Slip. (Locomotive Debit Slips or LDSs were the means by which the Traffic/Operations Branch brought to the attention of the Mechanical Branch Management matters for which the issuing officer thought they were responsible.) Such things could be loss of time in running against the timetable allowance, refusal to partake of crib where directed, or in this case refusing to carry out legitimate directions. The Mechanical Branch complained each time and each time the Traffic Branch withdrew the debit. Gutless.

Before electrification to Port Kembla, in about 1984, railmotors ran a shuttle passenger service between Sutherland, Heathcote, Waterfall and Helensburgh. The yard on the Down consisted of two sidings which held about 40 vehicles each and a shorter siding holding about 20. The Up was served by a refuge loop and three sidings, including a siding with watering facilities. Still existing, at the time of writing in 2001, it is one of the few water columns remaining in the State. It was a busy station for the station master and assistants who were responsible for the signalling and, for long portions of the day, were also responsible for ticket selling.

Helensburgh was a safeworking station only, with a crossover that allowed railmotors that were extended to Helensburgh and to return to Sutherland. At the time I learned Illawarra Control, Helensburgh was not more than a village.

Metropolitan Colliery was a coal mine which despatched around 18 BCHs (bogie coal hoppers) of coal to BHP at Newcastle per week day. A train with 18 BCHs and brakevan left Port Kembla each morning for the Colliery. I should qualify that by saying there were occasions when empties were short in the Port Kembla area and the Coal Clerk booked empties from Enfield to Waterfall. On these occasions, the train from Port Kembla was engine and van to Waterfall to lift the empties and then into Metropolitan Colliery. Access to the siding, was controlled by Metropolitan Colliery Junction Signal Box.

Sutherland railway station in November 1984 viewed in the direction towards Sydney.
John R Newland.

Waterfall railway station in April 1984 viewed in the direction towards Sydney.
John R Newland.

Helensburgh railway station in March 1985 viewed in the direction towards Sydney.
John R Newland.

Otford railway station in April 1984 viewed in the direction towards Sydney. Electrification works for the Illawarra Line are in progress. *John R Newland.*

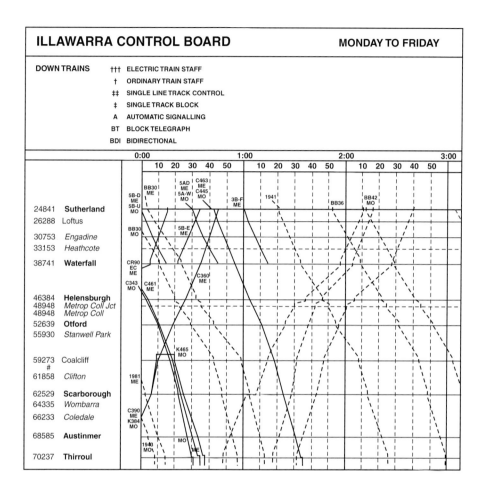

The engine ran around the train and proceeded into the Colliery. After six BCHs had been loaded, which formed a 48 Class load with the brakevan, the 48 Class took them into Waterfall and returned engine and van. Around 3.00pm, a 48 Class light engine ran to the Colliery from Thirroul and attached to the 48 Class and worked the balance of 12 BCHs into Waterfall. A variation to this engine rostering was that on occasions, a 48 Class was detached from a Down train, the crew coming passenger from Port Kembla to take charge of the engine at Waterfall, they then proceeded as light engine to the colliery.

Another ploy was to run a single load to Waterfall, where it stowed; before the engine and van was returned to Metropolitan Colliery with an engine off a Down train. At Waterfall, the loaded wagons were all put together and an 1800-ton load of coal headed for Newcastle, changing engines to three 46 Class electric locomotives, usually at Canterbury.

Otford was a safeworking point only, equipped with an Up and Down Refuge Sidings. Otford then, as it is today, could only be described as a village.

Coalcliff nestled at the foot of the Illawarra escarpment on the Sydney side, a couple of hundred metres from the ocean. This town with a million dollar outlook produced coal and coke from before the turn of the 20th century. Because of the single line section to Scarborough, tunnelled through the escarpment, facilities were provided to enable Up terminating empty coal wagon trains to gain admittance directly into the sidings, allowing Down passenger trains to be admitted to the platform and to complete their platform work while waiting clearance.

The terminating trains finished close to the signal box so that the station master had only a short distance to take the staff to the Down train after changing the Coalcliff—Scarborough staff. It was a safeworking requirement that a different staff had to be handed to the driver of a train waiting for the arrival of another. In other words, the incoming staff had to be placed in the electric staff instrument and another obtained for the waiting train. Each staff was numbered. The practice of not putting the staff through the instrument before reissuing it was known as 'swinging the staff'. I will not say that I did not 'swing the staff' at Orange East Fork on occasions.

A bank of coke ovens was situated on the Up side and had two sidings available for empties. Some of the wagons in the coke trade were stencilled *Coke Traffic Only*. These wagons ran between Coalcliff and the Newcastle industrial areas. Generally they were detached from No 701, nominally the pick-up goods. Coke was available tonnage every day, varying from two to six wagons. It was nearly always taken to Port Kembla and sent to its final destination from that point. A considerable amount of coke loaded for Broken Hill was despatched via the South.

The Down side had two storage sidings, which held something like 40 bogie wagons. The washery plant was situated off these sidings. While I was associated with Illawarra Control, generally about six or seven 13 BCH wagon trains, worked by 48 Class locomotives, were loaded daily and despatched to Port Kembla Inner Harbour. The Illawarra Coal and Coke Company owned the mine. It was a busy station with continuous safeworking movements with the coal trains arriving, the shunting of them to the coal mine, the placement of coke wagons, the departure of the coal trains and the safeworking associated with the through traffic. It reported all trains to the train controller.

The town was then, and in 2005 still is, populated by many retired people. The mine workers lived almost on the job. There were some Port Kembla steelworks employees who travelled by a 'Katie' train (more about 'Katies' later) which in the morning, ran empty from Thirroul and in the afternoon ran back to Coalcliff and returned empty to Thirroul.

Coalcliff railway station in June 1987 viewed in the direction towards Wollongong.

John R Newland.

Scarborough yard and signal box in April 1984 viewed in the direction towards Wollongong.

John R Newland.

Scarborough was, like Coalcliff, a small town with a million-dollar view situated on the Southern side of the Illawarra Escarpment, just as close to the ocean as its next door neighbour. In my early days in Illawarra Control, the local coal mine was working and despatched three or four 48 Class loads of coal to Port Kembla daily. It had an Up Refuge Siding and a number of sidings on the Up side where the mine was situated. In holiday times and in times of industrial unrest, these sidings were used for storage purposes. Because of the single line section, Scarborough and Coalcliff were key safeworking stations.

From my point of view, I found the officers at both points good to work with. If a direction regarding a crossing had not been already given, they invariably asked the question. Some of my colleagues put this down to lack of initiative, but I did not care what they put it down to as long as the two stations always asked the question of me.

It was a reasonably busy station which reported all trains, but which became less so when the coal mine closed in about late 1968. In the holiday times it attracted many tourists and holidaymakers, the local hotel being quite famous for its outlook and hospitality.

Coledale was an early safeworking station. However in my time, it was attended by a female station attendant, (a position similar to Blaxland, Warrimoo, and Faulconbridge I earlier described). The term and name was acceptable in 1968; not so today.

Thirroul was for all of the steam years, the rail depot for the industrial area of the South Coast. All traffic loaded at Cringila, Lysaghts and the other industries associated with the area, was transferred to Thirroul, where it was formed into trains. In the steam days, the locomotive depot was located at Thirroul, as were the drivers and guards. An Assistant District Superintendent was in charge of the area from Waterfall to Nowra, Unanderra to Robertson and the Port Kembla industrial area.

This all changed in 1965 when the South Coast became completely dieselised, and most depot functions were shifted to Port Kembla. Many of the Thirroul guards and drivers stayed with the Thirroul depot and maintained their own loco roster clerk. In the main, these men worked the coal trains which ran between Port Kembla—Coalcliff and Scarborough. The administrative office was shifted to Wollongong, when the area came under a District Superintendent, Wollongong.

The passenger trains that took the workers to and from Port Kembla were known as 'Katies'. I have not found out reliably to this day why they were so called, but I believe it was because they were mostly worked by 'K' Class goods steam engines. When I went to Illawarra, there were four morning passenger trains to Port Kembla from Thirroul and one from Kiama, which transported the workers. Two trains from Thirroul served the afternoon and back shift. The carriages, which consisted of light suburban types, were in

Thirroul yard and signal box in April 1984 viewed in the direction towards Sydney. The remains of the loco depot are to the left.   *John R Newland.*

Bulli Colliery overbridge and lead out from the Illawarra Line to the exchange sidings in March 1985 viewed in the direction towards Sydney.   *John R Newland.*

a deplorable condition and were stowed at Thirroul overnight. The rostering of the engines for these trains will be covered when I come to the rostering of engines. Thirroul Signal Box was the main point of contact for the controllers who reported all train movements.

Bulli was a town situated within five kilometres of Thirroul and mostly inhabited by a population associated with the local industries. It was a safeworking station without refuges, but it did have a crossover from the Up to Down. The Bulli Colliery line was situated a short distance from the station in the Thirroul section. This was an AIS mine. The company supplied their own wagons, locomotives and train crews to haul their coal to Cringila. However, haulage between the exchange sidings and Cringila was subsequently taken over by 48 Class diesel-electric locomotives. Entrance to the mine siding was gained when Bulli, electrically released the subsidiary frame known as Bulli Coal Sidings Box. The line from the colliery crossed over the main line and ran about three kilometres towards the ocean to exchange sidings where the trains reversed direction prior to proceeding onto the main line. Generally three or four trains a day ran between Port Kembla and Bulli.

Bellambi was another safeworking station that could not cut-out, due to the presence of an interlocked level crossing. It still loaded some coke in 1967, although before I left Illawarra Control, it had ceased to do so. In the early days, it was the junction for a mine that was situated at the foot of the Illawarra Escarpment. I was delighted to learn that a guard who used to visit Cowra barracks from Bathurst, and whom I remembered for his fastidiousness and willingness to help the juniors equip his brakevan, was an ASM at Bellambi. Above all else, I remembered his copy-plate penmanship.

Corrimal was another safeworking station that reported the passage of trains to the controller. Situated mid-way between Thirroul and Wollongong, it served a large residential area. In the early days, it also was a coal loading point, a junction line spurring off towards the Range. It also loaded some coke, but stopped doing so around 1967.

Mt Pleasant was a signal box with a coke siding that loaded three or four coke wagons each day. The siding had to be shunted for both lifting of loaded wagons and placing of empties in the Up direction. Access to the siding was on the Down side, gained by an Annett release, portion of the train always having to be left on the main line.

Wollongong could be described as the commercial heart of the Illawarra region, for in 1967 it had a population in excess of 200,000. While dieselisation had been completed on the South Coast, there was one train which ran with a 30 Class steam locomotive and two carriages. This was the *Moss Vale Passenger*, which left Wollongong after making a connection with a Down train from Thirroul in the late afternoon, returning the following morning. For this reason, there was still a water column and turntable at Wollongong. It also had storage sidings that accommodated the carriages for the terminating Sydney passenger trains, and an Up refuge loop in addition to two long storage sidings that were provided on the Down.

In February 1967 the steam train was replaced by a CPH railmotor with brakes slightly modified to handle the steep descent from Summit Tank.

Some goods traffic was handled at Wollongong Goods Shed that was also situated on the Down side. The dock on the Kiama end of the platforms was used for the 600 Class diesel passenger cars that plied between Wollongong-Kiama-Nowra and return. A number of small sidings were available on the Up which, in the steam days, had been where passenger engines were stowed overnight. A line to Inner Harbour was available from the Up direction. However it was necessary for the engine of the Up train to run around and attach to the rear of the train in order to run via the Up into Inner Harbour. In 1967, some coal traffic went there for shipment, but not very much. It was not until some years later that the bulk wheat terminal and coal shipping facilities were constructed. A double track from the Unanderra end was constructed into the Inner Harbour, and bulk wheat trains and coal trains were able to unload around a balloon loop that serviced both facilities.

Wollongong was to the passenger section what Port Kembla was to the freight section. It was a very busy passenger station. The through trains, the *South Coast Daylight Express* for example, worked by self propelled Budd cars (commonly known as 'the camel' from the shape of the cars) disgorged the majority of its passengers at Wollongong. The early morning Budd from Wollongong had a corridor attendant who worked back to Wollongong on the *South Coast Daylight Express*. This train stopped at Hurstville, Sutherland, Waterfall, Thirroul and Wollongong, then all stations to Bomaderry-Nowra. On the afternoon journey home, it stopped at the same stations. The District Locomotive Engineer Port Kembla serviced the Budd cars at Wollongong.

Local passenger services ran from Wollongong to Kiama and to Thirroul. An early morning 600 Class diesel started from Nowra and connected with a Sydney service. A conglomeration of 600 Class diesels and railmotors worked the daytime services. The only locomotive-hauled services were the 'Katies' morning and afternoon. It was not often that the controller was called on to make any adjustment to the carriage and self-propelled car rostering. However, the failure of a railmotor caused some havoc with the timetabling on the far South Coast if a locomotive-hauled set of cars was the replacement. If only one railmotor in a multiple set failed, I tried to maintain the *status quo* by reducing a service to one railmotor if this was possible, or juggling them so that it became possible.

The ASMs at Wollongong where generally very co-operative and had a good idea of where adjustments could be made in the rosters. This method may have caused some overcrowding, but I always believed this to be better than running loco-hauled carriages. The provision of a 48 Class diesel invariably cancelled a goods service. While I was learning, I spent two days in the area when my impression of the passengers services was that they could have been reduced by 50 per cent and still have sufficient capacity to meet the demand. This particularly applied to the 'Katies'.

Wollongong had a diesel fuelling point which I made use of on many occasions. This will be revealed later when dealing with engine rostering and the maintaining of that rostering.

Coniston was the junction from the main line to the Port Kembla network with platforms located a short distance on the Wollongong side. A small staff contingent attended to passenger services only.

Unanderra had the reputation, along with Orange East Fork and Werris Creek South Box, as being one the most difficult third class ASM positions in the State. From my observations of it, the reputation was well earned. It was the junction for the Moss Vale Line and the Port Kembla network. Unanderra, Allens Creek Signal Box and Wollongong (or more precisely Coniston) formed a giant triangle.

Every Down freight train from Port Kembla, whether to the South Coast or to Moss Vale, came via Allens Creek to Unanderra. As a general rule, after dieselisation, Down trains did not shunt, the exception being if the BHP works shunted empty limestone wagons into the sidings at Unanderra. The trains listed to take empties to Medway (Nos 861,863, 865 or 867) would depart Port Kembla engine and brakevan and pick up the empties.

The 1200-ton bogie steel loads with two locomotives, and the general goods trains with 800 tons with one locomotive each, had an assistant engine that detached at Summit Tank and returned light engine if a timetable path was available. If a path was not available, they attached to an Up Goods train at Summit Tank. This was a regular practice when the track capacity had been reached. The line to Summit Tank was steep with grades up to 1 in 30 and, as with the line from Valley Heights to Katoomba, every loaded freight train was assisted. The Medway trains conveying empties had 19 BLH/BCH hoppers and a brakevan for a load of 400 tons and were unassisted.

It would be fair to say that 95 per cent of Up trains from Moss Vale shunted at Unanderra. The interstate trains returning with empty bogie flatwagons would detach these wagons, which the BHP shunters would then lift from the sidings. The limestone trains detached their loads and then went engine and brakevan to Port Kembla.

The section Unanderra—Dapto had an intermediate staff instrument at Wongawilli

Wollongong railway station in April 1984 viewed in the direction towards Nowra. The yards are in the distance.   *John R Newland.*

Junction of the Moss Vale and Illawarra Lines at Unanderra in June 1984 viewed in the direction towards Sydney. Some rearrangement was effected shortly afterwards for the proposed line (later abandoned) to Maldon on the Main Southern Line.   *John R Newland.*

Junction near Brownsville, which was the junction for the private branch line to BHP's Wongawilli mine at the foot of the mountain, directly below Summit Tank. These trains came from the steelworks unheralded. The first information that the controller had, was when Unanderra advised him he had a Wongawilli waiting. The controller had to give him the first available margin, and there were times when it was 40 to 60 minutes before a margin was available, and this being in a 12 minute section for a goods train. There were also other times, of course, when a margin was immediately available, especially on backshift.

These trains, worked by BHP crews with BHP wagons and locomotives, loaded at Wongawilli and returned to Brownsville. Once again, the first information was when the guard sought an electric staff from the safeworking instrument. The Down trains from Port Kembla going to Shellharbour and Bombo and the Up trains returning, all passed through Unanderra. The single line from Unanderra to Kiama carried the maximum number of trains possible between about 6.30am and 9.30am and from about 3.00pm to 6.00pm. Each crossing loop was occupied during these times.

Unanderra served an expanding area; the population growth that went south from Wollongong found Unanderra as their station. Consequently its passenger revenue increased, making it a busy station, both passenger and freight wise.

Dapto could best be described as a small station that had everything. It was the type of station from which good juniors came. A small amount of inwards freight, mainly fodder for the local dairies, and 'out-ofs' from the Darling Harbour train that detached the empty milk vats each day and placed them in the dairy siding. At least two milk vans were loaded everyday, but on some days, and in the spring especially, three. The milk train returning from Nowra picked up the milk and ran direct to Darling Harbour via the Goods Road.

It was a busy safeworking station. There were few trains that passed that did not cross another train at Dapto. The safeworking staff worked from about 6.00am to about 10.00pm. After that, it was in automatic, which meant that the guard of the milk train was responsible for detaching and placing the milk vats. They were rostered guards and during my time not once did they fail to correctly place them.

There were early morning peak passenger train comprised railmotors or 600 Class diesels that terminated and formed services back to Wollongong and to the Port Kembla works. In the late 1960s, Dapto was starting to burgeon into a large shopping centre, serving the ever-increasing numbers who were finding employment in the industrial areas because of the buoyant economy.

Albion Park was similar in many respects to Dapto, except that it was not nearly as busy passenger revenue-wise. It was served with a crossing loop that, like Dapto, had a train in it for every train that passed there. Although it was predominantly dairying country, no milk was loaded, the milk being taken from the farms to Dapto.

Shellharbour was a beautiful seaside town in 1968, still untouched by the prolific development taking place north of it. In later years a very large club was built, but in the time of writing, it was as 'country' as you could get. I think I could have handled being Station Master Shellharbour! It was, however an important and busy station. A blue metal quarry about three kilometres away, was situated on a spur line.

As was the case in many different parts of New South Wales, a 1 in 40 gradient existed between Albion Park and Shellharbour; the gradient being at Oak Flats. Over the years this gradient cost the Department thousands upon thousands of dollars in man-hours and locomotive time. It really came down to whatever load that two locomotives could haul from Port Kembla to Enfield, would require three locos from Shellharbour.

On a daily basis, Shellharbour loaded approximately 24 BCHs of blue metal bound for the ready mix cement companies in the metropolitan area. This equated to the loads of 4 x 48 Class diesel-electric locomotives. Had the grade been as it was from Port Kembla to Enfield, two 48 Classes would have lifted 20 of these wagons, obviously the loadings would either have been reduced to 20 BCHs per day from Shellharbour or increased to 30 with the use of the third 48 Class locomotive. With the use of diesels, the additional locomotive did not require an additional crew, but in the days of steam, every engine, of course, was manned. The 1 in 40 gradient to Albion Park really cost in those days.

Bombo has the distinction of being the closest rail station to the ocean in New South Wales, the beach being about 50 yards from the platform. The New South Wales Railways own the blue metal quarry at Bombo. All the blue metal required by the Chief Civil Engineer in the Southern, Metropolitan and Western Divisions was mined at Bombo and despatched from there in BBWs (bogie ballast wagons), each of which held 40 tons of blue metal ballast. While the loading varied from day to day, the average would have seen at least one, and more often than not, two trains leave Bombo. Two third class ASMs manned Bombo. The same corollary, of course, could be applied to Bombo regarding engine power as that for Shellharbour.

Kiama was the main tourist attraction on the South Coast, at peak holiday times the population of Kiama trebled. It is a comfortable day return rail journey from Sydney, which many people took advantage of, adding to the numbers who spent holidays there. The majority of passenger trains terminated and returned to Wollongong. The *South*

Coast Daylight Express and two other trains were the only ones which ran through to Nowra. It boasted a turntable and storage sidings for about 20 carriages. There was little goods revenue in the mid 1960s. The passenger revenue, however, was considerable.

Berry is a very old town by Australian standards and was the centre of a large dairying area. It was also a popular holiday resort. It was, and still is, served well by craft and antique shops for which towns of its antiquity are famed. It caused Illawarra Control very little trouble. It reported the passenger trains and also the crossings if it had any, which was only on rare occasions. The Station Master Berry advised Nowra of the milk loading, generally three or four milk tanks daily.

Bombaderry is the rail terminus for Nowra was situated on the Sydney side of the Shoalhaven River. It was a busy railhead, serving some 400km of South Coast to the Victorian border. Daily coach services run by the Pioneer Coach Company connected with the arriving and departing *South Coast Daylight Express*, Mondays to Saturdays. The late running of up to 30 minutes of these coaches would always result in the controller authorising the Station Master to hold the *Express*.

Any later than that, he sought direction from the Train Control Superintendent, who in turn sought advice from the Passenger Train Manager. I knew of times when the train was held for an hour. On the very rare occasions, the coaches were later than this, arrangements were made with Pioneer Coaches to run coaches to either Wollongong or Waterfall, depending what connections were available. Nevertheless, it has to be said that for the long distance that they travelled, Pioneer Coaches had an enviable record of reliability.

The Australian Paper and Pulp Manufacturing Company despatched anything up to four bogie louvres of paper products daily by the milk train to Darling Harbour. The milk train was formed off the Down train that supplied the empty milk vats between Kiama and Bombaderry and the empty bogie louvred vans for the paper trade. The crew shunted and placed the empties as required on arrival. The locomotive crew stabled their engine and with the guard, they rested in the barracks, to sign on again in the evening to return to Darling Harbour. The station master gave the anticipated load for the return train to Illawarra Control. The controller then passed it on Goods Control. Bombaderry would advise control of the departure of the train; on most occasions it was not heard of until Dapto when the guard would give his times up to that point. I only heard from the guard once at Berry, and that being he could not get a staff from Kiama. I had to get the SM Berry on duty and institute pilotworking from Kiama.

Bombo railway station in June 1984 viewed in the direction towards Nowra. The turnout in the foreground serves the ballast quarry. *John R Newland.*

Bomaderry railway station and yard in June 1984 viewed in the direction towards Nowra and the terminus of the Illawarra Line. *John R Newland.*

Dombarton is situated on the Illawarra Escarpment where the gradients were 1 in 30, it was the only signal box in New South Wales that had a runaway that was not a derail; it ran up into the mountain beside the signal box.

If the Down train arrived first, it ran into No 1 Refuge Siding then propelled under the main line to No 3 Refuge Siding from which position it departed towards Summit Tank after the Up train had passed. If the Up train arrived first, it ran into No 2 Refuge Siding then propelled under the main line to No 1 Refuge Siding from which position it departed towards Unanderra after the Down train had passed.

If both and Up and Down train were required to cross another service, such as the passenger train, there was sufficient refuging space to accommodate both whilst the passenger train could proceed direct via the Main Line.

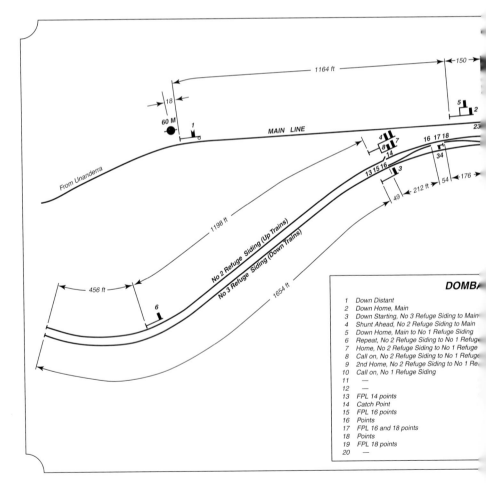

DOMB/

1   Down Distant
2   Down Home, Main
3   Down Starting, No 3 Refuge Siding to Main
4   Shunt Ahead, No 2 Refuge Siding to Main
5   Down Home, Main to No 1 Refuge Siding
6   Repeat, No 2 Refuge Siding to No 1 Refuge
7   Home, No 2 Refuge Siding to No 1 Refuge
8   Call on, No 2 Refuge Siding to No 1 Refuge
9   2nd Home, No 2 Refuge Siding to No 1 Re.
10 Call on, No 1 Refuge Siding
11 —
12 —
13 FPL 14 points
14 Catch Point
15 FPL 16 points
16 Points
17 FPL 16 and 18 points
18 Points
19 FPL 18 points
20 —

Because of the steep gradient of the main line through Dombarton, instructions provided that trains should not generally be stopped on the main lines but instead be admitted to the Refuge Sidings if a 'through run' was not available. In its original form, Dombarton was a slow crossing point. It generally took 20 minutes to effect a crossing.

When the proposed electrification to Maldon was being constructed, an additional track was built from Unanderra to Dombarton. When this took place, Dombarton was remodelled and today is controlled from the Wollongong Signal Box complex. Before an Up freight train is permitted to pass the Up Accept signal to Dombarton, the driver has assure the Wollongong Complex Signalman that he has his train under control before the signalman will clear the through road. If this assurance is not forthcoming, the train will still head for the 'scrub' via the runaway.

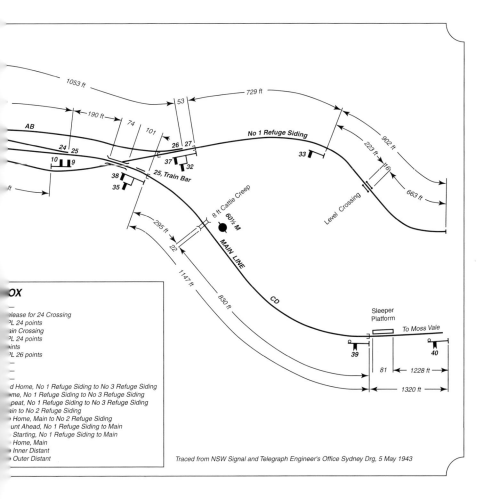

Traced from NSW Signal and Telegraph Engineer's Office Sydney Drg, 5 May 1943

Dombarton Signal Box and Refuge Sidings in November 1985 viewed in the direction towards Unanderra. The top photo shows the turnout to No 2 Refuge Siding and the lower photo shows the underbridge carrying the Main Line over No 1 Refuge Siding. John R Newland.

Summit Tank is on top of the escarpment, with magical views across Lake Illawarra, towards Dapto, Albion Park and Shellharbour and back into the escarpment and Brownsville mine. The gradients to Moss Vale were 1 in 60, enabling the bank engines to be detached and sent back to Unanderra, either attached to a train or as light engine. In the steam days, a turntable and water column and de-ashing pit were available. In my time in Illawarra Control, it was unusual for a train not to cross an Up train after detaching the bank engine. On weekdays, the section was so saturated that the train control diagram resembled a wire netting fence. The sectional running time from Summit Tank to Robertson was 58 minutes for a main line diesel hauling 800 tons. Theoretically, this allowed the section Unanderra to Moss Vale to carry 24 trains in 24 hours. However, the morning railmotor, because of its departure time from Moss Vale, eliminated a path, making the maximum 23 trains. Only on one or two occasions, when the gypsum trains were running did I see this happen. Summit Tank was manned by fourth class ASMs, residences being provided. Access by road, while possible, was difficult, especially at night.

Special regulations regarding fog signalmen appeared in 1932. Gangers were directed that, when they became aware of fog setting in, they were to proceed to nominated signals, even during the hours they were off duty, without being called to do so. The signals concerned were the Up and Down homes at Summit Tank and Robertson. During working hours, they were to supply qualified flagmen to the signals. To my knowledge, these were the only places in New South Wales where the ganger did not wait to be called to attend for fog signalling duties. If he was asleep in the wee small hours, I do not know how he was expected to be aware of a fog!

Robertson is a small town situated in the Southern Highlands, a very picturesque area, cold in the winter but very pleasant during the balance of the year. On occasions, strong winds made conditions unpleasant. Before the Centralised Train Signalling Control system was installed, it had a crossing loop holding about 56 vehicles. There were more major safeworking irregularities at Robertson in the 1960s than was reasonably conceivable. A fatality occurred when an observer was burnt to death. An Up train was approaching Robertson when the station was in automatic working; the observer had walked in from the home signal.

There is a level crossing on the Moss Vale side and for this reason the signals were always left at stop. The fireman spoke to control and was told to bring his train through on the main line and to work the Down train through the Loop. While he was speaking, the Down train passed the Down Home and continued on to crash into the train standing on the main line. The observer on the Down train was killed. It took days to clean up the resultant chaos. One engine, from memory 4460, was written off and two others were damaged to the extent requiring months of repair work to return them to traffic. It appeared from the report of the Board of Inquiry that alcohol had played a part in this accident.

Summit Tank in November 1985 viewed in the direction towards Unanderra showing the small platform, with signal box and loop. John R Newland.

Robertson railway station in December 1985 viewed in the direction towards Moss Vale. John R Newland.

One Saturday afternoon, I was on the Control Board when the guard of the Up railmotor from Moss Vale came on the phone and, with a panic stricken voice, said there had been a collision between the railmotor and a Down freight. The guard had not spoken to me until this time. On my calculations, the freight train should have arrived at Robertson in time for the observer to walk in, speak to Control and admit his train to the loop before the railmotor arrived.

To this day, I am not aware of what delayed the train after it left Summit Tank. The guard of the railmotor, not knowing he had a crossing, had admitted the railmotor to the main line. This was, of course, where it should have been to deal with passenger traffic. The Down train topped the rise about 500 metres from Robertson. The driver, apparently unable to control the speed of his train, passed the home signal at stop and collided with the railmotor standing on the platform. Fortunately, no person in the railmotor was injured. I still do not know if the guard got them out or not because he would have seen the Down train approaching. No damage was sustained by the locomotive, the railmotor however, suffered minor damage.

I advised Traffic Trouble and the senior mechanical officer in Wollongong, the District Superintendent Goulburn and the Chief Inspector Moss Vale. The section was closed for some 12 hours before traffic was again permitted to run. There was, of course, an inquiry, but I was not called. This surprised me, because I had made the decision, legitimately, to make the crossing at Robertson that resulted in the collision. I was not asked to verify the times that I was spoken to, or what action I took to advise emergency services. In fact, I was not even asked for a statement. The other surprising thing to me was why the railmotor driver, when he saw the inevitability of a collision, did not start going backwards to avoid it. In view of the fact there was little damage, he may have done so, another thing I did not find out.

At the insistence of the Unions after this incident, it became mandatory to have Robertson staffed for crossings and two permanent staff were appointed as a result. I remember being appalled at the weakness of the management in agreeing to the staffing. There are innumerable places in New South Wales that have longer and steeper gradients approaching stations and unattended crossing loops. With the short distance of the falling gradient, I found it then, and still do, unbelievable that management did not insist that train crews control their trains in such a manner that they approach the place safely, and if necessary, putting a speed limit from the top of the rising gradient into Robertson.

The embargo, even with the advent of CTC signalling, was not lifted; crossings were not permitted at Robertson unless the signal box was manned. After some time, reason prevailed and it became permissible for crossings to be made. The main reason? The Staff Superintendent (whose interest was not in safeworking) wanted to withdraw the staff.

Robertson is the centre of a large potato growing area. In the early days, many trucks of potatoes were loaded during each season and consigned from Robertson to the vegetable markets in Darling Harbour.

I have noted that Burrawang and Calwalla [now a crossing loop], before Centralised Train Signalling Control, were sidings, which up to about the mid-1970s received considerable amounts of fodder, especially in the winter months.

Illawarra Control was manned by four controllers each day and worked round the clock. At 5.30am an additional controller signed on duty to set up the freight train programme for the following 36 hours. This officer signed on Mondays to Fridays. In addition, the Illawarra/Goulburn Programmer that I mentioned when dealing with South Control, signed on duty at 6.00am. Each controller qualified for Illawarra Control worked the boards as well as the programme position. The addition of a second day work week was a plus for those who worked the board, a plus which was well earned because it was the busiest and most complicated of all the boards which extended outside the Metropolitan area.

In order to try and gain a continuity in my descriptions of the duties, I will start with the 11.30pm shift, leaving the duties of the 5.30am programme officer till last. Like most of the boards in Sydney, the period from midnight till about 2.00am was the quietest. The Up trains had mostly passed Sutherland heading toward Enfield, Cooks River or Chullora, which were the regular destinations. The last steel train would be around Robertson and generally there was a limestone train to make a crossing at Robertson, which as I have said, was manned. The train with the Up loaded milk vats was on its way from Thirroul towards Darling Harbour, while the Down train conveying the empty vats was between Kiama and Bombaderry.

There were coal trains running between Inner Harbour and Coalcliff/Scarborough, but these trains did not cause much problem. The crews, with one exception, were conscientious and realised the importance of their punctual running to the Department and the coal industry. I shall not take long to describe the other crew, but this driver was an obstructionist who had only one equal in my time as controller; his equal being at Hawkesbury River. BHP coal trains would be running between Cringila and Bulli. They caused little problem. If they were overtime at Bulli, which they often were, that was not the problem of the controller; all he had to do was to give Bulli a margin for the main line from the siding when the ASM Bulli asked for it. So, for the first two hours, the controller was maintaining the *status quo* and setting himself up for the busy time that was ahead. I normally had my sandwiches and cup of coffee around 2.30-3.00am.

The branch line or 48 Class locomotives which worked all trains, both freight and passenger, each week day morning from Thirroul and Port Kembla, returned from the metropolitan area on Down trains, having worked on the Up into the metropolitan area. The main line locomotives working the steel trains to South Dynon and empty BLH/BCHs to Medway, were either rostered from Up trains arriving from Moss Vale or were light attached to Down trains from Enfield.

There were 25 48 Class locomotives numbered from 4876 to 48100 allocated to Port Kembla, these locomotives being maintained by the District Locomotive Engineer, Port Kembla. The Liaison DLE in Engine Control advised each Friday the locomotives that would be required for inspection each day in the week following. It was the controller's responsibility to see that the nominated locomotive was available to the Mechanical Branch in time for it to be cleaned for the staff to begin work at the dayshift commencement.

From about 3.00am I used to start looking for the trains returning to Port Kembla. Three locomotives were required to run the 'Katies' from Thirroul, the first departing about 6.15am. The ideal situation was to be able to take a locomotive off the two trains returning as double 48 Class, then to have the train from Cooks River, with a single 48 Class, which usually was the first to return, run through to Port Kembla with its load and then send the locomotive back light engine to Thirroul.

It was very difficult to ascertain when the trains would leave Enfield. It was pointless ringing the yard controller or his clerk, for they knew not. I intend to write a chapter about Enfield so, for the sake of my present exercise, I will say I used to get the telephone boy at Enfield South Box on side. He would ring and tell me when the trains left the yard, and from that, I was able to fairly accurately work out when they would pass Sutherland. It would not be inaccurate to say that on at least two days a week, the trains returned from Enfield too late for the engines to work the 'Katies' as rostered. The trains which ran to Cooks River and Chullora were much more reliable.

On the majority of occasions, it was possible still to use the 48 Class by terminating the returning trains at Thirroul. This working delayed empties for the steel works and often affected the departure of trains the following day. On the occasions when the return trains did not arrive at Thirroul in time for the 'Katies', it was necessary to use extreme measures to obtain engines. No 801, which was a steel train set to depart from Port Kembla at 4.40am, was my avenue of escape. I used to put this train back to No 803's time at 8.40am and take the engines to work the 'Katies'.

This inevitably raised the ire of the Illawarra/Goulburn Programmer, who believed his engines were sacrosanct. My reply was that I would rather listen to you complain than have a thousand workers late for work. I will admit it made life difficult if No 803 was already scheduled to run; it too would then be laid back to the next timetable.

The backshift *amba* was sent about 4.30am. This *amba* included trains for the next 24 hours. Some controllers used to go further but I could see no purpose in that. The only stations to take the *amba* were the attended stations from Sutherland to Port Kembla and Unanderra.

When the returning trains arrived at Thirroul in time to stow the load and then work the 'Katies', the problem was finding a way to shift the loading from Thirroul. On many occasions nothing was available until late in the day. In addition to the 'Katies' engines,

engines were required to run 'H' coal trains. The coal trains between Coalcliff–Scarborough and Inner Harbour all had numbers beginning with the letter 'H'. The engines for trains that ran to Shellharbour and Bombo came from the engines which either worked 'Katies' or from returning Down trains.

As far as possible, the backshift controller entered the engine numbers onto the day's engine rosters for the programme man. This roster was an A4 page size that had the continuous rosters for the engines. There were 25 lines of rosters, including the locomotive scheduled for maintenance. This locomotive became available to the Operations Branch around 5.00pm. Main line locomotive numbers were recorded separately. In addition, he recorded the 6.00am tonnage figures for Illawarra—Goulburn and the Illawarra programmers.

Not only were engines often difficult to get back in time for the 'Katies', the main line locomotives to work Nos 801, 861 and 803 were rostered from returning Medway limestone trains, trains from South Dynon loaded with empties and trains from the metropolitan area attached to the returning 48 Class. It was a bonus sometimes to have them on the Enfield trains, because it was possible to take the 48s at Thirroul and run to Port Kembla with the main line locomotive. It was often necessary to put No 801 back 60 to 90 minutes, waiting engines.

One of my favourite tricks to avoid putting units into Loco at Port Kembla and losing them for hours, was to send them to Wollongong to refuel. The Chargeman as a rule had no objection, but he did get a lot of pressure from the fitters because they saw this as a means of cutting out their jobs. This was not the intention at all. I used to relieve No 864 limestone or 802 ex South Dynon with empties at Unanderra with either the shed crew (preferably) or the outgoing crew and arrange to have the train stowed at Unanderra. The units, when the shunting was completed, ran to Wollongong, re-fuelled and then ran straight onto the train either in Lysaghts or Cringila, if it was for a steel train and to Port Kembla or Unanderra for empties, if it was No 861.

The officer taking charge at 6.00am had to carry on the arrangements left for him. The train working which became virtual peak hour leading up to the 7.00am start for the dayshift staff at BHP, Lysaghts and other industrial firms, made the period up to around 8.00am quite busy. During this shift, he would see at least two trains go to Shellharbour and one to Bombo. While these were running, he had the 'H' trains running. A train that was virtually at the disposal of the controller conveyed empties to Mt Pleasant, Corrimal and Coalcliff for coke loading. It also cleared loaded coke from Coalcliff and any empties that had been placed the previous day for loading from Mt Pleasant and which could only be shunted on the Up. This train also cleared any loading left at Thirroul. The train that went to Waterfall and back to Metropolitan Colliery, sometimes engine and brakevan or sometimes conveying empties, started from Port Kembla around 10.00am.

On the mountain, he would have 861 with Medway empties, and at least one train load of Down interstate steel and sometimes two. On the Up, the passenger from Moss Vale, a load of empties from interstate and a limestone train from Medway would give crossings at Dombarton, Summit Tank and Robertson. The key to this section was how the trains came out of Moss Vale. If they followed on sectional running times from Moss Vale, a significant amount of standing time was going to take place at either Robertson or Summit Tank. It always seemed that the empty wagons were urgently required at the steelworks, which meant the Up train received preference and the Down trains took the standing time. The ideal situation was when there was sufficient margin to get a Down train from Robertson between the two trains. I was generally prepared (as I have just said) with the exception of urgent empties, to stand a train at Moss Vale for 20 to 30 minutes to produce this outcome. This working when a heavy programme was involved, would save far more in standing time during the next 4 to 5 hours than it cost.

By 10.00am, the controller had received the Down programme from the Chief Train Controller, the Up and South Coast programme from the Illawarra Controller, and the Moss Vale/Goulburn Up and Down programme from the Illawarra/Goulburn Programmer. These were entered in the *amba* book, sometimes by the Programme Controller, and the *amba* was sent. I used to do the *amba* in three sections, firstly Sutherland to Wollongong, then the South Coast from Port Kembla to Nowra and finally the Port Kembla— Unanderra—Moss Vale *amba*. This method was more time consuming but it was effective because, if an attempt to give the whole South Coast *amba* in the one go was made, the stations south of Unanderra would not come on straight away and finish up missing half the *amba*. By breaking it up into sections, no station had to wait on the telephone longer than necessary. Any station claiming they had missed the *amba*, and who tried to get me to repeat it after I had used this method, was doomed to disappointment and told to get it from the station next to him. After I had sent the *ambas*, I used to spot the next day's diagram. This entailed marking the diagram in pencil with the Up and Down trains and times that were programmed from their originating point, or where timetabled on the Down, past the border station. This duty was carried out on all boards by the 5.30am controller.

However, a co-operative progamme controller also sometimes did it. If the two controllers had a good working relationship, the two jobs were made easier. When I was on the programme job, I would normally send the *ambas* to give the man working the board an opportunity to have a tea break. Most controllers did the same for me, there was only one who would do no more than his job (or less), and in whichever position he was occupying. He was not a very easy person to work with but was a very fine train controller. The train working duties were enough to keep the controller occupied until his relief arrived at 11.30am.

The 11.30am controller was kept occupied with train working. He was responsible for seeing that the engines were in position for the afternoon passengers. He collected *ecces* from all wayside stations and sidings, including the milk lift for the Bombaderry—Darling Harbour train, which he passed onto Nowra. I found one area that needed watching was Metropolitan Colliery. On most occasions, a light engine was sent to run to Waterfall, to assist the coal train from Metropolitan Colliery on the second leg. When this train arrived at Waterfall, it attached the 600 tons of coal left on the first leg and formed an 1800-ton train that had the brakes tested by an examiner from Thirroul. The train changed engines at Canterbury to 3 x 46 Class and ran north to Morandoo.

I used to ensure that the colliery would load 800 tons before I despatched the light engine, because the colliery's loading record was, to say the least, unreliable. If I found they were not going to load the full complement, I would get an estimate from Helensburgh, who would contact the colliery by public telephone. This information was passed onto the Chief Train Controller. On most occasions, if the total load for the two engines was more than 1000 tons, the train was let run; if it were less than this, the light engine was cancelled and the single 48 Class departed from Waterfall with the 600 ton load.

One of the first duties of the afternoon assistant station master at Port Kembla was to check his yard to establish if the forecast loading for the Up trains especially had come from the various industrial areas. He spoke to the controller about 4.30pm with this information, and together with the controller worked out if the loading would meet the programme set. By this time, the controller knew what loading was coming from Shellharbour and Bombo. If the loading figures did not meet the forecasts, adjustments were made to the programme by reducing trains worked by two or three 48s by one or two engines. It was, of course, important to check the chief train controller's Down tonnage in Enfield before reducing the engine power on the Up trains. Heavy Down loading obviously meant the engines ran light attached on the Up. Generally speaking, the tonnages that came from the Port Kembla industrial area were far greater than that which came from Enfield. Zoned loads were formed for trains to run direct to Cooks River and Chullora. These trains formed return trains and could be relied upon to run to time, more than those trains that originated from Enfield.

When the afternoon programme was finalised, the controller ran through the programme with the ASM at Port Kembla, the guards and enginemen's roster clerks and the chargeman at Port Kembla. The controller then made a list of what each train would convey and passed it onto Goods Control, the Chief Train Controller and Engine Control.

The 5.30pm controllers' main task was, literally speaking, that of a maintainer. He kept a close watch on the engines to ensure that they were available for the trains to be rostered on and made adjustments if they were not. It was very important that the trains ran on time from their origins into the metropolitan area. Their on-time arrival into the metropolitan area gave the backshift man, when he was applying pressure to get his trains back out of the metropolitan area somewhere near to time, a basis from which he could agitate for his engines. He tried to make sure that the main line locomotives were in sight for No 801, the first of the steel trains, because they almost invariably came from engines off the limestone and deep South trains.

The Illawarra Up Programmer signed on duty at 5.30am. His first duty was to formulate a programme from the figures left with him by the backshift controller for the following 36 hours. A loose-leaf system with pages about the equivalent of four A4 pages was used, one sheet per day. This sheet showed all the trains in the timetable that ran in the Port Kembla area. He had to select from these sufficient trains to clear the Up loading, and sufficient trains to run to Shellharbour and Bombo to lift the Departmental and commercial usage ore, plus the 'H' coal trains, and to allocate engines onto each of these trains. The metal orders were advised on a daily basis by *mets* (this was the code word for the Rolling Stock Superintendent), his office being universally known as *Mets*. The orders from Bombo were given each Friday for the following week by a liaison officer of the Chief Civil Engineer's Office, who was situated in *Mets*. The order for the 'H' coal trains was given by the coal and mineral clerk in *Mets*.

The controller was responsible for the total Illawarra programme, and the Illawarra Goulburn Programmer was responsible for giving him his proposed programme before 8.30am. This program rostered the main line diesel locomotives and accounted for southern and south western traffic from the industrial works, in particular the oil, fertiliser and the interstate steel traffic from Lysaghts and Cringila.

When he had completed the programme for the next 36 hours, the telegraph operator at Wollongong connected the controller to a telephone hook up. The programme was then relayed to the locomotive roster clerks at Port Kembla and Thirroul, the guards roster clerk and the Assistant Station Master Port Kembla. The controller advised these key personnel of the train numbers that were to run, their destinations, the locomotives to work them, and the trains these locomotives were to arrive by.

After he had completed this, he would write up the particulars of the loading forecast of each train for the chief train controller. Invariably on week days, there would be a train to Morandoo with coal from Metropolitan Colliery, and others to Cooks River, to Chullora, to Darling Harbour with the South Coast milk and paper from Nowra, and two trains to Enfield with blue metal from Bombo and Shellharbour. In addition to these zoned loads, loading from the steelworks and the associated industrial areas, accounted for about 800 to 1000 tons daily; this loading being cleared by an Enfield train. This programme was extended to a 36 hour forecast, in order to give the chief train controller the assured loading for that day's trains and a forecast of the loading for the next day, for his own programme.

He was responsible for the rostering of the 25 x 48 Class locomotives, and providing to the Mechanical Branch the required locomotives for inspection each day. He did this by rostering them on a train for the metropolitan area that was timetabled to return to Port Kembla in time for it to be in Loco by 6.00am. The ideal situation was to avoid working the engine to the metropolitan area the previous evening, which was possible if the loading could be cleared without using it.

I would say, that on average, this would happen only once a week. He would complete the engine numbers onto the engine roster sheet and start the next day's roster off by pencilling in the engine numbers and trains by which they were returning. He would write up the next day's programme sheet showing forecast loadings and engine rostering.

Around 10.00am every morning, the Chief Clerk CMPC, the chief train controller, the main line diesel clerk, the 46 Class electric locomotives clerk and the train control superintendent examined the final programme for the metropolitan area. I will not go into the full detail here, suffice to say that at 10.00am, a set of alterations would come from the chief train controller outlining the amendments to the programme due to engine shortages. It rarely affected the South Coast 48 Classes.

The Illawarra—Goulburn Programmer would have main line locomotives taken from the Down trains on which he had ordered them to run his programme. In the majority of cases, these units would be light attached to Port Kembla. So as far as the chief train controller was concerned, he was happy to see those engines taken and used on loading from the metropolitan area on other trains. From Wednesday to Friday, it was almost a daily occurrence for the Illawarra—Goulburn Programmer to lose at least one main line locomotive and have to re-cast his programme. This done, he would give the changes to the Illawarra Programmer and the programmer in turn, would give those alterations to the respective roster clerks. It was generally very poorly received by the Mechanical Branch Roster Clerk at Port Kembla. We were all dimwits in his view.

After I had been in Illawarra Control about 12 months, the passenger train section introduced a new passenger timetable for the metropolitan area and the South Coast. I was given the special duty job of recasting the 48 Class rosters, which had not been amended since the complete dieselisation on the South Coast. The changes to the numbers of passenger trains were minimal, although in my view, there were still too many. I recall one occasion when a derailment in Thirroul yard locked in a set of carriages for the second 'Katie'. I saw no option but to cancel the first 'Katie' and run only one. Before I made the decision, I spoke to the station master at Thirroul and asked whether he thought one train would take all the workers. His response was,

"With room to spare."

I made 25 new rosters that reflected the change in the passenger train working, which also better fitted the changes that had taken place in the local freight working. I began this chapter by saying Illawarra Control was the complete Train Control Board. My experiences in the job, which I enjoyed, confirmed that. There were many challenges that did not arise in straight train working boards. It was certainly a great training ground for the chief train controller programme position.

Tank locomotive 3052 stands at Lysaghts platform with the afternoon workers' train in November 1952. This train with its end-platform consist would wait at the platform for the day shift workers from the nearby John Lysaght Company's works and the AIS flat products mill, then under construction, to board the train at the end of the shift. The train stopped at all stations and terminated at Thirroul.

On Friday afternoons, the 30 Class locomotive was detached from the train at Wollongong station, a 32 Class locomotive with additional carriages attached whence the train proceeded to Sydney Terminal.   *John R Newland.*

SENIOR TRAIN CONTROLLER, ILLAWARRA—GOULBURN PROGRAMME

THE DUTIES of this Senior Train Control position can be easily described; what cannot be easily described however, is the amount of attention to detail that was required to make it function. I learned the position in 1967 and relieved for holidays each year until I was appointed Chief Train Controller. I was also constantly called to relieve on days when the incumbent went off duty ill.

The first duty after signing on at 6.00am was to call into South Control and see how the limestone trains were running. I also checked to see where Nos 802 and 804 were, these being the trains which brought the empty steel flat wagons from South Dynon. Then I went into Illawarra Control to get the 6.00am tonnages. These tonnages revealed how much, if any, traffic was carried over from the previous day. The Senior's chair for this job was situated in the same room as the Livestock Agent, the Wheat Officer, the Interstate Transit Officer and Manna Wheat.

On returning to my desk, I used to speak first with the Steel Freight Manager from Lysaghts who would forecast how many tons of steel that he would load in the next 24 hours and at what time it would be available. From this information, we decided what trains he would require to clear his loading. The next officer spoken to was the Station Master Port Kembla who would have the steel loading from Cringila, the oil tanks loading from the oil depots and the fertiliser loading from Australian Fertilisers Limited, plus general loading from the industrial area.

When the controller had this information, he formulated a programme that generally saw three 1200-ton loads of steel to South Dynon, an oil train and a load of general goods including fertiliser for Goulburn, and mostly four train loads of empty limestone wagons. This working required 12 mainline diesels plus one to bank the trains to Summit Tank.

He then typed out a programme which showed each Down train departing and each Up train arriving, with their departure times and the anticipated arrivals of the Up trains. He showed on his typed programme where the locomotives to work each train were to come from. If he required locomotives from the metropolitan area, he showed the Down trains that he had ordered to be on. It was essential that he had this programme ready before the Illawarra Control programmer was ready to give his programme to the officers concerned. When it was received, it was incorporated into the Illawarra programme and given jointly with the programme.

The next duty was to contact the Assistant Station Master Moss Vale, who was the guards roster clerk, the station staff roster clerk and among other things, he was the liaison officer with Berrima Cement Works and the limestone quarry at Medway. The ASM at this time was able to advise the following day's limestone requirements of the cement works at Berrima Junction and the steel mills requirements at Cringila. The programme requirements for the following 36 hours were then worked out jointly (or at least, they were with me) and passed onto Goulburn Control, South Control and Chief Train Controller Programme.

The Marulan—Maldon limestone programme was also another responsibility for the controller. He conferred with the Station Master Marulan on a daily basis. If there were any amendments to the standard programme, these also were passed onto the ASM Moss Vale for inclusion in his programme. The duties associated with the programme side of the position were mostly completed by 11.30am.

There were also a couple of 'tack on' jobs associated with the controller's position. He was responsible for balancing the 4 EHG vans, each of which was a power van with one motor used to refrigerate containers of fruit and vegetables from interstate. To maintain control over these, he had a diagrammatic form that was able to show a running image of their use and where they were at any given time. It was not a difficult task, but was time consuming. In addition to this, he used to obtain a forecast of bogie empties arriving into the State for the following 24 hours. That was another relatively simple task that required time.

This position was by far the best of the Senior Controller's positions in Sydney. It was daywork from Monday to Friday but as a consequence, it was the lowest paying Senior's position. Every time I relieved in it, I seemed to work at least one Saturday and Sunday in the fortnight. The incumbent would not work overtime.

SENIOR TRAIN CONTROLLER, METROPOLITAN GOODS CONTROL

IN December of 1969, I began to learn Goods Control. There is not the slightest doubt that this was the most demanding Train Control Board in the State. The demand placed on the Goods Controller was equal to no other demand in the rail control system. He was responsible for seeing the daily sustenance arriving into the metropolitan area between the hours of 3.00am and 5.30am was placed for delivery. More than one controller in my period on the third floor was removed from Goods Control because he failed to achieve this target.

It was uncommon, but nevertheless I can recall two occasions when backshift train controllers were woken up at home at 9.00am and directed to report, in person, to the Train Control Superintendent who had been directed by the Goods Train Superintendent (The Great White Father) to take statements from them and then formulate defence against punishment charges, against the controller.

On one occasion, the wife of the controller answered the telephone call and when she was directed, not asked, to get the controller to the telephone, she refused. Despite the threat (and that is all it could have been), her husband would be held to account for her refusal and punished accordingly, she still refused. She agreed to wake him at 2.00pm, which was eight hours after he signed off duty. One of the controllers taken off Goods Control did not get back there for some years; the other was charged departmentally for failing to make proper arrangements to place meat at Kogarah for A J Bush & Co and at the Abattoirs Siding. A warning was issued together with the fine; one more failure to perform would see him removed permanently. So it was a no nonsense, no mistakes position. This knowledge was very stressful when things were not running according to schedule. It caused a lot of gut churning, mine included.

After the refusal of the controller to speak to anyone from the Department until eight hours had elapsed, this being the time the Salaried Officers Award decreed between sign-off and sign-on, the practice of demanding controllers (or any one else for that matter) return to duty to make statements ceased. And so it should have. It was vindictive and showed no consideration to the person concerned.

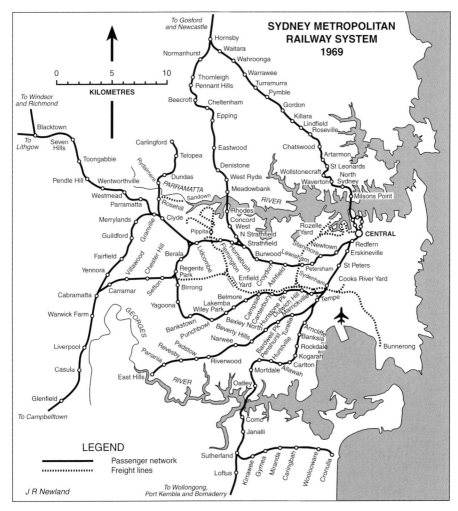

SYDNEY METROPOLITAN
RAILWAY SYSTEM
1969

LEGEND

Passenger network

Freight lines

J R Newland

The load of every train that departed from Broadmeadow, Lithgow, Goulburn, Port Kembla and even the milk train from Nowra, was despatched to Sydney Telegraph, in my time, by teleprinter. Sydney Telegraph sent the load messages to Train Control Telegraph, which was situated outside the door of Goods Control, by placing them in small cylinders and despatching them in compressed air-operated tubes. The telegraph junior delivered these loads messages to the board concerned and to Goods Control. It was his duty to deliver the loads every 15 minutes to the control boards. The receipt of train loads within an hour of their departure from the originating country depots of Goulburn, Lithgow, Broadmeadow and Port Kembla was absolutely essential to Goods Control.

In addition to these, were forecast loads of the two regular fruit and perishable trains from the Murrumbidgee Irrigation Areas, the fruit and perishable train from Orange and generally two perishable milk and fruit trains from the North Coast. These forecasts were mostly received between 3.00pm and 5.00pm. Over the 24-hour period, forecasts were also received for interstate trains from South Dynon, Clapham and Mile End.

I have already said it was the responsibility of the controllers working each of the boards with trains arriving into the metropolitan area to forecast their arrival times and to keep that forecast updated. It did not take long to find out who the good controllers were when it came to forecasting train arrivals. On backshift, I developed the habit of walking up the steps to the third floor and into and through the apparatus room that led into South Control. I used to glance at the diagram of the South, West and North as I went into Goods Control. Doing this gave me an idea if there were any trains running out of course on the Up, but it was to no advantage with some controllers who did not pencil the forecast running of their trains onto the diagram.

It was about the end of 1968 that an additional Train Control Board, known as No 2 Goods, was introduced. It was graded as a First Class Train Controller position. Initially it was worked by second class assistant station masters who were experienced in metropolitan depot working and with the geography of the area. The purpose was twofold; firstly, to maintain control over the light engines for outgoing trains going to the several depots and for the return to Delec (the name of the Mechanical Branch Depot at Enfield) of engines arriving, and to have oversight of trip trains working at the Goods Controller's directions. The second reason was to take some of the pressure off the Goods Controller.

Prior to the introduction, the standing times of incoming engines en-route to their locomotive depot, Delec were not far short of criminal neglect on the part of depot officers, head/senior shunters, signalmen and the goods train section administration. The introduction of No 2 Goods Control was a genuine effort, albeit a very expensive one, of remedying a state of affairs that had existed for far too long. This neglect applied especially to trains whose crews had been relieved at Enfield on their way to Rozelle, Cooks River or Darling Harbour. The relief crews would be in no hurry to return to Delec. The shunting staff would oblige and lock engines into sidings while they shunted. They would be held unnecessarily by signalmen claiming no margin for them. It was all a culture that developed over many years and was so ingrained, that for some time, No 2 Goods Control was ineffectual. Many of the signalmen had not reported to a control officer before, other than to Traffic Trouble, and had no intention of doing so.

It was not until pressure was put on them by the controllers and inspectorial staff that an improvement was seen. The delays made a mockery of Commissioner McCusker's edict that diesel locomotives should be productive 23 hours per day. A chapter will be devoted to No 2 Goods Control; the purpose of mentioning it at this juncture is to set a proper foundation in the reader's mind of the working of Goods Control.

The Metropolitan area in the late 1960s was a hotchpotch of depots that came into being because Enfield did not function properly. The depots, or more correctly, mini-depots were:

North Strathfield was manned by an assistant station master. It detached Ashfield wire traffic, and Darling Harbour perishable traffic from trains that conveyed predominantly Enfield area traffic. Arnotts biscuit factory loaded traffic and the White Rose flour mill received wheat wagons. Arnotts was shunted in the afternoon by a trip train; the north bound biscuit vans were placed for pick up by a train departing Enfield about 9.30pm. The Western Line biscuit vans were taken to Clyde for a train that ran from Darling Harbour via the main line to pick up at Clyde.

The Main South biscuit vans went to Enfield and received transit by a train departing Enfield around 10.00pm almost every evening. A train load of wire for Ashfield came from the industrial area of Lysaghts at Newcastle. Unless Ashfield had not unloaded the

A portion of North Strathfield Yard in September 1954 located to the right of the Short North flyover bridging the Western Line, viewed from the Parramatta Road underbridge. A Garratt locomotive hauling a goods train is approaching from the Western Line. The White Rose flour mill and Arnott's biscuit factory sidings are located behind the photographer.

C C Singleton, ARHS Rail Resource Centre 5624.

wire from the previous day, which was uncommon, this train ran direct to Ashfield, arriving around 3.30am. In the majority of cases, it placed the wire and returned light engine to Delec. It was a common occurrence for the overflow wire from the manufacturer to receive transit from Broadmeadow by one or more trains a day. Mostly, it was detached at North Strathfield and placed at Ashfield by trip trains. When deciding whether to detach it or let it go to Enfield, the controller had to take into consideration the time of day, and whether, by detaching it at North Strathfield, he would take up too much of the limited room at that point. I would not detach it after about 9.00pm because I did not have the opportunity to transfer it to Ashfield before the backshift transfer perishable traffic arrived.

On the backshift every night of the week, milk for Pippita and meat for the Abattoirs was detached from the north trains. The fruit express conveying the Darling Harbour fruit for COD (short for Committee of Distribution, a commercial group of agents who were responsible for the fruit after it was placed in fruit sidings), was a high profile train and invariably ran to North Strathfield or Darling Harbour via the main line. The controller who, in his wisdom, (*or* lack of it), sent the train to Homebush Saleyards to detach then to Darling Harbour, found that when the delays were perused by management—he was in big trouble. Sometimes on a Sunday and Monday morning, milk for Darling Harbour would be detached from various north trains.

Trip trains transferred this traffic. North Strathfield was a busy and important cog in the metropolitan working. The amount of work performed there by one officer on each shift was many times that performed by individuals at Enfield.

Homebush Saleyards became as busy as Flemington had ever been with the closure of Flemington and the transfer of all the livestock industry's requirements to the Homebush Saleyards. The sales were held bi-weekly on Mondays and Thursdays. The country stock trains I have spoken so much of coming from west and south, all ran into Homebush Saleyards. Although there was not much room to store traffic, it was easier to handle because it was, in effect, a large balloon loop. Trains with traffic for the yards were able to run in, detach and keep going to their destination in the direction of travel. In effect it became another metropolitan depot. Trains arriving into the metropolitan area on backshift with stock (naturally), milk and meat and not requiring to go to Darling Harbour, were shared by Clyde and Homebush Saleyards, before terminating in Enfield.

The forming of bogie interstate trains, for which Homebush Saleyards were not designed, became almost standard practice on the off stock days. Trains arriving from South Dynon with the bulk of their loads for Brisbane either went to Clyde or Homebush Saleyards to attach, detach, do brakes, change engine/s to 46 Class electric/s and depart for the north. The saleyards was a difficult place to manage from a controller's viewpoint. He often had no recourse other than put more work there than he wanted.

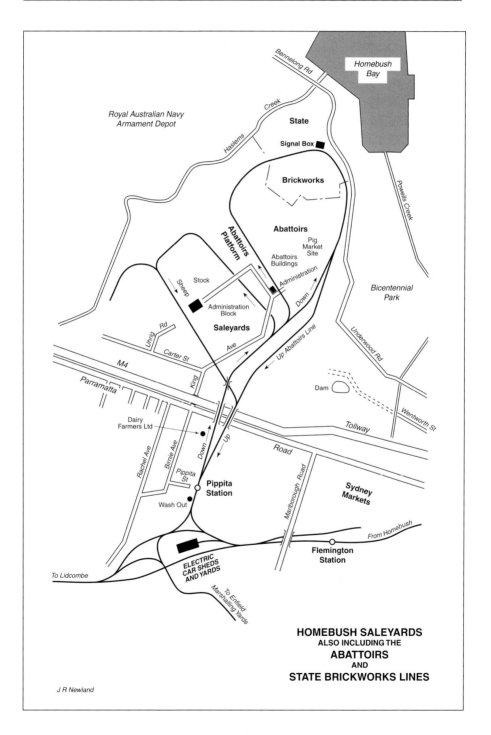

HOMEBUSH SALEYARDS
ALSO INCLUDING THE
ABATTOIRS
AND
STATE BRICKWORKS LINES

J R Newland

Homebush Saleyards Loop and Sidings (above photo) and the Abattoirs Sidings (lower photo) viewed from the Park Road overbridge in April 1985. The Abattoirs ceased operation later that year and the Homebush Saleyards finally closed in June 1991. The whole area has been developed for the Sydney Olympic Park and new Showground, opening in 1998. John R Newland.

The shunters were not as co-operative as they were in other depots and perhaps, more importantly, with one exception in my time, the assistant station masters were not strong enough or experienced enough to maintain control over the working. The daywork station master was the only officer I found who directed the shunters and saw that they carried out his directions. With the ASMs, the shunters said what they would do and got away with it. To their credit, they picked the trains they would delay and I, at no stage, had reason to complain about the way they despatched the trip trains with the milk and meat to Pippita and the Abattoirs.

The clearance of empty stock wagons to Enfield was critical for two reasons; firstly, to give the saleyards room to move ,and secondly, to meet the stock wagon book out for the Wednesday from Enfield. Sometimes they were cleared by attaching to trains which had detached, this move was objected to by crews who had come from barracks and they would do no more than to detach the stock. The option then available was to get them relieved by a Delec shed crew. The overflow was cleared by trip trains. Sometimes train loads of empties for the country book outs left Enfield lightly loaded to attach empty wagons.

The empty TRC and MRC meat wagons from the Abattoirs were washed out at Pippita wash-out sidings and were usually ready by about 3.00pm; the same applied to the milk vans. These were shunted out by a trip train and taken to the saleyards. From there, they went as directed by the chief train controller, mostly to Clyde for the West train from Darling Harbour to attach, and the Short South milk pots went to Enfield for the Moss Vale pick-up. A special shunt, which had started earlier from Darling Harbour to the washout sidings, often brought the first of the clean empty TRC/MRC meat wagons to the saleyards for a north afternoon train to pick up.

Clyde Yard was a depot station in its own right, supervised by a station master and shunting yardmasters. Goods controllers worked closely with the yardmasters. Up trains from the south and west regularly detached Clyde area traffic. The advantage of having Clyde area traffic marshalled together, one of the banes of my life as a shunter at Parkes, was quickly appreciated when I became a goods controller. Clyde was the centre of a heavily industrialised area. The Shell Oil Company refineries were nearby; Hardies building supply manufacturers were on the Sandown Line nearby; Clyde Engineering and Chamberlain farm machinery were the leaders of the many large engineering businesses in the region. The Clyde Wagon Repair Siding was across the way on the Down side of the main lines.

A number of Down trains originating from Enfield, Botany and Darling Harbour were timetabled to shunt and pick up at Clyde. The south and west oil trains from Botany picked up on weekdays. A far western train from Darling Harbour attached biscuit vans

Clyde Yard and the Western Line viewed from Clyde 'D' Signal Box in September 1951.
C C Singleton, ARHS Rail Resource Centre 7031.

from Arnotts. Other traffic was arranged by the chief train controller with the assistance of the goods controller, whose job it was to land the traffic to Clyde from whatever point the chief had nominated. It was also a common occurrence at Clyde for an interstate bogie express train from South Dynon to Brisbane conveying metropolitan traffic, to come into Clyde and, after detaching, to attach Brisbane bogie traffic, again as arranged by the chief train controller, and continue to Brisbane after the 46 Class electric locomotives had been attached.

Clyde yards became very important on backshift, No 416 fruit express from the Murrumbidgee Irrigation Areas invariably detached meat for the Abattoirs and stock for Homebush Saleyards, and then proceeded to Darling Harbour. No 418, the second fruit express, mostly shunted at Clyde, then went to Darling Harbour. Sometimes this train did not convey Darling Harbour traffic; when this was so, it ran from Homebush Saleyards to Enfield.

No 310 West conveyed Darling Harbour fruit from Orange, meat from the Abattoirs at Dubbo and Orange and, on occasions, livestock from the Orange open sales. This train detached at Clyde then ran direct to Darling Harbour. No 78 South pick-up detached milk at Clyde for Pippita. This train also conveyed bulk cement for Clyde, some of which went to Hardies and the balance to the bulk concrete company at Granville. On the occasions No 78 conveyed milk for Darling Harbour, it was detached and despatched by trip train around 11.00pm direct to Darling Harbour.

Pippita station in February 1985. Locomotive 48151 is travelling light engine to the Homebush Saleyards to relieve another locomotive. John R Newland.

It was another important cog in the metropolitan scheme of things which always seemed to run smoothly. I took a lot of care to see that I worked in with the yardmasters, avoiding where I could, putting more than one train at a time in there. I was rewarded by having yardmasters who would go the extra 'mile' if I was in trouble, which in Goods Control, irrespective of who the controller was, was often the case. An easy way of getting into trouble, and over which the controller really had no control, was when trains needing to go to Clyde arrived from the west and south simultaneously. This occurred more often on backshift with the fruit expresses when they ran late.

Alexandria was almost redundant as a receiving station for perishable and empty return traffic by the time I came to Goods Control. It had in its earlier years been a very important industrial yard. Before all empty returns were directed to Cooks River, many of these were dealt with at Alexandria.

There were still a few trains that went to Alexandria including trips from Enfield. Some next day delivery for South Dynon was loaded there. If insufficient for a train load, it was transferred to Cooks River by the engine and crew of the train to work the South Dynon load from Cooks River. A shunting trip from Darling Harbour in the morning and evening delivered empty bogie louvre vans and cleared urgent intrastate loading. The return of the Enfield trip that had provided the shunting engine, cleared the balance of loading at the end of the day. Alexandria finally closed down in 1970.

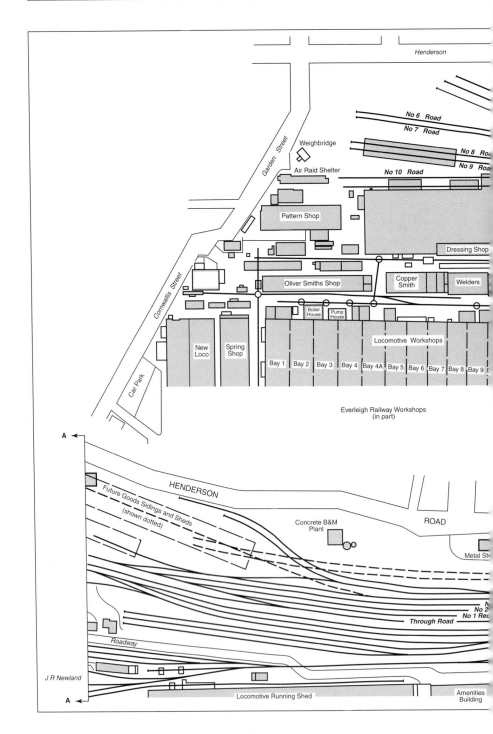

Everleigh Railway Workshops
(in part)

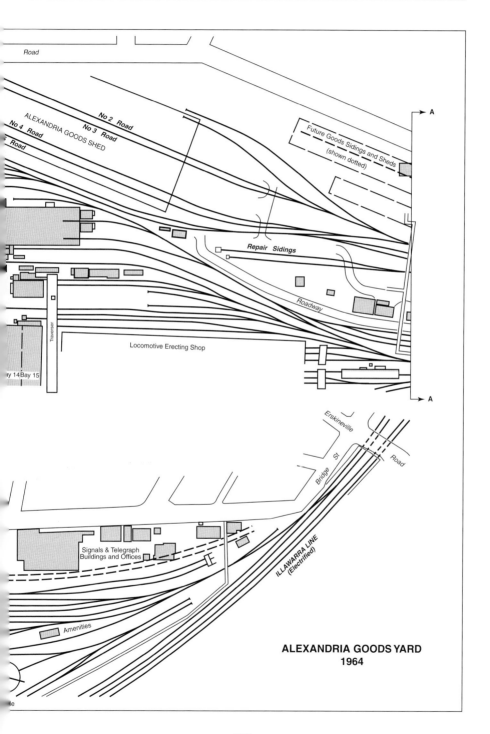

Road

No 2 Road

No 3 Road

ALEXANDRIA GOODS SHED

No 4 Road

Road

Future Goods Sidings and Sheds
(shown dotted)

A

Repair Sidings

Roadway

Traverser

Locomotive Erecting Shop

Bay 14 Bay 15

A

Erskineville

St

Bridge

Road

ILLAWARRA LINE
(Electrified)

Signals & Telegraph
Buildings and Offices

Amenities

ALEXANDRIA GOODS YARD
1964

Two views of Alexandria Goods Yard taken from the pedestrian overbridge, sometime before 1970 looking westerly (top photo) and easterly (bottom photo). The goods yard was demolished and removed during the 1990s and is now the site of medium density housing development.

Photographer unknown.

Darling Harbour could be described as the railway heart of New South Wales, because it was from here that every southern, western and a large number of north western and northern towns received their groceries. Every weekday from this point, train loads of loaded louvre vans, 'S' and 'U' trucks covered with tarpaulins, went to the country areas. Such was the organisation at Darling Harbour, that trucks to be loaded with 'out of' traffic for one or two stations on a branch line, that the goods were not only loaded in the truck, they were also loaded on the side of the wagon which was the platform side at the unloading point.

As an example that I knew of, was the 'out of' truck on the Eugowra pick-up. This would be loaded with 'out of' traffic for Bangaroo, Billimari, and Goolagong with the balance for Eugowra. Goods for each of these places would be loaded together. It was only rarely when I was at Eugowra that I found a consignment that had been over carried. It would be difficult to know how many such trucks were loaded on a daily basis at Darling Harbour, but there was certainly quite a large number.

Again, referring to my own knowledge when I was shunting at Parkes, there was always one 'out of' truck on the Parkes—Narromine train, one on the Tottenham Line train and one on the Condobolin train. In addition, there were bi-weekly Darling Harbour

A view of portion of Darling Harbour Goods Yard in May 1955 looking east towards the Sydney city skyline.   *C C Singleton, ARHS Rail Resource Centre 1307.*

trucks for Tottenham, Tullamore, Trundle, Condobolin and Peak Hill. These trucks, of course, were loaded on certain days to connect with the service that ran from the country depot.

On a daily basis, wagons were loaded for the larger stations. Dubbo, for an example, was a depot for Permewan Wright wholesale distributors. This company received two and three wagons daily. Tooths and Tooheys breweries loaded all their kegs and cartons of beer, generally into the trucks loading with others' groceries, etc. The amount of work that was involved in the supervising by the staff of the loading the 'out of' trucks and the making of Guards Road Van waybills, was huge and employed large numbers of staff. The invoicing which was done in the afternoon was a monumental task.

Once again, from my own knowledge, I know that it was on very rare occasions that the invoices for a Darling Harbour truck did not arrive on the mail train, or its connection, before the arrival of the wagon, despite the fact they were mostly next day delivery. It was a simple matter to check the invoice against what was loaded onto a carrier's vehicle. It was not so simple when every item had to recorded, if there was no invoice.

In addition to its outwards loading, Darling Harbour in 1969 received all wool loaded in the southern and western areas of the State. All fruit consigned from all parts of New South Wales, the MIA (Murrumbidgee Irrigation Areas), the west and North Coast was received at Darling Harbour. Dairy Farmers Ltd received milk from the Illawarra, southern and northern dairies at their nearby Ultimo depot. The milk tanks returning empty received the attention of both the chief and goods controllers. The empty north milk tanks departed on a train from Darling Harbour and the southern ones to Enfield for the Moss Vale pick-up. A train ran from Darling Harbour to Nowra with empty milk tanks plus empty bogie louvre vans for the paper mill.

Darling Harbour ran smoothly mainly because the shunters who had their very busy times worked hard to get their work done. When it was done, they downed tools and often on the afternoon shift went home, leaving perhaps a shunter for emergencies. This practice was known to the administration. However, they condoned it for the sake of harmonious relationships and a smooth running ship at Darling Harbour. Had they not turned a blind eye, Darling Harbour would have been a nightmare with work to regulation shunters.

Rozelle became a depot after the Second World War where the Grain Elevator Board's bulk grain terminals, were located. Rozelle grew very rapidly when coal exports boomed in the early 1950s. The advent of containers saw that depot become even busier. I mentioned in my description of South Control the fact that a yard controller was in charge and that he was replaced by a station master in 1964.

This officer, by virtue of two things, his expertise as a depot administrator and his ability to have the respect and loyalty of his staff (given the fact he replaced a yardmaster, which was not an easy task), turned Rozelle around and made it function as a depot should. He did not make many friends with the running staff, however.

I will deal more fully with Rozelle in my description of the chief train controller positions of programme controller, wheat officer, interstate transit officer and container programmer.

Cooks River became a depot in the early 1950s, being the original home of the 'piggyback' method of interstate transport, an innovation of Thomas National Transport (TNT). As time went on Brambles, Mayne Nickless and a number of smaller transport firms established themselves at Cooks River. Before the opening of the standard gauge to Melbourne, their wagons were bogie changed at Albury. After the standardisation, TNT's piggyback method became used less and less. They hired their own wagons from the NSWGR, as it was then, and later from the PTC and still later, the SRA. With these wagons, they ran a daily train with containers of general goods and perishable traffic to South Dynon.

The train left Cooks River at about 2.30pm daily running at A or B schedule with a maximum speed of 115km/h. The cut-off loading time was about 1.30pm. They arrived at South Dynon for unloading at 7.00am the following morning. They were, of course, recorded delay trains, and their running was supervised by the assistant goods trains

Cooks River Goods Yard in April 1954 .   C C Singleton, ARHS Rail Resource Centre 5796.

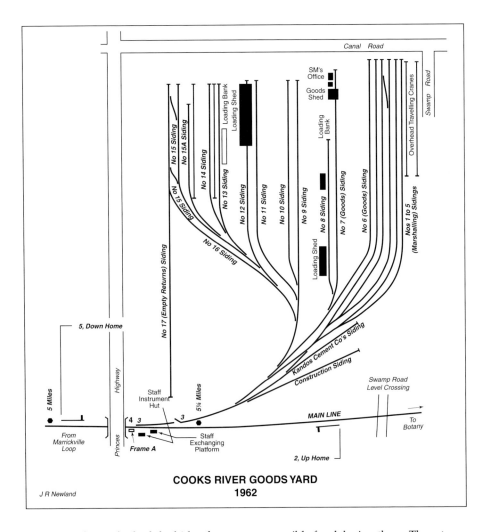

COOKS RIVER GOODS YARD
1962

J R Newland

superintendent, who had the hide of anyone responsible for delaying them. The return train that loaded in South Dynon was due to arrive Campbelltown at around 6.10am, assuring it a path ahead of the peak hour. When referring to Alexandria, I mentioned that all empty returns were directed to Cooks River. This began in the very early 1950s. When I was at Parkes, the Weekly Notices on a regular basis were directing the attention of staff that all empty returns were to be invoiced and directed to Cooks River.

Cooks River was a very busy depot. Besides the South Dynon loading, interstate loading for Brisbane (Clapham and Park Road) was conveyed by a train departing Cooks River daily, and Western and South Australia interstate loading was conveyed to Enfield for trains which ran Monday to Friday with interstate loading for the two States. This, of course, did not commence until the standard gauge link between Broken Hill and Port Augusta was completed. The South Australian traffic for Mile End was bogie exchanged at Peterborough. Cooks River is situated on the Botany Line and was well clear of the main line. A train could be delayed outside the home signal waiting admittance without causing the controller ulcers, as it would have done with stations situated on the main lines. The single line section from Marrickville Loop to Cooks River was worked by electric staff.

I will begin my descriptions of how the goods controller managed to get the traffic that came into his control area by trains conveying milk, meat and fruit to its final destination. To simplify the description, the traffic was detached at either Clyde, Homebush Saleyards or North Strathfield and was delivered from these points by trip trains. It was very important, when taking over on any shift in Goods Control, to read all the files on the back loads (or anticipated loads) and to go through the pigeon hole that was on the controller's right side.

The controllers placed telegrams regarding perishable or important traffic arriving in this pigeonhole, as well as notes to one another as reminders of track work or power off, in fact, anything that affected the working. For every vehicle that did not go direct to Enfield, the controller made a file. These files were usually made on the backs of old local STNs, the passenger sheets which came up from 'Coach' and the backs of any other unwanted used paper from the offices; these were torn in half and an A4 sheet of paper made two files.

As each load came into him, the controller placed a line under every vehicle, or group of vehicles. He copied these onto a file showing in the top left hand corner, the train arriving in the middle, the date, the station at which the vehicle was detaching the right hand side, and the trip it was to receive transit on. As an example:

310W	12 Dec 1969	Clyde 35T
2TRC ex Dubbo		Abattoirs
Yardmaster 2.40am		

This procedure was adopted for 15 trains on an average backshift, but on stock nights the number got to about 20 trains. Clyde dealt with Nos 416 and 418 South and 310 West. After detaching, these trains almost invariably went to Darling Harbour, although there were exceptions sometimes with No 418, if No 416 conveyed all the MIA perishable traffic for Darling Harbour. A trip train moved any stock or meat on these trains from Clyde.

On the majority of nights, at least four trains conveyed perishable traffic ex Broadmeadow. Two of them went to Darling Harbour after detaching at North Strathfield and the other two mostly went to Enfield after detaching the milk and meat. They would have detached something like 8-10 milkpots and about 6-8 TRCs of meat. A trip train took these to Pippita and Abattoirs Sidings. By the time the controller had dissected all the train loads, made out his files and began to arrange his requirements with each station, it was generally around 1.45am.

After he had completed each load, he gave it to the No 2 Goods Controller to route. For trains from the south and going to Clyde, this officer advised Cabramatta, Granville and Auburn signal boxes; from the south going to Cooks River, he advised Cabramatta, Sefton Junction, Chullora, Enfield South and Wardell Road signal boxes; from the south and going to Enfield and then Rozelle, he advised Cabramatta, Sefton Junction, Chullora, Enfield North and Wardell Road signal boxes; and for trains going direct to Enfield, he advised Cabramatta and Sefton Junction signal boxes.

For trains from the west going to Clyde then to Darling Harbour via the main line, he advised Granville, Clyde, Auburn, Lidcombe and Flemington Goods Junction signal boxes; for trains going to Enfield, he advised Auburn and Lidcombe and Flemington Goods Junction signal boxes; for trains going to Homebush Saleyards and Enfield, he advised Auburn and Flemington Goods Junction signal boxes.

For trains from the north, the signal boxes at Epping and North Strathfield were advised of the destinations irrespective of where they were destined. After trains came round the Homebush loop towards Flemington Goods Junction, this signal box and Chullora were advised for Enfield trains. For trains going beyond Enfield, the Enfield North and South and Wardell Road signal boxes were also advised.

When the No 2 Controller had routed the trains, I obtained the loads from him and attached the matching files to each one. I then rang the respective stations with the programme of trains that they would receive. As I gave them each detach, I recorded on the file both the time and the trip train that the goods were to receive transit by. I normally began with Clyde, then Homebush Saleyards, North Strathfield and finally Darling Harbour. The files were lined up along the top of the desk in trip train order. When I had finished, I had in each bundle of files the traffic that each trip train would convey.

One of the difficult wagons to place was the A J Bush and Sons TRC/MRC, which mostly came from Yanco on No 416, but on occasions, they received transit by No 418. It was common practice to detach this consignment at Clyde and run with 20T, 35T or 11T. The Bush's representative used to ring every morning at around 4.30am wanting to know where the meat was. There were many occasions when the area around Enfield South and Canterbury was congested. If the No 2 Goods was not 'on the ball' and failed to check Enfield South before he let it pass Sefton Junction, it could be delayed for long periods getting past Enfield. The secret was to have Sefton call the train from Lidcombe and when he did, advise him to send it via the Bankstown line to Canterbury and bypassing Enfield, if it was blocking back or delaying trains.

I found a very good train clerk at Darling Harbour. This officer worked only backshift because he lived at Woy Woy and the train service suited his travelling requirements. I never met him, but I imagined he was an older man. By the time I started to give him the programme it was around 3.00am. He knew precisely what could be done at the Harbour, and how many trains the shunters could or would handle in a shift. There were often occasions when an additional train conveying Darling Harbour non-perishable traffic would be coming from the north. Knowing him, I always left this train till last on the programme. If he thought the train could not be handled, he used to say gently,

"I don't know about that one."

I used to take the hint and, depending on the type of engine, would route it to Darling Harbour via the goods road. If it was electrically hauled, I would try and get a diesel engine onto it at Enfield. Failing that, it went to Enfield and the loading was worked forward on a regular trip train from Enfield, as the line from Rozelle to Darling Harbour was not electrified.

Trains regularly blocked back at Sydney West Box on the Up main line waiting for admittance to the Harbour. I mentioned earlier about a controller getting into trouble in Goods Control. This controller insisted that Darling Harbour take a train that the train clerk had said that they could not handle. At 7.00am, as the peak hour was beginning, this train was sitting on the main line. Furthermore, it sat there until after the change of shifts and was taken into Darling Harbour at about 7.40am. This caused chaos to the morning peak hour traffic. I was determined that this was not going to happen to me. Generally speaking, it took about 20 minutes to give Darling Harbour the programme. By this time on most mornings, the back of the work was broken. I used to have my meal when I had completed Darling Harbour.

I used to do a check around the depots around 4.00am to make sure that the trains had come in where they were forecasted and that the trip trains would leave to place the milk and meat at the Abattoirs and Pippita. The staff at these two places used to start around 4.30-5.00am. It was essential to have some of the perishable traffic delivered by 5.00am. North Strathfield relied very heavily on the trip train guards. Generally speaking, they were rostered guards who knew 'the ropes'. I used to get the regular guards on 20T on side early in the week.

On the slack mornings, which were Mondays and Tuesdays, I would try and work them into position so they had an hour or so before the trains started coming in. In return for this, I expected and mostly got, their co-operation on the busy nights. If a guard unfamiliar with the working at North Strathfield was on either 35 Trip or 20 Trip, I worked that train and guard away from there into Clyde or Homebush Saleyards. I was in Goods Control for a long time and during that time, I did not have a complaint about late placement that I was responsible for. I certainly had complaints, but it was generally brought about by the late arrival of the traffic into the metropolitan area. The controllers in Goods Control were picked for their ability, and the colleagues I had all the time I was there, achieved the same results that I did.

No 23 Trip train regularly ran from Darling Harbour to Cooks River, leaving at about 6.00am. It conveyed the Cooks River traffic which had accumulated at Darling Harbour during the previous 24 hours and TRC/MRCs meat vans for the Glenmore Meat Company, whose siding was near Marrickville, but on the goods road. The rollingstock superintendent used to come into Goods Control about 6.45am (when he was later the Freight Train Manager, he still did) and ask the same question every morning,

"Where is the Glenmore meat?"

After the first couple of mornings, I knew he would ask this question, so at 5.30am, the first thing I did was find out where it was and what time it had, or when it would leave, Darling Harbour. If he got an answer straight away, he went away without comment. If he did not, he asked questions about a variety of things, all of which were difficult to answer without some effort. I have to say that, among my colleagues (despite what I said in the previous paragraph), there were some slow learners!

By about 4.30am, the loads for trains that would arrive in the metropolitan area after the peak would start coming in. Every train load was examined and its destination decided. If a train from Goulburn was conveying say 500 tons of wheat for Rozelle and the balance for Enfield, the controller would route it Enfield—Rozelle. Mostly the *zona* clerk (the name for the Mechanical Branch Roster Clerk) responsible for crewing arrangements, would relieve the crew before the train went to Rozelle. If there was any traffic on the train that appeared urgent, or was for a metropolitan siding serviced by a trip train, the controller listed the traffic with the traffic clerk at Enfield onto the respective trip train. On backshift I used to start to compile a handover at about 5.00am or a bit later. This was hand-written and conveyed to my relief controller, the loading of each trip and their destinations to which I had planned. There were no *ambas* to worry about: No 2 Goods Controller was responsible for them and the recording of the delays.

On 5.30am shift, I used to catch the 4.32am from Turramurra that enabled me to be in the control room at about 5.10am. It was my practice to go to each board and to record the trains arriving for the next couple of hours, come back and go through the forward files attached to the forecast loads, then be ready to take a handover at about 5.35am. Most controllers were able to catch a train home just before 6.00am. It was an accepted practice for the 5.30am shift to arrange his take-over so that the backshift could get away. When I was on backshift, I generally caught a train at 5.55am.

The first part of the daywork shift was to supervise the trip working, in conjunction with No 2 Goods Control. It was important that the trip trains did not get locked away somewhere for the duration of the peak hour. After taking over, I generally went through the trip train loads again to make sure I had in my mind, what each one had and just as importantly, that they were in the process of placing the perishable loading at Abattoirs and Pippita milk sidings, especially. Another trip I mentioned earlier was the Darling Harbour—Cooks River trip, because I knew that I would be asked the question I had mentioned earlier. I also checked that the Glenmore meat was listed on it and checked Darling Harbour for a forecast departure time.

Most of the clerical staff of the rollingstock superintendent began work at 7.30am, in particular the clerks in charge of the coal wagons and the bogie covered vans. It was unusual if one of these officers did not require wagons placed somewhere urgently or lifted from somewhere and placed elsewhere for loading. The wheat officer would often come looking for wheat wagons from a wheat siding somewhere if the grain elevator staff had not unloaded sufficient wheat wagons for his early trains. Places such as McLeods at Merrylands, Allied Feeds at Rhodes, White Rose at North Strathfield and Mungo Scott were mills which unloaded early.

Often the chief train controller would require interstate traffic that had arrived overnight at the outer depots to be taken to Clyde to complete loads for his interstate trains. The controller's job was to accommodate the requests of these officers. On all week days, two trip trains were available, and sometimes by adjusting the working of the fixed trip trains, they also could be diverted to deliver wagons.

Short supply of book-out from Enfield of bogie covered vans was another feature that occurred far too often. The Department's clients at Railor at Granville and Tattersalls at Auburn were repeatedly left short. When the bogie covered van man came to me saying he was short supplied to these points, I used to give him preference. The worst feature of this was that mostly the vans were in Enfield and getting a trip train in and out of Enfield without at least an hour's delay, was impossible. If the vans were at Clyde or even Cooks River, they could be placed without the customer going to road transport because he had no vans.

I enjoyed a good rapport with the clerks and always did my best to meet their requests. Some of my colleagues, I unfortunately have to say, thought they were pains in the 'butt' and would not co-operate at all. Others were of my feeling and did their best. It was to the Department's advantage, not the clerks' nor the controllers', that they did co-operate. Those who continually did not co-operate finished with the assistant train control super-intendent directing them, or working on another board.

While the pressure of the backshift was not present, the shift was always busy. I have outlined the arranging of the trip trains to meet requirements, the routing of the incoming trains, the writing of files from forecast loads, especially interstate ones, and the transferring, after being washed out, of milk pots from Pippita at Homebush Saleyards for afternoon trains to lift were duties which saw little idle time being available. The supervising of the wheat trains from both west and south with No 2 Goods Control, to ensure that they were not delayed getting to Rozelle, was also very important. The locomotive crews were nearly always relieved at Enfield on the through road by the *zona* clerk. Generally the guards worked through. If the trains were full Rozelle shipment wheat loads, the wheat officer used to rely on these wagons being unloaded to meet his afternoon program.

It was also often necessary to shunt Ashfield to lift the empties and to place the loaded wagons. On occasions, wire would be left at North Strathfield by the backshift and if so, it would have to be moved to Ashfield and the controller was pretty much at the mercy of the signalmen at Strathfield and Ashfield boxes in finding timetable margins. For this reason, if I had to take the loaded wagons from North Strathfield, I gave directions that the trip train after placing the loaded wagons, the train was not to pick up the empties from Ashfield but to come away engine and brakevan. Lifting the empties meant sending the trip train to Enfield and to risk losing it for hours, especially if change of shifts was imminent. Around 11.15am, I used to write up the work that the trip trains were doing and that which I had planned for the two hours for my relief.

The first hour or so of the 11.30am shift was probably the quietest period of the day. The supervising of the trips, the routing of trains arriving, and watching that the empty milkpots and TRC/MRC meat vans were coming from the Washout Sidings and Pippita in time for their nominated departure trains. It can be fairly said that the turn-around of these wagons from these two sidings was such that it was only on rare occasions that they did not receive transit from the metropolitan area in the afternoon or evening of the day they were placed loaded.

From about 2.00pm onwards, the side telephone never seemed to stop ringing. All the stations with sidings under their control and who had loadings of their own that would be cleared by trip trains, would ring with their *ecces*. Although they had begun to close, there were still many sidings in the metropolitan area. As an example, on the main line, the stations at Newtown, Ashfield, Petersham and Burwood had *ecces*. On the north, the stations at North Strathfield, Concord West, Rhodes, West Ryde, Epping and Pennant Hills all had sidings under their control, including the very busy Allied Feeds at Rhodes.

On the west, the stations at Homebush, Lidcombe, Parramatta, Wentworthville, Seven Hills and Blacktown, and on the south, the stations at Sefton, Leightonfield and Liverpool, Cabramatta to Fairfield and Merrylands had sidings under their control; for those sidings between Enfield and Botany, Canterbury, Cooks River and Botany, gave the *ecces*.

On the Illawarra Line, the stations at Sydenham, Kogarah, Rockdale, Hurstville and occasionally Mortdale and Sutherland had sidings under their control. The gathering of all these *ecces* usually took up to two hours.

Around 4.00pm each day, a telegram known as the *Frut* wire was despatched from Griffith and went to Mets, Darling Harbour, Clyde, Homebush Saleyards and Enfield as well as *syco* South and *syco* CTC. This telegram advised the anticipated loading and marshalling of the two fruit and perishable trains from the Murrumbidgee Irrigation Areas. The controller, on receipt of these, compiled the files for each load. This was not a mandatory task for him, but he did it however, which lent much-needed assistance to the backshift controller, who had only to check the files with the load when it was received from Goulburn. If the afternoon controller was too busy to do them, which was not often, it was standard practice to tell his relief so that he could. It was my habit to write up the trip train working for the 5.30pm shift at about 5.15pm or so.

The 5.30pm shift on Sundays and Mondays was a reasonable shift. However, it was quite busy on Tuesdays (especially), Wednesdays and Thursdays, and as with the other shifts, the supervision of the trip trains was time consuming. One of the trips would be involved in transferring perishable or urgent bogie interstate traffic for the chief train controller. Often traffic would emanate from Clyde for a South Dynon-bound train from Cooks River. Before Alexandria closed, it was often necessary to pick up from there and deliver to Clyde, Cooks River or Homebush Saleyards. Finding margins for these movements anywhere near the peak times was difficult. I used to become annoyed when the chief train controller said about 4.30pm or so, that he wanted something from Alexandria for a train around 7.00pm from Clyde.

When I started in Goods Control on Tuesday evenings, there was a back-up controller who used to sign on at 10.00pm. His job was to keep the forecast loads up to date with files and to do the files for loads as they came in. Because there was no transport home at the 4.30am finishing time, I used to drive in when I did it. It was cut out about three months after No 2 Goods Control came into being. The fact that this assistance was supplied to the 5.30pm and 11.30pm shifts on stock night is an indication of how busy the job used to get.

From about 8.30pm onwards, the train loads were coming in with every telegraph delivery. The volume of work involved in the load files, the supervising of the trips, watching that the trains from Darling Harbour picked up traffic as they were supposed to from North Strathfield and Clyde, and watching that the empty bulk wheat trains departing Rozelle had full loads, ensured that there was no time for idle chatter.

Goods Control, probably more than any other board, was good training in-as-much as we learned that the moment there was seemingly idle time, never to accept that it was time that could be relaxed in and to look around on the back desk and make sure that there was not something you could do.

An indication of the complexity of the trip working will be gleaned from the following trip train summary taken from an early 1960 Metropolitan Goods Working Timetable:

22T Tuesdays to Saturdays conveys from Enfield traffic for Homebush, Burwood and Ashfield. Traffic for Burwood to be overlanded to Ashfield and returned by No 15 Suburban

Goods Train to be marshalled: engine - brakevan - Homebush traffic - Ashfield traffic - Burwood traffic - brakevan.

330 Trip runs with full load to Ashfield conveying traffic for Homebush, Burwood and Petersham. On Mondays also conveys traffic for Newtown. Two guards are to be supplied to shunt Newtown. Burwood traffic off Nos 330 and 22 Trips to be stowed in the terminal road at Ashfield for No 15 suburban goods to lift and place at Burwood.

No 26 Trip formed by a light engine from Sydney Yard, shunts Newtown and Petersham, conveys Up traffic to Darling Harbour after placing Down traffic in readiness for No 23T. On Monday nights, terminates at Newtown and returns as No 26T to Darling Harbour. Two guards to be supplied . Brakevan to be supplied by No 316. When brakevan not supplied, No 21 light engine to attach van from Sydney Yard. Tuesdays to Thursdays, from Enfield, conveys livestock, marshalled next to the engine, then ordinary goods and perishable traffic marshalled at the rear, shunting Newton and Petersham.

No 32T from Enfield conveys livestock marshalled on engine, then perishable traffic followed by ordinary goods.

No 194 from Enfield conveys load of Darling Harbour Goods. When it is necessary for 194 to convey perishables and shipment traffic for Darling Island, such traffic is to be taken through to Darling Harbour and returned as arranged by the Metropolitan Goods Superintendent.

No 64 from Enfield conveys load for Alexandria, including traffic for Sydenham received after departure of No 624. Sydenham traffic to be returned by the Wolli shunter.

No 316 conveys from Enfield traffic for Homebush, Burwood, Ashfield, Petersham and Newtown. Returns as No 337. Train to be marshalled as follows: engine-Petersham traffic-Newtown traffic two brakevans-Ashfield traffic-one brakevan-Homebush traffic-Burwood traffic-Brakevan. One brakevan is to be detached at Ashfield for No 8 Suburban Goods the following day. Burwood and Homebush traffic, not to exceed 24 vehicles in length, if stowed in terminal road at Ashfield, whilst other traffic is shunted to the yard and Ashfield traffic detached. Station Masters Homebush, Burwood, Ashfield, Petersham and Newtown to advise the Chief Train Controller and Yard Supervisor Enfield by 6.00am daily the number of vehicles that can be accommodated off No 316.

Nos 318 and 320 conveying traffic Homebush to Newtown runs as required to clear loading.

No 624 from Enfield a full load for Alexandria.

No 31T conveys bogie contract loading for Melbourne to Alexandria.

No 664 from Enfield runs via Homebush Saleyards and clears perishable traffic to Darling Harbour.

No 900 Mondays only conveys grain traffic for Mungo Scott siding.

No 904 from Enfield conveys traffic on the goods road Rozelle to Darling Harbour.

No 922 conveys traffic for Shell sidings, Pyrmont, including Shell oil tanks and traffic for Wattle Street, including McWilliams wine tanks, traffic for Darling Harbour and City Council sidings. On Saturdays also conveys traffic for Canterbury, Rozelle and Darling Harbour.

No 984 conveys Darling Harbour, also traffic to and from Comets siding, Great Western Milling Company and Mungo Scotts.

No23T conveys from Darling Harbour traffic for Suburban stations, lifts Down journey traffic from Newtown and Petersham. On Sundays shunts all Suburban goods stations.

No 37T conveys from Enfield traffic for Stockmans Siding, also stock for Homebush Saleyards and Abattoirs area.

No 59T, formed by Abattoirs shunter. conveys refrigerator cars from Abattoirs to Flemington and shunts at Flemington as required.

No 199 runs from Darling Harbour via Wells Street and conveys empty refrigerator cars for Washout sidings and loaded refrigerator cars for Abattoirs and Petersham. Lifts traffic at Homebush Saleyards and then to Enfield.

No 201 from Enfield conveys contract and general traffic for Chullora Industrial sidings.

No 221 Mondays to Fridays, conveys bogie contract traffic from Alexandria to Enfield North for 421 South, worked by assisting engine for No 421 South.

No 203 from Darling Harbour conveys interstate contract traffic for Rudders, Rozelle, Sanatorium siding and Enfield Yard traffic.

No 43T from Enfield shunt all sidings Chullora area as required.

No 205 from Darling Harbour attaches and conveys from Alexandria composite trucks for the Southern and Western lines, which should be marshalled next to the brakevan followed by traffic for Rockdale to Heathcote, then for stations on the Bankstown line, with ordinary traffic and empties marshalled next to the engine.

No 207 From Darling Harbour conveys all traffic for Nos 401 and 41A South and Carlingford line. Bowral, Moss Vale and Exeter traffic to go forward by 401 South. Out-of-van for Glenfield to Campbelltown to go forward on 41A. Out-ofs for Menangle Park to Maldon to be loaded into bogie brakevan of No 205, which goes forward on 401 South. Also conveys brakevans for 69 West and traffic for stations Rockdale to Heathcote for conveyance by Nos 27 and 167 Illawarra.

No 555 From Darling Harbour conveys traffic for stations Toongabbie to Kingswood, Richmond line, Lidcombe, Regents Park, Epping to Hornsby, Asquith to Point Clare. Also conveys traffic for Auburn, Granville, Parramatta and Wentworthville. Out-of traffic for Westmead and Wentworthville (to be loaded in brakevan for No 5 trip) and traffic for stations and sidings North Strathfield Junction to West Ryde for Nos 2 and 4 trips.

No 591 conveys traffic from Alexandria sidings to Enfield.

No 631 From Darling Harbour conveys traffic for Enfield, including milk vans for North, South and West (except Penrith)

No 715 From Rozelle conveys load for Enfield, Lewisham Sub-station siding and Long Cove siding.

No 943, Mondays to Fridays, conveys traffic from Rozelle, and works Mungo Scott's, Lewisham Ice Works, Great Western Milling Co and Dulwich Hill Goods siding. Load of No 943 must be restricted in length so that the train will not exceed equal to 50 four-wheeled vehicles on arrival Enfield.

Shunting trips, worked by Sydney Yard stand-by pilot engine conveying milkpots off arriving passenger trains from Sydney Yard to Darling Harbour and, on return from Darling Harbour' goods traffic for early morning paper trains.

The Illawarra shunter runs from Alexandria to Rockdale Mondays to Fridays, and shunts all stations to Rockdale and return, leaving Down traffic beyond Rockdale at Rockdale for No 24 trip.

No 1 conveys traffic for Richmond line only, and shunts all stations and sidings from

Blacktown to Richmond. Small out-of consignments for Marayong to be put out at Blacktown and despatched by passenger train. Large out-of consignments to be taken through to Riverstone and returned to Marayong. Train to be provided with LHG or PHG brakevan.

No 7 conditional train starts from Homebush Saleyards on weekdays, and from Enfield Yards on Sundays. Conveys meat vans and goods trucks for Riverstone and beyond; traffic to be marshalled in station order; stock, then tallow trucks casks to be marshalled next to the brakevan. On Sundays, conveys meat vans etc, landed to Enfield by 15 Suburban from Homebush Saleyards.

No 69 conveys traffic all stations Blacktown to Kingswood. Picks up all loaded traffic and open empty trucks for Penrith and stations West thereof. Stops at Granville to pick up out-of traffic from Southern stations. Traffic for Ropes Creek must be marshalled together, detached at St Marys and subsequently picked up by branch shunter.

No 2 Works all stations and sidings Richmond to Mulgrave inclusive, detaches at Riverstone, out-of van to be marshalled next to the engine, Darling Harbour stock and meat to be marshalled next in order. On Sunday nights, shunts where required between Richmond and Riverstone and to lift meat at Riverstone for Wollongong, Kogarah, Hornsby and St Leonards.

No 8 conveys from Richards siding (Riverstone) meat and other traffic for Granville and Darling Harbour.

No 64W works all stations Kingswood to Wentworthville. When required to shunt Mt Druitt, load not to exceed 100 tons less than the fixed load for the engine employed. Traffic off Up trains terminating at Penrith for stations on the Carlingford line, Sandown branch, Auburn goods and meat sidings, Tanner and Middleton's siding, sidings in Clyde Yards, Brunton's and Clyde Engineering Company's siding, is to be despatched from Penrith by Nos 64 and 64A.

No 207 from Enfield conveys traffic for and picks up at Epping, Pennant Hills, Gonarro Siding and Hornsby.

No 231A conveys brakevan and limited number of trucks from Enfield to North Strathfield Junction, unless otherwise directed. Places traffic ex Arnotts at North Strathfield in readiness to be attached to Nos 663 and 258. Shunts sidings between North Strathfield and Rhodes, and places such traffic, as directed by 'Control', for No 487 to lift.

No 205 conveys traffic for Hornsby and North Shore line.

No 258 lifts traffic on hand Hornsby ex North for North Strathfield goods siding and Down relief line to Rhodes for transit by No 4 trip.

No 272 conveys from Hornsby traffic for and works all stations. Brickworks siding to North Strathfield. Down journey traffic from Brickworks siding to be detached at Pennant Hills, for Down train to lift as directed by 'Control'. Places in position West Ryde traffic and lifts outwards Up traffic from that Station. Detaches perishable and other traffic at Darling Harbour for transit by No 274. Station Master Hornsby to provide assistant guard, who will remain at North Strathfield and assist with the shunting of No 274 and other trains, returning to Hornsby on No 207 as assistant guard

No 232A conveys from West Ryde traffic for Enfield and empties required for Darling's siding, Rhodes. Places traffic in readiness at West Ryde for No 272 to lift. Brakevan to be provided at West Ryde for No 4 trip. Lifts outward traffic from Tulloch's, Timbrol's and Darlings sidings and traffic at North Strathfield as required. Detaches Darling Harbour traffic at North Strathfield for No 274.

Nos 7 Trip, 11 Trip and 23 Trip convey traffic from Enfield for the Botany line. The station Master Marrickville must ascertain from the Traffic Supervisor, Enfield, when trains convey loads hauled by two engines and arrange for an employee qualified as a signalman to be in attendance at Marrickville loop signal box for the passage of the train/s concerned.

Traffic from Botany is conveyed to Enfield by the return of these trip trains and, when more than 54 vehicles in length, the guard must advise the Yard Controller Enfield. Nos 7 and 11 Trips shunt all intermediate sidings.

By the time I entered Goods Control, the trip train working was dieselised utilising 73 Class shunting locomotives, the exception being Nos 20T and 35T, which were used solely at the goods controller's discretion and often conveyed loads in excess of the capacity of a 73 Class and were worked by a 48 Class.

The working on the Suburban Line between Newtown to Homebush had been greatly reduced. Newtown with Cragos Flour and Produce Mill received loaded wheat wagons, but loaded very little outwards traffic. Petersham received some inwards loaded daily, and out loaded bogie louvre vans of contract interstate and intrastate loading. Ashfield received anything up to 60 trucks of wire a day and Burwood was shunted only on rare occasions. The Suburban Line was serviced by the one trip daily—No 22 Trip. It was not often that Ashfield wire landed in Enfield, so the only traffic for 22 Suburban was wheat for Newtown and the loaded traffic for Petersham.

A train still ran daily from Darling Harbour to the Washout Sidings with milk vans and TRC/MRC meat vans. Alexandria had all but closed, but for the first few months, the traffic for 421 South was still loading at Alexandria and receiving transit by 221A. After the closure of Alexandria, this traffic was mostly loaded at Darling Harbour. The interstate bogie traffic, however, was loaded at Cooks River and received transit from there.

Regular trip trains worked to Botany, to West Ryde and Hornsby. The malt siding at Gonarro (near Thornleigh) received heavy traffic after the barley harvest, but when there was no traffic for Gonarro, the trip train did not run past West Ryde. Allied Feeds at Rhodes received bulk wheat wagons on a daily basis, Monday to Friday all year round. A trip train ran to Hornsby then to St Leonards, generally the only station on the North Shore (Point) Line doing goods work by 1970. Lysaghts loaded some steel, but the Chief Civil Engineer's Branch St Leonards Depot provided most of the work. This trip generally returned via North Sydney and over the Sydney Harbour Bridge; the last timetable margin ahead of the peak hour trains from St Leonards being just before 5.00am.

Trip trains also serviced the Chullora industrial sidings; and trains ran to Richmond, returning with sand and blue metal for Enfield. They also ran to Emu Plains for the same purpose, except the destination was Wolli Creek. There was little goods traffic at Wentworthville, Seven Hills, Blacktown and St Marys. No 69 that ran to Penrith serviced them. No 69's engine shunted Penrith and the sand/blue metal quarry at Emu Plains and returned home assisting the Wolli Creek train from Penrith.

On the south, No 41A still served all stations Liverpool to Campbelltown and Menangle, then it continued on to Moss Vale. If required, it shunted Thirlmere on the Picton Mittagong Loop Line, the train running from Picton to do so, and returning to Picton to continue on its journey. Hurstville, Kogarah and Rockdale had also almost stopped receiving inwards loaded traffic and certainly did not load any out. Kogarah, with the Bush's meat, was the only regular receiver of any traffic. They were serviced by a trip train that ran from Enfield in the afternoon.

The Botany line had changed considerably. Botany itself had become a container depot and oil depot. Nos 7 and 11 Trips still ran, but the major change to the working was that oil trains originated at Botany and ran to the west and south.

One of the hazards of being a goods controller prior to the introduction of No 2 Goods Control, was the inability of the controller to know where his trip trains were. This was brought about by a number of means, the least excusable being the changing of numbers of a trip train. A trip, for example, would leave Cooks River for Clyde and be given out by Cooks River as 20 Trip, but by the time it passed Enfield South, it would be given another number, say 35T. Enfield North would come and ask Goods Control where 35T was going to and if the controller had it programmed to North Strathfield, then that is where the trip would go. When it arrived at North Strathfield, the assistant station master would naturally come and ask what was on 20T for him. He knew it was 20 Trip because he had asked the guard when he passed the Office.

This was still happening when I went into Goods Control, although not nearly as often, because when the telephone boy gave the times, the No 2 Goods Controller would know if he had been given a wrong number. It was something that always baffled me. It happened with engines going to trains on leaving Delec to go, say, to Homebush Saleyards for a train, and despite being given correctly by Enfield North, it would finish up in Clyde. The misnaming of the trips conveying perishable traffic could be costly in time and could also affect on-time delivery.

I set out to find out if it happened with certain signalmen only, but it appeared not to and I never found out why it happened so often. There really, to my mind, was never a legitimate reason for it happening. If you challenged a signal box, the signalman would say it was given to him as a certain number. If you then challenged the signal box that passed on the trip number, he would deny that he gave that number. I sometimes wondered whether there was conspiracy between the trip train crews and the boxes. I must say it happened more often in times when it was not all that busy, which appears to lend credence to my theory. It was one of the things that really frustrated me, more probably than it should have done. After the advent of No 2 Goods Control, it occurred mostly on week-ends.

When the trend towards shipping containers had begun in earnest, container depots set up by the shipping companies were built indiscriminately in the metropolitan area. I say that from a transport point of view, not of the shipping agents. Obviously, they built where their warehouses had originally been established. Depots were at Chullora, Homebush Saleyards, Leightonfield, Enfield and Botany. A huge container terminal was built at Rozelle where containers were unloaded onto flat wagons from the ships or direct onto the wharf.

The responsibility for the movement of the shipping containers from the container terminals at Rozelle and Botany, to the shipping agents' depots and the return loaded (or empty) from the shipping agents' depots or warehouses, was given to a chief train controller. I will detail his duties more fully in a chapter on containers. The duty of the goods controller was to see that the container trains provided for the purpose maintained their schedules and did not stand avoidably idle. No 2 Goods Control had oversight over their movements and advised the goods controller, especially after hours, if they were waiting loading, or their loads had not materialised, or would be seriously delayed waiting. The goods controller had a number of options; he could turn the container train's engine into Loco, or if he had sufficient work for it, he could convert it to his own use for the period of delay then return it to its timetable. If he terminated the train, he generally ordered the engine back out again when the next turn of shift was due.

On a regular basis, out-of-gauge trains ran from Port Kembla to Brisbane. These trains were out-of-gauge to the extent that a Down train could not pass an Up out-of-gauge train in the section. In the early days, they were accompanied by a traffic officer whose duty it was to confer with the controller and to ensure safe and proper arrangements were made for its passage. I was very meticulous with them; I would never let an out-of-gauge into a section until I had an assurance from the signalman in advance that he could accept the train. I obtained an assurance that he would not allow another train into the section until it had arrived complete at his signal box.

In about 1972, the traffic officers were taken from the trains. They rarely made any contribution and were not really required. The only thing this did was to place a bit more onus on the controller. This annoyed some, but I did no more than I had always done. On one occasion an out-of-gauge was going north and had left Chullora heading for Flemington Goods Junction. I had received the assurance I required from Flemington Goods Junction, and I recorded the time I had obtained that advice from each signal box on the diagram. I rang Homebush Signal Box and received no answer, but I have to mention that Homebush was not required to speak to Goods Control regarding the movement of normal trains. This was the duty of North Strathfield and Flemington Goods Junction. When I had no response to the Control phone, I rang Homebush on the side telephone. He answered straight away, when I said,

"Goods Control here."

He hung up in my ear. I then rang Flemington Goods Junction and told him not to let the out-of-gauge pass his signal box until I directed that he do so. I also suggested to him that he get the signalman at Homebush on the phone and to tell him the train would stay at Flemington Goods Junction until he spoke to me and I did not care how long it stood there, because he would answer for every minute of the delay. I told the trouble officer what was happening and suggested that he ring Homebush; his response was to tell me that I was being too pedantic. If anything, he was taking the part of the signalman, who had apparently already spoken to him saying he was not going to talk to any goods controller. I told the trouble officer the train would stay at Flemington Goods Junction until he did.

The reason I 'stuck to my guns', was the fact that until it arrived at Flemington Goods Junction, it was on the Goods Road and I had a good idea of where the other goods trains were, but after it left Flemington Goods Junction, it was on the main line and I had no idea where the passenger trains were. After about five minutes the trouble officer came to me and said,

"That out-of-gauge has not moved from Flemo."

I replied,

"Until that signalman at Homebush speaks to me it will not, either."

Another five minutes had elapsed when a voice came over the speaker,

"Homebush Signal Box."

I replied in accordance with the laid down procedure in the General Appendix Part 1,

"Speak Homebush."

He said, "You want me?"

I then said,

"Can you accept No N405 out-of-gauge in accordance with the Regulations?"

He said, "Yes."

As I was being accused of being pedantic, I was, so I then said,

"Finished Homebush."

I then directed Flemington Goods Junction to despatch the train. I did not report the delay or the fact I had the run-in with the signalman. I was on duty for out-of-gauge trains many times after that. The word must have spread because I had nothing but co-operation from all the metropolitan signalmen who operated on the section of track that the out-of-gauge trains ran over.

On Saturdays, No 445 South from Botany picked up to a full load of oil at Clyde. As the No 2 Goods Controllers did not work on Saturdays or Sundays, it was the responsibility of the goods controller to route the train from Botany to Clyde. A file was made out for the lift from Clyde and, on that file, was recorded the time each signal box was told where to send the train. On this occasion, I informed Cooks River, Enfield South, Enfield North, Auburn and Clyde. The missing link from this was Chullora.

I remember to this day ringing Chullora, but that is all. He did not answer and I went doing something else and forgot it. This signalman was one who, unless he was specifically directed, would send a train to its ultimate destination, Goulburn. The fact that it was timetabled via Clyde on Saturdays and he knew that it picked up at Clyde every Saturday, did not matter to him. The first I knew was when Sefton came on and gave me 445 South as it passed his signal box.

I immediately rang Chullora and asked where the train was, he told me it passed at such and such a time heading south. When I challenged him, he said I had not told him to send it to Clyde. I could not deny that. I immediately rang Campbelltown and told the signalman that the train was to be stowed there while the engine and guard returned to Clyde, for the balance of the loading. I told Clyde what had happened and asked him to attach it to a brakevan. He replied it was already sitting on one. The engine duly returned to Clyde, picked up the loading, and in about 15 minutes was gone again to Campbelltown. The train was delayed about an hour and a half, which was of no consequence because the train was stabled at Goulburn until Monday morning.

About a fortnight later, I received correspondence from the freight trains manager, with the copy of a letter of complaint from the assistant station master at Campbelltown complaining about the train shunting his station. I was asked to report. I replied to the effect that I accepted full responsibility that I had not told Chullora, who routed the train directly south. Not long after the correspondence clerk came into the control room with a paper in his hand. It was my reply. The freight trains manager had written on it 'File'. He (the clerk) told me,

"You have not seen this."

Honesty did pay.

I worked for a long time in Goods Control. Around 1972, it was made a Chief Train Controller's position. I was appointed a Chief Train Controller in March 1972. I worked as a Chief in Goods, as the Chief Train Controller Programme, Chief Train Controller Interstate Traffic, Chief Train Controller Container Traffic and finally Chief Train Controller as the Wheat Officer until 1979. I worked about 50 per cent of the time in Goods Control; about 40% as Chief Train Controller Programme, and the balance relieving the incumbents in the other positions for holidays.

As long as I worked in Goods Control, it was never easy. However, knowledge and experience gained over time made for confidence and it became much easier to assess a situation quickly and to give decisions that one knew were what was required.

No 2 GOODS CONTROL

T HE senior train controllers who were qualified for Goods Control were considered to be qualified for No 2 Goods Control. I suppose if all the time I worked this board was put together, it would not amount to much more than a month. I detested the job. The train control diagram was to my mind a monstrosity. I suppose that, no matter how it was set up, it would be difficult to make a diagram that was easy to read. Enfield was the centre of the control diagram; on the Up it ran towards Canterbury, Wardell Road, and thence to the Illawarra.

The Botany line was also shown from Wardell Road as was the Goods Road to Rozelle and Darling Harbour. The result was that to diagram a train from Botany to Clyde, a number of breaks were necessary. First it was diagrammed to Wardell Road. Because the Illawarra and Rozelle sections divided the Botany—Wardell Road segment, a break in the diagramming of the train was necessary. It was next diagrammed from Wardell Road, but this time on the Enfield side.

The south section again caused a division at Enfield North, the section to Cabramatta separating the western and northern Lines. The train had to be re-diagrammed on the Chullora, Lidcombe and west section. In effect, the train was in three positions on the diagram. A section was from Parramatta to Darling Harbour, which also accommodated trains from the north at Strathfield. The north was a through section from Enfield North and the west was a separate section starting at Lidcombe.

The first and most important duty of the No 2 Goods Controllers was the oversight of engines travelling from Delec Depot to the various points in the metropolitan area from where trains commenced their journeys. Equally important was the oversight of engines arriving into the metropolitan area terminating points. Sometimes engines ran straight onto other trains without going to the Delec Depot. An example was the coal train from Metropolitan Colliery and Waterfall that invariably changed engines to three 46 Class engines at Canterbury and then proceeded north. It was the duty of No 2 Goods Control to see that these engines, which may have worked a train to Rozelle, for example, were directed to Canterbury. He was responsible for seeing that the outgoing crews were sent to Canterbury.

At other times, engines from incoming trains were despatched to Delec for a mechanical service before working a train. It was important for the sake of maintaining the goods programme that these engines did get to Delec without being delayed for long periods. No 2 Goods Control was introduced for the purpose of recapturing train working in the metropolitan area and making signal boxes, depot stations and shunters aware of their responsibilities and duties. To maximise the use of not only rolling stock, but also, and probably more importantly, maximising the use of engine power.

I have already said that the introduction of No 2 Goods Control was met with a lot of passive resistance by the operating staff, particularly signalmen. Some of these men had worked decades in signal boxes in what was known as the 'blackout area', without ever answering to anyone. The only signal box I found to be always co-operative was Enfield South, which was a key box. The telephone boys in this box were very good. Nothing seemed a problem, a fact that I appreciated when I was in Illawarra Control. Enfield North and Chullora signal boxes were difficult. In the end, it was necessary to have inspectors spend shifts in the boxes and to instruct the signalmen in their duties to No 2 Goods Control.

Perhaps one of the reasons for this resistance was not so much in the introduction of No 2 Goods Control, but in the gradual change to trip train working. In the days before dieselisation, the trip working was much more rigid, the trains worked to the instruction laid down by the Metropolitan Goods timetable. An example of this stereo type working is shown in the extracts from the 1960 timetable. The goods controller had only one trip train at his disposal, it being used for day to day special requirements. The set shunting/trip trains performed the balance of the work. The controller did not know where they were and was never told. A Botany trip, for example, could run out and back without him ever being aware that it had left Enfield.

With the introduction of diesel trip trains, and the rationalisation of the working giving a far greater flexibility than ever before, the goods controller had a better oversight and input into the working.

I suspect that the reason signalmen were loath to report was the fact that for so many years, the set working had, to their minds at least, worked successfully, so why change it? In point of fact, it had not worked economically in the last few years. The closing of goods sidings by the drove, coupled with the proliferation of road traffic, meant that the trip trains were grossly underused and a fair estimate would be that they were all 50 per cent under utilised.

By taking away the rigid adherence to a timetable and directing train controllers to use them on a needs basis, the numbers of trip trains were reduced, probably by about 25 per cent. This reduction, and the placing of greater onus on the goods controller for their efficient working, brought a larger degree of productivity than had been achieved since the early days. The set timetable trip trains achieved their targets up to the end of World War 2 and for a period thereafter. The advent of the motor lorry as a means of transport saw the necessity for the reduction in the number of trip trains.

When the goods controller had routed a train, he handed the load to the No 2 Goods Controller who advised the respective signal boxes of its destination. He also received a continuously updated advice of the workings of the trip trains.

There were trains that ran into depots like Cooks River and Chullora from the Illawarra Line and returned working trains back to the Illawarra. No 2 Goods Control was responsible for seeing that they were not unduly delayed getting into the depots. Each train had a turn-around of about 90 minutes which, provided they were delayed for no longer than about 20 minutes, was sufficient time. The Illawarra Controller was soon on his back if they were not leaving on time on the return journey, for reasons that I stated when writing about Illawarra Control.

There can be no doubt that No 2 Goods Control did make a difference to the working and in the savings it made in standing times, which resulted in the better utilisation of engine power. This made the introduction if No 2 Goods Control worthwhile. Another area where better savings were made was in the better movement of trains around Enfield. The controllers would be able to see where trains were likely to bank up because of engine changes, or crew reliefs at Enfield, and they were able to use the Bankstown line as an alternative route for trains to Cooks River or Rozelle. The only problem was ascertaining if the crews knew the alternative road.

During all my writing I have often said things that I have done, and in so doing, I have tried to keep a balance. In particular, I have tried not to convey the impression that I had ability any greater that my colleagues had. I will say more of this towards the conclusion, I say this now as a precursor to what may appear undue immodesty. Without being asked, I was marked up on the roster to learn Traffic Trouble, something I would not have minded at all. The Freight Train Manager came into the Goods Control room shortly after the roster appeared and said,

"You are not going into the bloody Trouble Office; you are staying right here."

He was not a friend of mine in the terms of friendship, but he was, however, someone with whom I had a good understanding. The trouble officers came under the jurisdiction of the Passenger Section and as a consequence, when a controller went to Traffic Trouble, he was, as a general rule, lost to the Freight Section. His clear implication was that he did not want to lose me. The crunch came when the roster for the following fortnight went up. I was shown in No 2 Goods Control and was actually working in there when he came in again. He had come into Goods Control seeking information regarding something else, and was about to walk out when he saw me.

"What are you doing in here?" and before I could answer, he continued,

"I told that bloody roster clerk you were to work only on Goods Control or as Programme Chief."

Next day, when I came to work, I was in No 1 Goods Control. I was in a group of about six that came under this direction.

As I said at the beginning. I detested No 2 Goods Control as a job as I did not like the working. However, it was not because I did not want to answer to another controller as one does become used to running one's own race, but I detested it mainly because it was a job that you could not plan ahead.

It was certainly possible to start chasing engines when they were due from Delec, provided you could get Enfield North to answer the telephone. You could chase engines from terminating points, which perhaps were required to work continuously on another train from the metropolitan area. This particularly applied to electric locomotives.

The faithful application of this 'chasing' was fundamental to economical engine working and productivity.

A view of portion of Darling Harbour Goods Yard in June 1985 looking south east shortly before its closure and removal. Some of the Sydney city skyline can be seen and, at right, work has commenced conversion of the former Ultimo Power Station to the Powerhouse Museum.
John Hoyle, ARHS Rail Resource Centre 7402.

CHIEF TRAIN CONTROLLER, PROGRAMME

I BEGAN to learn the Chief Train Controller Programme in mid 1971. I was happy to do so, and I must admit not a little proud, something I kept to myself. Probably the only person I let know my feelings was Mamie. I, along with a couple of colleagues, created something of a history when we begun to learn the job. It was only seven years since we had come to Sydney as senior train controllers, and the usual length of time to achieve that what we had, was not less than 12 years and mostly 15 years. In the 1950s, it was rare to be appointed a chief under the age of 55 years. I was 42 when I began to learn. I had not been appointed when I began to learn the position.

This was quite a culture change. To begin with, there were 8-hour shifts, the hours of duty, commencing at 6.00am, 1.30pm and 10.00pm. The Chief was responsible for the clearing of all loading emanating from the metropolitan area. This loading came from the oil sidings at Botany and Clyde, the empty stock wagons returning to country areas, the empty meat wagons, the empty milk wagons, the empty wheat hoppers from Rozelle, the containers from Chullora, Rozelle, Leightonfield, Homebush Saleyards and Cooks River, the loading from Darling Harbour to all country areas, the empty cement wagons, the loading which arrived at Enfield from all the metropolitan sidings serviced by trip trains, and the bogie interstate loading from Cooks River, Enfield, Clyde, Auburn, and Chullora. The empty wagon book-out from the rollingstock superintendent for interstate and intrastate destinations and the interstate perishable fruit from Queensland to South Dynon and South Australia. In addition, there was coal loading from Metropolitan Colliery, the interstate steel from Port Kembla to Brisbane, the coal arriving from the west and going to Inner Harbour for shipment, the through interstate trains from Victoria to Clapham, and the interstate loading arriving from Western Australia and South Australia. As I attempt to outline the duties of the Chief Train Controller, I will explain how he came by all the information regarding the traffic that he was responsible for moving from the metropolitan area.

The 6.00am shift began with reading the handover and going through the files left by the backshift officer, who had mostly gone off shift between 5.30am and 6.00am. I should say, that while certain signing on and off times were laid down, the chiefs generally set their own pattern. Mostly the 6.00am shift saw the incoming man there at 5.50am, the 1.30pm shift saw him in at 12.45pm. In the 45 minutes before starting time, he had the *ambas* typed up by the secretary to the interstate transit officer (designated as part of her duties), the 10.00pm man was usually in at 9.30pm to type up his own *ambas*. So it was on the afternoon and backshift that the officers went when they had finished, mostly about as early as they had arrived.

To continue the 6.00am chief's tasks, after he had been through the handover, they mostly, and I certainly did, would go into goods control and look through the incoming loads for tonnage that would work through Enfield, especially, and had become Down loading for connecting trains. While it was the duty of the goods controller to give the chief files for any large amounts of traffic that would become Down traffic off an Up train, I felt that by going through the incoming loads I had a 'feeling' for what was happening, that I would be able to get a 'gut' feel about the availability of wheat wagons by seeing where the wagons were to tip and form the outgoing trains were, and at what time they could be expected at Rozelle.

This exercise probably took about 20 minutes and to me, it was time well spent. The backshift chief left a form typed up with the interstate loading in the metropolitan area and where it was situated. This was set out in train form and was used by the 6.00am chief as the basis for his daily interstate freight trains. The chief was personally responsible for the loading which went onto all interstate trains. The Yard Controller Enfield, for example, was responsible for forming trains in his yard with available tonnage. The chief nominated to the originating station every vehicle that was to form an interstate train.

A comprehensive yard report was taken by the yard porters at Enfield three times a day and was available at the commencement of each shift, that is 6.00am, 1.30pm and 10.00pm, and was relayed to the chief by the train clerk at Enfield. The report contained the Down tonnage, the number of stock wagons, the number of bogie open empties, empty BCH and BWH hopper wagons and interstate empty wagons returning to their home state. This information was the basis of the tonnage balances kept by the chief, but whilst it was supposed to be accurate, there were occasions when it was wildly inaccurate. Sometimes this was caused by not taking into consideration trains that had either departed or arrived in the hour prior to the report being given. It always showed before and after trains, but with the late arrival of Up trains or late departure of Down trains, this information was always suspect.

The 6.00am chief set up a forecast programme for 36 hours commencing from 6.00am the next day. Permanent programme sheets for the Southern, Western, Northern and Illawarra Lines were printed from the working timetable. There was a set of sheets for

Mondays to Thursdays, a set for Fridays and a combined set for Saturdays and Sundays. The chief took a set of sheets and set up a skeleton programme to begin from the following morning. The Darling Harbour permanent trains, the oil trains from Botany, the regular interstate trains from Cooks River, Clyde, Homebush Saleyards and sometimes Flemington Markets were all shown on these sheets which formed the basis of the *ambas*. The trains not required were crossed out in pencil; pencil because sometimes it became necessary to add them to the programme.

The time was fully occupied with this work and tonnage balances until about 9.30-10.00am. At this time every day, the main line diesel, the electric locomotive and the 48 Class diesel respective engine roster clerks had balanced the engines and set engines onto trains for the next 24 hours. It is not inaccurate to say that every day of the week, Mondays to Fridays, there were not enough engines to run the set programme. There were Mondays when this was not so, especially if there were no shipment wheat or coal programmes running. The obvious question is:

"Why would the chief set up programmes if there are not enough engines to run them?"

There are two reasons: firstly, the Operations Branch, the providers of the service, wanted to show the Mechanical Branch every day that insufficient engines were available to run the programme without delaying traffic on a daily basis; and secondly, the chiefs themselves set a programme that was required to shift the traffic offering. If they did not, and the 6.00am traffic/tonnage reports showed traffic standing, their necks were on the chopping block. From the chief's viewpoint, if there was loading at 6.00am, the report itself would have shown the trains cancelled due to shortage of engine power.

The Centralised Motive Power Control (CMPC) engine roster Clerks balanced the engines available onto the trains that fitted the time availability frame of the locomotive. The chief clerk in charge of CMPC took a list of the trains that were programmed to run even if main line diesel, electric and branch line locomotives were not available.

A conference was then held between the Train Control Superintendent, the Chief Train Controller and the Freight Trains Manager or his assistant. If the chief was overloaded with work, he did not attend. I always tried to do so, feeling that by being there I could have my 'tuppence' worth and perhaps get the changes I wanted, rather than what someone else wanted. After this conference, the Chief Clerk CMPC gave a list of the agreed alterations to the Chief Train Controller (if he was not present), who then proceeded to make the necessary programme alterations.

Effort was always made to avoid cancelling trains. This was done by reducing trains to single loads, setting trains back to another timetable so that engines were available, by running a train to Waterfall and terminating it and letting Illawarra Control arrange clearance from Down trains and returning the engine to run continuous to another train.

There were times when the Wheat Officer's trains were altered. This invariably brought about a fight with him. When you saw the door burst open after the alteration had been given, it was almost a certainty he would be behind it, he would rant to all concerned about the importance of his wheat trains to the department and the economy and demand that other trains be cancelled to provide him with engines. It worked only on rare occasions.

The truth was that when a wheat train was cancelled, things were desperate. He was in fact, a very good officer. In each position that he had been employed in, he regarded it as the most important position on the third floor. He gave every position he worked in this philosophy, so that he could obtain the maximum benefit for it. He was certainly among the elite of chief train controllers. I sympathised with him more much later when I became the Wheat Officer.

The chief, when he had amended his programme sheets, issued what was called 'The alterations to 10.00am Programme'. These alterations went to the control boards for inclusion in their 10.00am *ambas*, and to all the guards and Mechanical Branch roster clerks, and to the yard controllers at the various depots and the outlying country control areas.

From about 10.30am, he was able to concentrate on the bogie interstate loading. This loading always seemed to come from the 'woodwork'. The Interstate Transit Officer provided the forecast loading from Tattersalls at Auburn, (which usually found its way onto 421 South), interstate loading from Jonlaw at Clyde, from SPD at Enfield and from Brambles Ltd and Mayne Nickless.

Around 11.00am the Station Master Cooks River gave the forecast loading for each bogie train departing from his depot. These loading figures were transferred onto the interstate bogie sheet and running totals kept. The precision required will be gauged by the fact that, in the late 1960s, a system was introduced which provided for every north bogie train leaving the metropolitan area being equal to no more than 56 four-wheeled vehicles in length when worked by a single engine, and 52 when worked by two locomotives.

This was done by providing the exact length of every bogie vehicle in service, including other systems' vehicles; for example, a VLX (a Victorian covered van) was equal to 2.2 four-wheeled vehicles. The table of vehicle lengths was printed in each working timetable. The reason for these lengths was that it facilitated the crossings of trains north of Maitland to Clapham, Acacia Ridge and Park Road in Queensland. The majority of crossing loops were equal to 56 and one engine, which meant that the problem of crossing over-length trains was solved. The time saved and the improvement to the on time running of interstate trains far outweighed the revenue loss when trains ran lightly loaded because of length restrictions.

A fresh interstate sheet was typed up at about 12.00pm for the afternoon chief. The forecast loading was given to the chief on the programme in Newcastle. Included in these figures was the loading on trains from Darling Harbour conveying empty milkpots and loading for the north west. It also included the biscuit loading from Arnotts at North Strathfield.

The coal shipment requirements were arranged by a first class clerk in the office of the Rollingstock Superintendent. This officer was responsible for the overall total of the coal programme, in the Western, Northern (Hunter Valley), South Coast and Glenlee Coalfields. He advised the chief on a daily basis of the amount of coal required at Rozelle and Port Kembla for shipping and the names of the ships which were loading coal and their estimated departure times. From this advice, and in conjunction with him, the chief set up the coal programme that was to appear on the *ambas*. Because the turn around times for the unloading and despatching of empties from Rozelle was, of necessity, very tight, it was often necessary to adjust the departure times of empty trains.

This was done with both the Coal Clerk and the Station Master Rozelle, who kept a very close eye on both the empty coal and wheat wagon train departures. The coal trains were somewhat easier to adjust than the wheat trains, because mostly the electric engines arriving on a coal train stayed at Rozelle to convey the empties after unloading, or to go onto an empty rake waiting transit. The Coal Clerk in my time was a most efficient officer, who died not very long after taking an early retirement; it was very sad. By the time I was appointed chief, the line to Glenlee had been electrified and the problems I mentioned earlier when describing South Control, associated with the 60 Class engines did not exist. Better communication facilities had also been installed and the South Controller was able to control the train movements much more effectively.

The wheat officer presented the chief with a copy of his programme around the same time as the coal officer. I will not go into the wheat programme, because in another chapter, I will detail the duties of the Wheat Officer.

Although the afternoon chief signed on duty at 1.30pm, he invariably put in an appearance around 12.45pm, the reason for this was that the typist assisting the interstate transit officer, the wheat officer, manna wheat, livestock officer and the statistical officer was available to type the afternoon or 4.00pm *ambas* from around 1.00pm. She took an early lunch to be available for this duty. The typist, with the *ambas* being read to her was able to type them in around 20-25 minutes. The typing of the full *ambas* used to take me about an hour and a half. It was a considerable time saver. The only chief I knew not to use the typist was in fact himself, a 40 words per minute typist and could type the *ambas* much more quickly on his own.

The incoming chief received a handover between 1.30pm and 2.00pm. The outgoing chief went over the bogie interstate loading sheet that he had typed in detail. He also went through the *amba* sheets and pointed out any unusual loading listed, and urgent trucks which were specially required at destinations. Often there were telegrams associated with these trucks. To advance my knowledge further of what was happening, I used to go around the boards and look over the controllers' shoulders and see where the trains that would interest me were and then went to the Goods Board. I used to discuss with the Goods Controller where he had the interstate traffic that had to transfer and by what trips he was transferring them with.

After arming myself with all the information I could gather, the next task was to set about preparing the *ambas* for publication. The truck clerk from *mets* generally had completed his bogie wagon book-out sheet around 3.00pm. This sheet was about the size of twelve A4 pages. It contained a comprehensive inventory of the bogie open and covered empties in the metropolitan area. The book out for all these wagons was shown, with the varying interstate vehicles mostly nominated for their home state.

At this time, it was customary for the states to levy charges on their wagons if they had not been returned to their home state within a certain number of days after entering loaded to another state. The states returned as many wagons as they were economically able to load; in other words, interstate wagons would be held only for short periods to enable them to be loaded for return to their home states. It was an effective method for avoiding shortages of wagons for NSW's own requirements. It was the duty of the chief to record the departure of all empty wagons on the sheet and to record the book-outs for empty wagons given to the Yard Controller Enfield.

In many respects, the compiling of this sheet by the chief was a complete and utter waste of time. Although the chief gave the yard controller a book-out on both afternoon and backshifts for every wagon in his yard and nominated the train for which each wagon was to receive transit, the shunters ignored it. It is fair to say, however, that on most occasions at the end of the day, the wagons nominated had been despatched from Enfield to their required destinations. The preparation of this sheet probably occupied something in the order of two hours over the afternoon and backshifts, the chief being obliged to record the empties on the trains on which he had instructed Enfield for despatch. This information was transferred on the *amba* sheets.

Finally, he had to record the empties actually despatched on his shift. It was the recording of these that showed how the nomination of specific wagons to specific trains was futile. I suspect that the truck clerk, when he took the completed sheet the next day, filed it and at the end of twelve months, or however long the department were obligated to keep them, they were dispatched to the incinerator.

Before he completed the *amba* sheets, the chief conferred with Enfield Yard controller, the Yardmaster Clyde, Assistant Station Master Homebush Saleyards, Assistant Station Master Cooks River, Assistant Station Master Botany, Assistant Station Master Rozelle and Train Clerk Darling Harbour. With each of these officers, he confirmed that the loading already set on trains was available, making adjustments where anticipated loading had failed to materialise or had exceeded the forecasts. These adjustments ranged from the alteration of engine power to arranging the transfer of additional loading to complete a train load. If it was at all possible, I avoided putting a train into Enfield to complete loading. (I have previously stated what happened to trip trains put into Enfield; trains put into Enfield received the same treatment). The afternoon *ambas* were generally ready for printing around 5.00pm. The junior who copied and distributed them took the originals to the telegraph section on the first floor to be copied.

After the *ambas* had been completed, I usually had my lunch and from around 6.00pm, I began checking that the bogie interstate loading was in place and that the connecting and transferring trip trains were in place for on-time departures. A fresh bogie interstate loading sheet was typed up for the next 24 hours. Much of the loading for the pm trains for the following day was forecast loading. It was, however, an indication of the loading that would be available and also an indication that the running of the train was justified on the forecast loading in sight.

The pressure started to come off around 8.00pm. I spent the time from then until about 9.00pm typing up an *amba* for the backshift. The CMPC supervisors usually typed at least one *amba* leaving the backshift with two *ambas* at the most to type. I also attended to any correspondence and was ready to catch a train for home at 9.10pm.

I found the backshift a drag. I had never worked eight hours from 10.00pm to 6.00am. I had of course worked 8 hour shifts commencing at 11.55pm at Orange East Fork. A number of things seem to get to me. Firstly, I had become used to going to bed after dinner and even if I did not sleep, I rested. Having to catch a train at 9.10pm curtailed the time available severely. Secondly, the conditions in the Centralised Motive Power Control office, where about 12 people were working, and the majority of whom smoked, were not conducive to a good workplace environment. The air became fetid, despite the fact that it was air-conditioned.

After three or four hours in these conditions, my eyes used to sting and I became very sleepy, no matter how well I had rested. The same thing occurred to me on the morning shift. By 10.00am I was yawning all the time. I used to get out for a few minutes as often as I could. I washed my face at least every half-hour to freshen up. The more I think of that room, especially with benefit of having worked in other air-conditioning since, the more I am convinced that it re-cycled too much stale air without taking in air from the outside atmosphere. Sometime after the installation of air-conditioning in CMPC, all the control rooms were air-conditioned and I could work in these rooms without suffering like I did in the CMPC room.

After arriving around 9.45pm for backshift, I firstly went through the handover left, then checked the bogie loading sheet and, after going around the boards, set about typing up the remaining *ambas*. The train clerk at around 11.00pm usually passed on the 10.00pm yard figures from Enfield. It was usually around midnight when the *ambas* were finished and a tonnage balance had been run up from the Enfield figures to make sure the programme would stand up. There were occasions when it was necessary to adjust engine power from a double to single load. This was especially so on the north, it seemed forecast loading failed to materialise more often on the north than elsewhere. It was not often necessary to cancel trains outright for want of loading. Cancellations were more likely to take place on loads of empty coal hoppers from Rozelle, where the unloading was slow or the anticipated inward loaded to make the empties, arrived late or did not arrive at all.

Until about 2.00am the backshift was all about supervising the existing programme arrangements and starting on the bogie open book-out sheet and recording the empties that had already left Enfield. The train clerks at Enfield would mostly give this information, which made the chasing through train loads unnecessary. I usually had my meal around 2.00am. When I had finished the serious business of completing the book out sheets, I used to give them to the train clerk at Enfield in return for favours already received.

When the sheet was completed, it was necessary to show on the *ambas* the individual types and numbers of empties booked on each train. I generally found I was completing the *ambas* around 4.00am and had the printed copies back for distribution about 4.15am. This *amba* was known as the 4.00am *amba*.

It was from this *amba* that the control boards sent their all station *ambas*. It was the basis for train running information made available at 7.30am to gangers by signal boxes and station masters throughout the Sydney *syco* area. The *ambas* conveyed all the information that any person from rostering officers, to shunters, to outlying control areas and wayside stations needed. Each train was identified by number, by originating station, by the departure time, by engine type/s and, if required, light engine departure time from Delec. The type of loading the train would convey was identified, especially those showing livestock or perishable traffic. They were, in fact, complete in the information they imparted.

The responsibility involved in putting out *ambas* to the Southern, Western, Northern and Illawarra Lines over a 36-hour period involving around 60-70 trains in normal times and many more when coal or wheat lifts were in operation, was enormous. The task of checking each train listed to see that the information was correct was time consuming, but also vital to the integrity of the *amba*.

I recall, one afternoon around 8.00pm, the Chief Operations Manager coming into the room with a group of businessmen with whom he had been attending a transport conference. He was explaining the functions of the engine controllers and others in the room before coming and standing near the chief's desk. He introduced me to them and then told them the chiefs were charged with one of the most responsible and difficult positions in the rail transport system. He finished by saying it was only men of ability, coupled with a vast experience, who were able meet the demands the position placed on them. I did not forget to tell my colleagues of his words. While it may have come in a roundabout manner, the fact that the Chief Operations Manager spoke to the obvious leaders of industry in the manner he did, was pleasing to us all.

I believe I should not let these recordings of my experiences as a railwayman pass without recording my opinion on what was once and should have remained the hub of the metropolitan goods railway working. I refer to Enfield marshalling yards. There is no doubt that in the years prior to World War 2, it served as it was designed. One only has to read the early instructions in the Metropolitan Goods Working Timetable to see and to realise the great attention to detail that was required to make Enfield function.

The number of trip trains that ran to service the number of goods sidings in the metropolitan area was testimony to this—a metropolitan area that did not know road transport unless it was with a horse, (or a slow motor lorry in the 1930s). Enfield required yardmasters, head shunters and senior shunters who knew their sections and, above all, took pride in what they did. These were the times when it took 10 years to progress from a shunter to a senior shunter class 2.

An assistant district superintendent, whose staff consisted of a special class yard controller on day work and two special class yard controllers on night work, administered Enfield. The out depots to Enfield were Alexandria, Darling Harbour and Clyde. Each of these depots had its own shunting staff. Trip trains were despatched on a daily basis. The engines of these formed the shunting engines for the depots and returned after working one, and sometimes two, shifts as loaded trip trains. Rozelle was a depot in as much as trains commenced from there but they were, however, only ever trains that conveyed empty wheat wagons, RUs and KUs (sheeted U trucks used for wheat conveyance in the harvest season) and empty coal hoppers used in the export coal trade, at that time a fraction of what it is today.

Whatever goods came from Rozelle was the result of trip train working on the goods road to Darling Harbour and from the short Illawarra, and this was cleared to Enfield by trip trains. It would have been unheard of to start a goods train from Flemington, unless it was a full load of stock wagons; I believe this was a rare occurrence. Enfield was really the axle or hub and the out depots the spokes of the complete wheel.

From being the hub of the metropolitan area, it began to become in the 1950s, a lumbering giant of a place that became a barnacle on the rump of the railway's progress. The shunters, courtesy of union agitation and demands which were acceded to by an administration, from the Chief Traffic Manager down, who were unbelievably weak. They allowed shunters half-hour shower time before finishing work and allowed them some 30 minutes to sign on and get into the yard. Effectively every shunter was employed for 8 hours and worked seven—less, if a legitimate crib allowance was considered. Although sign-on times were staggered to meet these arrangements, the disruption to the orderly working of the yard was felt from shift to shift.

I have always believed that while there were many good and conscientious shunters of all grades, they were a group lacking in the qualifications for decision making. The only qualification required of them was shunting. It always stretched my imagination beyond the limits when I thought about the qualification requirements for special class clerks, special class station masters, chief inspectors, chief train controllers and special class locomotive running inspectors. I then thought of special class yard controllers, whose only qualification, as I have mentioned, was shunting!

I am saying, in essence, that the yard controllers of Enfield, Darling Harbour and Sydney Yard should at the least have been qualified in safeworking. Beyond the grade of special class senior shunter, they should have had to qualify in an examination based on shunting yard management and some minor form of mathematics and English in order to gauge whether they had the thought processes required beyond that grade.

I must repeat, lest it be thought I am being unfair, that there were yardmasters and yard controllers who would have held their own anywhere; they were shunters because they enjoyed the job and were good at it. There were those also who were shunters for all their days because they were either too lazy or could not qualify for anything else. Enfield, being the size that it was, attracted many of them, but even those who commenced there pre-war became reasonably efficient because of the long periods it took them to advance in any grade in those days.

At the beginning of the decline in the late 1940s and early 1950s of Enfield, it was not uncommon for crews who signed on to work a train from Enfield to Lithgow to be on duty for long hours at Penrith. The reason for this was that they were four to five hours late in departing from Enfield, and thus were on duty for about six hours when they did leave. The *zona* clerks at Enfield often sent crews to Penrith or Valley Heights by passenger train to relieve them. Lithgow had stand-by crews rostered there and these often found themselves at Katoomba relieving men who had been on duty 10-11 hours after working from Enfield about six hours away by a Down goods train. Enfield used to become grid locked and it was not possible to work trains in there or to get them out. No goods controller was game to put a trip train into Enfield for urgent traffic, for if he did, he lost that trip train for hours. I used to try and get the train clerks on side and to be sure for the traffic required got onto a trip train, and this was in the late 1960s! The success rate using this method was less 50 percent.

The administration, in an effort to overcome the problems of Enfield, took the easy way out. Instead of trying to make it work like it did in its hey-day, they attempted to by-pass it all the time. For example, all empty returns were sent direct to Cooks River. There was nothing wrong with this, but instead of going into Enfield and on to trip trains, as many trains as possible were sent Enfield to detach, then sent to Cooks River, an unnecessary expense, especially when the trip trains ran lightly loaded from Enfield. It is probably fair to note that the scheduling of a train into Enfield to detach took up the shunters' time, time that could have better been utilised shunting the whole train, which should have seen the traffic on the next trip train. (Was Enfield not designed for this?) The problem was that it only rarely got on to the next trip, staying in Enfield for up to 36 hours. As a shunter in Parkes, I recall the constant reminders we had of keeping Cooks River traffic together. The same thing applied to Clyde area traffic, but this was of course much more legitimate, the Clyde area being detached at Clyde on the way to Enfield.

Cooks River became the main depot for TNT and other container companies. Mayne Nickless and two other small interstate freight forwarders were at Enfield, but the traffic from these clients was taken to Cooks River to be part of interstate bogie trains commencing from that depot. The administration did not have the fortitude to let the trains commence from Cooks River and attach at Enfield. Ground plants with compressors to supply air for the testing of the Westinghouse air brakes were available. The use of these meant that wagons could have the brakes tested prior to being attached to a train.

Another station that was used to avoid Enfield was Canterbury. Many trains changed engines there, either coming from the west with coal to Port Kembla prior to electrification or for South Coast trains going north. Every time this happened, it caused delays, although they were only on the goods road. Nevertheless, they cost money in unproductive wages and loss of engine-hauling revenue. Good management would have seen that these changes took place at Enfield. While many would disagree, I am sure, the facilities to do so were available at Enfield.

The difficulties associated with Enfield were evident, as I have said, from the late 1940s until I left the Freight Operations Branch in 1979. I do not believe they improved until Enfield was finally closed for re-development and the working shifted to Rozelle. I believe the blame for what Enfield became can be fairly laid at the feet of unprincipled unionism and at the feet of management who were not prepared to take the unions 'on'. I also believe that some of this reluctance was political.

I have no desire to be seen as a union 'basher'. The principal union associated with the Traffic (Operations) Branch was a moderate union, which through the years acted responsibly. However, the Enfield delegates were radical left wing who were backed by a minor union that was nothing short of a socialist organisation. This combination held far more power than their numbers should have dictated.

An example of the recalcitrance of the shunters was the treatment handed out to a particular timber company. The company, whose owner had political connections, regularly received a truck of timber from Gwabegar station on a Thursday. All the goods controllers watched this timber very carefully and made sure that it was listed from the arriving train onto the appropriate trip train.

The owner expected (and quite rightly so) for his timber to be on the trip train on a

Monday but it invariably did not arrive on this train. His first call was to the Freight Train Manager, who, on feeling the lash of his intemperate tongue (probably justifiably also; but he did not have to be so rude!) made the Train Control Superintendent personally responsible for seeing that the timber was delivered by 8.00am the next day. There was little that the goods controllers could do other than remind the yard controller of the brawl that would occur if that delivery was not made. Despite all this, it mostly did not arrive until Wednesday. I recall the Train Control Superintendent's direction to organise a trip train one afternoon at around 1.00pm for the timber to delivered to the client. The truck of timber was still there when I had finished my shift. The assistant superintendent had been directed to personally supervise its attaching to the train, but the shunters fixed that; they contrived to get the truck derailed and it ended up in the repair siding. The treatment this company got was quite scandalous.

I was appointed Chief Train Controller in May of 1973 at the age of 42 years. I spent the next seven years doing the rounds of the chief train controller positions. In fact, I was the holiday relief. Aside from Goods Control, which was by now a chief train controller's position, I worked as chief on the programme, as wheat officer, as interstate transit officer and as container officer. With the advent of the 19-day month, I relieved the three isolated daywork chiefs each on one day a month. The peculiar thing about it was that they were getting a day off and on most occasions, it was a day's overtime for me.

During the 15 years I was on the third floor, I probably, with one exception, worked more overtime than anyone else did. There were two reasons. Firstly if anyone went sick during the night or late evening, the chances were I was qualified for the position, so the trouble officers who were responsible for filling shifts when anyone went sick, called me before anyone else, if I was available. The other reason was that I would always come to work. There was only one occasion in those 15 years I declined to come to work; Cathy had been having a bad night and when the phone rang at 4.30am, I had had no rest and was just too tired. There were those who would not come out for 5.30am if they were asked to lift up from 11.30am.

I was repeatedly called out at 6.00am for the Illawarra/Goulburn programmer's job. It used to be annoying to have an 11.30am shift rostered and to have the telephone ring at 4.00am and say the officer had gone off sick. I invariably came because I was the only one who knew the job besides the incumbent. I was probably used to a degree, however I have to say, the overtime and the money that went with it kept me financially afloat. For this reason, I never complained and accepted the good alterations with the bad. For long periods in the late 1960s and early 1970s, the vacancies which existed meant nearly all controllers were rostered for one day's overtime. When I was on the 10-day fortnight rosters, it was on rare fortnights that I did not work at least two and sometimes three days overtime a fortnight.

The third floor was a good place to work. In the main, the people I worked with were good conscientious railwaymen who took pride in what they did. The personnel, and I include the total staff of the floor, had, by the time they got there, stepped up from the levels of management that were required in station working to a level that was much more mentally stimulating and responsible. It also carried the respect of the ranks from which we all had come. This respect however, was something one began with. To keep it, required attention to detail, consideration and to my mind, above all, courteousness to those with whom we worked on the floor. It also applied to those who were charged with carrying out our directions at station and depot level.

'Out of the blue' in April 1979, when I collected my correspondence one Saturday morning, was the offer of promotion to Assistant District Superintendent, Coaching Rolling Stock Section, in other words 'Coach'; the position you will recall me saying as a junior porter at Cowra that was on the right hand of God. I had been appointed Wheat Officer; a Chief Train Controller position that was permanent daywork. The shift I was working was the last day of the fortnight and the last I was rostered to work as chief on the programme. I was take up the Wheat position the following Monday.

The offer caused me much deep thought. I certainly aspired to the position. The fact though that I was now assured of daywork via the Wheat Officer's position, which because of my family circumstances I was desperately in need of, made me hesitate. On the other side of that coin was the knowledge that if a drought season was experienced and there was no wheat to shift, which I had seen happen, I would be back on shiftwork. The appointment to 'Coach' would assure me of daywork to retirement, I was then 50 years of age. When I accepted the promotion offer, I was not at all sure I would get it. I did and was appointed to the position.

CATHY: SCOLIOSIS AND THE OTHER CHILDREN

THE years of the late 1960s saw a gradual improvement in our financial position, so much so that we went for a holiday on Boxing Day of 1968. We drove to the Gold Coast, where we had 14 days of very pleasant relaxation. This was the second holiday we had had since we were married. This period of Cathy being well and leading as normal a life as someone who is mildly developmentally disabled can lead, was drawing to a close.

In the early part of 1967, an incident that could only be described as traumatic occurred. As was usual on a Sunday morning, the family, myself on backshift excepted, went to Sunday school and church. One day at about midday, the telephone rang and woke me. Cursing, I answered it, to hear the voice of Roy, who was trembling telling me that Cathy had been knocked over by a motor car. At the least she had a broken leg and that Mum had gone with her in the ambulance to Hornsby Hospital. I went to the church to find Roy and Faye.

I found them both upset, Faye especially, because after Sunday school, she had gone with a friend across the street, where Cathy had seen her and had just run across the street without looking and straight into the path of a car. The lady driver was coming to pick up her own children from the Sunday school. Faye blamed herself for going with her friend. It was not her fault. As a general rule, Cathy's Sunday school finished at the same time as church. On this occasion, she had wandered from the Sunday school, something she did if she was bored and went looking for Faye. On other occasions, when she did this she went into the church to find Mamie.

When the ambulance picked her up her right leg was almost at right angles with her body. The bone was broken to the extent that the x-ray showed about half an inch separation of the thigh bone. She spent a long time in Hornsby Hospital. Surgery was required to pin the thighbone together. A scar extending from the hip joint to the knee was the result. I do not know how many stitches were in it, but what I do know is that, when we took her to the orthopaedic surgeon to have them out, something we were both dreading, the surgeon cut a stitch at the bottom of the scar and pulled on this little piece of stitch and as he did, it started unravelling. Cathy was so surprised she did not do anything, just looked. He finished with a piece of suture material about two feet long (610mm). The x-rays taken after the operation showed a piece of material inserted into the marrow of the bone, together with about six screws that were through the bone. Because it was not the driver's fault, the insurance company would not pay any compensation. I knew this would be so because I had already contacted the NRMA legal department who said that the insurance company was not legally liable, but that some companies under these circumstances might make an *ex gratia* payment. This one did not.

I felt very sorry for the lady driver who was very upset. To the police who interviewed me, I said firstly that I knew what had happened and I did not attach any blame to the driver. The police sergeant then asked me did I know how serious my daughter's injuries were. I replied her injuries were not the issue in the conversation. So far as I was concerned, as unfortunate as it was, it was an accident. It appeared that when she was hit, she was thrown into the air, first landing on the car bonnet and then landing on the road. It was nearly six months before she was able to walk again. In fact, she never fully recovered her gait to that she had before the accident.

In the early part of 1970, she began to become unstable on her feet, and as a result, she quite often fell, especially if she started to hurry. Our doctor at this stage had a handicapped child of his own and he was very sympathetic and caring to Cathy. It was in 1970 he discovered she had developed scoliosis, which is curvature of the spine. This of course, had much to do with her being unstable. He referred us to us to an orthopaedic professor who had rooms in the city and ran a clinic at the Royal North Shore Hospital. When we first went to his rooms for a consultation, I became aware, very quickly, that we had come to visit a very caring man. He examined Cathy and made measurements that revealed she had a 28 per cent curvature of the spine. He said we should wait another two months before seeing him again and that he would make further measurements, from which he would gauge whether the scoliosis was still developing or whether it had stabilised.

Before we left his clinic he asked,

"What support do you have and how long is it since you have had a break away?"

The answer was we had no support from any government agency and not much family support because they all lived in the country. We had not had a break away from Cathy since she first became ill. Such was the nature of the man that he arranged for respite care for her for two weeks. Mamie and I went on the *Indian Pacific* to Perth on our third holiday in 17 years. It was a good battery recharger.

Like so many things in Cathy's life, it did not improve and, in fact, the curvature was slightly more pronounced. The professor advised us that the only remedy to correct it was what was called a Milwaukee brace, invented after a surgeon in that city. The best way to describe it would be to say that it was an instrument of the devil. It fitted tightly under her chin, similar to a collar brace. Under the chin it fitted like a tight fitting bodice, that was tightened with leather laces threaded through eyelets on the back. A flat piece of steel was joined to the neck brace from the point where the brace was laced up, to the bottom of the back, to about three inches below her hips.

In the measurement of the time, the piece of steel would have been about an eighth of an inch thick and about an inch wide. It was on an angle of about 20 degrees from the collar and flattened out at about six inches from her back and came back on the same angle to connect with the steel band around the bottom. The main body part was of stiffened leather. She had to wear this contraption 23 hours a day. It would have been possible to pick her up and carry her like a suitcase, using the steel bar as a handle, when she had it on.

As parents, we could not begin to believe how uncomfortable it was. To have to insist she wore it was very distressing. It was not possible to comfort her by cuddling and holding her; she could not be nursed. We thought at this time that things were about as bad as they could get. We were wrong, so very wrong. After some 12 months, the professor came to the conclusion the brace was not doing what it was supposed to. In fact in that period the scoliosis curvature had slightly increased. He said he thought the best thing for Cathy was to discontinue its use. He was of the opinion the scoliosis would eventually develop to the point where she could not walk. This was something, of course, we did not want to hear, but in our hearts we suspected he was correct in his assessment.

In 1970, she developed the first of a long line of water blisters, which first appeared on her heels. They would ultimately burst or have to be lanced. In each case, the healing was a very slow and difficult process. Each time she got one, it meant a spell in hospital. The hospital of the Crippled Children's Association at St Ives was Margaret Reid Orthopaedic Children's Hospital. She went on each occasion to this hospital, which was close by and could be reached from home in about five minutes. I spent hours each day there. If I was on the 5.30pm shift, I went in the morning and helped her with lunch. If I was on an 11.30am shift, I went for short time in the morning. On 5.30am and 11.30pm shifts I went in about 4.00pm and helped with her dinner. Mamie also went every day, the idea being to alternate our times there so she had one of us for a portion of every day. It was important to her; tiring for us.

One Saturday morning, when only one nurse was on duty in the ward, an incident that would not occur in hospitals today, did occur. The nurse had Cathy in a shower chair and was showering her when the telephone rang. The nurse answered it, leaving Cathy in the shower. After being in the shower for some time, she got sick of it and, as she thought, turned the water off. However, all she succeeded in doing was turning the cold water off and scalding herself with the hot. She was blistered on her chest and buttocks where the water lay in the chair. When we got there, the poor nurse was in terrible state. She had nursed Cathy for some time in the hospital and was very kind to her. When I saw the nurse, I put my arms around her and assured her that we would not blame her. It was, however, another incident in the life of Cathy that was unnecessary. She had enough to put up with without this type of thing. The healing process was very slow and required many months to pass by. It is government regulation today that hot water in children's hospitals is of such a temperature that it will not scald.

We may well have had a case for compensation in the courts. We thought of it and decided not to. The launching of an action, while Cathy and therefore us who were still involved with the hospital system, would have placed a strain on everyone concerned with her care. We felt we could all do without that.

We were no different from any other caring parents when it came to the way our two older children conducted themselves at school. In school and at play, we wanted them to be successful and to achieve those things they set their hearts on, but above all else, to be respected members of their school community. They both were. Their school reports were always in the upper brackets of achievement. Roy was, on occasions, urged to work harder, so he could achieve better results, as he did only that which he had to.

He represented Ku-ring-gai High School for four year in gymnastics. He and his team, under the Olympian Mark Foulkes as coach, won the Combined High Schools Championships twice and were second on the other two occasions to Cleveland Street Boys High School. He came overall ninth at the State Gymnastics Championships in 1970. He also played golf and hockey for the school. He became friendly with the professional coach/manager of North Turramurra Golf Course and spent most afternoons there from 4.00pm. He looked after the office, doing his homework at the same time. He sat for the Higher School Certificate in 1972 and achieved a good pass that gave him matriculation to all Universities, except Sydney.

He had not really made up his mind what he wanted to do in life, so he applied and was accepted into the University of New South Wales in an arts degree course. On 20 February 1973, he responded to an advertisement in the *Sydney Morning Herald* that invited those interested to join the then Department of Justice. On 21 February, our 20th wedding anniversary, he commenced work in the Bridge Street office of the Courts of Petty Sessions. He did not proceed with the arts degree.

Faye was a brilliant student, but I must be careful and not overstate. However what I write is a true record of her achievements. In her final year at North Turramurra Primary School, she attained either an A or A plus in twelve and B plus in two of the 14 examinations she sat for. Throughout her six years at Ku-ring-gai High, she was in the top class in all her subjects. We belonged to the Manly–Warringah Leagues Club; so she applied for the

Club Scholarship in 1971, when she was in Year 10. There were some 650 applicants for six scholarships. She was short listed, interviewed and won a scholarship, which was to assist in Years 11 and 12. To continue with the Manly-Warringah Leagues Club, she again applied for a university scholarship in Year 12 she was again short listed and interviewed, but because she had already won a scholarship, she received the congratulations of the Board, but no scholarship!

She also had sporting prowess and represented the school in softball at the Combined High Schools level. In 1973 she won, with her team, the Combined High Schools Championships at Lismore. In the School Certificate of 1972 she scored six As. Whatever results she got she deserved, because although her mother in good humour accused her father of allowing her to get away with not doing any work in the house on the grounds that she was studying, she did study hard and long. In 1974, prior to sitting for the Higher School Certificate, she was offered one of 200 places that the Australian National University was setting aside for outstanding students.

With the place in the University went residential accommodation in Burton Hall. After much thought and family consultation, with Faye herself, being reluctant because of Cathy's failing health, she eventually accepted the offer. When the Higher School Certificate results were published, she received the 95 to 100 percentile mark; she was in the top 5 per cent in the State! We were justifiably proud of her.

In 1974, our number one daughter left home to go to the Australian National University, where she studied Asian Civilisations as a history subject, in which she majored. To this subject she added Indonesian, French and German as language subjects. Her intention was to enter the Department of External Affairs at the completion of her degree. When she left home, Roy was at Wagga Wagga, where he was sent shortly after joining his employment. We were left with Cathy, who missed her siblings more than we expected.

Roy showed much aptitude for his position, studying speed reading and the internal requirements of the Department in his first year and in his second, he completed typing at 40 wpm. In 1974, he commenced a law degree by correspondence with Macquarie University which was the first time that this course was offered by that University. It entailed six years of study by correspondence with two in-house periods of two weeks each year. Some 180 students commenced the course, but six years later there were eight people who received their degrees of BLegS. (Bachelor of Legal Studies). He was one of the them.

During his final year in his law degree, he also studied for the Barristers Admission Board examinations. He passed his law examinations and his Barristers Admission examination in late 1980. It was a very big thrill for us to attend his graduation ceremony and admittance to the Bar in the Banco Court in early 1981. He was appointed to Wagga Wagga as the Senior Legal Officer in the Attorney General's Department shortly after.

Faye succeeded at the Australian National University to the extent that she was offered an honours year at the end of the first year. In this time she had met Phillip, a distant cousin, through Roy. They very quickly fell in love. She declined the honours year and applied for a teaching scholarship with the University, which she obtained.

Phillip was studying at Wollongong University, also on a teacher scholarship, which he completed in 1975. They were married in December 1976. Faye completed her degree in 1977 and then did her Diploma in Education at the Canberra College of Advanced Education. Her first appointment was at Dunheved High School, teaching Indonesian, French and German.

During the time Faye was at Burton College, she had as her room mate a young lady named Catherine Sykes (Cathy to us), a former foreign exchange student to America and the daughter of a Uniting Church minister and his wife. Faye introduced Cathy to her brother, they fell in love and were married in 1977. Cathy was of great assistance to Roy in his final years of study, because also being a university student, she realised the importance of quality study time and saw that he got it.

THE WHEAT OFFICER

I learned the Chief Train Controller, Wheat Officer position sometime in 1971 and relieved in the position for rostered days off and holidays until I was appointed to it in 1979. The incumbent was universally known as the Wheat Officer. In a nutshell, he was responsible for bringing the State's wheat crop to the seaboard for shipment, and the domestic use wheat to the metropolitan flour milling companies' sidings. He was assisted by (or worked with, was my attitude) a first class clerk whose position was known as *manna wheat* (of all the code words and abbreviations for names, I thought this was the most apt).

The wheat officer was a position which carried a heavy responsibility; failure to meet the Grain Elevators Board's (known as the GEB) shipping programme because of insufficient wheat would have been very seriously viewed both by the GEB and the Freight Train Manager. However, I felt it did not have the pressures of backshift goods control and backshift chief train controller programme. If something went wrong, there seemed to be more time to retrieve the situation.

The week's work for the two really began on Friday morning when the GEB's representative rang *manna wheat* and advised him of all the wheat that was required for the following week to meet milling and shipping arrangements. This information was later available in telegram form from the GEB. The early advice enabled the wheat officer to set a programme on Friday for Monday that reflected the requirements of the GEB.

The information from the GEB was very detailed; it contained information of which the following is an example:

Gilgandra silo 800 tons NH1 (Northern Hard Grade 1) shipment by Shinto Maru Rozelle Friday (date).

This format was followed for every silo from which wheat was to be despatched for the following week. There were quite a number of types of wheat, which were selected for special shipments, and ordered by overseas milling companies.

The grades were:

- ASW (Australian soft wheat, in earlier times was known as FAQ - Fair Average Quality);

- NH1, NH2, (Northern Hard);
- SH1, SH2, (Southern Hard);
- Second Grade, (shot or sprung wheat which had been rain damaged during or just before harvesting, the excess moisture causing the grain to swell and partially to germinate); and
- Durham (a soft wheat with high gluten content used for noodle making).

Durham was a variety introduced in the 1970s and became quite a sizeable portion of wheat grown in NSW. The second grade wheat was almost exclusively used by the stock feed companies, such as Allied Feeds at Rhodes.

Special types of wheat such as NH1 were almost exclusively shipment wheat, the exception being the White Rose Mill, which was Arnott's mill, that took in small quantities of the special wheat to mix with other wheat to make a suitable flour for their products. The reward to the farmer for producing a hard wheat was something in the order of $30 to $40 per tonne additional to ASW quality wheat.

The wheat officer signed on duty at 6.00am. My first job was to go to goods control and go through his files looking for wheat trucks that were coming forward both by full train load direct to Rozelle or for trucks of milling wheat which would be delivered for the following day's unloading. The yard figures from Enfield were examined to see what Rozelle wheat was on hand there to receive transit by a trip train that left Enfield about 8.30am. I also contacted the train clerk at Enfield to see if the wheat listed on trip trains to the various mills had received the listed transit. If it had not, I re-listed it. My earlier criticism of Enfield was again justified on many occasions. The listed wheat, despite having arrived in ample time to make the trip train, was still in Enfield yard when the trip train departed.

My predecessors would try and get Goods Control to put a trip train in. I know this because I was often the goods controller asked to lift the wheat to the flour mill in question. I knew the futility of this when I became wheat officer. By the time I had collated all these figures, it was getting on towards 7.00am. The Station Master Rozelle would call me with information regarding the number of bulks placed to unload at the silo, and whether the GEB employees, who were members of the AWU and were very militant, were working or not. We would assess then whether the programme set up for the day would stand or whether it needed adjusting. If it did, I went straight to the chief on the programme with the adjustment required.

I had a very good relationship with the Station Master Rozelle. I was very much aware that he not only dealt with shipment wheat, but he also dealt with shipment coal and container traffic; this was in a yard, which to say the least, was not designed for what it was now doing. Because of his trust in me, I often received information that was 'off the record' but which nearly always came to fruition, (it generally concerned what the GEB employees were going to do or not do). It saved me, on more than one occasion, from setting unworkable programmes and pushing wheat into Rozelle that they could not handle because of the congestion. One of the complaints of the Australian Workers Union was dust from the wheat. It certainly was a problem, but they were, however, supplied with breathing apparatus that stopped them inhaling the dust. They would work for a period and perhaps unload 60/70 wagons and then find some reason to call a halt for the day, which would make programme setting very difficult. They were a very militant union and while they were a source of annoyance to the Freight Train Section with their constant stoppages disrupting the wheat programme, they were a far greater source of annoyance to the Grain Elevators Board and the Wheat Board. Their aim was to delay shipping waiting for wheat, as a lever to gain demands that the GEB was not prepared to accede to.

The country management of the transport of the wheat harvest was by a series of key officers working from the offices of the country district superintendents. Each morning, the wheat officer would confer with these officers. He would advise them of the bulk wheat trucks he anticipated they would receive. Already having the silos from which wheat was to be loaded, they would set up trains from the depots in the districts to the silos. For example, the wheat clerk at Orange arranged with the senior train controllers at Orange and Dubbo for those Station Masters at those points to run specials from their depots.

After the country programmes were set by the officers from Lithgow, Goulburn and Junee, the Wheat Officer spoke to them again around midday, when he obtained from them the silos to which they were despatching trucks, the trains on which the wagons loading that day were to receive transit, and the destinations of the mill wheat. If he agreed with the way the country officers had programmed the wheat, he said so. If, however, and this happened to me quite frequently, he did not agree, he would nominate the order he wished the wheat to depart from the country depots.

The main reason for any alteration was to expedite Rozelle shipment wheat. I was careful to tell the officers in the morning, when the programme was being formulated, if the Rozelle wheat loading was for shipment for a ship that was approaching Rozelle or loading there. Having to give preference to Rozelle wheat often meant shunting otherwise through loads in the depots. I had more trouble getting the wheat in the order I required from the officer at Orange than I had with other officers. Although he was a train controller, he had been a clerk in the office when I was ASM at Orange East Fork, and for some reason, which I suspect may have been subconscious, he found taking direction from me irksome. It also annoyed me if I had to change their loading programme, because they had already been given the preferences. The bulk of the work involved was with Junee and Orange. Lithgow and Goulburn had a smaller number of silos in their districts, and their truck clerks were usually responsible for the arrangements with the Wheat Officer.

While the Wheat Officer was dealing with the southern and western areas, *Manna Wheat* dealt with the wheat officer at Werris Creek. All the wheat from the north western area of the State, including that from the Binnaway to Werris Creek Line, went to Bullock Island. The wheat officer at Werris Creek, always an experienced train controller, set up the programme of trains each day. Each morning, he gave *Manna Wheat* particulars of wheat trucks in his district that were loading for that particular day, and the trains by which they would receive transit. In the afternoon, the wheat officer spoke to him and was given the trains that were to run from Bullock Island and to where he was despatching the empty bulks to after arrival at Werris Creek.

After I had the number of trucks under load at Rozelle at the beginning of the day, and adding those that would arrive by direct train and by No 898, the trip train from Enfield, I made a running balance, which showed whether the programme set for the day was achievable. I continued the balance with the forecast arrivals for the next 36 hours, which was the basis on which I formed the programme for the following 36 hours. Each train conveyed 29 BWH wagons and a brakevan. As block loads on the main line, they ran at 'D' schedule. ('D' schedule was a special sectional 80km/h running time, provided in the working timetable, for block loads of bogie empties of any type). The amendments to the original programme had to be in the hands of the chief train controller in time for him to include any alterations for the day on his 10.00am alterations. If I was delayed and could not get the whole programme out, I went and verbally told him of any early alteration.

The programme for each day was between five and nine trains per day, Saturdays excepted. On some occasions, the GEB would put on two shifts. It would be fair to say that the average overall would be five trains a day of empties from Rozelle. The mill and stock feed wheat used to go to Newtown, Homebush, Parramatta, Merrylands, North Strathfield, Rhodes, Mungo Scotts Siding (on the goods road) and Gillespie's (on the goods road between Rozelle and Darling Harbour). In the barley season, Gonaroo siding (near Thornleigh) received malting barley.

On most days, there were sufficient empties to make a trainload of bulks from Enfield with those that returned from these sidings. I made the habit of checking with the Programme Chief before I set a train to depart from Enfield because, on many occasions, west and south trains set from Enfield would be lightly loaded. Provided I could have some assurance that these trains would not terminate at Lithgow or Goulburn and leave no ongoing connection for the bulks, I would let them go on these trains. It seemed eminently reasonable to me to do this. One of the reasons it did so was because, as a Chief, I had on many occasions to make alterations because, if this was not done, I was then left with insufficient loading for two trains.

So it was that six or seven trains per day ran to the country areas with empties and generally that many came back loaded. One of the constant considerations I had was the quick turnaround of wagons. It was very difficult to have each wagon turned around twice in a week. For the bulkheads at Parkes, Junee, the short distance silos on the Eugowra and Grenfell branches, between Molong and Dubbo and Wellington and Dubbo, two turnarounds a week were achievable.

For the areas beyond Junee towards Narrandera and Griffith, beyond Cootamundra to Griffith, beyond Temora to the plethora of silos that were on the branch lines, beyond Parkes to Tottenham, Condobolin and Peak Hill, beyond Dubbo to Nyngan, Coonamble and Binnaway and Gwabegar the average turnaround was four days.

Not long after I first learned the job, I was given a 'special duties' job of re-timetabling all the regular wheat trains on the Southern and Western Lines. After spending some time going over the existing timetables, I came to the conclusion that the best idea was make a completely new timetable for all the wheat trains that could be required to run when a full harvesting and export programme was required. I re-numbered all the Southern trains so that their first number began with a '9', which would immediately tell anyone from rostering officers to train controllers that it was a wheat train. The same thing on the West where I gave the number '7'. While there had been some change when I left the job in 1979, the basis of what I had done was still being used.

The Wheat Officer used as a record and as a working document, a book that recorded everything that occurred each day. It showed the incoming trains, the outgoing trains, the destinations to which each district was despatching wagons, the points to which those wagons were loading, the destinations they were loading for, the running balance for each district and the trains by which the wheat was being forwarded to the metropolitan area.

It was during the taking of these facts, that the Wheat Officer would, if it was necessary, change the consist of trains to give him the first preference wheat. The book also contained the wagons on hand at each metropolitan mill, the trip trains of empties that were anticipated to be cleared from the mills, and a running Enfield balance that showed the trip train empties that were arriving. The Enfield balance also showed the trains that the empties were to receive transit by, a running balance of the Rozelle working and the programme set from that point. It was a complete record.

When I heard that the incumbent planned to retire and had been told that the job was mine, I expected to see out my time to retirement in the position. I have already said I had been offered the 'Coach' position on the last day as Chief on the Programme, and it was during the second week in the wheat job, that I accepted that position. I had some regrets about leaving the third floor. I had been there for 15 years, and having occupied the positions I had, I was considered very experienced. To leave that experience in the Freight Section behind, and go into the Passenger Section where I was not known, was like a new beginning—a new challenge which, when the surprise of the appointment had abated, I looked forward to.

CHIEF TRAIN CONTROLLER, CONTAINER SECTION

I N 1974 I learned a Chief Train Controller's position known as The Container Programmer. After learning it, I relieved the incumbent for holidays that year, and each year until I left the third floor. It was a job I always felt I did not have a grasp of, the reason being, I think, that it was the type of job that was constantly changing.

It entailed setting container trains to clear inwards containers from the container wharves at Rozelle and Port Botany, delivering them to the container depots, and picking up containers from the depots and taking them to the wharves for outwards loading onto container ships.

There were container depots at Chullora, Leightonfield, Yennora, Homebush Saleyards, Port Botany and Clyde. The container ships from overseas unloaded containers at Rozelle for OCL and Seatainers Limited. Overseas shipping containers for various other companies were received at Port Botany.

The first daily duty of the Container Chief was to go to No 2 Goods Control and see whether the container trains he had set up the day before had maintained their working or whether the Goods Controller had found it necessary to make alterations. This was frequently the case, because despite the best endeavours of the Container Chief to set a 'loose program', or in other words, set something he thought that would be realistic, it was virtually impossible to set such a programme. There were many variables that would result in changes being made, the major causes being the failure of the shipping companies to unload their forecast number of containers and the failure also of the loading terminals to load to their forecasts. It was almost a daily occurrence for at least one train load to be cancelled either from the container loading depots or the unloading wharves.

After gathering the running sheet of the container trains from No 2 Goods Control, the Container Programmer then contacted all the loading depots for their daily forecasts for container loading for the next 36 hours. The next step was to speak to the Officer in Charge of containers at Rozelle, who was situated in an office on the wharf, and obtain from him his forecast of unloading numbers from the ships, and the depots to which they would proceed. The same procedure was followed with Port Botany.

The container trains were run by 48 Class locomotives and generally consisted of fifteen 20 metre flat wagons which would hold two 9.7 metre or three 6.7 metre containers. The container programmer found mostly that he had between 400 and 500 containers a day to shift. With this number, it was necessary to run two trains continuously for the 24-hour period to transport all the containers. There were occasions when a shipment of outward-loaded containers was being loaded; this applied especially to Leightonfield and Yennora. When this happened, it was generally necessary to run a third train.

When the container programmer set his daily programme, he gave it to the programme chief and the depots concerned. His next task was to plan the 24 hours work for the trains. It mostly took around five hours to do each container run, that would start from a depot, go to, say, Rozelle, and lift another load and then return to a receiving depot. It was legitimate to set a container train five runs in 24 hours. The programmer had to show each run the train was planned to do, the numbers of containers forecast, and their destination. It was a timetabling effort that simply showed the starting and destination times. While it has not taken long to write about it, it was a very time consuming exercise. There were no *akrus* or timetable telegrams despatched.

The completed programme was set out for No 2 Goods Control in diagrammatic form. Their task was to follow the programme and to route the trains as they came loaded from each depot. The proper supervision of these trains was the key to their successful operation. Those controllers, who maintained constant touch with the depots when departure time was near, and who put pressure on depot staff to supervise crews to ensure that they carried out their tasks without 'laying down' on the job, achieved a much better result for the department than those who did not.

A first class clerk was employed to keep records of the container movements for statistical and freight charging purposes. This position was a little like *Manna Wheat*; a very important one that involved much attention to detail if the proper charges were to be levied and the department recompensed for the containers moved.

CHIEF TRAIN CONTROLLER, INTERSTATE TRANSIT

ONE of the 'plum' jobs on the third floor was the Chief Train Controller position of Interstate Transit Officer. The position was a sinecure, if ever there was one. That is not, however, to say that it was not important in the knowledge it supplied to the department's clientele. When the position was created, a Chief Train Controller was appointed to it, not because it warranted that exalted grade, but because it said thank you to a long-serving and faithful Chief Train Controller in his final years. The other side of this coin was, of course, that clients, when they knew they were speaking to a Chief Train Controller, spoke to someone with some authority and whose word they could accept. Upon the retirement of the original incumbent, the position went to the Illawarra/Goulburn Programmer, another daywork position!

I had learned the position sometime in 1974 and had relieved for holidays each year and for rostered days off on a monthly basis. My day began by going to Goods Control about 6.50am. It was a 7.00am start and this was to check to see if the urgent traffic files which had been left in Goods Control on the previous day were referenced off. It was rare to find that traffic of that nature was not delivered. On most occasions, Goods Control would detach the traffic short of Enfield and run with it. On the occasions they did not, stock nights for example, it rarely missed transit from Enfield.

Very soon after 7.00am each morning, representatives of TNT, Mayne Nickless, Brambles and Railor would be trying to trace their interstate traffic, especially that from the west. The first duty in occupying the chair was to speak to Broken Hill, if he had not already rung in. He gave the complete train loads coming towards him from Mile End and Elizabeth in South Australia and Forrestfield and other depots in Western Australia. The practice was to write the wagon number, destination and consignee into a large plain page book.

Each day filled the best part of a page. With this information, it was possible to satisfy the inquiries from the transport companies. TNT was also early on the telephone checking the numbers of each wagon that was arriving on their train. If it was late, a blast about the efficiency of the railways could be expected. Sometimes it stopped there and sometimes they took it to the Freight Train Manager.

One of the important duties was to collate, for the Chief Train Controller, all the interstate traffic emanating from the freight forwarders as they were known. This traffic came from Tattersall at Auburn, who loaded beer for both state and interstate destinations, Railor at Clyde, Mayne Nickless and Top Transport at Enfield, Brambles and TNT at Cooks River. This was traffic that would load that day for afternoon trains going north and south from Cooks River.

A train started from Cooks River with South Australian and Western Australian loading and ran to Enfield. This loading was attached to the South/West Australia traffic loaded at Enfield for the only interstate train that attached at that depot. South Dynon and Brisbane traffic was loaded at Enfield and transferred by one of the outgoing engines and crew to Cooks River. The firms were very quick to advise of any changes to their forecast loading. This information was usually in the hands of the Chief by 10.00am. The latest acceptable alteration was around 1.00pm.

It is difficult to portray with any degree of accuracy the things this officer did after say 10.30am. The telephones seemed always to be ringing with inquiries from the department's clients (often the forwarding agents) seeking advice on transit for anticipated interstate traffic. The information required was for their clients who were seeking the transit arrangements of goods ordered through the forwarding agent and also from clients trying to trace their one-off consignments of traffic coming from interstate.

The files made out for Goods Control prior to finishing duty were a result of the inquiries made. A number of statistical forms were kept which had running totals of interstate traffic loaded. This seemed to be mainly at the behest of the Commercial Manager, who was obviously trying to keep a finger on the interstate traffic that the department was keeping or not keeping.

MORE CATHY

URING 1974, 1975 and 1976 Cathy, became progressively more unstable and finally was not able to walk. During the original tumour operation, a ventriculogram shunt was placed in her head, the purpose being to drain excess fluid from brain cavities via a tube that was placed just under the skin and continued into her abdomen. The tube and a return stop valve could be felt in her neck. In 1975 this shunt became infected and had to be replaced.

In 1976, she became very unsteady and appeared to be deteriorating. We went to the neurosurgeon who had taken over from Dr Schreiber. She was admitted to the Royal Prince Alfred Hospital for further neurological tests which resulted in the very worst diagnosis conveyed to us; her brain tumour had formed again. We asked the inevitable question, what if she did not have it removed. The answer was the same as the first time; she would not live long. The second question was: would she recover and be able to walk; there was some glimmer of hope that she might. The time was nearing Faye's wedding, so we postponed any action until after she was married. The last time Cathy stood unaided was when she stood against the side of the car for wedding photos taken when Faye was getting in the car.

She entered Royal Prince Alfred Hospital and was operated on 16 December 1976 (my birthday). The balance of the tumour was successfully removed and a plate was put into her forehead in an endeavour to normalise the appearance of it. On Christmas Day, the hospital sent for us, saying she was critically ill. We had intended taking some Christmas lunch to the hospital and sharing it with her. When we arrived she was conscious. She was lying flat on her back and had an array of gadgets attached to her that was apparently measuring activity in her head.

It was heart rending to watch. She was not able to eat and neither were her parents. She had a very gradual recovery and we went to the hospital nearly every day that she was there. After about 14 days, her body began to reject the plate in her forehead; she had to go back to the theatre to have it removed. It had become seriously infected and would not respond to antibiotics—another blow. The faint hope we had of her walking did not materialise.

During the latter part of 1976 she began to become slightly incontinent. Initially it was controllable with pads, but in late 1977 it became so much of a problem that we sought medical advice. We were referred to an urologist at Royal Prince Alfred Hospital. This doctor refused to treat her, saying that we could use a catheter. I said this placed an unfair burden on her mother. He said,

"You could insert the catheter as well."

I replied, "She is my daughter and no way would I humiliate her or myself by doing this."

We returned to the neurosurgeon again with this news. He referred us to a very caring man at Royal North Shore Hospital. He said what the medical profession had to do was to make life as comfortable as possible for Cathy and as convenient as possible for those caring for her.

He performed an *iliostomony*, which operation diverts the urine into a bag via a stoma. This stoma is attached to the wall of the abdomen muscle and an adhesive pad that covers the stoma leaving a hole through which the urine enters the bag attached to it. The bag is attached to the adhesive pad. The medical profession has trained sisters who are known as stoma therapy sisters, and one such sister showed Mamie how to manage the whole business. The constant attention this demanded in the changing of the bags daily, the replacement of the adhesive pad, and the care of the skin under it was very time consuming. It did, however, make Cathy comfortable again.

The stoma pads, the bags and the recommended cosmetic creams and powders that made the wearing of the bag more comfortable were then quite expensive. By joining a Stoma Therapy Society we were able to purchase those at minimal cost. There was, of course, a limit to the number of bags that could be purchased at one time. Every time they were required, a trip into the city for supplies was necessary. This in itself was not a burden, but all the things that were building up in the care of Cathy were stretching our capacity to the limit.

In 1981, she started to become incontinent in the bowel. This was intolerable. She had a colostomy operation, which then made her an illiostimate, having two bags.

Not long after this her legs began to draw up into the foetal position, making even lying in bed uncomfortable. Once again we were faced with surgery, this time to release the abductor tendons. I was starting to feel guilty about the continuing need for surgery and the need for us to have to agree to it. The operation was not a major one so, for the sake of her comfort, we agreed; it was the last surgical procedure she had.

ASSISTANT SUPERINTENDENT, COACHING ROLLINGSTOCK SECTION

I N early June of 1979, some 33 years after I was a junior at Cowra thinking that 'Coach' was at the right hand of God, I arrived into the position, finding that it was not really! I have to say I reflected a good deal on that fact after I was appointed and before I took up. I realised I was going into a new world where I was dealing with people and not freight. I was now a member of the Passenger Trains Section and the recipient of a 'Book Pass', an all lines First Class pass covering sleeping berths. The Coach's title was the Coaching Rolling Stock Officer and the position carried the rank of an assistant district superintendent. I have mentioned once or twice to date that I was pleased with being appointed to a position. Probably this position carried the most satisfaction, because in it, I was on the administrative staff, albeit on the very bottom rung of a tortuously long ladder—a ladder that in my time was to be very heavily criticised.

My appointment caused a furore among the traffic inspectors, who historically had regarded promotion to 'Coach' as their right. One chief inspector appealed the appointment only to be told that I was the senior applicant and that he had no right of appeal. This chief inspector was the one who was designated to teach me the duties of the position. The outgoing coaching rolling stock officer gave a week's notice of his intention to retire. It was early in the learning process that I realised the inspector teaching me, was to say the least, battling. He had had to learn in a week from the coaching rolling stock officer, who was a bitter, almost alcoholic man. He had little intention of teaching anyone anything. It was a sad ending to a career, that except for the last couple of years had been a very productive one. His lifestyle in retirement changed dramatically back to that which he was proud of in earlier years.

Hence the handover to this new, in my earlier mind, exalted position was not what it might have been. While the position placed the incumbent in control of all passenger rolling stock, he had particular responsibility for the air-conditioned stock. The yard controller Sydney Yard was responsible for the formation of the non air-conditioned trains. A passenger train composition book showed the marshalling order and types of carriages that were to be conveyed by every outgoing train from the various mails to the interurban trains. It also included all the air-conditioned services.

The method of working was from a large daily diary that did not have the train load compositions, but the amendments to them. There was no attempt made on any day to balance the rolling stock. Under the system, the coaching rolling stock officer had no idea what air-conditioned carriages that he had in Acdep, the abbreviated name for the Air-conditioned Train Depot at Eveleigh. I could see there would be little assistance from the staff, not that it was their duty to be of any assistance at all. The Class 2 Clerk was a tradesman-like person, who seemed very reluctant to come into my office, and operated from bits of paper that were periodically dumped on his table.

The balance of the staff consisted of a correspondence clerk, a typist and a junior porter. In the first week, I made it very clear to the clerk that there would be no more bits of paper dumped on his table, but that each morning, we would go through the programme together after it had been settled. I had two reasons for this: firstly, I wanted him to feel that he was part of a team effort; and secondly, if I made any blunders, he would pick them up during our going through the programme that I had set. He appreciated my openness, and as a result we had a very good working relationship for the whole time I was in 'coach'.

During the learning time, I went to Melbourne to meet my counterpart in V/Line. I was anxious to see how they maintained records of their rolling stock. I was appalled at the way our coaching rolling stock section was run. I soon found that the Victorians regarded the NSW side of the two state agreement as a joke. Whilst I did not go along with that out of loyalty, I had to confess to myself that they were correct. They maintained on a daily basis, the code and number of each sleeping car, dining car, lounge car, power van and brakevan of the *Southern Aurora*, *Spirit of Progress* and the *Intercapital Daylight*. I returned to Sydney determined that some type of system that gave me control over the situation would be implemented.

With the commissioning of the *Southern Aurora* and the extension of the *Spirit of Progress* to Sydney in 1963, a number of carriages sufficient to make two *Southern Auroras*, with spares, was jointly purchased by the NSW Railways and the Victorian Railways. These vehicles consisted of: -

4	MHN	Brakevans
4	PHN	Power generating vans
4	ABS	Dining cars
4	BCS	Lounge/cafeteria cars.
12	LAN	Sleeping cars with 20 single cabins. Each had a toilet and hand basin with showers situated at each end of the carriage.

12	NAM	Sleeping cars with 10 compartments, each with an upper and lower berth and an en-suite,
2	DAM	Sleeping cars with 8 ordinary compartments similar to the NAM and with one compartment the size of two normal compartments. It was known as the deluxe suite.

This made a combined total of 42 passenger vehicles jointly owned by the NSW Railways and the Victorian Railways.

Verification of this fact was carried on the sides of each vehicle, they being stencilled NSWGR/VR. I have long forgotten the serial numbers of the joint-owned stock vehicles; suffice to say that they were numbered. During my stay in Melbourne, it was kindly suggested to me when I got back to Sydney, that I check the numbers and see how many were running north and, at the same time, was reminded that, on the train I arrived in Melbourne on, there were two wholly-owned New South Wales vehicles. My reply to this was,

"Give me a fortnight to get my feet and after that only emergencies will see sleeping cars on a train they should not be on."

The *Brisbane Limited Express* and the *Gold Coast Motorail* were a mixture of air-conditioned sleeping cars and sitting cars. The sleeping cars solely owned by NSWGR were:

6	NAM	
6	LAN	
10	FAM	9 cabin 18 berth sleepers, similar to NAMs, with a little more room.

New South Wales owned a variety of power vans, with 8 PHSs and 4 PFH vans, which were originally part of the *Newcastle Flyer* consists. These vans having a passenger seating capacity of 35 Economy Class; and a PHV which was made for the Commissioner's train.

Without identifying them by type, there were 72 air-conditioned carriages available. These carriages were used on the *Brisbane Limited Express*, the *Gold Coast Motorail*, the *Intercapital Daylight*, and the *Central West Express*. Two sets formed the four air-conditioned *Newcastle Flyers* and one carriage was attached to the *Indian Pacific* to be detached at Broken Hill. The total number of carriages rostered every day was 64. Of the balance five were under overhaul in the Carriage Works and the other three were for stand-by. More often than not, one or two of these were in local repairs.

The joint-owned fleet was maintained by the two systems, each system having vehicles for which they were responsible. There was nearly always a LAN and a NAM under overhaul, one by each system. The same applied to the power vans and brakevans; these vehicles required little in the line of interior maintenance, the changing of bogies and generator motors being the main items.

The Coach's day began at 7.00am, a heavenly difference to the 5.30am and 6.00am starts that had been my lot for a long time. I went to the Station Master's office and collected the *cana* sheets and after a quick chat, I then went to the Yard Controller's Office situated on No 1 platform, about four doors from the Station Master's Office. It was not essential to do this, however, but it was good 'PR' and besides that, I went into the office knowing if anything had occurred overnight that might attract the attention of the Passenger Train Manager, that I should be made aware of.

I was therefore in a position to answer straight away any question. That paid dividends more than once. From a quick look at the *Central West Express*, I knew if any failures had occurred overnight, I also knew that this would be the train to suffer. If failures left no air-conditioned stock available, it was supplemented by a First Class BS non air-conditioned car from Sydney Yard.

I was generally in the office by 7.15am. At about this time, the supervisor of the Central Reservation Centre arrived with a printout of all the bookings for every train, both air-conditioned and non-air-conditioned, that were advertised as booked seat or berth trains, for the next seven days. Each train conveying sleeping car accommodation or sitting accommodation was entered in the reservation section's computer with a basic composition. As an example, the *Southern Aurora* was entered with six sleeping cars only; the full complement being 10 cars. The printout, which showed the exact number of sleepers or seats booked and the numbers of each type that were still unbooked, was examined each morning.

It was Coach's responsibility to see that the accommodation was added to each consist so that there was not a time when the trains were classified as booked out. The only times this condition was not met was 'Black Thursday', the day before Good Friday, and on Christmas Eve; the *Southern Aurora* and the *Spirit of Progress* having being entered into the computer with full consists.

Care had to be taken with adding sleeping cars because of the staffing factor. An additional conductor was required for the first sleeper added, but in most cases a second could be added without an additional conductor being required. The rule of thumb was two conductors for three sleeping cars. The unions were very strict about staffing levels. It did not take me long to realise that these trains filled faster for a weekend and that if, say, on a Tuesday, there were only 10 sleeping berths available on a Friday train, I would attach an additional car immediately. If however, the day was Thursday, I would not add an additional sleeping car. I would wait until there were only one or two berths vacant before I would attach a car for a Saturday or Sunday train.

I would not attach an additional sleeper less than three days from departure because the chances of even half filling it on a weekday were very slim. It made economical sense to decline one or two applications for berths than to run a sleeping car for that number and pay a conductor the equivalent of two and a half day's wages. While this attitude contradicts the previous paragraph, I took the view that people wanting sleeping berths should book at least seven days in advance. Friday and Sunday nights were the big nights.

The addition of sitting cars to the consist depended, of course, on their availability. The *Brisbane Limited* and the *Gold Coast Motorail* were the two trains most likely to need additional seating accommodation. In contrast to the position with sleeping cars, the set composition for sitting carriages was always maintained. It was generally only when large groups booked that extra carriages were required outside holiday periods. The *Intercapital Daylight* was run with New South Wales carriages only. I would not attach additional carriages to the train outside peak periods. When it was fully booked, that was it.

One of the reasons for this decision was that it was timetabled with a limited load and the additional extra tonnage resulted either in the attaching of an additional locomotive or the permissive loss in running time, which on the Up journey was quite substantial. During the summer school holidays, an additional car was attached to each consist and an additional locomotive supplied. In this period, locomotives were readily available.

If I was going to place an additional carriage on any train, I did so as soon as the reservations clerk requested, or if I saw during the examination of the print-out that a train was filling with, say a week to go before departure, then the carriage would be attached. My predecessor, I was told, would wait and wait and give it on the day before and then, when it had not had time to fill and ran almost empty, he would say,

" See, you did not need that car".

The next set of passenger figures that came out in the Commissioner's Annual Report showed a 2 per cent increase in the number of passengers carried on the Country Services. The Officer in Charge of the Reservation Centre when asked in a conference what he attributed the increase to, said immediately,

"Better utilisation of the rolling stock."

He went on to say the current practice of putting carriages on trains early as opposed to the last day was the main contributing factor.

The *Northern Tablelands Express*, the *Canberra Express* and the *Riverina Express* were all self-propelled 900 Class air-conditioned carriages, commonly known as DEB sets. The *Canberra-Monaro Express* ran daily with four cars, namely a power car with Economy seating, a brakevan with Economy seating, a buffet carriage with First Class accommodation and a composite car with First and Economy. The *Riverina Express* ran with a similar set of carriages to Griffith five times a week and to Albury on the other days. The *Northern Tablelands Express* ran with seven carriages, and was divided at Werris Creek. Three carriages went to Moree and the other four to Glen Innes. It was only in cases of very heavy bookings, holiday times for example, that eight carriages were attached to the *Northern Tablelands Express*, and then only after consultation with Mechanical Branch. The haul over the Liverpool Ranges was such that unless the two power cars were in tip top condition, they would not make the Murrurundi to Ardglen section of the Liverpool Ranges.

Every morning at 9.00am the Sydney Telegraph Office obtained a line to my Melbourne colleagues through the departmental system, which was a permanently booked call. If the departmental lines were out, the call was placed through Telecom Australia. During the morning's conference, we advised each other of the changes that had been made for the following week to the composition of the *Southern Aurora*. The *Spirit of Progress*, which had only Victorian carriages, was also checked. In the event of Sydney receiving a request for a bulk booking, which sometimes happened when the Department of Sport and Recreation took children interstate, it was necessary to advise V/Line who would send a car empty from Melbourne on the *Spirit* for the booking.

After the morning's conference with the reservations clerk, and checking the changes with my clerk, with V/Line and the Yard Controller Sydney, it was Acdep's turn. Each morning at about 10.00am, I went through the full composition of each air-conditioned train. We used to commence from the brakevan and nominate the types of carriages and its number on the train. For instance, the *Southern Aurora* started with 'MHN, NAM 1, LAN 2, NAM 3' etc. It did not take very long doing this each day to learn the composition of each train. Before we began, the Acdep clerk gave me the repairs on hand and also advised of any car arriving next morning that was likely to need attention.

Soon after I arrived back from Melbourne, I went to Acdep and spent some time with the DLE (District Locomotive Engineer in charge of Acdep) and the train clerk that I had my dealings with. It was from that moment that the Melbourne cars began to get onto their correct trains. The shunters threatened all sorts of trouble when they knew they had to swap cars from one train to another. To them they were all carriages; who owned them did not concern them. The Yard Controller Sydney was in charge of the shunting staff at Acdep, and I found it necessary to have a talk to him to get the matter straightened out.

After the clerk in Coach had received the changes for the next day's trains, he typed up the list in chronological order, showing the full composition for each train. This information, together with any amendments to the current day's trains, was printed and distributed by the junior to traffic trouble, chief train controller programme, CMPC supervisor, diesel and electric engine roster clerks, *syco* west, south, north, Illawarra and goods control, the Yard Controller and Station Master Sydney, the guards foreman and chief inspector carriage sheds. A telegram was also despatched to the country super-intendents advising changes and total load of trains.

Sydney Parcels Office was in full swing in 1979. They loaded vans for the mail trains (including the DEH for Broken Hill) in Regent Street Platform, which was really an extension of the Mortuary Platform. I had worked with the parcels and luggage agent at Orange East Fork when we were both third class assistant station masters. In addition to these wagons, Darling Harbour loaded next-day delivery traffic for Dubbo, Tamworth, Armidale, Cootamundra and Griffith. A special shunt ran from Sydney Yard about 6.00pm and picked up the loaded vans, returning to place them on the lead of their trains standing at platforms on the main station.

The DEH of the *Forbes Mail*, which trailed from Sydney, although a light draw gear vehicle, had been converted to Westinghouse airbrake compatibility, but it was also still compatible with the pneumatic air brakes of the *Silver City Comet*. A brakesman was employed from Sydney to Lithgow. The vehicle was reversed at Orange, so that it became the trailing vehicle again.

The clerk gathered all this information from Darling Harbour and Sydney Parcels before putting out his composition lists. When I became Coach, it had been the practice to put out two composition lists, one in the morning without the information concerning the bogie louvre vans that were to attach to the mails, and a second which contained all the information. I knew from my experience on the control boards that the first programme that came from Coach was thrown straight into the waste paper bin, or in goods control at least, folded and torn in half to make files. Some three months after I had been there, I wrote to all concerned saying that the first programme would be discontinued and henceforth only one programme would be issued.

This bought an immediate reaction from the yard controller and the country passenger services manager. After much doubt and conference between the three of us, it was decided to give it a three-month trial. At the end of the three months I did not say a word, but when I left about nine years later, there was still only one programme. I estimated that we saved two reams of paper a week. The clerk thought it was a wonderful idea, but then of course he would! It saved him a lot of work.

I was amazed at the antagonism of the Traffic/Operations Branch toward the Carriage Works and the Mechanical Branch. The Passenger Section Administration were of the opinion that they were the only ones with any concept of conscientiousness or intellectual capacity. The Manager Carriage Works especially was regarded as nothing but a 'stirrer' who could not manage the Works efficiently. This attitude offended my consensus style of doing things, and even though I was very new in the job, I determined that as far as I was concerned that attitude would not prevail.

The Assistant Manager Carriage Works rang me early in my tenure and said that an SDS (an air-conditioned First Class carriage) had come into the shops for repairs. He said he was going to take it for general overhaul because another carriage that was due in three months ago had not turned up. I did not say anything to him, partly because I had nothing to say anyway and secondly, I did not want to reveal my ignorance. While I had no idea of what the procedure was, I knew there must be some sort of Workshop schedule available somewhere. I set about going through all the material that had been gathering dust for years in the large cabinet and found nothing useful, except old Workshop schedules. I kept on looking and found folded tightly behind the cabinet, the current Workshop schedule.

I was amazed at what was on this schedule. Besides the carriage the Assistant Manager had mentioned, there were two that were a month overdue into the shops and one that was due the next week. On the following Monday, I made an appointment with the Workshops Management. I found they did not have two heads and were as intelligent and conscientious as any one in the Operations Branch. We had a long and fruitful conversation, in which I guaranteed them that in future the cars would come into the shops as scheduled. In return they guaranteed me that if I did this, they would return them to operational use on the due date.

The criticism of the Works Manager was unfair. Many of the times when he was being regarded as a 'stirrer', he was trying to get into the Workshops the carriages that the maintenance schedule said he was entitled to. The continual and deliberate ignoring of the maintenance schedule hitherto was a blight on the management of my predecessor and the Passenger Trains Manager and his assistant.

Of concern to me was the way the schedules were drawn up. There was no thought given to operational requirements, although I suspect that was as much the fault of the Operations Branch as the Carriage Works. An example of this was the schedule for that year. There were five RDH type cars, which had 36 First Class seats and a small buffet type kitchen that provided take-away meals in service. Two of these five were scheduled together in the shops, but the daily requirement in service was four. Obviously it was not going to be possible to maintain the service with two in for overhaul. During our conversation we sorted this out by re-arranging their timing into the shops. Simple, really.

We agreed that in September, when the schedules for 1980 would be made up, that I would spend time with them and we would arrange a programme suitable to both our requirements. This mutual drawing up of the schedule left me in the position of being able to be sure I could have the vehicles available on the date they were required and guaranteed them continuity of work. Consensus worked again and I made friends in the Workshop, which in the long run paid dividends. Especially at holiday periods, the management made every effort to see that anything in for running repairs was available on the Friday of a long weekend. This, I might say, did not go unnoticed by the Country Passenger Services Manager. He made mention of the fact he had not heard from the Carriages Works Manager for ages, I simply said a bit of co-operation worked wonders.

The night mail trains in 1979 were really horror trains to travel by. When I took over

Coach, the *Forbes Mail*, the *Western Mail*, the *South West Mail*, the *North Coast Mail* which terminated at Kempsey and the *North West Mail* were still running. The *North Coast Mail*, the *North West Mail* and the *Western Mail* conveyed Travelling Post Offices (TPOs). After something like 80 years of useful and reliable mail service to country New South Wales, they were to be discontinued during the next year.

The TPOs carried a varying staff level, usually three or four in the off-peak periods. In the heavy Christmas periods, the staff levels were significantly increased to cope with the extra mail. Many country post offices addressed mail bags to the TPO, and these were loaded directly into the van. The TPO staff knew where to expect bags and generally were in position to take them. The mail from these was sorted and placed into bags for the sorting room at the GPO (in those days).

The rolling stock supplied to these trains was not heated, with the exception of some open area Waddington cars that were gas heated. This was not particularly effective. The cars were drafty and unless the passenger sat under the heaters, they received no benefit. Of course, by this time there were fewer passengers to sit under the heaters. The eight passenger compartments in these cars were not heated by reason of the regulations of the Occupational Health and Safety Act, which forbade it. Non-pungent gas leakage in such a confined area could well have been fatal.

The Sydney footwarmer boilers were still operative and footwarmers from these were placed into the carriages about 20 minutes before departure. There was not an operative boiler left in the country areas. I doubt the footwarmers were even taken from the carriages at some termination points. The non air-conditioned, old-style sleeping cars were still in use and percentage wise were probably better patronised than the sitting cars. They were reasonable enough to travel in, but they all seemed to have a musty smell in them.

The revamped BAM, which were refitted from, I think, TAM sleepers were better. They had 14 beds that were placed in the direction of travel from Sydney with the head of the bed nearest the engine. Returning from the country the passenger's feet were nearest the engine. They had gas heated showers and had hot water to the hand basins in the cabins. I travelled often in these in later years and, to my mind, they were the most comfortable sleeping cars in the fleet, including the air-conditioned ones.

When the air-conditioned carriages started coming on line in the early 1950s, Carriage Works stopped doing overhauls on long-distance non air-conditioned rolling stock. The carriages were repaired as required and returned to traffic. Under-floor requirements were stringently met, to ensure the safety of the cars, but the above floor work, however, was always just maintenance only. The carriages were, to my mind, a disgrace. The trim on the sliding doors on nearly every carriage was either missing altogether or had pieces missing, so that no matter what a passenger did, the drafts could not be kept out. The rolling stock for urban transportation was maintained to a much better standard; carriages were regularly overhauled. The interurban electric fleet in 1979 did not nearly meet the number of trains that were required to run in morning and afternoon peak hours. There were still three locomotive hauled trains from Gosford each weekday. These were open type carriages that had been stripped and between 60 and 70 seats built into them. The seats could be turned or rolled over to suit the direction of travel. The Moss Vale and Goulburn passenger trains were formed from similar types. These carriages were all gas heated.

Not long after I took up Coach, the District Superintendent Wollongong wrote a stinging letter about the condition of the carriages that formed the 'Katies'. I went to Wollongong and went with him and the senior inspector to Thirroul to see these carriages. One word came to my mind when I was walking through the first set; it was 'gross'. These cars were in a deplorable state. They were made up of a mixture of close-coupled sets of the LUB, SIB and LOB type cars (close coupled, high density sets used in the metropolitan area prior to electrification). They were clean in as much as they were swept and dusted daily.

The only redeeming feature I could see was that passengers were in them for no more than 30 minutes if they came from Coal Cliff, but as the majority came from between Thirroul and Wollongong, they were only on them about 20 minutes. To my mind, there was no way that they could be brought up to a decent standard. Despite the urgings of my good friend, the late Brian Daly, I could see no way of supplying anything better until more electric interurban cars came into service on the Gosford run. I have to confess that these carriages were still in use when the Illawarra Line was electrified some five years later.

On a regular basis, the Department of Sport and Recreation ran country camps for city children. These camps were at Wagga Wagga, Dubbo, Tamworth and on the North Coast. Every three months, they sent a copy of the programme to the Passenger Train Section, from where it found its way to Coach. My first experience with them was not a good one. The June long weekend of 1979 occurred at the end of the week that I had taken up Coach. On the Thursday prior to the weekend, the yard controller advised me that he could not meet the orders for the Department of Sport and Recreation. I had no option but to inform the Passenger Trains Manager, who in turn advised the Department, that they would have to provide road coaches to the camps. This went down very badly with them, and so it should have.

During the next month, the programme for the following three months including the October long weekend arrived. I rang the Sport and Recreation Officer in charge and asked her to come and see me. We met and had a very fruitful discussion about how we might prevent another fiasco like the one that had just occurred. I also learned from her that they also required carriages at times to run empty to the country to bring country children for their camps on the Central Coast. After this meeting, I allotted the carriages they required and gave the allocations to the yard controller, the Reservations Centre, the Station Master Sydney and the Passenger Trains Manager.

There was not another occasion when their requirements were not met during my time as Coach. Some 12 months later, the Director General rang the Operations Manager and requested that I be given leave for a day while they took me out on a tour of their Central Coast camps. I had a very educational day, that made me even more determined to meet their requirements. The strange thing was that when I allocated the rolling stock up to three months in advance, the yard controller made no complaint about not being able to meet the demand.

Another area of difficulty concerned the GPS Schools at the beginning of holidays. Some two months before the date they were due to travel, each school sent to the Reservations Section a list of the pupils who would be travelling by train and of their destinations. The Reservations Section clerk in charge of school bookings would break the list up into the trains for which travel was required and then come to Coach seeking the carriages required. It was mandatory to supply the carriages as required. I had no problem with this.

My problem came on the day of travel when some of the carriages went out empty, the schools having made other arrangements to send the children by road coach because parents had complained of the students' behaviour on trains. Some parents actually came from the country to travel on the trains, the *Dubbo Mail* especially, to ensure the conduct of the students did not exceed that which was acceptable. Although the carriages for boys were separated from the girls, they seemed to be able to mix, for which I blamed the conductors for not making them stay in their seats. The conductors said to me,

"You should try it!"

Fair comment. One very large school that offended the most, when they were contacted regarding the failure of the children to travel by nominated trains, were very off handed and gave the impression that they could not see what the complaint was. It took senior management to see the Principal, and to have him understand the basis of our complaint.

Some six months into my time as Coach, a re-arrangement of the offices on the second floor took place. The Passenger Section was moved from the eastern side of the building (or that side nearest Elizabeth Street) to the northern portion (or the portion that faced Eddy Avenue and Belmore Park). I had a pleasant office, which was glass partitioned from my staff. This shut us off from other sections. Before going into this office, I had been trying to devise a method whereby I knew where every air-conditioned vehicle in the fleet was at any given time. I still had the feeling that the system was running me, rather than the other way round. Before we moved in, I had the inkling of an idea, and went to the Container Section where as I have described, I had worked. On the wall, still not being used was a large magnetic board, originally designed to keep track of containers. I asked the Container Officer if he used it. The answer was, "No."

My next question was, "Can I have it?" His answer, "Yes."

Pleased with myself, I contacted the Way and Works Branch carpenter and asked him to fix it to the wall of my office, which was the dividing wall and therefore solid. He did so. Using my budget, I then purchased two 'Dymo' machines for pressing letters and numbers onto metallic strips and several strips of metallic tape. I then charged the junior with the task of making the serial number and letters of every vehicle in the fleet, including power vans and brakevans. For example, for SDS2220, he made these figures on the 'Dymo' tape and then placed it on the magnetic tape. When this was finished, he made out the names of all the trains; such as the *Brisbane Limited*. On the Down journey, they were coloured green and red for the Up journey. He then made out names for the varying types of ways in which a vehicle could be utilised, such as 'Spare', 'Repairs', 'Overhaul Workshops' and 'Wheel Lathe'.

It took us about a fortnight to set it up after we moved into the new office. The junior had been so enthusiastic about doing all this that I decided to let him have the responsibility and gave him the daily task for bringing the board up to date each morning. When I got the repairs from Acdep, he moved the cars around to show the state of the repair fleet. He also made it his business to get the incoming loads of each train and check them against the board. When I had done the programme, he took cars off the consists or added cars to them to reflect that day's compositions. He was appointed to Riverstone station when he became 18½ years. I lost track of him but I often think of him; he took so much obvious pleasure from having the responsibility I gave him.

The addition of this board completely changed my ability to manage the fleet. I knew where every vehicle was. I could see from the board how I would be placed for cars a fortnight ahead. When the reservations clerks came in for the morning conference, I could say "Yes" or "No" to their requests with confidence. Before, I used to give them cars and hope I could find them. This way, I knew.

The crunch came one morning about 11.00am. The Deputy Chief Executive wanted to know how every car in the air-conditioned fleet was being used by 1.00pm that day. It was simple; it was all on the board and a reply was faxed to him within 30 minutes. With the previous method it would have taken hours to track each vehicle down. The additional advantage to me was that it told the Deputy Chief Executive that I had a 'handle' on the job.

The Assistant Yard Controller Sydney was so taken with the board that he had one made for the Yard Controller's Office. He very soon saw the benefit of knowing where every vehicle was and described the idea as 'a bloody bottler'.

It was recognised, before I became Coach, that the air-conditioned rolling stock was reaching the stage where its capacity to continue to support the requirements of a State whose population was increasing, was becoming increasingly difficult. The interiors of some of the original economy cars were very 'tatty' indeed. The roll-over seats were uncomfortable for long distance travel, while many of the rotating and reclining seats used in the original First Class cars were in an almost deplorable state. Many of the seats would not recline, and if they did, they went right back. The seats were hard from years of use, resulting in a continual flow of complaints from the travelling public.

Tenders were invited for two groups of vehicles, locomotive hauled long distance cars and for underfloor-engined railcars for shorter distance services. Other more innovative solutions were also to be considered in place of the specified cars.

Two companies responded with alternative ideas; a French Consortium and Comeng, who offered a version of the British Rail and the English firm which had built the much-vaunted HST. Both companies sent representatives to New South Wales, fortunately at different times. The French were first putting forward a slightly modified version of the TGV. (*le Train à Grande Vitesse* – translation: High Speed Train.) The carriages were shorter articulated and than those of State Rail, something like 40 feet as opposed to 72 feet overall for our carriages. The purpose of this was to enable them to take curves at a much faster speed.

The French were not taken with the idea of not fitting-out the cars in France to the passenger comfort they thought should accompany their vehicles. I agreed with them. The air-conditioning system was unique to each vehicle; hence a power failure in one car did not affect the whole train. They were also providing the vehicles only; at the time only a Turbine powered prototype had been tested and we were to supply the locomotive power. This fact put them in a difficult position when the request was for self-propelled trains. They had mock-ups of their vehicles which looked very impressive. The TGV ran from Paris to Lyons at very high speeds, far higher than would ever be achieved in this State. I was impressed with their presentation, but not really 'blown away' by it.

The Comeng submission was based largely on the British Rail's High Speed Train, commonly known as the HST, but using trailer cars to a new Australian design, and was accepted. The Mechanical Branch, especially, was very anxious that these trains be the future of State Rail passenger transport. This concept consisted of the push-pull method that in the New South Wales system would be adequate for the 1 in 40 and 1 in 33 gradients for either five or seven carriage sets. The power units each had a Paxman diesel engine supplying about 1980 horsepower (1500 kilowatts), making the hauling capacity of each power car approximately the same as single 44/45/421/422/442 Class diesel-electric locomotives.

The main drawback I saw with them was the amount of power syphoned off to run the electrical power for the train. Approximately 15 per cent of the output of one unit was required to maintain the buffet car and air-conditioning—this reduced the traction power available if one power car failed. They were to be known in New South Wales as the 'XPTs'. Comeng built the power cars under licence in New South Wales.

There was much discussion regarding the seating that should be placed in them. For ease of management and cleaning, the Mechanical Branch were pushing very hard to have fixed seating installed in Economy Class, fixed in as much as the seat frame was fastened to the floor and could not be moved. However, by the use of a small lever on the side of the seat, it was possible to move the seat forwards or backwards to give somewhat of an impression that the seat had reclined. I argued that there would be uproar. Passengers in New South Wales had been used to facing the engine on long distance trains since the inception of air-conditioned trains. These seats, based on those in the French TGV, were adopted in both classes, with 2+1 across in First Class and 2+2 across in Economy Class.

I suggested, with the Chief Executive present, that we were buying a Rolls Royce train and putting Model 'T' seats in it. This received a cool reception. However, the Chief Executive listened to what I had to say, but unfortunately, I was outvoted. I was right about the uproar! I always had the feeling that the whole deal of the purchase of the XPTs was driven by the Mechanical Branch, and we finished up with what, in my opinion, was a second-rate train when it came to passenger comfort. I also said at one meeting that the seating of the Victorian cars that came into Sydney on the *Spirit of Progress* was far superior to that in any NSW State Rail train, including what was going into the XPTs. Again it was not appreciated, but it was the truth.

We received a litany of complaints in the first month of operation about the fixed seating. I knew this would happen and was disappointed, I guess, at the lack of support from my own Branch. They were too frightened of the Chief Executive to say what they thought. The thing that most disappointed me was the seating. After about six months, they were behaving in the same way as they had in the First Class loco-hauled air-conditioned cars. It cannot be said that the XPT made a very marked difference to the quality or comfort of the service provided in this State. Had they originally been furnished with the seating they have today, I am sure they would have been accepted more readily, and become much more popular as a means of transport.

After many trials and crew training along with a State-wide demonstration tour, the XPTs came into service on 8 April 1982 working the *Central West Express*. As the four train sets were delivered, later services commenced on 31 May 1982 with the *Mid North Coast* and, on 23 August 1982 with the *Riverina Express*. The Up *Mid North Coast* was a morning departure from Kempsey with the Down being an afternoon departure from Kempsey. When the *Riverina Express* changed to an XPT, it was an early afternoon departure from Sydney and an early morning departure from Albury which enabled one train to work the Up *Riverina* and then form the Down *Mid North Coast*, etc. In early 1984 two more sets came on-line and the country passenger services were re-organised. The sets, when introduced, each had five carriages, with the buffet car in the middle. The trains were designed to run approximately 1,100 kilometres before requiring fuel and toilet decanting. The rosters for the trains were formed with this in mind.

While I cannot recall the exact rosters of each set, they worked the *Northern Tablelands Express* to Glen Innes, where extensive electrical work was undertaken to provide for the

415 volt power needed to maintain lighting for the cleaners. Engine warmers which also required an external power source, were used in the winter months to ensure the engines were warm and would start. There were numerous occasions over the years when the DEB sets on this service would not start. The catering staff did not go past Armidale. The 415 volt three phase AC supply had been installed at most sidings or platforms where Daylight Express trains stabled so that electric power was available for the stationary train without the need for the engines in the power van to be working.

As well as the *Riverina Express*, the *South XPT* was introduced in June 1984 as an overnight sitting car only train to Albury which meant that the XPT no longer stayed overnight in Albury. The train could be kept under cover; the carriage sheds that stabled the overnight passenger trains at Albury were still available. Again, extensive electrical work was required. The *Central West Express* ran a round trip to Dubbo, departing around 8.08am and returning around 9.30pm. The catering crews worked continuously on this. The corridor attendants were Dubbo-based.

During mid 1974, the DEB sets based at Dubbo to work the Nyngan/Bourke/ Brewarrina and the Nyngan/Cobar services were withdrawn. They were replaced by three GM and three Leyland, which in 1977 were fitted with GM engines, road coaches. A much improved passenger service came into existence with the implementation of these coaches. An additional service was provided to Lightning Ridge, connecting with train services to Walgett.

In addition to the GM coaches already in service at Dubbo, 17 further GM engined coaches were obtained during 1981-86 and another 20 Scania coaches were purchased in 1985-85. The idea of the purchase of these coaches was to keep the XPTs on the main lines only. The coaches were to, and did, provide the rest of the State with a branch line feeder service that was to become known, sarcastically, as the 'rubber railway'. Coaches were situated at Cowra, Cootamundra, Wagga, Parkes, Dubbo, Tamworth and Grafton. The only depot with coaches and qualified coach captains was Dubbo. It was necessary, therefore to select and train (pardon the pun!) drivers in the art of coach driving. It was agreed between the Department and the Unions that these positions were to be open to guards only. It fell to my lot, with a representative of the Personnel Department and an independent person, to interview and select from the applicants the required number of coach captains for training. As the railways were part of the Public Transport Commission during 1972, they were trained by instructors from PTC Bus division, Dangar Street School at Randwick and examined in their driving skills by their inspectors.

The Country Passenger Operations Manager who did the north area of the State, and I conducted the trials for the timetables. Prior to going out, we had, with the Country Passenger Services Manager, worked out what we thought would be approximate times by using an average speed of 70km/h, which took into consideration the stops required and the speed restrictions through built-up areas. This proved an accurate measure and when we returned from the trials, very little alteration was made to our notional timetables. I went south and conducted trials from Cootamundra to Griffith and Hay, and to Tumut via Gundagai. We arranged permanent accommodation at a local motel at each point, but getting the most competitive price was not easy. The coach captains wanted the best accommodation, of course. We were prepared to give them three or three and a half star accommodation. On each of the trials, representatives of the Australian Railways Union and the National Union of Railwaymen were present.

After Cootamundra, I went to Wagga Wagga, where we did trials to Tumbarumba, Narrandera, Leeton and Griffith. When these were complete, we took the coach to Blayney, where it would connect with the XPT, and travelled to Cowra and on to Grenfell and return to Cowra. The following day, we went to Eugowra. I had contacted my mother at Canowindra, as she was active in the Senior Citizens group. I suggested that she get a group of them together for a ride to Eugowra and return for nothing. I do not know whether it was an embarrassing moment or a proud one, but my mother made the most of it. This was her son and she made sure the 30 or so who joined the coach knew it. It was a good thing to have done. From Eugowra we went back to Cowra via Canowindra, then on to Blayney to connect with the Up *Central West Express*. The Country Passenger Services Manager had run trials from Tamworth to Moree and Narrabri and from Grafton to Casino and Murwillumbah.

The coaches received their maintenance from the local agents in the country towns, when they were due for major regular maintenance or required extensive repair work, they were transferred to the Departmental motor garage at Clyde.

The Mechanical Branch, despite having a very large facility at Acdep, decided that they required an XPT depot and built one at Sydenham (Meeks Road), probably at a cost approaching the cost of the XPT contract. While I was and still am, to a degree, critical of this decision, I have to agree that they were justified in building it. There were certainly drawbacks at Acdep, but whether half the money spent at Sydenham would not have fixed them, I am not prepared to guess.

With the bedding down of the XPTs and the successful launch of the new coach routes, I felt that I had control of all aspects of the job. I had repaired the distrust between the Operations Branch, the Carriage Works Management and the Mechanical Branch. The Workshop schedules were being adhered to and the winner was the Department. I would have been content to stay there until retirement. It was not to be.

STILL MORE CATHY

AFTER Cathy had the colostomy bag inserted, I (or we did) made the decision that we would not agree to further surgery, because by this time she had had some 40-odd surgical procedures. I do not now, nor have I ever, criticised the medical profession for this, because I am sure that up to that point, every procedure had been made with the interests of Cathy as number one priority.

I believed, however, that enough was enough, both for Cathy and her parents. I also made the decision after she had recovered from the colostomy surgery, had come home and then returned to hospital with a huge water blister on her heel, that the time had unfortunately come when we could no longer look after her at home full-time. The demands were just too much. She slept irregularly and would be awake for hours every night, which meant one of us was awake. I found that I was getting so little sleep that I was dozing off in the middle of the morning when I was working. We had reached the point, that if we tried to continue, one of us would have had a breakdown. If this happened, we could not have looked after her, nor would we have been able to devote the time to her that we did after she finally went to full time care. It was a very sad decision.

While Margaret Reid Hospital was operating, we had no problem but when the hospital closed, we had all sorts of difficulty finding a placement for her. She was placed in a nursing home at Turramurra with disastrous results. She was so heavily sedated because she was noisy and disturbed the other old people that, when she was awake, the effect of the drugs made her worse than she was normally. Finally the administration of the home rang one morning and said that Cathy and her things would be on the footpath at midday.

We had the best efforts of her social worker working for us, but this was not finding her accommodation. Finally, that afternoon, she was taken to North Ryde Psychiatric Centre. She was placed in a security ward that housed people suffering dementia, severe retardation and physical disabilities. One of the occupants was a male whose arms and legs were no more than 20 centimetres long. The torso was about a metre long while the head was that of an adult. In addition to these physical disabilities, he was deaf, dumb and blind. He used to be placed naked in a large bouncer that had a small amount of water in it; he was able to move on the bouncer and from the appearance of his face received some pleasure when he did so. It was one of the most distressing sights I have ever seen. While I sympathised with them, I was appalled that I had to leave Cathy in these surroundings. Either Mamie or I, or both of us, went there every day for the whole time she was there.

After she had been there some time, she dehydrated and the doctor ordered a saline drip. The staff who did the 'cut down' (which is the term used for placing a long term needle in the vein) missed the vein in her right arm with the needle. As a result, a full bag of saline drained into her arm. It become grossly swollen and remained so for a long time. She never used the arm again. In fact, over time the hand became clawed to the extent that her fingernails used to mark the skin in the pulse area.

Shortly after this, the hospital rang Mamie about 9.00pm one night to say that Cathy had been transferred to Royal North Shore Hospital suffering pneumonia and that her condition was critical. Mamie went straight to the hospital to find her in the emergency ward. She was blue. I was at Lodge in the Artarmon temple, and the Hospital Registrar arranged for the police to contact me. I, of course, also went straight to the hospital. After a period of time she was stabilised and the doctor said she was not in immediate danger, but that she was very seriously ill and to expect anything to happen. We came home. Next afternoon, we spoke to a cardiologist who said straight out that he did not expect Cathy to recover. Once again, she beat the odds that were stacked against her and did recover, although it took a long time. I still have the 21 pages of pathology tests the hospital sent accompanying the account, which was about $2000.00. The hospital accepted the Medibank payment as full payment.

During the time she was in the hospital, she was accepted into one of the first Richmond scheme homes. These were homes in the community for people like Cathy. There were five people in the home she was in. It was the first time she had been placed where she was treated like a member of an ordinary household, where she paid rent and contributed to the household food costs from her invalid pension. When I went to the North Ryde Psychiatric Hospital to collect her belongings, the head sister (a male) said,

"I am glad she did not 'cark it' here; I shudder when I think of the paperwork I would have had."

I did not say anything, but just looked at him. He must have seen how angry I was, for he had the grace to suggest it was an unfortunate remark. I think that was the only time in all the hospitalisation that Cathy had, that I felt any animosity toward someone who was caring for her. The young people of our church banded together and raised money to furnish her bedroom. It took a load from us. In the early part of her residence I went and helped her with her dinner every night on my way home from work. After a period, I stopped this, partly to give her independence and partly because I was starting to wilt under the strain. We brought her home every Saturday and Sunday for lunch and took her back in the afternoon.

THE 1979 REORGANISATION

THE early part of 1979 saw wholesale changes in the administration of the New South Wales transport system brought about by the appointment of a new Chief Executive. The Public Transport Commission became the State Rail Authority. Out with the old letterheads. Hang the expense. Print new ones with a new logo and the new name. The cost was thousands of dollars; it was not good enough for typists to 'X' out the old name and type in the new one, not even in inter-departmental correspondence.

In 1981, further wholesale changes were made. The old Chief Traffic Manager position, which had become the Operations Manager, was abolished. In its place there were two positions; General Manager Passenger Services and General Manager Freight Services, who answered to a Chief Operations Manager in Transport House. The Passenger Section, with which I was associated, was managed by a Country Passenger Services Manager; a Country Passenger Operations Manager and I became the Country Passenger Facility Manager.

Progress was progress. I was sad, however, to see the positions of Chief Traffic Manager and Passenger Train Superintendent, which had existed from almost the beginning of the NSW Railways, disappear. These positions had been held by many very distinguished railway senior officers over time. I doubt that any recognition of these men will be found in the histories that have been written of their era. There are records of some of the Chief Mechanical Engineers, notably Mr E E Lucy, 'The Man of Steam'. His life was depicted in a book of the same name. The romance of steam engines from early times made them, and often their designers, attractive subjects about which to write. Something as mundane as the Traffic Branch, despite being regarded as the service branch and therefore the senior branch, failed to attract historians.

In this set up, I became a Senior Officer Class 2. I still had overall control of the rolling stock, with the added responsibilities of its presentation in terms of cleanliness, passenger comfort, interior maintenance and Workshop maintenance schedules, plus the responsibilities for the onboard train staff train staff including the catering staff, which under the new regime belonged to the Passenger Services Section, a fact not pleasing to the catering or hospitality staff. It was, from their point of view, the beginning of sweeping change. The same criteria applied to conductors and corridor attendants. In a previous chapter, I outlined the events surrounding the acquisition of the XPTs and coaches. All this re-organisation took place in this period. In addition, the Chief Inspector Carriage Cleaning Sheds and his staff of 320 cleaners became answerable to me.

The new General Manager Passenger Services came from another Government Department not associated with transport. To me this was not a problem, although it was to others, especially those who had missed out on the position. The age old cry,

"What would he know about railways", came quickly to the fore.

I held the view, which I expressed to not sympathetic ears on a number of occasions, that his job was to manage; he had officers like us to advise on the running of the show. He had to manage budgets and carry out government policy.

He fairly quickly revealed that he believed the section employed too many people. The one area he failed to mention was the Central Reservations Centre. I have always believed, and still do, that this area took far more of the earnings of the passenger section by way of salaries, than it ever went near to earning. At this time, there were 12 trains daily which were compulsory seat or berth-booked trains. To man these trains, the section employed something like 40 people. The Reservation Centre was open seven days a week from 6.00am to 10.00pm. In my time, at least three senior officers spent months each on special duties attempting to set up computer programmes that would work efficiently. The introduction of a computerised reservation system was supposed to reduce staffing levels; the same numbers of staff worked on the computerised system as there were on the old manual system.

There were people in the centre who I believed were the laziest I had ever seen. The favourite trick of one person was to sit there with his computer turned on, but with the telephone head piece not properly plugged in. All the while he had it like this, he had no calls. In one of the branch conferences, I suggested that there should be an audit run on the computers on a particular day to see who were working conscientiously and who were not. The Clerks had to enter their own number into the computer before they began a call. An audit would have been simple to do. This could not be done; they did not want to upset the union.

Despite the desire of the General Manager Passenger Services to rationalise staff in an endeavour to reduce the numbers and therefore costs, he set up an Advertising Section, which he headed up with a lady from a prominent advertising firm. She was employed as a Schedule 8 Senior Officer that was equal to the grade of the Passenger Services Manager. Among her staff was a Senior Officer Grade 4, together with ancillary staff. I had no objection to having a lady in the position, if there had to be an Advertising Section, the work of which had been formerly done with much less outlay by the Commercial Section.

The problem I and my colleagues had, was that the Advertising Section put forward suggestions that could not possibly be made work with the rolling stock and equipment we had. When I tried to point out to her that no one had ever succeeded in putting a quart into a pint pot, I was informed I was being negative. I tried to assure her that the reverse was the case and that I would be the first to assist in any realistic programme.

One of the schemes was to run a special train to the Brisbane Expo conveying sleeping cars and First Class sitting cars. I suggested that we did not have the rolling stock for this and I doubted that people would pay an additional 50 per cent on the fare for a chocolate on their pillow and not much else for their money. Had we been able to provide the rolling stock, the Mechanical Branch would not have been able to supply the power vans required.

In their wisdom, the Advertising Section decided that they would 'tart up' a sleeping car and run it on the regular service, and add a surcharge for the chocolate and breakfast. After an advertising campaign that would have cost plenty, the response was so poor that they cancelled the idea in the second week. To my mind that section was empire building by the General Manager Passenger Services.

One of the good ideas the General Manager had was one that was to affect me greatly. He introduced the idea of multi-skilling of the train hospitality staff and the conductors and corridor attendants. This idea, of course, brought forth the wrath of the unions. They were not interested in the idea and even refused to come to the table to discuss the matter. I was nominated to run the trials for the envisaged manning levels of all trains from XPTs to the overnight interstate expresses.

The Industrial Section became heavily involved when the unions refused to even consider the ideas. The conductors had attended to the comfort of passengers from the beginning of the railways and the Trading and Catering Staff (ex Railway Refreshment Room staff) had attended to the passengers' catering requirements. The unions were not going to see this changed. The most belligerent of the unions was the NUR (National Union of Railwaymen). Together with the ARU (Australian Railways Union) they covered all the employees concerned with the proposals. The idea of multi-skilling was good; but its implementation time was long, frustrating and arduous from my personal point of view. In view of the changes to the original position of Country Passenger Facility Manager, I became the Country Passenger Operations Superintendent.

When the General Manager first gave the directions that the staff become multi-skilled and share in the workload on the train, he indicated that he expected to see the proposals operating within three months. Three months had passed before the Industrial Section got the unions to come to the discussion table! I knew most of the conductors and was on reasonable terms with them. They indicated early in discussions that they would accept me as the departmental representative in the on-train trials.

We began the trials on the *North Coast Daylight*, which by this time had become an

XPT. The staff was four catering, (a cook and three counter staff) from Sydney and two corridor attendants, one of whom was Newcastle-based. The Sydney attendant left the train at Broadmeadow and returned to Sydney on the midday *Flyer* as a ticket examiner. The Newcastle man also left the train at Broadmeadow to be replaced by another Newcastle attendant who worked to Grafton. The purpose of the two from Sydney was to have the tickets checked in the five carriages prior to Broadmeadow, thus giving the attendant to Grafton the job only of patrolling the train, making stopping announcements and keeping the rubbish removed from carriages and keeping the toilets clean.

It became abundantly clear in the first half hour of the trial that this was going to be a difficult process. The initial trial was to assess the work carried out by the attendants and to see what assistance the catering staff could give. The unions demanded that on every trial we conducted, a member of each of the ARU and NUR be present. The NUR demanded at the beginning that, aside from me, a senior officer of the Catering Section also be part of the trials. This was refused by the General Manager who said, under the new formation of the branch, I as Country Operations Superintendent, was representing the Department from both the old Operations and the Trading and Catering Branches, and that the two were now part of the Passenger Services Branch. The solving of this alone took something like a month; it had gone to the Industrial Section, which backed the decision.

It must have either looked comical or stupid from the passengers' point of view to see two union nominated representatives and a senior officer (not that they knew who we were) watching every movement of the attendant checking tickets and marking the seating diagram. The NUR representative was offering advice continually to the attendant, suggesting things that would slow his progress. I took him aside at Gosford and told him he was there as an observer and not to interfere with the attendant, telling him it was my intention for the three of us to discuss the day's proceedings in the hour prior to arriving at Grafton. The ARU man agreed. The NUR man was making the checking of tickets farcical. I told him any comment he had to make about the poor work method of his member, would be taken into consideration at this discussion. He did not appreciate that remark.

On arrival at Broadmeadow, the tickets for the whole train had been checked, and the required telegram showing the seats which had been booked but had not been occupied due to the passenger failing to show, was compiled ready for despatch to the Reservation Section. These seats were entered back into the system, making them available for day of travel seat bookings for stations Maitland and North thereof. I had been warned by the Chief Inspector attached to the General Manager's personal staff, of the laziness of the corridor attendant who joined at Broadmeadow. He came under notice almost on a regular basis by the inspector and by public complaint. I realised I had to put this from my mind, and although I said nothing about him, I knew from the attitude of his union representative, that he was not happy that he was the person around whom the test was to evolve. Shortly after leaving Broadmeadow, I took him and the union representatives in the leading brakevan and explained to him what we were doing. I made it clear to him that I did not want him to 'burst his boiler', but that he did the work that was required in his normal manner and we would judge from that. The NUR man accused me of pressuring him; the ARU man said he thought my comments were fair.

This attendant was lacking in any purpose or planning, he just muddled through. By the time we had arrived at Wingham, the whole train was in a mess. There had been no rubbish run, no tables cleared from lunch left-overs and the toilets had not been looked at. After we departed Wingham, I spoke to the ARU man who was the attendant's representative and suggested to him, that he guide him in the manner of the performance of his duties, and saying at the same time, that I would not consider this train run as part of the long term trials that were going to be necessary, before we got to a point that satisfied the General Manager and the unions. He agreed with me. My thinking was that if we could get someone to give the attendant a duty plan, the day would not have been altogether wasted. I did not consult the NUR man and did not much care what his reaction would be. I think his brother representative must have spoken to him, because he was very amenable. While from the viewpoint of a trial this was not a successful trip, it was from another point quite successful. I learned a lot about how the catering staff operated what meal breaks they took, and when their slack times were. It was good information.

Perhaps the most important duty of the corridor attendant on any train, was the closing of doors after each stop. He was duty bound to see that each passenger was aware of their approaching station of disembarkation via the PA system. He had to ensure they were able to handle their luggage and to lift it off the racks if necessary and place it near the door. If the passengers were alighting from more than one carriage, he had to make a judgment as to which passengers required his assistance the most to alight. After passengers had alighted and the train started to move, his first duty was to close the doors. In my XPT travels while conducting tests, the number of times I found doors not closed was unbelievable.

The first tests conducted without assistance from the catering staff, had the unions on the 'front foot'. They believed they had proved to me that two corridor attendants were required on all XPT journeys. This was not so. I was however of the opinion, that on the *Grafton XPT* at least, there was more work than what one person could perform, if he was to carry out the laid down duties for corridor attendants. The union representatives of course were familiar with these. They also, of course, demanded these duties be carried out in their entirety while we were doing tests. In my first report to the General Manager, I stated that I believed that we had a difficult task ahead of us to reduce the overall staff by more than one person on any XPT. He was looking for at least two off every train. At this point in time, the unions had not accepted the multi-skilling concept and were not about to.

Despite the General Manager's ingenuousness in the belief that all that had to be done was for him to say to the unions,

"This is what I want, and this is what will be done."

Nothing like that happened. In a very short time, we were in the Authority's Industrial Relations Section. After months of wrangling, the unions agreed to trials without obligation for multi-skilling. They attached, however, a number of demands to this agreement which were to be guaranteed by the Authority before we conducted any more trials. Among these was a new classification of passenger attendant for the base grade and that of chief passenger attendant for the person in charge of the on-train crew. Hand-in-hand with this demand, went a new wage scale that was, of course, quite considerably more than what was the current rate for on-train staff. It was about this time that productivity trade-off became quite the 'in' thing. These demands went to the Industrial Commission and after much haggling, a deal was struck. The General Manager thought he was now in the box seat and expected multi-skilling to be introduced forthwith.

He was doomed to disappointment because the trials of multi-skilling and manning levels came down now to the nitty gritty of staff numbers on trains. The unions were demanding that we trial with six people to begin with. It was generally agreed that when conducting the first of the multi-skilling trials, those who had been attendants should remain as the people who checked tickets. The catering staff were to be utilised to assist with the seating of passengers entraining at the main stations after departure, for example, Strathfield, and at the timetabled metropolitan stations.

Despite the union demands for six people, the trials, after further Industrial Relations Section action, began with five people. Part of the concept of multi-skilling was to provide a better service to the on-board passenger. The catering staff was expected to take meals to those who requested meals at their seats and to those incapable of moving to the catering area. Much better use was made of the PA system on the train; the attendant announcing the approaching stations, making announcements concerning connections, and the catering staff announcing meal, morning and afternoon tea times. This provided better and more useful information to the passenger.

The first of the trials with five people proved successful, from my perspective, and of the Authority's, which followed. The catering staff, without any direction or suggestion from me, removed rubbish from the seats as they moved about in the carriages. The union representatives, especially the NUR, tried to push them away, maintaining that it was not their duty. I came back with the reply that what they were doing was the nexus of what multi-skilling was all about. I must say the staff themselves were aware that six people on the train was one too many. Five staff, excluding the guard, was my recommendation to the General Manager, a figure that the unions accepted. We had, in fact, reduced the staff on the train by a little more than 16 per cent, a very considerable saving in wages over all trains in a 12 month period.

In my initial reports, I submitted this to the General Manager, who was not satisfied; he wanted two people off the train. He was frustrated to the point of exasperation by the unions continually running to the Industrial Section. To make matters worse, he did not believe the Department's industrial officers were supporting him in the Arbitration Commission. He also believed, I am sure that I was too sympathetic towards the unions, saying I seemed to be too friendly with them. I told him I could not stand a bar of the NUR representative; for the sake of any possible legal action, I will refrain from saying what I told the General Manager. The ARU man I had known and respected for some time. I did not agree with him on many aspects of what he was trying to achieve, but that was no reason to become unfriendly with him. We in fact respected one another. In my discussions with the General Manager, I told him that, given the new awards that had been approved for the multi-skilling, there would be times during a ten-hour journey when a staff of only four was on meal breaks provided under the conditions of the awards, there would insufficient staff to maintain the required standard of service.

One of the suggestions I made to the General Manager and to the unions was that if they wanted more working staff off the trains, they should dispense with the guard and make the chief passenger attendant responsible for the guard's duties and at the same time, be a working attendant. Not surprisingly the unions would not have a bar of this and made all sorts of threats should it even be thought about. To my surprise, the General Manager agreed with them. I assured him that the guard on the *North Coast XPT* did approximately 30 minutes work each time he signed on. It is with some satisfaction I note that since I retired, there is no guard on XPTs and the chief passenger attendant does exactly what I had recommended.

Agreement was finally made by the General Manager that there should be five staff on the XPTs working with five carriages, which was the standard composition for XPTs in the initial stages. When the XPTs were increased to seven cars, agitation from the unions demanded an additional staff member. After much haggling, this was not agreed to and eventually the unions settled for five staff, but left themselves an out by demanding a review within 12 months.

The trials on all the XPT services ran for months. I was heartily sick of train travel between Sydney, Grafton, Albury and Dubbo. I often consoled myself, thank goodness, that I did not do this for my living! After the start of the XPT trials, movement was made by the General Manager to have the overnight trains to Melbourne and Brisbane, together with the *Indian Pacific* and *The Ghan*, manned by multi-skilled crews.

The total number of staff who signed on duty to work the *Southern Aurora* was sixteen. Yes, sixteen! They included the driver and observer, guard, four conductors, three waiters, one bar attendant in the lounge car, two chefs, an assistant chef, a kitchen hand and a galley hand. The catering staff all booked off in Goulburn and worked the Up *Southern Aurora* from Goulburn to Sydney, the next morning.

It was very difficult to rearrange the staff to make reductions on this train. I had meetings with the General Manager, the Manager Trades and Catering and the chief inspector attached to the General Manager's personal staff. The biggest hurdle was the fact that the *Southern Aurora* was placed on No 1 platform at 7.00pm so that business men, especially, could entertain guests to dinner on the train prior to departure. The travelling populace often used this facility. Parents and grandparents would use the dining car as a means of saying thank you to siblings who had entertained them on holiday. People travelling on the train often used it; they would have their meal while the train was stationary and then either adjourn to the lounge car or to their cabins.

The unions claimed, with some justification, that the conductors were required at the door of their sleeping cars to book people in and to assist them with their luggage, and they therefore were not available to act as waiters before the train departed. This was especially so since the allocation earlier of the two sleeping cars to one conductor. The more we looked at this train, the more difficult it became. My suggestion finally was to bring the train to the platform at 7.00pm and dispense with the dinner availability on the platform. This went down like a lead balloon with the unions and did not get much support from the General Manager. I told him privately, that if he wanted staff reduced on the train, he had to make concessions. The days of eating cake and retaining it had long gone! Up to the time I retired in 1989, the problem still had not been resolved and the staffing arrangements had not changed. The fact that it had not was one of the reasons for its ultimate demise.

The *Brisbane Limited Express* and the *North Coast Overnight Express* to Murwillumbah (commonly known as *Norco*) were trains with similar staffing arrangements. Each of these trains had a dining car and back up takeaway (RDH) buffet. From the buffet car could be purchased pies, sandwiches, tea, coffee, cakes, confectionery, soft drinks and alcohol. In contrast to the *Southern Aurora*, these trains had as many as six sitting cars on them. Passengers from First Class and the sleeping cars were entitled to purchase a meal in the dining car. Poor old economy had to do with the take-away style.

As with the *Southern Aurora*, it was difficult to be able to utilise the conductors as waiters. Both trains stopped at Strathfield and Hornsby to pick up, so the unions were able to say that the conductors were required to be at the doors of their respective carriages when the train stopped at these points. It was hard to argue against this. The dining car staff from Sydney on the *Brisbane Limited* and the *Gold Coast Overnight Express* booked off at Casino and returned on the Up journey in the evening. Casino staff worked to Murwillumbah and to Brisbane. I found the Casino staff very efficient and customer oriented.

The difference between the *Southern Aurora* and the two north expresses was that there was no lounge car attendant and no chefs. The staff consisted of a cook and assistant, three waitresses in the dining car, and one person in the RDH take away. However the manning levels were looked at, the conducting staff was not available to assist in the dining car until around Gosford, approximately an hour from Sydney. By this time, most of those who wanted a meal in the dining car were seated and being attended to by the waitresses. The number of conductors was, of course, governed by the number of sleeping cars the train conveyed.

My suggestion, early in the trials, was to reduce the dining car staff when there were only three or four sleeping cars attached instead of the six allocated. This was strongly opposed by the unions and equally strongly supported by the Trades and Catering Section and the General Manager. To me, it was logical and the neatest way of reducing the staff, without affecting them when the train conveyed a full consist. If two thirds of the sleeping cars only were used, the reduction of one waitress, being a third of the full staff seemed logical to me. The problem was that the word did not appear in the union vocabulary. The arguments were still in progress when I retired some four years after we first started on manning levels.

New South Wales manned the *Intercapital Daylight* (ICD) with three waitresses, a chef and an assistant to the chef, who was also a general hand assisting with presentation of meals in the peak time and washing up as time permitted. I thought when we started looking at the staffing levels, that we may have been able to reduce the waiting staff by one. I deliberately chose days when the bookings were heavy to try this theory. I was convinced with 75 per cent capacity or more, which was not very often, three waiting staff, were necessary. Below this they were not. The corridor attendant, if he did his job properly, had no time to assist. The corridor attendants were Albury-based and were probably the best workers in the service.

The majority of the Sydney staff excelled in the service they provided to the passengers at any time and letters of commendation were received on a regular basis from passengers who had benefited from their service. In the event of staff shortages, which were not uncommon, the Sydney staff would work with three or four in the dining car. To enable them to cope, they would close off about a third of the places in the RS cars, which had bar like stools for people to sit on. (The RS dining cars differed from those on all other trains in that they had a long counter and fixed stool-like swivel seats were provided for patrons). The Sydney staff worked to Junee and they were relieved by the Victorian crew who had worked up on the *Spirit of Progress* the previous evening.

The Victorian unions refused to allow their members to take over the till from the NSW crew, demanding that all cash be counted up, money removed from the till and a float left for them. This most unreasonable action meant that the NSW crew had to start compiling a handover about 12.00pm when they were around Harden to enable the required handover to be ready. In fairness to the NSW crew, I have to say, that they made sure that announcements were made throughout the train, so that passengers were aware of the break in service. This gave passengers an opportunity of ordering meals before the dining service closed.

The Victorian crew demanded a half-hour to set up their way of doing things. In essence there was no service on the train from midday until about 1.45pm. To my mind, this break in service at lunchtime was scandalous. I broached this subject on a number of times with my Victorian colleagues and the union delegates. On one occasion, I was told by a female delegate to 'butt-out'. She told the gathering that the convenience of the travelling public was secondary to the convenience of the Victorian staff. The Victorians had seven dining car staff and if there was only one staff member short, they would shut the dining car down.

I was present at Junee when the Victorian staff came into the RS and found only four NSW staff. The abuse dished out by the Victorian union representative was disgusting, particularly coming from a female. I intervened and told the NSW staff just to leave and not respond to them. The New South Wales management at times thought their unions were not reasonable. I found out very quickly they were amateurs when it came to Victorian left-wing unions. They were totally obstructionist.

The *Indian Pacific* and *The Ghan* had between 13 and 15 staff, depending on the number of sleeping cars. The difference with these trains was that NSW and Australian National staff manned them; the Australian National staff, working into Sydney on Thursdays to return on Saturdays, and NSW staff manned the other two trains. We tried a number of options on these trains. On each occasion, when we arrived at Adelaide, the Australian National Railways union representatives, who belonged to the AWU, would inspect the train before deciding whether they would take it on from there. They of course knew how many staff that we had left Sydney with and were looking for any reason to create an industrial situation at Adelaide.

As an idea of how militant and unrelenting they were in their demands, the Australian Workers Union so exasperated the Australian National Management that on one occasion, the *Indian Pacific* was cancelled for three months. Australian National finally became so frustrated with their unrealistic demands, that they took action and told the crews that when they were ready to resume work under the terms that the Australian National had years before agreed with them, the train would run again. They eventually returned under Australian National's terms.

The concept of multi-skilling and job sharing on the State Rail Authority was really an effort by the General Manager and his administrative staff to rein in the costs associated with operating the passenger services, which at this time required that for every two dollars earned, three dollars was spent. This situation had been occurring for far too long and had contributed to the railway deficit each year, which was something like $400 million.

I put to the unions both officially and privately that if they wanted to keep long-term jobs, they had to assist with reducing the costs of running the passenger services, even if this meant they had to relent and meet at least half-way, the demands of multi-skilling. I emphasised, privately that if they did not, trains like the *Southern Aurora* and the two northern overnight expresses would cease to run. I was told this would not happen and if it were threatened, they would bring the system to a stand still until such times as they were re-instated.

It was around the beginning of 1987 that multi-skilling was achieved on the XPTs. When I retired in 1989, the overnight expresses still were not multi-skilled and never became so. After my retirement the *Southern Aurora*, the *Spirit of Progress*, the *Brisbane Limited Express* and the *Gold Coast Overnight Express* were all dispensed with. Additional XPTs formed a rationalised service to Melbourne and Brisbane.

Single locomotive 8152 awaiting at No 1 Platform of Sydney Terminal on 2 August 1986 for departure at 8.00pm with the last Southern Aurora *train for Melbourne. At 8.05pm, single locomotive 42203 departed from No 3 Platform with the last* Spirit of Progress *train.*

John R Newland.

THE BICENTENNIAL YEAR PLANNING

AROUND mid-1983, I received a letter that had been written by the Chief Executive, to the General Manager Passenger Services, who in turn passed it on to the Country Passenger Services Manager, seeking a senior officer for secondment to the NSW Bicentennial Steam Train Committee and to the Railways of Australia Bicentennial Committee. On the letter was the one word,

"Congratulations!"

This secondment bought about what was the culmination of my career. No other project I had ever undertaken came anywhere near to what this was to be. The ultimate pleasure and sheer joy of bringing to so many people, all over this great land, especially children, so much happiness and wonderment at watching the railways of a bygone era, was indeed the jewel in the crown of my career.

A committee known as the Steam Preservation Committee had met on a monthly basis in Room 513 of Transport House. This group consisted of members of the NSW Rail Transport Museum, the Lachlan Valley Railway Society, and the Department's Chief Accountant (an avid steam enthusiast), and it was generally chaired by the Commercial Manager. I became part of this group in my capacity as Country Passenger Operations Superintendent.

In early 1984, it became the driving force behind what was to become the New South Wales Railways response to the Bicentennial Year. The meetings in 1984-85 broadly discussed the 'what if' suggestions that were thrown up. We discussed what steam locomotives would be available and also the passenger rolling stock required to form trains for the various locomotives. Towards mid-1985, a small committee consisting of myself as the Passenger Services Branch Representative, a Bicentennial co-ordinator from the Commercial Branch, a representative of the Chief Mechanical Engineer (it was not uncommon for him to join our deliberations), representatives from the NSW Rail Transport Museum, the Chief Accountant, and from 3801 Limited and the Lachlan Valley Railway was formed.

The stated aim of the Bicentennial Steam Committee of New South Wales was to see that every country school child either rode behind or saw a steam engine in 1988.

It was at that time we began to get serious with our planning operations. The State Rail Secretariat became very supportive, the Chief Executive being very mindful of the importance of exhibiting the earlier modes of steam transport to the general public all over the State. I have generally refrained from using many names since I completed my time at Cowra in the first weeks of 1947, but I will name the Bicentennial Co-Coordinator, and an erudite young man—Owen Johnson-Donnett. Owen and I worked closely from then till the end of the Bicentennial Year. Owen had in his unit a number of people who were responsible for contacting schools, both public and private, over the whole of country New South Wales.

The NSW Government had formed the State into zones, each zone having responsibility for the Bicentennial events in its defined area. Owen and I went to each zone headquarters and spoke to the zone bicentennial director. We visited Wagga Wagga, Dubbo, Narrabri West, Armidale, Grafton, Newcastle and Wollongong. Aside from the regional zone headquarters, we visited Albury, Junee, Narrandera, Griffith, Leeton, West Wyalong, Forbes, Parkes, Condobolin, Peak Hill, Narromine, Orange, Bathurst, Lithgow, Tamworth, Werris Creek, Armidale, Moree, Casino, Lismore, Coffs Harbour, Taree, Muswellbrook, Scone, Maitland, Wollongong, Kiama, Moss Vale, Goulburn, Canberra and Queanbeyan.

Before leaving on our extensive tours of the State, I informed each district superintendent that we were going to be in his district. I invited each one to accompany us. I also advised them that when we had completed our rounds of the various Bicentennial Statewide committees, we would then visit them with the programme that we had devised for each area. Although they were initially slow to realise the import of what we were trying to achieve, they all became enthusiastic supporters of the Bicentennial State steam programme.

The State Rail Authority, largely through the initiative of the Commercial Manager and Owen, hired a hot-air balloon from Balloons Aloft, which was based at Canowindra. The balloon, together with the steam engine, drew large crowds all over the State. Because balloons are largely early morning and late evening attractions, they were used to give free rides before and after the day's steam train runs. It was a hugely successful venture, enjoyed by thousands Statewide. There were handouts for school children; prizes for colouring in 3801, pages for excursions listing some history of steam, State Rail biros and many other trinkets were given to many hundreds of children.

When we went to the superintendents with these plans, which did not fall into their jurisdiction, but were to be significant functions and bring many people to railway stations, they really began to realise the magnitude of the undertaking. One of the early snags I foresaw was the inability of the Timetable Section to cope with anything unusual or time-demanding. I spoke to the officer in charge of timetables and advised him that we would be looking for timetables all over the State, and that these would be required in concentrated periods. The answer was that they could not and would not entertain the idea of providing timetables for steam trains all over the State.

This left me with only two options: to push the matter with the General Manager Passenger Services, who did not like 'dirty old steam trains' or to arrange with the districts to issue their own Special Train Notices for the special steam trains. I chose the latter, knowing that had I pushed the matter, we would not have received one timetable on time from the Timetable Section. I made out skeletons of the timetables that we required and passed them on to the country assistant superintendents. We had no trouble statewide with timetables. Each district produced the STNs in ample time.

As our meetings with the Steam Committee continued, the Chief Mechanical Engineer appointed the Locomotive Superintendent of the Western Division to liaise and be responsible for the Mechanical Branch's part of the steam train programme being met. Again I am going to name a name, for he became an essential cog in our team. Tony Gogarty and I toured the State looking for what facilities were left in the country areas that would facilitate maintenance and servicing of the locomotives.

Despite asking every superintendent before we left to outline their facilities, we found in one town a turntable that was operative and an ashpit that was not shown as being available. In this particular town, a junction station, the turntable made a huge difference. We had to find where the water hydrants were at stations. If they did not have one, we had to locate the nearest. We spoke to many country fire brigades about supply of water. Every brigade officer that we spoke to was full of enthusiasm. A number of cartons were left in the care of these officers after our visits, as tokens of appreciation when we left for the next stage of our journey.

Before every trip, Tony Gogarty wrote an action plan of mechanical requirements for each day that we would be away. This plan really became the trip 'bible'. I have to say it rarely required adjustment and was one of the main reasons we so often ran on time and achieved the goals we set out to attain. Obviously there were no coal loading facilities anywhere in the State. Tony arranged with his staff to have coal loaded into industrial one-tonne bottom discharge bags. I forget the number of bags our committee purchased, but it was in the order of 100 bags. They were loaded in the large erecting shop at Eveleigh using the travelling crane. After the wagons were loaded with the bagged coal, they were despatched to their required destinations by freight train. The wagons were always on hand when we arrived at stations at which we required coal.

To load the bags, the loaded coal wagon was placed over a pit which had kibbles strategically placed so the coal would drop into them from the bottom discharge wagon.

The wagon was then hauled away. The kibbles were lifted with the crane and the coal dumped into the bags that were supported by a hoop type affair, high enough to hold the bag fully extended. At the locations where it was necessary to coal the locomotives, the bags were lifted above the tender by a crane and the coal dropped into the engine's tender. It was necessary to arrange the means of lifting the coal above the engine's tender wherever we coaled. Local cranes were hired for the purpose. Per Way trucks with cranes were used and in some cases, station cranes were put to use. The height of the tender from ground level is 3.9 metres.

Toward the end of 1987, I called a meeting of the committee and invited the Chief Mechanical Engineer to attend. I did this for two reasons; firstly, the enthusiasm of the CME demanded I do it and secondly, prior to his appointment, he had been Chief Production Engineer in the Carriage Works. The plan was to discuss what rolling stock would be required and what rolling stock would have to be brought into use to meet the demand.

At the commencement of the meeting, the CME offered to have DUB 66 made available. This was wonderful news from my perspective. DUB 66 was a light drawgear eight car close-coupled set that had something like 450 seats. We used this set mostly behind 3026 in the west; behind 5910 in the south and southwest; and behind 5367 in the northwest. The use of the DUB set meant that we were able to meet the balance of requirements from existing stock. The Carriage Works returned to service four FS type carriages that were going to be condemned for the duration of the programme. This proved a very productive meeting. It gave me, as the Passenger Section Representative, enough carriages to be able to move onward with confidence. I did not realise at that time the response we would get from the public; I might, however, have been a little less confident if had I done so.

THE RESTORATION OF 3801

S OMETIME in early 1982 when the far-sighted Chief Executive Officer of State Rail realised the significant opportunities that would exist to display to the Australian people at large during the Bicentennial Year. The available historical forms of transport, including steam engines still in service, static engines, old carriages from the Governor's car to the prison van at Thirlmere, old freight rolling stock including stock wagons, four-wheeled hook drawgear wagons and a host of other types that formed the railways of the early part of the century, were all part of the rich heritage available.

One of his imaginative ideas was the restoration of steam locomotive 3801. At an Australian Railway Historical Society social function in early 1983, over dinner, he proposed the idea of returning 3801 to operating condition. Those present agreed that it was a great idea. It was only about a month or so later that the real implication of this agreement became clear when one of State Rail's most senior officers started forming a small working party to investigate the feasibility of the idea. Among those he approached were Professor John Glastonbury, Dean of Engineering, Sydney University and President of the Australian Railway Historical Society.

3801 was stored in the open at Thirlmere following a major boiler failure in 1976. Inspection revealed that a new inner firebox and other major boiler work would be required. This work was going to be extremely expensive as the tools, trade skills and labour were no longer available. Through the network of 'interested' people, the project was introduced to the Head of the Apprenticeship Section of the then Department of Labour and Industry.

At that time there was a recession in the Hunter Region and a training company (the Hunter Valley Training Company) was established by the late Hon Pat Hills (a very caring man and Minister for Industrial Relations) to train apprentices for the electricity generating industry, using job skill training funds provided by the Commonwealth Government to support apprentices who had been indentured to small firms which had become bankrupt. Mr Milton Morris, a former Minister for Transport (another very caring man), was and still is Chairman of HVTC. The proposal was that the funded 'out of trade' apprentices would continue to learn their skills by working on the restoration of 3801 and would have the motivation to complete their training by being associated with such a high profile project. While the project team were uncertain of the capacity of partially trained apprentices to undertake such a specialised task, the condition was laid down, "that it was the whole locomotive or nothing at all".

Thus it was that restoration of 3801 became possible.

Mr Morris, together with the Minister for Industrial Relations, the Hon Pat Hills, who shared Mr Morris' concerns for the apprentices, will be long remembered and thanked by a grateful Hunter Valley community. The Hunter Valley Training Company still exists today and carries on the work of training youth for the benefit of future generations.

And so it was that 3801 was towed behind diesel locomotive 8111 on a tour train on 20 November 1983 to Newcastle and ultimately to the Newcastle State Dockyard for restoration to commence. Before the locomotive had been fully restored some 300 apprentices had gained their trade certificates. Had the locomotive never turned a wheel again, it would have served a most valuable training purpose, but turn a wheel it has done, probably millions of times. As there were some additional costs to be met, a fundraising committee was established under the chairmanship of Mr Geoff White.

Locomotive 3801 undergoing restoration at the Hunter Valley Training Company's workshops at the former State Dockyard, Newcastle in September 1985. The boiler barrel and firebox components are to the left and the locomotive's frame, wheels and smokebox are to the right of the photo.   *John R Newland.*

Approaches were made to the related industries, special lunches were held and the upshot was that a foundation was formed that supported the project and ultimately became the 'not for profit' company, 3801 Limited, that continues to operate the locomotive today.

The locomotive's restoration was completed in November 1986. The Chief Executive issued a direction that he wanted the oldest retired driver in the State qualified to work 38 Class locomotives to be the driver from the State Dockyard into what is known as traffic (or the mainline). A retired driver aged 92 years and living at Muswellbrook was found. This man, although his legs were not all that sound, had to receive some assistance in climbing onto the locomotive, but certainly proved there was nothing wrong with his mind or memory. I doubt that in all my life I have seen a face light so much as his did when he got onto 3801. Although the temptation to become emotional was probably there, he did not. There are no prizes for guessing that the Chief Executive was the fireman! He took great pleasure in seeing the locomotive restored. There was of course a qualified crew on the locomotive. On 15 November 1986, just one week short of three years, 3801 left the State Dockyard under its own steam to run an inaugural train to Maitland.

After doing further running trials in the Newcastle area, 3801 left Newcastle with passenger cars on Saturday 29 November 1986, headed for Sydney. After stopping at North Strathfield for external cleaning and watering, the train pulled into Strathfield station and picked up its special guests. The second ever Railway Ball to be held on the concourse at Central station had been arranged as a celebration for the restoration of 3801 and to mark the State Rail Authority's very significant efforts to celebrate the Bicentennial Year. This really was a huge show and was very well supported.

3801 with the train of official guests was due to arrive at 8.00pm. Everything on 3801 was going fine; the train was on time into Strathfield and left on time for the 16 minute run into Central. Alas, the short sharp grade out of Strathfield to Burwood caught yet another driver unaware! The train pulled almost to a stand and lost about 15 minutes before it got going from Burwood. The Chief Executive was waiting for it at Redfern. He was livid! We were all going to be hung, drawn and quartered! It later transpired that the driver was not altogether to blame. The valve settings were not right and it was not until a couple of experienced fitters got to them that the engine performed to its capabilities. Despite being about 15 minutes late, the engine was the centre of attraction among many other attractions that night. I was glad when the night was over!

During the latter part of 3801's restoration at the State Dockyard, a Railways of Australia Commissioners' meeting raised the issue of the Bicentennial Celebrations and the potential involvement of Railways of Australia was discussed. The Chief Executive reported later that he had presented to his Railways Commissioner colleagues the idea of having the restored 3801 with its tour train run into every State and capital that had standard gauge. The suggestion it be a joint venture was warmly embraced. He left the meeting with their blessing.

We had a number of exciting times that were virtually trials for what was planned for the Bicentennial. The Maitland Steamfest commenced in 1984. In that year and again in 1985, it was organised between Steamfest and the Rail transport Museum. Unfortunately, during those years, there were some timetabling problems due to Maitland being a very busy junction.

In 1986 an approach was made by the Maitland City Council Steamfest Committee to join with them in the planning of future events. In that year and until 1989, I represented State Rail and from 1989 until 1995, I represented 3801 Limited as a member of the Maitland Steamfest Committee. By having the Station Master Maitland also a member, we were able to work out realistic timetables that mostly ran to time.

On each occasion 3801 would travel between Sydney and Maitland on the Saturday and the Sunday. On the Sunday it would run a shuttle to Paterson and return to Maitland and continue to Newcastle to take part in the 'Great Plane' race; a Tiger Moth from the local aero club would race 3801 from a point near Hexham to East Maitland. These races caused great excitement and on each occasion people sharing the experience booked the train out. The locomotive generally reached its maximum speed of 115km/h for a short time. The races were genuinely close. It seemed the honours were equally shared between 3801 and the plane year about.

One of the long trials was between Sydney and Albury at Easter time in 1987. This trial was really one we termed as 'a shakedown' experience. Its purpose was to get the crews, the engine maintenance staff and the train catering crews familiar with what would be required to run long distances over a period of time extending into weeks.

To make it a viable proposition, the journey was marketed and somewhere in the order of 200 passengers accompanied us. Morning and afternoon teas were available on the train from the FNR (a buffet car) that served hundreds of light meals and morning teas during 1988. It would probably be more correct to say thousands rather than hundreds of people were served. They were overnighted in motels at Cootamundra and Albury.

After leaving Sydney on time and arriving at Moss Vale, also on time, water was taken from a hydrant on the end of the downside platform. The next stop was Goulburn, where the engine was detached and went to the locomotive depot, where the fire was cleaned and the fitter had a look under the locomotive. On returning to traffic, it hooked up to the train and took water from the water column at the Yass end of the platform. The passengers were given a salad lunch on the platform by the ladies of a local church group. I quickly learned that the engine crew thought that everything revolved around them. It was difficult to get them to understand that this trip, and future trips, were not the traditional enthusiast trains where timetables did not matter, where the passengers were all enthusiasts. While agreeing with the philosophy that enjoyment of the day was paramount, I pointed out what we were now doing was somewhat different.

I had difficulty getting the message across that if we were going to successfully run a

Bicentennial programme that encompassed the State and beyond, we had to run to time and be reliable. All the timetables we would run to would be achievable, was the message I got across, and would include time allowed for engine inspections and for locomotive purposes. It took some cajoling, in a couple of places on this trip, when 'Control' was asking questions about our preparedness to leave with a small margin ahead of an XPT.

By the time we arrived back in Sydney, I had got their understanding and realisation of the importance of being on time. When they realised that six or seven coaches would be waiting for the train and that they would charge waiting time if we were late, and that we had dinner at the RSL Club at Cootamundra, Parkes, or Casino for 350-400 people timed for 8.00pm, they saw the importance of what I was saying.

We ran shuttle trains from Albury to Table Top on the Sunday and, on the Monday, ran a trip from Albury to Cootamundra and back. Every one had a day off on the Tuesday and we came home in one day from Albury. The trip was a success; the coaling method worked well, the watering arrangements were satisfactory, in fact, it was a good 'shake-down' trip—a foretaste of what was to come.

It was agreed that 3801 was ready to meet whatever task was to be put to it in the Bicentennial Year. It is recorded on a plaque on the side of the cab that 3801 in the Bicentennial year travelled 25,000 kilometres. There were very few of those kilometres that I was not behind it.

The special tour organised for locomotive 3801 'official' return to service at Narara on 29 November 1986. A celebration was held in Sydney Central Station that evening.   John R Newland.

THE BICENTENNIAL YEAR

THE true test of whether the celebrations being organised throughout the year would be a success or not, was the Australia Day of 1988. The emphasis of the celebrations was situated around the Opera House, Sydney Harbour foreshores, the Rocks area and Sydney Harbour itself.

The entry of the 'tall ships' and their sailing up the Harbour was a magnificent sight that attracted tens of thousands of people. From early morning, the suburban trains were packed with happy people out to enjoy their nation's two hundredth birthday. In all my years of being associated with people using trains and travelling generally, I have to say that the mood and gaiety of the people will live with me as my outstanding memory of a day filled with extraordinary events that went like clockwork. I was particularly pleased to have been a railwayman. The co-operation of the train crews and staff contributed largely to the successful day that State Rail and the City of Sydney enjoyed. Mamie and I went into the city early and watched the tall ships, and wandered around the Opera House. At noon I had to present myself for work. Mamie joined our daughter and her children. Later they settled themselves under the bridge at Milsons Point and stayed until after the fireworks. When they went to go home, they had to let five trains pass before they could squeeze onto one at Milsons Point.

I was placed in charge of passenger movement at Central Station. The fireworks, the finale of the day, saw an estimated 750,000 people wanting a train about 9.30pm. Circular Quay was closed early in the piece, followed by Wynyard, Town Hall, St James and Museum. To have allowed more people on these platforms would have been dangerous. At around 11.15pm, there was a line of people trying to gain admission to Central Station that stretched into Eddy Avenue and further into Elizabeth Street.

Many of these people were interested in catching interurban trains to the west and north, while others wanted trains to the South Coast. My responsibility was to people travelling to destinations outside the area served by the suburban network. We had two stand-by sets available; one, an interurban, was utilised to go north. When the last South Coast train left, there was still a train load of people on the platform. I went to the second stand-by driver, who had a loco-hauled set of cars, and asked if he would go to Nowra. I thought I would have no chance, but I was wrong. He said,

"Yes mate, on one condition."

I asked what that was and he said,

"That I turn around and come back empty cars."

I said, "Done."

This was symbolic of the effort railwaymen performed that night. At around 1.00am, the platforms were clear of people.

I was not able to accompany many of the country New South Wales excursions, because of the demands put on my time organising the final arrangements for them and the interstate journeys 3801 was to take. In addition, my own position of Country Passenger Operations Superintendent placed further demands on my time. The staff allocated to the State Rail Authority's steam programme, from the very first event, reported on the huge crowds that the steam trains were drawing, not only school children, but adults as well. The accompanying hot-air balloons added to the attractions. The programme ran almost continuously from March to November before the whole undertaking we originally set out to do, was completed.

When Owen Johnson-Donnett and I went to Narrabri Council Chambers, where the North Western Zone had its headquarters, we received an enthusiastic welcome from the Mayor, councillors and representatives from a wide area of the north west. I began by saying that we would have 5367 available with carriages that would accommodate about 400 passengers.

The tentative plan was to work our way up from Werris Creek, staying overnight at Gunnedah and Narrabri, and going as far as Moree, from where we would run shuttles to the north west. As I sat down, a very tall lady from Warialda rose and asked would we come to Warialda?

The lady had a very imperious bearing, making me a little hesitant about saying "No". I knew, however, that there had not been a steam passenger train on that line since 1963, and that when I was the Wheat Officer, we ran with BWH hoppers only that were limited to 40 tonnes of wheat in each wagon. The speed of the line was 25km/h, rather a slow haul.

In view of this, I said to her that I did not think we could do that. She rose again and said if you do not come to Warialda there will not be a Bicentennial function within 100km of the town. This floored me! There was an expectant hush in the room that I could feel. I finally said,

"Yes, we will come."

The first thing I did after the meeting was to almost genuflect to the Divisional Engineer, who was stationed at Narrabri and tell him what I had done. He firstly reflected on my parentage and secondly on my intelligence. Nevertheless, he agreed that he would make the track safe for a passenger train, but that the speed would be 25km/h. I had no trouble with that. I was just pleased that he agreed to let us run out to Warialda.

We arranged for 5367 to run tender first from Moree to Warialda. It was then to run a shuttle to Gravesend and back to Warialda before returning to Moree. In the meantime, the lady from Warialda's committee got busy, and did she get them busy! Warialda that day had a golf tournament, a bowls tournament, a tennis tournament and a host of other functions that were to entertain the people who came to ride on the train, but more importantly, for those people who came from Moree to occupy their time for the approximately four hours the train was running the shuttle.

On the Tuesday before the event, the station master from Moree rang me to say that he had booked all the seats on the train from Warialda and could I send him two more carriages to fill his waiting list. I did this. On the Wednesday evening around 10.00pm, my phone rang again, and as soon as I heard the voice, I knew who it was. Yes, he had booked those last two carriages and could he PLEASE have another one. The Yard Controller Sydney was less than pleased the next morning when I asked for another carriage, because by this time they were getting very 'tight'. The carriage arrived at Moree about an hour before the departure time on the Saturday morning.

On his day off, the Station Master Moree went with the train. He told me on the Monday morning that it was a most memorable day. From Moree there was a crowd of 500 on the train. He estimated that were 700 people on the shuttle to Gravesend. People had come from as far as Goondiwindi and from over the Queensland border to see a steam engine. There were many there that had never seen one.

Narromine was another town where unexpected numbers turned up to board 3026 and the DUB set. We were not expecting Catholic schools, but somewhere the system broke down and their applications were not included in the numbers. Schoolchildren came from as far south as Tomingley West, and west from Trangie, Nevertire and Warren. We crammed them all in after sitting some of the kindergarten children two to a seat.

These two examples were spread over the whole of New South Wales. I have a book of press clippings that is about six centimetres thick. I have to say I owed, and the Authority owed, a debt of gratitude to the staff of the Country Passenger Operations Manager. They worked very diligently to see that all the correspondence that flowed as a result of the organisational arrangements was in the hands of those who needed it without delay. In addition, the clerk kept a running financial statement which showed how much was spent on wages, coal, crane hire and the sundries that were charged to each excursion. At the end of the year, when everything was balanced up, the New South Wales Bicentennial Train projects had returned a profit of $41,000.00—a most pleasing result. In an overall look at the money expended on the Bicentennial Year by the State Rail Authority as a whole, the Financial Manager commented favourably on the efforts.

THE BICENTENNIAL YEAR OF THE RAILWAYS OF AUSTRALIA

A T THE conclusion of the Bicentennial year celebrations, Tony Gogarty and Ron Preston wrote a book entitled *A Diary of the Bicentennial Train*. Professor John Glastonbury wrote the introduction and, with the permission of the author and Professor Glastonbury, I quote from it:

> In late 1985 with much enthusiasm, the then Chief Executive of the State Rail Authority, David Hill, told me he had persuaded his fellow Railway Commissioners, to agree in principle to, 3801 operating a series of tours to all the Australian mainland capital cities during the Bicentennial Year. Whilst very exciting, the idea at that time seemed distinctly unreal - 3801 was still a year away from full restoration in Newcastle. The company, which had been formed to operate the engine, had no carriages, equipment or staff and not much money. 1986 passed quickly with all efforts being concentrated on the completion of the restoration of 3801 and its return to service in November 1986.

At a time near this announcement by the New South Wales Chief Executive, Owen Johnson-Donnett and I were seconded to the Railways of Australia Bicentennial Steam Committee, which was headed by the Executive Director of Railways of Australia, Michael Schrader. Michael was and is a dedicated steam enthusiast; but he found this project both daunting and exhilarating. I might add he was not the only one.

We first met with Michael Schrader in the Melbourne headquarters of the Railways of Australia on our own. Michael was anxious that we, as the provider of the locomotive and train, gather up some of his thoughts and to add our own on what might be a suitable programme for 1988. We started off from the sound footing of knowing that what we proposed, as a programme would have the in-principal agreement of the Commissioners of the other States. We felt, and correctly so it turned out, that co-operation would be the operative word of the systems. I must say on my own behalf, that before going any further into the events that were to follow, that I received nothing but courtesy and co-operative involvement from every person with whom I dealt from any other system during the whole of 1988.

At our first meeting, which lasted from the time the *Southern Aurora* arrived at Spencer

Street station in the morning, until an hour before its departure that evening, we had a very rough idea of what we might do and how we might achieve it. Michael's staff recorded the minutes of our meeting and forwarded them to the appointed personnel of each system, with a request that we meet in Melbourne at ROA offices the following week.

Representatives from South Australia and Victoria were present at that meeting. Queensland advised by fax that they would afford every consideration to the Bicentennial Train with the large crowds it would generate for two reasons; one, it was the Bicentennial Train and secondly, 3801 would be the first steam locomotive to cross the bridge over the Brisbane River and arrive into Roma St. The Queensland historical societies indicated that they would meet the train and accompany it from Clapham with a steam locomotive. Western Australia also advised that they would welcome 3801. However, they thought it best that we should visit them when we had prepared our plans.

This meeting confirmed the sketchy plans we had drawn up, which would take us to Brisbane, Melbourne, Adelaide and Perth. We were also to visit the Australian Capital; these arrangements however, were to be left to New South Wales. We had not involved the Mechanical Branch people from any system in the preliminary planning. Guidelines for each system in respect to operating, to commercial aspects, to insurance cover for each system and for 3801were the first priority. Before we met with the Mechanical Branch people, proposed timetables were necessary. The group agreed that timetables would be prepared for the next meeting that would concentrate on the visit of the train to Melbourne.

We met the following week with timetables I had prepared for New South Wales and V/Line had prepared for Victoria. We agreed on them. We then set about trying to ascertain what would be a reasonable fare for passengers travelling Sydney to Melbourne by 3801 and accompanied in parallel running between Albury and Melbourne, with photo stops thrown in for good measure. This process had to be undertaken also for the Canberra, Perth and Brisbane trips.

We booked motels and buses connecting to them at Taree, Casino, Brisbane, Canberra, Parkes, Broken Hill, Peterborough, Perth, Cootamundra, Albury and Melbourne. Owen and his team did this in New South Wales. They also arranged for the hot-air balloons to be at each overnight stop in New South Wales.

When we had completed draft timetables and had an action plan to show, we invited the Mechanical Branch people of each system to gather at the ROA Office in Melbourne. Tony Gogarty and the late Pat Rea represented New South Wales. Representatives from Victoria, South Australia and Western Australia were present. On this occasion, we stayed overnight in Melbourne. The first day, our plans were presented and agreed to by the Mechanical Branch representatives. So far as New South Wales was concerned, I took care to see that the timetables were easily achievable. Although the State Rail Authority had placed 100km/h bogies under the water tanks we were to use, we did not table the train to run constantly at this speed. The timetable speed I made out was close to Schedule 'D'. We visited the locomotive depot in South Dynon. This was Tony's domain; he and the Victorian people got on with it 'like a house on fire' and enthusiastically made arrangements that ultimately saw great success.

The journey to Melbourne however, paled into insignificance when we started looking at the logistics of the transcontinental journey. To begin the planning of this epic journey Tony Gogarty, Owen Johntson-Donnett and I went to Adelaide where Michael Schrader joined us. We met with the operations representative of the Commissioner, the Head of the Timetable Section, representatives from the Mechanical Branch, including the Chief Mechanical Engineer, his Chief Travelling Inspector and representatives of the Chief Civil Engineer. In the morning session, we met as a total group. I had prepared what was purely a speculative timetable for our stay in Adelaide, where we expected to run local excursions with SteamRanger on our return from Perth. The forward journey was to see us run from Broken Hill to Peterborough overnight, thence direct to Port Augusta, where we would have an overnight stay while the train was being serviced for the run across the Nullarbor.

There were a number of difficult issues confronting us, particularly insurance and costs that were to be applied by Australian National Railways. The morning meeting broke up on this issue. After lunch, the Mechanical Branch representatives met to bring together the plans that would be needed to ensure a trouble-free journey. We of the operating and commercial side continued in the afternoon, the insurance issue finally being handed over to the legal section for clarification.

It was known from the beginning that we would need to hire sufficient sleeping cars and support vehicles from Australian National Railways to enable the majority of our passengers to have air-conditioned sleeping accommodation from Port Augusta to Perth. We sold a small number of tickets for people who wished to use sleeping bags, four to a compartment, in FS type economy carriages. We were able to have the showers at Tarcoola, Cook and Rawlinna available for them. They had meals in an economy cafeteria car. There were something like 10 sleeping cars, a power van, a staff sleeping car, a lounge car, a dining car and a brakevan, which was really a transcontinental composition. The total weight of the train was to be 1220 tonnes and 29 vehicles in length.

It was necessary for our Mechanical Branch to supply the drawings of 3801 and of each individual carriage to be conveyed on the train, together with records of their inspection and maintenance histories. Tony Gogarty knew this and had with him all the required paperwork. I must say that the Chief Mechanical Engineer of the Australian National Railways, whom I had met previously, was an outstanding person, both personality-wise and ability-wise. His enthusiasm for this journey seemed unbounded. It followed that the Mechanical Branch people all got on very well and that they had but one aim, which was see that one of the world's great steam journeys would succeed.

Whilst Australian National Railways went out of their way to assist in the operation of the train, they were hard-nosed when it came to costing the air-conditioned sleeping cars and staff that were a necessary part of it. This was not unreasonable from a commercial viewpoint; without knowing these costs when the trip per passenger was being costed long before we spoke to them, we built into the fare a significant sum which was close to that charged. I forget the exact sum and the amount that Australian National charged.

We came back to Sydney fired with enthusiasm, knowing the trip would be a huge success, if for no other reason than every person associated with it wanted it to be so. The amount of hard work ahead of Tony Gogarty and myself was unbelievable. His was the important task of being sure the train was equipped for the journey. I do not intend to get into his area of endeavour; that has been well chronicled. My efforts were concentrated on timetabling, and arranging with Owen Johnston-Donnett, for accommodation at Parkes, Broken Hill, Peterborough and Port Augusta. We also arranged tours of the Silver City for those interested and also a trip to the Pichie Richie Railway while we were at Port Augusta.

One of the important carriages in the consist was the FNR, a buffet car. Phil Sutton, who had long been in charge of all things connected with the buffet on our journeys, was in charge again. The amount of organising, calculating, providoring and plain hard work that went into the journey from Phil and his crew before we left Sydney, was amazing.

Before we left Sydney, two wagons loaded with bagged coal were despatched from Eveleigh. The required amounts of coal were then unloaded en-route at Bathurst, Parkes, Ivanhoe, Broken Hill, Peterborough, Port Augusta, Tarcoola, Cook, Rawlinna, Kalgoorlie, Meriden and Perth. Australian National Railways had arranged water supply at Tarcoola and Rawlinna in 10,000-gallon tanks. We had two water tanks, one of which had a petrol water pump, enabling water to be pumped into the tender while travelling.

Before arrangements were complete, Tony Gogarty and I went to Adelaide for the final briefing and were given a 'Cooks tour' of their workshops and the areas where they intended to stow the carriages and the locomotive. We also met the SteamRanger people and came to an agreement on the excursions to be run jointly and separately. We then flew to Perth where we were greeted with the same enthusiasm as we had been elsewhere. We found the timetabling experts had been busy, in fact, we were presented with completed timetables. The Mechanical Branch people were just as enthusiastic, taking us to Forrestville Workshops where the train would be stowed and the locomotive serviced. We flew back to Adelaide and came home on the *Indian Pacific*.

PERTH: A GREAT RAILWAY STEAM JOURNEY

O N Wednesday 27 April 1988 at 8.20am, the momentous journey to Perth began. Before it did however, Mr Pat Johnson, the retiring Chief Executive, presented gold medallions to the crews of 3801 and the assisting 3642. He then donned a boiler suit and rode 3801 to Strathfield, where an unscheduled stop was made to let him off. The presentation of these medals was one of his last official public duties.

Departure was near to time. The 200 passengers were filled with excitement, which could be felt as I walked through the train, the first of many times before we arrived in Perth. On arrival at Penrith, the train set back to take water from the column at the Sydney end of the Up platform. An electric locomotive 4623, was attached to assist between Valley Heights and Katoomba on the 1 in 33 gradients.

One of the insistences of Michael Schrader was that photo stops be provided for the passengers. I did not disagree with this in principle, but I was not in favour of having one between Lawson and Wentworth Falls on the double line. I was overruled. Time was allowed in the timetable and all the necessary precautions were taken to protect passengers crossing the Up line to an embankment. The train duly ran past them and then set back on the 1 in 33 grades. Special authority was given in the Special Train Notice to allow this. It still did not thrill me! We had many photo stops after that, but none on double lines and gradients like that. We arrived Bathurst about 20 minutes late for an overnight stop, to be greeted by a platform full of people and the All Saints School Band.

The station staff cleaned the carriages. Before the shops closed, Phil Sutton was able to purchase his requirements for the next day. The passengers were met by buses and taken to their motels. After they had time to shower and change, the buses took them to the RSL Club at Bathurst, where we had a most enjoyable meal. It was good to get to bed that night.

The next day saw us leave bright and early to face the challenge of Tumulla Bank. The run to Georges Plains left behind a trail of steam that stretched for a couple of kilometres, 3801 and 3642 performed as they, and their counterparts had done for many years hauling mail trains and holiday period loads. This very demanding 1 in 40 gradient, extends for seven kilometres and the section Georges Plains to Gresham was run exactly to the timetable sectional running.

Continuing on, we were hijacked by an 'outlaw' gang at Newbridge who held the passengers to ransom. At Blayney, a play by Blayney High School students was carried out to a successful conclusion in the courtyard area at the eastern end of Blayney platform. That was one of the highlights of the trip and we left Blayney some 40 minutes late as a result. Some spirited running to Orange regained some of the lost time. The train ran into Orange station, where the passengers were taken by coach for a tour of the Nashdale and Mt Canobolas areas. A picnic lunch was provided at Lake Canobolas.

In the meantime, the Orange shunter and the two engines hauled and propelled the train to Orange East Fork, where the engines went to Loco for servicing. The train then ran from the East Fork triangle to Borenore and was pulling in as the passengers arrived by coach. We missed the crossing with the *Silver City Comet* cars from Parkes at Manildra and waited for it at Molong. We arrived about 40 minutes late into Parkes after a very enjoyable day. Once again the passengers were taken to motels for a clean up and then to the Parkes RSL Club where a very good meal was provided, along with entertainment. It was almost 11.00pm before we left the club. We were due to leave Parkes at 5.40am.

Early on the third day, 3642 ran light engine from Parkes to Ivanhoe to work the train to Menindee, while 3801 was serviced and coaled at Ivanhoe. The plan came unstuck; the inexperienced crew on 3642 could not maintain the running time and lost considerable time. The passengers were given their evening meal in Underdown's Hotel. We arrived at Broken Hill some 90 minutes late. The passengers were happy that they had had a day of running singly with 3801 and 3642, and then with both engines from Menindee to Broken Hill. The following day was a rest day at Broken Hill.

An overnight stop was made at Peterborough. This was enjoyed by the local school children and 'children' of a much more mature age, who clustered around the locomotive until dark. There was no staff provided at Peterborough to clean the carriages, which of course, after travelling through dust for most of the day from Broken Hill, were very dirty. I said earlier that I never liked cleaning carriages; I did not like cleaning these either, especially when everyone disappeared and I was left on my own.

Continuing on to Port Augusta the next day via Coonamia, and thus by-passing Port Pirie, the arrival at Port Augusta was some 16 minutes late after stopping to pick up the Mayor, one Joy Baluch, a character if ever there was one. Her responses to certain questions have been well documented and would be out of place here.

Another rest day, this time at Port Augusta, was used to prepare the locomotive for the epic experience ahead. Australian National supplied GMs 1 and 2 as pilot locomotives across the Nullarbor, not because they did not believe 3801 capable of performing the task on its own, but for commonsense reasons. A failure of any kind would seriously delay the many trains that used the line and also could leave passengers stranded for lengthy periods awaiting assistance.

A photo stop was made just west of Bates at Yorky's Crossing and passengers, together with most of the crew, alighted and waited while the train set back. 3801 showed just what a remarkable locomotive it is. The control fuse on the GMs blew and both diesel locomotives lost power. Not to be bothered by such a minor detail, it kept going with both diesels dead attached and made a 'grandstand' run past the photographers, on what was probably about a 1 in 100 gradient. The message had been received by the photographers via an inspector's two-way radio. There was much cheering when the 'old girl' thundered by.

We were not long out of Port Augusta when the Australian National crew attending the sleeping cars walked through the non-air conditioned portion of the train. After returning, they made it very clear that they would have nothing to do with these carriages. Guess who looked after their cleanliness all the way to Kalgoorlie? About every two hours, I went through the cars with a kerosene rag and wiped all the windowsills and dusted the seats. Many of the passengers would have nothing to do with the air-conditioned cars and only had their meals in them. It is a long way from Port Augusta to Kalgoorlie under these conditions! While I shall refrain from being critical, I found that my colleague's disinterest in cleaning carriages stemmed from the thought that it was beneath his dignity.

The timetable provided for another rest day at Kalgoorlie, the reason being to give the locomotive maintenance crew and the catering crew a break. During the day, 3801 ran two shuttle trips with loads of school children; their excitement was a pure joy to behold. I was a little less enthusiastic when it came to cleaning up after them, but this time; however, I had so much assistance from the staff at Kalgoorlie that we were finished in about an hour.

We set off in the evening from Kalgoorlie with an 'L' Class Western Australia mainline diesel as a pilot. The idea was to spend time at Merriden in the morning for breakfast and to be on show for the local school children. The locomotive was to be serviced and coaled prior to the run to Perth for arrival at around 2.00pm.

Alas! Trouble at 1.35am at about two kilometres from Koolyanobbing—3801 had been running on the pilot valve, but the West Australian crew were keen to have the locomotive doing some real work. The 3801 representative agreed to this. When the regulator was wound forward about six turns and pressure applied, a loud thumping noise was heard. The train was immediately stopped.

Tony Gogarty was disturbed from his rest and took charge of the situation, which to say the least was heartbreaking. The driver's side big end bearing was red hot, and was glowing in the darkness. It was essential that the thing be dismantled and the driving rod placed in the spare parts van. Placing of the side rod in the van was only possible because of the immense strength and ingenuity of Ian Thornton, a member of the staff and a chief locomotive inspector in New South Wales. Steam locomotive 3801 then ran on one 'side' into Perth. (A term used when one cylinder has failed or, as in this case, a hot big end problem. The locomotive is worked by the remaining cylinder.)

It was not until I had surfaced for breakfast that I became aware of what had happened. I had woken a few times during the night and we were stopped on each occasion, but I had not thought the reason was anything other than for train working purposes. We arrived into Merriden, where we were to have breakfast about three hours late. We were met by crowds of school children who were wildly excited at seeing a locomotive the size of 3801.

The locomotive was prepared at Merriden, by having the fire cleaned, water tanks and tender filled and coaled. A concerted effort by the Mechanical Branch staff, even though delayed by a signal failure at Merriden, saw the train ready to depart 77 minutes late from Merriden. An on-time arrival at Perth was thought to be achievable but a slower train ahead caused some delay. The original intention was to take the diesel assisting off at Merriden, together with the air-conditioned carriages, and for 3801 to work the train into Perth on its own. However, with 3801 working on one cylinder it was deemed wise to leave the diesel attached. Shortly before arriving Perth, the diesel and silver carriages were detached and 3801 worked into Perth, some 30 minutes late, to a magnificent reception. The train was taken to Forrestfield where the carriages were stowed and the locomotive was placed on the Transit Road.

That evening at 7.30pm, the whole crew was entertained to dinner by the Westrail's senior management, a most generous gesture somewhat spoiled by the disappointment of the disaster of the previous night.

I am not going to detail all the heartbreak we felt, the repair of the locomotive and all it entailed; it was a Mechanical Branch responsibility and is fully detailed in *The Diary of the Bicentennial Train* by Tony Gogarty and Ron Preston. I will say that I was standing alongside Tony Gogarty when he stripped the crank pin, stood back and looked at it and said,

"That is bent" or words to that effect.

I thought he was 'nuts'. I could not see it—he was not, and it was.

The assistance given by Westrail in undertaking in a short time what was a major task went far beyond what could have been reasonably expected of them. Another whose great assistance had an important bearing on the successful repair of the locomotive was Ian Willis of Willis Engineering Perth. If you have the chance to have a look at the driver's side crank pin on 3801, you will see 'Willis Engineering Perth' inscribed on it. The course of events that took place was that, after the crank pin had been made fit to receive the big end again, the locomotive was trialled in Forrestfield yard and even after running up and down the yard a couple of times the bearing was found to be warm. Proof positive that the crank pin was bent. The major work began then. Very long hours were worked by all the Mechanical Branch people, and while this has been acknowledged before, I should say it from the Bicentennial Committee's perspective and extend its thanks to them.

All the events that had been planned in Perth were cancelled; but the Herculean effort saw the locomotive being ready for service the day prior to its scheduled departure. During this time, I tried to make things as easy as possible for the crews by getting meals, and morning teas, etc. I also cleaned the exterior of all the carriages. While this was a difficult time for the crew, it was also one for me. I left Perth before the job was completed and came back to Sydney on the *Indian Pacific*. I was very tired and I enjoyed the deluxe suite, which was not booked and which the Westrail head conductor suggested that I use, for which I was grateful to him.

It is fine to detail all the work that was undertaken, but it would also be remiss not to mention that, despite the great assistance by Westrail, there was very heavy expenditure involved. The NSW Chief Mechanical Engineer being aware of this via Tony Gogarty, met with the Acting Chief Executive, The Acting Deputy Chief Executive and the Director of Engineering. The decision was that costs would be met on the condition that 3801 worked the Bicentennial Train from Perth as planned and that it fulfilled its obligations in South Australia. It did both. I doubt that Executive Group have ever been thanked or offered congratulations for their support of the Bicentennial Train. On behalf many people, I do so now.

I returned to Adelaide in time to meet the train as it arrived into the main platform at Keswick Terminal. A much happier crew greeted me. Things had returned to normal, so much so, that during the run from Port Augusta, Ian Thornton decided to give the 'Old Girl' her head and was running at a decidedly rapid speed when a police highway patrol car travelling on the road running parallel, put his speed camera on the locomotive in the vicinity of Bowmans. When the train stopped at Two Wells, the police officer presented Ian with a completed traffic infringement notice stating he was travelling at 141km/h!

A pleasant few days were spent in Adelaide, running local trips and having a great train race with SteamRanger's 621 Class. The poor water quality was the reason for 3801 priming a good deal while in Adelaide. A 'secret' mixture of tannin and whatever else brought the priming under control. I left Adelaide by *The Ghan* on the day prior to 3801 leaving Adelaide. There are a number of funny instances recorded in the *Diary of the Bicentennial Train* that I should not in fairness report here. I suggest that if the reader's curiosity has been aroused, they should obtain a copy of the *Bicentennial Train*; there may be still some about.

5910 and 3801 with the Bicentennial Train at Picton on 15 October 1988 en-route to Melbourne for the Austeam Celebrations. *John R Newland.*

British locomotive FLYING SCOTSMAN *and 3801 at Sydney Central on 24 March 1989 prior to departure for Brisbane.* *John R Newland.*

BRISBANE AND MELBOURNE

THE next major trip for the Bicentennial Train was to Brisbane in September 1988. As with all trips, much planning had been done and, with this one, I had perhaps given more input than with the other journeys, especially the Perth trip. This journey was under the auspices of the State Rail Authority from beginning to end. Not only did 3801 venture onto the North Coast Line, but 3642 and 5910 did also. The overnight stops were Taree and Casino. One of the largest crowds we saw during the Bicentennial Year gathered at Coffs Harbour to see 3801, 3642 and 5910 lined up on an angle at Coffs Harbour railway yard. The police estimated there were something in the order of 5000 people.

A touch of history was made when 3801 headed onto the North Coast Line at Maitland. It was the first time that a 38 Class had been on the line since the first 38 Class ran to Casino during the war on a trial run. It did so much damage to the perway that they were banned until the track was upgraded. The northern working timetable in the section showing where particular types of rollingstock were permitted to run, showed 38 Classes were not permitted beyond Maitland on the North Coast and North West lines.

Shuttle trains were run all the way from Maitland to Casino, Lismore and Murwillumbah with 3642 and 5910. They were so employed for 14 days. 3801 worked the Brisbane to Casino shuttles after its arrival at Roma Street.

The first overnight stop for the Brisbane bound 3801 was at Taree. The hot-air balloons were also in attendance. Huge crowds were on the riverbank watching them on a balmy spring night.

The second overnight stop was at Casino. This day was marred by very poor judgment by the train controller who held a train load of passengers 70 minutes to cross an unimportant freight train. The resultant delay meant that we had to delay the dinner arranged at Casino. Also at Casino during shunting operations which had to be carried out by 3801 because there was no other shunting engine, a serious misjudgement by a shunter brought 3801's train into violent contact with other vehicles in the yard. Although no damage was done, considerable time was spent examining vehicles to ensure that there was none.

The next day, which saw 3801 again performing majestically over the range, was pure enthusiasts' joy. The huge number of cars in the motorcade that followed us from Border Loop in the Macpherson Ranges down to Tamrookum and then through to Brisbane, was almost unbelievable. I did not count them, but I would estimate something in excess of a hundred vehicles were running in parallel or trailing behind us. The Queensland Steam Society was as good as its word and one of their locomotives ran parallel with us from Clapham for some distance. On arrival at Roma Street, the Queensland Minister for Transport entertained us to afternoon tea.

After two rest days, two round trips were made to Casino and on four days, two round-trip shuttles to Kagaru were made. All these trains were filled to capacity. The Bicentennial Train certainly proved a hit 'north of the border'. After 13 days in Brisbane, 3801 and its train headed south to return home. I have not taken much space to say what was done in Brisbane, but believe me, it was a busy time for all concerned. The catering crews, the on-train crews and the Mechanical Branch people all enjoyed Brisbane and would not have missed it. Nevertheless, some very tired people left Brisbane.

In terms of people actually seeing and riding behind a steam engine, I think this was the most successful trip we undertook. The efforts of all concerned on the North Coast, with the exception of the train controllers, was appreciated. As an old train controller, I have to say I was disgusted with some of the decisions they made.

The final interstate journey was to Melbourne and commenced from Sydney on 4 October 1988. The Mechanical Branch people and I had given much thought to the planning for this journey, and sadly, a lot of it was for nought. Some months prior to September, confirmation was received that the *Flying Scotsman* would visit Australia and was forecast to arrive in Melbourne in early September. It was soon discovered that the locomotive would have to be unloaded in Sydney, because it was stated that Melbourne did not have a suitable crane. However, this was incorrect; the real reason being that the Port Authority in Victoria wanted in excess of $30,000 to unload the thing. The Titan crane people in Sydney unloaded it for less than a quarter of that amount.

The indication that the arrival date in Sydney would be about a week prior to the departure of 3801 to Melbourne, looked at one stage to be achievable. All the necessary transferring of the *Flying Scotsman* from the docks at Rozelle to Eveleigh, the re-assembling of the locomotive and the trials necessary, prior to its approval to run on the NSW system, would take about a week. With this in view, the Mechanical Branch people set about organising their testing and trialling arrangements. On our return from Brisbane, a number of plans had gone awry. The ARHS Canberra locomotive 3016 which was to accompany 3801, and to assist it from Albury to Melbourne, would not be ready in time. The next news was that it was highly unlikely that the ship carrying the *Flying Scotsman* would be in Sydney prior to the departure of 3801 to Melbourne.

This left Tony Gogarty with no alternative other than to approach the RTM for the use of 3642. There was no problem there, and without being critical, the monetary return to the RTM during the Bicentennial Year was very rewarding indeed. Alas, on the weekend before the Melbourne trip, 3642 suffered a hot big end on a local trip and had suffered axle damage. It would not be ready in time. This left us with 5910, a goods type locomotive limited to 70km/h per hour. I was thrown into a spin when I heard this. I knew that the timetable to Melbourne was for passenger engine working and the timetable would be shot to ribbons. It was too late to try and adjust the timetable. The timetable section would not even have considered the idea, so I just let it ride. The problem would not be so great on the forward journey because we had an overnight stop at Wagga Wagga. The assisting 5910 was detached on arrival at Wagga Wagga and it returned that evening light engine to Thirlmere. The following morning, 3801, assisted by a green liveried 4836 to Uranquinty, showed exactly what it could do on the run to Albury, given its head. Many excited passengers gloried in the high speed running, and many car drivers following us stared at their speedometers in disbelief.

After some delay at Albury due to poor water flow, 3801 crossed the Murray River into Victoria, nearly 20 years after the first run to Melbourne before its restoration. We were met in grand style by Victorian R761, a most majestic locomotive, totally resplendent in its black and red colours. This was one of the most exciting steam train journeys I have ever experienced; two magnificent locomotives of a bygone era ran parallel and past one another for mile on end between Albury and Seymour. We arrived in Spencer Street after having, by some expert timetabling and direction by V/Line's Bob Evans, to have R761 run under the flyover near Spencer Street as 3801 ran over it. A tremendous sight! On arrival at Spencer Street, V/Line's General Manager, Mr Keith Fitzmaurice, and his senior management met us. We were later entertained in the GM's private dining room.

The excitement of 3801 being in Victoria has been well documented and I do not intend to labour it here. I will, however, mention the great Day of Rail at Spencer Street. I think probably that it was the most representative gathering of steam, diesel and vintage rollingstock ever assembled at one point in Australia. Present that day were two Victorian K Class locomotives, R761 and R703, several early Victorian diesels, 3801, 1210, 3112 and diesel locomotives 4201, 8168 and 42218 and the *Flying Scotsman*, which had arrived from Sydney in time for the exhibition. The two vintage NSW locomotives 1210 and 3112 had steamed together from Goulburn to Melbourne and subsequently returned together.

1210 was the locomotive that ran the official train to Canberra for the opening of Parliament House. This locomotive, built in 1879, stood on a plinth outside Kingston railway station in Canberra for some 25 years. Activity from ARHS Canberra resulted in a Federal Government Bicentennial financial grant being provided for its restoration. 3112 is a tank engine that was restored privately and is owned by Barry Tulloch. It saw its final Departmental service as a shunting engine at Bathurst. Diesel-electric 4201 is owned by the RTM and is still an active locomotive.

I returned to Sydney after arrival in Melbourne and returned the following weekend to assist the crew of the train in the shuttles that were to be run from Melbourne to Seymour and from Melbourne to Albury and back. Finally, we were to return home after one of the most successful Bicentennial journeys, if not the most successful. While I have stated success in terms of people on the North Coast seeing the train and riding it, the Melbourne trips were by far the most financially successful. The Victorian people did not just see 3801; in true Victorian style, they got out and rode behind it.

We left Melbourne and ran through to Albury. Owen and I had arranged a river cruise on the steamboat *Cumberoona* to be followed by a woolshed dance and dinner. The first disaster was the *Cumberoona*, which ran aground. As a result we were late for the dance. However people did not mind; it was one of the most entertaining nights of the Bicentennial Year. There were some tired people next day!

We left Albury early with 3801 running unassisted to Wagga Wagga. Here, 5910 which had returned from Thirlmere, had gone to Albury to be turned and prepared for the homeward journey and ran light engine ahead of 3801 to Wagga Wagga. The reason for this was that 3801 ran to Wagga Wagga at timetable schedule. After attaching 5910, the delays I knew that would occur, did occur between Wagga Wagga and Goulburn and we were some 90 minutes late. Owen Johnston-Donnett was beside himself. He could not understand why we could not go faster. Despite being told of 5910's limitations, his concern was for an on-time arrival into Sydney for the last run. After coaling at Goulburn, 3801 set forth on its own accepting the challenge of running the last journey of the Bicentennial Year in style and at great speed. Some 30 minutes was regained between Goulburn and Sydney; some of that due to not taking water at Moss Vale and some due to expert driving.

My last major effort for the Bicentennial Year concerned the return of the *Flying Scotsman* to Sydney. The story of the arrival in Sydney of the *Flying Scotsman*, numbered 4472, is not generally known, especially in Victoria. The locomotive and tender were unloaded separately at Rozelle. The two were joined and the locomotive was hauled to Eveleigh by State Rail diesel 4472. With his penchant for figures and matching, Bill Casley, the Chief Mechanical Engineer, directed the despatch of 4472 to lift 4472 to Eveleigh.

Because the official arrival of *Flying Scotsman* had been heralded to be in Victoria, and as I have said, it was at Spencer Street as part of the Great Rail display. Secrecy surrounded its movement in New South Wales. The first trial was run in the evening with a load consisting of the dynamometer car and a couple of carriages to Port Kembla, where it went around the balloon loop and returned to Sydney. It left for Melbourne very early in the morning and was clear of the metropolitan area by 7.00am. Our concern was that the press might get wind of it being in Sydney, but fortunately they did not. It arrived in Melbourne under cover of darkness and was announced to the public when it was on the platform at Spencer Street. Much was made of this. A cover had been erected around the loco and when the announcement was made to the press and TV stations, a large number of people were present to see it.

The *Flying Scotsman* arrived back into NSW and was stabled overnight at Junee on the evening of 6 December 1988. We in New South Wales set out to give it a royal welcome into Sydney. The official welcoming ceremony was to be at Moss Vale, where 3801 and 5910 met it. The District Superintendent Goulburn and myself were conscious that it would attract a very large crowd, and accordingly, arrangements were made to meet with the traffic sergeant of police at Moss Vale. When I expressed the opinion that there would be something in the order of 5000 people to witness it and that they would follow in lengthy convoys along the roads, he laughed, saying he could not believe that many people would want to see a steam engine. I told him of some of the experiences we had seen, and been part of, in Victoria, and he opined the Victorians were always mad anyway. He refused point blank to even so much as advise the staff who would be on duty to keep an 'eye' on the traffic build-up.

I made the timetable for the *Flying Scotsman* from Albury to Sydney. When the Victorian SteamRanger timetabler saw it, he rang and told me it would not work 'in a fit'. He disconcerted me somewhat, so I went over it again and could find no reason why it would not work.

The trains worked by 3801 and 5910 were packed to capacity. We had sold tickets for 3801 to Moss Vale and the *Flying Scotsman* for Moss Vale to Sydney. In addition, many people had travelled to Moss Vale by regular services and came home either on the *Flying Scotsman* or 3801. At 2.00pm, 3801 was placed in the loop and 5910 on the goods road. 5910 just leading 3801. The *Flying Scotsman* was due in Moss Vale at 2.10pm. At 2.00pm, the movements that saw 3801 and 5910 placed were completed, and as they were completed, the fireman of the *Flying Scotsman* rang from the Up Accept Signal. The *Flying Scotsman* drew into the platform at 2.10pm to great applause. The police estimate was that were 7000 people in Moss Vale for the arrival of perhaps the most famous locomotive of all. To his credit, the police sergeant, dressed in mufti, sought me out and apologised to me for doubting us. On seeing the crowds, he had done some pretty fast footwork; there was an obvious police presence. The crowd estimate was his.

The *Flying Scotsman*, after the welcome by the Deputy Chief Executive, left first, followed by 3801 and then 5910. The *Scotsman* travelled via Cabramatta—Sefton to Strathfield where it went onto the Main Line. The New South Wales pride, 3801, travelled via Cabramatta—Granville to Strathfield and went onto the Local Line. They ran in parallel to Central. The traffic trouble officer who let a Down suburban train run between them around Ashfield was not popular. There were many people at Central to meet *The Scotsman*.

I look back on that day when not a thing went wrong; when the people at Moss Vale spilled out onto the running lines to get photos and followed the directions of the staff without query, with a great deal of happiness and pleasure. It *was* my last major effort in the Bicentennial Year and also of my career.

I was sixty in December 1988 and I retired on 7 January 1989.

Whenever it was in Sydney, the British locomotive ex-LNER 4472 Flying Scotsman *made regular short weekend journeys round the suburbs with the Bicentennial Train. On this fine Sunday morning of 7 May 1989 (which was a 'rare' event for sunshine in that year), the locomotive demonstrates its paces as it dashes past on the Down Main at Stanmore.   John R Newland.*

FAREWELL

MY farewell was held at the NSW Bowlers Club in York Street. I had no idea of what the response would be. The week before, I had been to the farewell of an inspector who had about 60 people attend. Based on that, I expected about 70-80 if I was lucky. Merv Cherry, who was the Country Passenger Operations Manager, organised it. He had invited Roy, Cathy, Faye and Phillip. Our Cathy was in hospital with pneumonia.

When we arrived, Merv met us at the door and said to me,

"This ought to please you!"

It was a masterly understatement. There were in excess of 140 people present. I have never before attempted to explain my feelings, but if you can wrap them around the words—emotional, proud, humble, excited and thankful—you will have a gauge of how I felt. Senior management was represented in the form of the Deputy Chief Executive, Chief Operations Manager, General Manager Freight Services, General Manager Passenger Services and the Mechanical Branch Maintenance Manager.

Many of my train control colleagues, colleagues from the freight and passenger train sections had come. The unions were

The author leaving home on his last day of work.

represented by two of those conductors with whom I had conducted the manning level reviews. I was thrilled to see all these, but I think I received the greatest thrill and surprise when two station assistants from the cloak room at Central station were there. I thought this the ultimate tribute. I had been to many farewells to senior officers and to inspectors and never seen a station assistant. I made sure that not only did I personally thank them for coming but made sure my family did likewise. I was floored when one of them said,

"We came because we admired the way you made us feel important in what we did."

Among the apologies was one from the newly appointed Chief Executive. The State Secretary of the Australian Railways Union apologised and sent me a letter, the contents of which I value greatly.

We sat down to a delightful meal, interrupted between the main course and desserts by speeches. There were many speakers who all paid tribute to me in one way or another. I will not elaborate; modesty should bid I do not. However, one phrase from the Deputy Chief Executive pleased me. He said,

"He was totally honest."

If I had achieved nothing else in my career, my honesty being recognised was sufficient.

I was very careful in my reply not to overstate anything I had done. I had sat and listened before to an officer being farewelled who went through every thing he did in his life. I was not going to fall for that. In my prepared reply, I told of some of the things I had done that reflected the more humorous things that had happened. For example the lighting of the signal at Newnes Junction in the wind and walking past the Distant Signal at Wentworth Falls.

I said that during my life I had always tried to work with my fellow workmates in whatever position I held. I quoted from the Franco-American Quaker Stephen Grellet, who said:

I expect to pass through this world but once. Any good thing therefore that I can do, or any kindness that I can show to my fellow creature, let me do it now; let me not defer or neglect it, for I shall not pass this way again.

When I said that, that was the premise on which I had worked all my life. My colleagues to a man and woman rose and applauded. I was near to tears.

CATHY, THE FINAL CHAPTER

THE period from when Cathy went into the Richmond Scheme home at Wahroonga until the time I retired, was perhaps the most settled of her life. She was loved and cared for by staff who were unbelievably dedicated. Her fellow residents all had serious physical and mental developmental disabilities. Most of the time, there were four other residents, none of whom were able to speak. Cathy all her life was able to speak clearly and distinctly. Being able to do this was, of course, a very great advantage in the Richmond Scheme home situation. During the times there was only one staff member, they had someone to talk to, albeit on a limited range. It was still, however, a voice and company.

We brought her home every Saturday and Sunday, something she looked forward to. Cathy at this stage weighed about seven and a half stone, but as I grew older, I found it more difficult to lift her in and out of our station wagon. By this stage, she was a quadriplegic and, as a result, was not able to help herself. She was able to hold a spoon or fork in her left hand with her thumb and index finger and move the arm to her mouth. She was not able to make any other movement which made the lifting of her very difficult. During the last two years, the Hornsby Ku-ring-gai Area Health Service provided a bus with a hydraulic chair lift that made life much easier. The Richmond Scheme staff used to bring her home and return her after her visits home.

On most Saturdays, at that stage, Faye came home with her two daughters, to the delight of both Cathy and her mother. Faye and Phillip, when they first came to the metropolitan area, lived at Cambridge Park. They later sold there and bought at Kings Langley, where they currently live. They now have three daughters. Phillip taught at Marayong Primary School, where he became Deputy Principal. He was appointed Principal of Lalor Park School in 2000. At the beginning of the 2003 school year, he was appointed Principal of a new Primary School called Caddie's Creek, which is in Glenwood (adjoining Parklea). Faye teaches languages at Parramatta High School on a part time basis. She is also on the Examination Committee for Indonesian Studies and assists with the preparation of the Higher School Certificate. She has been a marker of the Higher School Certificate examinations for nearly 20 years. Faye was Marking Supervisor in the subject for 10 years, the maximum time the Department of Education permitted. She continued on after this period as a marker.

After about a two-year period in Wagga Wagga, Roy accepted a position with the Director of Public Prosecutions in Darwin, and within a six-month period, he became Deputy Senior Crown Prosecutor. In 1987, he was appointed a Crown Prosecutor in New South Wales. In 1996, he became a Deputy Senior Crown Prosecutor, with responsibility for major trials, although he spent a great deal of his time in the Court of Criminal Appeal. In 1999, he was appointed a Deputy Director of Public Prosecutions. There are two deputies to the Director. Roy and his wife Cathy have two daughters and a son. They have both created, with their spouses, wonderful homes for their children. These children—our grandchildren—have responded to their home environments, and thus are a joy to have as grandchildren.

We are justifiably proud of Roy and Faye; they have reached the top echelons of their professions with probity and have the respect of their peers. They attend, and have taken part in, the life of their respective churches. They will both say they are better and more compassionate people for having had Cathy as a sister. Mamie and I are also better people for having had her as a daughter.

As time progressed, Cathy suffered several severe attacks of pneumonia and on one occasion, near fatal dehydration. Each of these took her to Hornsby Hospital. When she was in hospital, we saw her on a daily basis. Because she had lost the ability to move any part of her body, her lungs became very congested. Each time in hospital saw this fluid removed but unfortunately the length of time between the clearing and another attack of pneumonia caused by another build up, decreased.

On the evening of Saturday 30 July 1989, Roy and I saw her in hospital. She was having extreme breathing difficulty. We were about to leave the hospital at 9.00pm when the sister asked if anything happened to Cathy, did I want her resuscitated? Although I knew and understood what was happening, this question hit me very hard. I had to make a decision on whether my daughter should be let die, or whether I said to resuscitate her with the extremely faint hope that she might recover. With a very heavy heart, I said if she passes away, leave her in peace.

At 4.20am on Sunday 31 July, the resident doctor from Hornsby Hospital rang to say that Cathy had passed away a few moments earlier. He asked did we wish to come and see her. We both said no. We held a family crematorium service and a thanksgiving service for her life in the Uniting Church at Turramurra. One of the most moving things from our viewpoint, and also that of the congregation, was when the residents of the Richmond Scheme home were either wheeled in or walked into the Church and sat in the front row. Many people saw at that time a part of their community they did not know existed, and their presence caused a good deal of emotion.

To us, her immediate family, we felt a tremendous loss. The indomitable spirit of Cathy had finally surrendered. It was a spirit that had carried her and us through many difficulties, through many painful processes and through many good times. The grieving processes that parents go through, especially mothers, at the passing of a child are difficult to adequately define. Her mother worried whether she had done everything possible to make her comfortable; whether her care for her had been sufficient. It had been.

No person could have done more than she did, or express so often so much love to a child. I think she accepted this, but that did not stop the grieving, which after all these years is still felt at special times. As a father, I persecuted myself by wondering whether I should have allowed all the medical procedures that she endured. In my more rational periods of thought, I realised that whatever had been done, was done only with her best interests at heart. We both had long periods when we were unable to sleep. This gradually passed with time.

The thing that remained rock solid through all the years of trauma and tension was our marriage. This happened because of our deep commitment to and love for one another.

LIFE AFTER RETIREMENT

SOME six months into retirement, I found that all the jobs that needed doing had been done. I determined long before I retired that whatever I did, would not interfere with anything that Mamie did. I was determined that I would find things to do that were independent of her. I felt I had seen too many retired husbands pushing the shopping trolley behind their wives and offering unsolicited advice on what ought to be purchased.

I became friendly with the financial planner who had set up my retirement

The author on a 3801 Limited tour on 7 December 1991.

investments. When he suggested that I accompany him for a couple of days a week to his office to research for him, I accepted. This continued into 1990 and in the mid June, we set out on a round the world trip that extended for 89 days, together with Mamie's sister whose husband had died in the March. It was just fabulous.

Shortly after I arrived back, I was approached by a representative of 3801 Limited who asked if would I be interested in becoming Marketing Manager and Tour Organiser for the company. I agreed. At the same time, Tony Gogarty was appointed General Manager. We took over something that was floundering. There was no forward planning for future excursions. I was somewhat apprehensive at playing second fiddle after having for so long virtually run my own race. I reasoned, however, that Tony and I would be able to get along without too many hassles. In the main, we did. I agreed to work part-time three days a week. It was not long, however, before I was working five days a week with the remuneration arrangements not changing.

I began by setting out a programme for the balance of the year. This was advertised in various media outlets that resulted in us obtaining good early patronage. My next task was to try and sell the train to charity groups. This turned out to be a very successful business. The first charity I approached, was the Fred Hollows Foundation with a plan for running a train exclusively for them. I was told they would not try to organise it, but I could use the Hollows' name in advertising it. The first train was so successful that over time, we ran two more trains for them. As a result, we donated something like $20,000 to the Fred Hollows Foundation. During the time I was associated with 3801 Limited, many trains were run for charitable organisations: the Adventist Hospital, Royal North Shore Hospital, Sunshine Homes plus many schools and other organisations. I have estimated using the train raised a total of around $100,000.

For every journey we undertook, I submitted an application to run a train, and a suggested timetable to the State Rail Authority. The Timetable Section had not changed much. The special train notices, on which the timetables and authority for the train(s) to run were printed, were rarely received before the Thursday prior to weekend departure. The timetables I submitted mostly were not significantly amended. 3801 Limited was able to make its own crewing arrangements from my suggested timetables.

A major trip to Alice Springs was organised and took place in 1992. I do not intend to go into detail about it, suffice to say, that the trip was very successful and that the Company was well rewarded financially for the journey.

I was also associated with the *Flying Scotsman's* journey to Alice Springs in 1989. This journey actually began in Melbourne, and it was the first steam train (in fact of any type of train) to depart from Melbourne for Alice Springs via Albury, Cootamundra and Parkes. Roland Kennington, the engineer in charge of the *Flying Scotsman* in Australia, was determined to break the record for the longest non-stop steam journey in the world while he was in Australia.

The only place he could do it was between Parkes and Broken Hill. The *Flying Scotsman* held the previous record when it ran non-stop on a circuitous route from Edinburgh to London; the reason for this route was a mishap on the main line. The distance travelled was 407 miles: the distance between Parkes and Broken Hill is 411 miles.

Much organisation was required to achieve this. The Country Passenger Operations Manager became very interested in the record attempt and set about making the arrangements to see it come about. There had never been a train run non-stop to Broken Hill. The reason for this, to a railwayman, was obvious. The safeworking system was staff and ticket, which meant that every train had to stop at each of the unattended stations and speak to the train controller. To overcome this, arrangements were made to have a Per Way four-wheel drive vehicle used as a means to transfer a safeworking employee from station to station ahead of the *Flying Scotsman*. Because the train was limited to 80km/h, it was not difficult to keep ahead of it with the road vehicle travelling on what was known as the 'Per Way Highway'. Because the Chief Civil Engineer's Branch had become totally mechanised, the roads running beside the railway line were in daily use and well maintained.

To ensure that sufficient coal and water were available for the journey, three 7000-gallon water tanks were attached to the train, the trailing tank being fitted with a petrol driven water pump. The tender, by using what is known as 'hungry boards', was loaded well above tender height with coal. The concern was to see that the tender springs were not overloaded.

Because it was necessary to change crews half way, L516, 3801's crew van, a converted sleeping car with an end access door to the next vehicle, was placed next to the tender so that crews could walk from the van onto the *Flying Scotsman's* locomotive via the walkway that was part of the *Flying Scotsman's* tender. It was common practice in England to change crews on 'the run'. Doing this meant that it was necessary to run an extended water hose from the water tanks to the tender, running around L516.

The train had arrived at Parkes on the previous day after having entertained many children on a cold brute of a day between Stockinbingal and Parkes. Fortunately, we ran on time, so the children at Weedallion, Quandialla, Bribbaree, Red Bend and Garema were not waiting long. A very large crowd welcomed us at Forbes. Arrival at Parkes was about 5.00pm. As on all previous occasions when I had been to Parkes with a steam train going interstate, we were entertained for dinner at the Services Club, a most successful evening. I will not mention the name of Mike Greenwood, Mr Tourism at Parkes at that time, except to thank him for all his efforts during the Bicentennial Year and for the *Scotsman* in 1989.

We left Parkes at 8.40am on the day of the momentous non-stop effort. Everything went smoothly. At each of the unattended staff stations, the Per Way vehicle had the safeworking man waiting for us. That is until we were approaching Kaleentha. It could be seen a long way from Kaleentha that the vehicle was not there. The driver immediately steadied down to a slow walking pace. Even so, as we passed the landmark there was no sign of the vehicle. The driver steadied to a crawl. I can and always will vouch that the train did not stop. I was at a door looking at the ground and could see that we moved continuously.

We were near the home signal when away in the distance a great cloud of dust signalled the approach of the Per Way truck. The signalman opened the door of the staff hut as the train neared the little platform and handed the driver the staff for the Menindee section. The reason for the delay, which none of us had tumbled to, was that the Per Way road deviated from the train line at Gum Lake, which added some distance to the truck's journey.

As we exceeded 407 miles of non-stop running, a huge cheer went up on the train, celebrating the creating of the longest non-stop steam train journey ever undertaken. I would be confident that the record will never be beaten.

When we arrived at Broken Hill, the train had been in motion for nine hours and 40 minutes, also a record for being the longest time a locomotive had run non-stop. There was about a tonne of coal left in the tender and about four thousand gallons of water in the tanks, some of which would not have been accessible. It was estimated that there was sufficient water only for another 40 miles. I will not go into any more detail on this trip, except to say that it was most enjoyable and that, in the main, the *Flying Scotsman* ran well.

Toward the end of its proposed stay in Australia, Ian Willis, proprietor of Willis Engineering, Perth who had given so much support in Perth to 3801 Limited, wanted the *Flying Scotsman* to come to Perth for the benefit of West Australian folk. Ian and the mechanical crew of 3801, along with myself, maintained a strong friendship after 3801 had returned east. In fact, Ian was staying at our home when Cathy died.

He had the full support of 3801 Limited. Because there was no standard gauge rollingstock in West Australia, Ian had to purchase six carriages from the State Rail Authority of NSW that were about to be condemned. The condition of their purchase was that they were not be returned to New South Wales. He was able to dispose of them, to farmers and school communities. Today there are still NSW carriages being used as amenity units and store sheds over a large area of Western Australia.

The English Great Western steam locomotive *Pendennis Castle* had been at Dampier and used by Hammersley Iron and the local steam enthusiasts. Negotiations were made by Ian to have the locomotive transferred to Perth by Brambles, who gave him a very sympathetic price. When the *Flying Scotsman* and the *Pendennis Castle* touched buffers on Perth platform it was the first time they had done so since the great Exhibition at Wembley in 1925.

The purchase of the carriages was really the least of his problems. I had agreed from the beginning to assist with bookings and timetabling in New South Wales. Ian negotiated the problems of insurance and all that goes with it. I went to Perth to assist there and assisted Ian with the ticketing arrangements, although I must say in his usual efficient way, he had a good system in place. We also spoke with Westrail, regarding stowing and cleaning of the train. The unions drove a hard bargain and insisted that they clean the carriages, an expense Ian could have done without. One of Ian's ambitions was to get the *Flying Scotsman* and/or *Pendennis Castle* to Esperance.

We set out from Perth and went to Kalgoorlie and tried to speak to the Mayor, but got nowhere with him. He was not interested. We made our arrangements there without any assistance from anyone. We then went to Esperance, calling in at Norseman to arrange water supply and to Salmon Gums, where the publican thought we were the greatest things since sliced bread. We arranged for him to supply three meals there, one going to Esperance, one on a round trip shuttle from Esperance, and one on the return journey.

Some 14 days prior to departure from Sydney with about 120 people booked on the train to Perth, the infamous airlines strike by Qantas pilots began. With no resolution in sight, the passengers who were relying on airlines to fly home, cancelled en masse. There were 14 hardy souls who could see that one of the great steam journeys of the world was being undertaken and weren't going to miss it. The cancellations threw into doubt the financing of the journey but after much thought, Ian decided to proceed with the project.

The *Flying Scotsman's* engineering crew decided that they would attempt to steam across Australia unassisted. Australian National Railways did not argue with this, but they insisted that a diesel locomotive be attached to the train for back up purposes. The completion of this journey unassisted would mean another world record for *Flying Scotsman*; it being the longest steam journey ever accomplished by one steam locomotive.

After leaving Broken Hill on time and were about the area of Yunta, one of the carriages developed a hot box. This caused several hours delay. The train was due to run to Port Augusta in the day. It was obvious that it would be something in the order of 10-12 hours late into Port Augusta for, not only did we have hot box problems, we also had air brake compressor problems which took a considerable time to repair at Peterborough. I cancelled the motel accommodation in Port Augusta and went to the local hardware store and purchased 12 sleeping bags. Two wise individuals had their own. It was close to dark when we left Peterborough and early morning when we arrived at Port Augusta.

The air compressor* again caused trouble at Port Augusta. Many hours were spent trying to make it work, and eventually, at about 11.00pm, we departed from Port Augusta 15 hours late. During the day, I had gone to the local store and purchased provisions for our meals. I also had to cancel the arrangements we had made for meals at Tarcoola, Cook and Rawlinna. The buffet on the train was a BSR hired from ARHS at Canberra. It

---

* The system of pneumatic braking on the *Flying Scotsman* was not compatible with the Australian Westinghouse air brake system. A Westinghouse compressor that had been brought from England was attached to the *Scotsman* at Eveleigh, so that it was compatible with the rollingstock in use.

had a small gas stove and refrigerator. I prepared all the meals for the passengers from Port Augusta to Perth. At Tarcoola, Cook and Rawlinna, provisions were bought. We had frozen vegies with each meal; twice we had steak, once frozen pizzas and once frozen pies. Each main meal, we had tinned fruit and custard. Lunch each day consisted of sandwiches.

I was so concerned about the air compressor that at the first safeworking stop after we left Port Augusta, I went to the engine to see how things were going. The driver told me the pump had failed again. The English engineer was trying to get the driver to continue without air, saying that on this flat country, the engine brake would be sufficient. I would not agree. The decision, of course, was not mine but the driver's and he would not agree either. I then asked if the support diesel locomotive was started and ran in idle to provide air from its compressor, would he be able to manipulate the air brakes from the *Flying Scotsman*. Both the driver and the engineer agreed that it could be done, so I then said to the engineer that he had no alternative, that the diesel would not be working, there being no crew in it; and that would not stop him from being able to claim the *Flying Scotsman* had steamed across the country unassisted. This was agreed to.

The further the *Flying Scotsman* went into the Nullarbor, the more it suffered from poor quality water and the continuous work it was called upon to do. In the middle of the night, between Rawlinna and Kalgoorlie, I am not going to suggest that the *Flying Scotsman* did at any stage stop steaming. If it did get a bit of a push up on a couple of occasions, I would not say so. In Kalgoorlie, it was necessary to hire an air compressor from Coates Hire. The compressor was placed in a wagon next to the locomotive and the assistant engine taken off at Kalgoorlie.

By the time we arrived in Perth on the Sunday evening, the brick arch in the *Flying Scotsman's* firebox had collapsed, the third cylinder was scored, the boiler needed a wash out, and a number of fire bars were missing. It was sick, very sick. The first shuttle train was planned to run on the following Wednesday, with four daily trips to Merriden, each one being booked out.

After arrival at the depot on that Sunday evening for our meal, the English engineer said that he was going to cancel the first three trips and run on the Saturday. Tony Gogarty, knowing the financial position Ian Willis was in, said in Tony Gogarty speak,

"We are not cancelling any *** trips. There are two whole days before Wednesday and three hours in this *** day. Let's get started."

With Gogarty leading the way, work started that night. I know for a fact that Tony did not go to bed until Tuesday morning when it was daylight. The boiler was washed out, the fire bars replaced, the brick arch renewed and the cylinder rebored. The fire was lit in the locomotive about 3.00am on the Wednesday morning. It ran the first shuttle without a trial—successfully, I might add.

I will not go into the Kalgoorlie to Esperance and return trip with the *Pendennis Castle* in great detail. The first of its many delays was at Norseman when the taking of water was much slower than anticipated. There was another problem; although the water tank attached to the *Pendennis Castle* was nearly full, there was no water going into the tender. It appeared from peering into the tank that a large lump of coal was blocking the outlet. One of the crew stripped to his underwear and dived into the tank. As the tender was shaped like a petrol tanker, he was able to this, and after a number of attempts, he had removed it.

We arrived at Esperance around 4.00pm, some three hours late. The plan was to prepare *Pendennis Castle* for the journey and run tender first to Salmon Gums with a load of people from Esperance, who were to have dinner and entertainment at the hotel. We left Esperance about 6.00pm. The driver originally rostered, who was very keen to be part of the weekend, became ill.

A replacement driver could not be found on a voluntary basis. The Westrail people leaned on a driver, who protested vigorously, but in the finish he was directed to go. He had the last laugh, however. He lost nearly two hours running tender first to Salmon Gums, the arrival being after 11.00pm. The passengers had a ball. They were having such a good time that we had difficulty in getting them to return to the train . The publican did not seem to be pushing them very hard; they were spending like it was going out of fashion!

Next, or I should say, that morning, a family shuttle was run to a siding I think was called Grass Patch. The families loved it. We left for Kalgoorlie, running tender first about midday and arrived without a hitch or loss of time, arriving at Kambalda about 11.00pm, where the *Flying Scotsman* was waiting for us.

Pendennis Castle was cut off and went for water. The only time I had words with the engineer of the *Flying Scotsman* then took place—he refused to run onto the train and be ready for *Pendennis Castle* to be attached for the run to Kalgoorlie. The two locomotives were required because of the gradient to Kalgoorlie. No Great Western engine was going to lead his engine! I told him in no uncertain terms that the passengers had been stuffed around from the time we had left and I was not going to delay them any more because of his pride. I told him it was dark and no one was going to see who led the bloody train into Kalgoorlie. He agreed in the finish. I had not been to bed from the time we left Kalgoorlie and I was not very good company at that point.

The *Flying Scotsman* came back to New South Wales attached to a freight train. It steamed all the way but did little work. I came back on the *Indian Pacific*.

Ian Willis lost a considerable amount of money on this tour. 3801 Limited picked up the losses initially, but Ian Willis, being the totally honourable man he is, repaid 3801 Limited within a relatively short period of time.

BACK TO THE TRACK

I N EARLY 1995, a man came into the office of 3801 Limited and asked straight out could 3801 run to Alice Springs? I was a little taken aback and replied, very cautiously, yes it could, but whether it would, was another matter.

He then went on to say that his name was Warren Brown and that he was the cartoonist for the DAILY TELEGRAPH, and a member of the Australian Ex Military Vehicles Collectors Society (AMVCS). I have to say here, I developed a very quick rapport with Warren and found him one of the most genuine young men I have ever met in my lifetime.

After the initial shock of the question, we discussed what it was that AMVC wanted to do. They had, as a group, developed the idea of performing a re-enactment of a wartime convoy from Alice Springs to Darwin, using their restored vehicles for the purpose. The concept called 'Back to the Track', appealed greatly to my patriotic instincts. In Warren's words,

"I embraced the concept from the start."

I knew that the standardisation of the track from Adelaide to Melbourne, due for completion some two months before the planned trip, would allow the re-enactment train to run via Melbourne and Adelaide. This was something the AMVC did not know. When I told Warren this, he was very excited that Melbourne's AMVC group would be able to participate from Melbourne. Warren, in his usual professional manner, drew up a format with the rough idea of what the journey was all about, for 3801 Limited. The problem with this was that it was so professional, that when the committee members of 3801 Limited saw it, they thought the journey with 3801 was a *fait accompli*. I had a good deal of trouble convincing some of them that this was not so and that I had not given any indication on behalf of the company that 3801 was available. I told the Chairman exactly what had transpired, and he accepted my word.

The Department of Veterans Affairs, which had early in the 1995 year celebrated 50 years since the cessation of hostilities, set-up a planning group known as 'The Australia Remembers Committee' under the chairmanship of a very senior officer, Tony Ashford. The Minister at the time was the Hon Con Sciacca. They also embraced the idea of the celebration of 'Back to the Track' with enthusiasm and financial support. The NSW Director of Veteran Affairs was another distinguished officer, in the person of Commissioner Geoff Stonehouse. There were very many other ladies and gentlemen in Veterans Affairs who ably assisted. In keeping with my general policy through this writing, I shall not name them.

While the tussle about whether 3801 would be used, or whether 3801's rolling stock or that of ARHS at Canberra would form the train continued, I had several meetings with the players in the game. I met with AMVC's people, formally and informally, together with the Department of Veterans Affairs, in Elizabeth St. The chairman for this meeting and of the many others we had, was Geoff Stonehouse. Tony Ashford attended some of them. I gathered the impression fairly early in the piece that the 'Australia Remembers Committee' was having budgetary problems, they having, of course, arranged outstanding events all over Australia. They were anxious to minimise costs, but were having difficulty seeing how. I had given them a very substantial sum as an indication of what it would cost to take 3801, again, I might say, without commitment.

At the first meeting were a Major Eastgate and Lieutenant Wilkinson of the Australian Army. They had been seconded by the Australian Army to assist with Army logistics and public relations. It was agreed that I would accompany them to every point between Sydney and Alice Springs where the train would stop. My task was to provide a timetable and to ensure that the points where we were to stay overnight were able to accommodate us.

To my profound disappointment, before we left, 3801 Limited decided they would not take part in the venture. I have to say that I was not greatly surprised at the decision, but my main disappointment was in the lack of vision they displayed in summing up what the journey might become. I immediately asked could 3801 lead whatever locomotive was used out of Sydney to give the 'Back to the Track Train' some authenticity as a troop train. This was agreed to.

Before we left on our reconnoitre, the NSW State Rail Authority, with Simon Foster as its representative, came to the party in a big way. Much of the success of the whole re-enactment was due to the efforts of State Rail and Simon Foster.

Major Eastgate, Lieutenant Wilkinson and I left Sydney very early one morning in a rented car, driving first to Canberra. On the way, however, we called at Goulburn. Due to the early hour, we did not call into Moss Vale, but visited it later. At every point we went to we spoke to the local mayor or shire president or their representatives and, where possible, the RSL club for the area. The local newspapers were visited and given historical detail concerning the conditions between Alice Springs and Darwin, during the war. They were informed of the fact that it took 11 days to make a return trip from Alice Springs to Laramah (the railhead on the North Australia Railway), and that the maximum allowable speed was 20mph. This speed was imposed in order to conserve fuel. The final information given was that the AMVC vehicles were to be unloaded in Alice Springs, and they were to do a re-enactment of a wartime journey from Alice Springs to Darwin.

On arrival at Canberra, we went to the office of Australia Remembers, for discussions with Tony Ashford and received a significant amount of money to cover our expenses for the time we would be away. After leaving Canberra before midday, we headed for Yass. We soon set a pattern; first find the office of the local newspaper, then to the RSL club and council chambers, if the town had one, of course. On this day we continued to Harden, Cootamundra, Junee and finally at Wagga Wagga. I had already made up my mind that Cootamundra would be as far as we could hope to get on the first day's journey, so I booked motel accommodation for 40 people. This number we reasoned would cover accommodation for the veterans, their carers, train staff and the organisers.

We went directly to the Kapooka army base, where we stayed in the officer's quarters as guests of the camp commandant. We paid the going rate, which was eminently reasonable. On the second day, we completed arrangements in Wagga Wagga, Albury, Wodonga, Benalla and Seymour. The train was to stop at all the places we visited, of course, but it was not easy arranging inspections of the army vehicles in Victoria because of the distance the standard gauge line was from the broad gauge platforms. On the second night, we stayed at Puckapunyal army base, again as guests of the base commander. My colleagues, especially the major, were very well known.

Next day was to Geelong, bypassing Melbourne. Because the standard gauge line does not go right into Geelong, we selected a station named North Shore as the area to exhibit the train and to have a ceremony. The siding would enable the train to be off the main line. We then headed west calling at Ararat, Stawell, Horsham and to Dimboola, where we stayed overnight. I had felt Dimboola was as far as it was practical to go in a day. There were also facilities there for stowing the train and engine, which was an added incentive.

The following day saw us in Nhill, Bordertown and Murray Bridge before arriving in Adelaide. A full day was spent in Adelaide where we spoke with Australian National Railways (AN), who as I have always found, were co-operative in the extreme. We anticipated that the train would have something like a hundred restored vehicles of varying types when it left Adelaide for Alice Springs.

After Adelaide we called at Port Pirie. I was very concerned about Port Pirie, because the line runs into a dead end and the locomotive has to be reversed to get the train away again, which in effect, turns it. I knew this would be unsatisfactory and I was not inclined to include Port Pirie, and the AN people agreed with me. We continued onto Port Augusta where we stayed overnight. We met the good Joy Baluch, the Mayor of Port Augusta and arranged an overnight stop for the train. We had lost our good car at Adelaide and were now driving a dual-cab utility, nowhere near as comfortable!

The next stop after Port Augusta was at Pimba, then Coober Pedy, Marla overnight, and finally at Alice Springs. After a day we left by road again to come home. We arranged an overnight stay at Coober Pedy; but their enthusiasm frightened me a little. The train was to stow in the refuge siding at Manguri and the passengers were to be transferred by bus. I reminded myself to keep on the fringe of the celebrations that they were going to have when we arrived there with the selected WW2 personnel!

After we arrived back in Sydney, the work of organisation really began. I liaised with officers from FreightRail to procure car carriers for the jeeps and flat wagons for the larger type field ambulance, blitz wagons and a Studebaker, a dual differential and gear box huge transport lorry. I had imagined there would car carriers available, because the transport of new cars was no longer a railway function. I was mistaken. After much searching, I finally found some in South Australia which were eventually despatched to Enfield. Finding flat wagons was even more difficult because these were in huge demand for container traffic. After a concerted effort by the rail officers concerned, we were able to obtain sufficient wagons. Pressure was placed upon repair depots to get the flat wagons into service they were waiting to be repaired, ahead of other rolling stock already scheduled for repair.

Warren Brown in his book acknowledges the effort made by Simon Foster and myself in obtaining the wagons. I should note here that the efforts of the FreightRail personnel have not been sufficiently acknowledged. Had they not wholeheartedly supported the concept, the wagons would not have been available and the greatest tribute paid to the soldiers/drivers who were responsible for the transport of goods between Alice Springs and Larimah would not have taken place. If I were able to recall their names, I would name them.

I had great difficulty contacting the management at South Dynon in Melbourne. Time and time again I left messages with the assurance that I would be contacted, but I never was. I finally contacted Faye Powell, whom I had known and worked with and who was respected in the NSW State Rail system. She was now a very senior person in the National Rail Corporation. The next time I rang South Dynon, I spoke to the manager and received all the assistance I required. We wanted to stow the train overnight in South Dynon yards. It also had to be turned so the wagons ran the same way from Melbourne as they did from Sydney. In addition to this, another 10 wagons were required for Melbourne-restored vehicles taking part in the 'Back to the Track' re-enactment from Alice Springs.

I had known the timetable personnel in V/Line previously, and when I contacted them with the proposed timetable I had, they were very keen to assist. The timetable they gave us did not vary very much from the one I suggested. There were crossings I did not know of to be worked into the timetable, but I had been very liberal with my times, so in the end, they worked out well.

Similar arrangements were made with Australian National Railways in Adelaide as I had made in Melbourne. Nothing was a problem for them. Approximately another 10 wagons were to be attached in Adelaide for restored vehicles, including some from Western Australia. We anticipated that the train would be 700 metres long when it left Adelaide.

Simon Foster had arranged availability of AAH 19, a carriage belonging to the Commissioner's train, together with an RDH buffet with 36 First Class seats, an SDS a 64-seat First Class carriage and a power van. The seats in the RDH buffet were allotted to the 14 selected veterans, their caring staff, Veterans Affairs staff, executive staff of the 'Back to the Track', Simon Foster and myself. The Commissioner's carriage was used as an office. It had six sleeping berths that were to be available for veterans if they wished to have a 'camp' during the day. I might say, I did avail myself on a couple of occasions. The First Class carriage was for the use of the drivers of the restored vehicles. The buffet was manned and supplied by 3801 Limited staff, in the names of Don and Joan Brand. They did a tremendous job. I did my share in it so they could also get much needed rest.

So the great day arrived when all the restored vehicles had been loaded, the carriages had been worked in from Eveleigh by 3801 and 8180, the diesel locomotive allocated to the train had arrived from Delec. 3801 led the train from Sydney to Moss Vale, to lend authenticity to the claim that the 'Back to the Track' train was a true re-enactment of a wartime train. The train was despatched with speeches of good wishes by the Minister, the Hon Con Sciacca, Warren Brown and Geoff Stonehouse, Veterans Affairs Commissioner. All of us who worked so hard to bring this to fruition and who had suffered so many frustrating moments, were overjoyed at the experience of departing Sydney to the fanfare we had.

I always had some misgivings about the reception we might receive from the stations, towns and cities we were to visit. I knew that Major Eastgate and Lieutenant Wilkinson had worked very hard to promote the venture and that when I was with them, the press in every place we visited were enthusiastic. Despite this, I was still concerned.

After arrival at the Moss Vale platform, our first stopping point, my fears melted away like snow in a spring breeze. The platform was packed. A path was left along the platform coping to enable 14 high school girl captains from the local private and public schools to escort the 14 veterans along this path, accompanied by music from school bands, and present them to the mayor. The local federal member was present, as were representatives of the RSL, local churches and businesses. Of significance was the re-forming for this day of the Blue Gum Ladies. During the war these ladies volunteered at Moss Vale station and provided meals at all hours of the day and night to soldiers passing through on troop trains. On this day, they served morning tea to the veterans. It was a very emotional and moving time for them. I do not know how many people were present, but Moss Vale platform, which covers a much larger area than most, was packed with school children and local residents. My mind went back to the day the *Flying Scotsman* arrived; there were similar crowds on the platform.

I do not intend to outline the reception we received at every point; Warren Brown has done that in his book. On this day alone, however, the crowds that greeted us at Goulburn, Yass Junction, Harden and Cootamundra were far, far in excess of anything I had imagined. It was just a wonderful day and experience. At Harden, the local mayor presented each veteran with a replica wartime bottle of beer and a fifty cent piece in a medallion-like form, representing a soldiers pay of 'five bob' a day, and a bottle of beer. A well thought out touch, equally well received by the veterans. I think at the end of the first day, some of the veterans thought they were film stars!

The following morning we left Cootamundra a bit after 8.00am. Arriving at Junee some 40 odd minutes later, there were school buses from areas 150 kilometres away. Once again, the platform was packed. This began another tremendous day that saw us eventually arrive in Melbourne. A rest day was had in Melbourne. The train was exhibited on the platform at Spencer Street and was the centre of attraction to many people all that day. The vehicles that loaded in Melbourne were attached.

The following day our first stop was at Sunshine. From this point, the Victorian G Class locomotive that was hauling the train, played up all day. We were late into Ararat and Stawell. Despite the atrocious weather accompanying us, there was unbelievable enthusiasm at each of these places. Local politicians were present at each point as were the commissioners (as they are called in Victoria) of the local government areas, local bands and hordes of children and adults on a non-school day. There was local entertainment and BBQs before we arrived, which had to be held under the cover of the station platforms, while those being entertained got wet.

Arrival at Horsham was 90 minutes late, and it was raining horizontally! When the train stopped, I tried to get off. Impossible! There was so many people on the platform, I could not get off. We finally set off for Dimboola. We were feted by the locals in the local School of Arts and entertained with songs and comedies from the wartime era. Unbelievable!

The following morning we set out for Nhill, and this time the same locomotive performed perfectly all day. I was stopped in my tracks at Nhill. An old soldier from the First War who was 100 years old, played the Last Post. This man was so much like my father, I could not take my eyes off him. It was uncanny. I spoke to him and sure enough he was a Londoner, as was my father. At Murray Bridge and Bordertown, we were greeted just as enthusiastically.

Late afternoon saw us arrive in Adelaide, the first special events train to run on the standard gauge line between Melbourne and Adelaide. The Australian National Railways Commissioners greeted us. The Veterans Affairs Commissioner for South Australia, RSL dignitaries and a large number of people were also present. We spent a rest day in Adelaide getting ready for the long and last leg of our journey. When we left Adelaide, the train, as forecast, was about 750 metres long. There were 90 restored vehicles of varying types that were a good representation of army vehicles of the era.

I learned during the lay day from the AN people that the mayor of Port Pirie, when he found the train was bypassing his town, nearly tore the place apart. The reason told to him of the operational difficulties cut no ice.

"Fix it," he said.

To enable the train to go into Port Pirie and come out without turning, AN arranged for a diesel locomotive to be on the Coonamia Loop. When the train passed into Port Pirie, the locomotive came behind and attached to the rear of the train.

When the train was ready to depart, the diesel locomotive hauled it back out onto the mainline, heading in the direction of Adelaide, when clear of the points leading into Port Pirie, the signal electrician reset the points and signals for the mainline. The train departed north and the diesel locomotive went back to its depot. But did the mayor turn on a show! He sure did. The veterans were treated like heroes. The train stood on and blocked a level crossing for the whole time we were there, the local police directing traffic to a detour. We stayed overnight at Port Augusta, where we were met by the redoubtable Mayor Joy Baluch, but not as many people.

The following day, we set out for Manguri, a siding some 30km from Coober Pedy. On the way, we saw several isolated groups of people, who had travelled from nearby stations, to see this great celebrity train pass. The school children of Tarcoola welcomed us with a programme one would have thought was beyond their ability and years. Some of their sketches were truly outstanding, as were the words of Warren Brown. He proceeded briefly to entertain them; the eyes of some of them were nearly popping from their heads in wonderment.

Members of the local RSL, who had commandeered school buses to take us to Coober Pedy, met us at Manguri. One of the sights that will remain with me, was looking westward as we travelled from Manguri and seeing the train silhouetted on the skyline, it was a ghostly sight for about five minutes after the sun had disappeared. The mayor gave a Coober Pedy-style of welcome to us, one full of gusto and sincerity. While he was intent on entertaining the war veterans, especially, he took time in his welcome to become serious and to recognise the sacrifice made by so many on the 'Track'.

He was also lavish in his praise for the organisation that saw the 'Back to the Track' train stop at Manguri. After the meal, I left with many of the organising group. The celebrations continued, but I believe they were quite sedate by Coober Pedy standards.

An early departure from Manguri on the following morning saw us in Marla around 11.00am. One of the most moving and emotional ceremonies I have ever witnessed, took place here. A dance by seven aboriginal women, who wore skirts only and had their breasts painted in white stripes, performed to the beat of wood on wood as they danced they moved barefooted towards two older women from a distance of about 10 metres. There was something in their movements that created a sense of urgency and a sense of security at the same time.

The performance lasted for about 15 minutes. At its conclusion the local school children sang *I still call Australia Home* and *Advance Australia Fair*. I have heard both sung better on countless occasions, but I have never heard them sung with greater effect. I asked one of the women who danced why they went to the trouble they obviously had done. She said,

"To say thank you to the men who saved us from the Japanese."

That to me, was what this journey was all about.

Arrival at Alice Springs was on time. The boundless joy that was shown by some, particularly Major Eastgate, at the success of the journey was sufficient thanks to me for my efforts, which modestly had contributed significantly to the journey. I came home from Alice Springs.

I had been home for a couple of days when I received a call from Tony Ashford's office wanting to know if I would like to go to Darwin and be there when the 'Back to the Track' vehicles arrived. I obviously said,

"Yes, I would."

I also said that I would not go on my own, that if I went my wife would accompany me and, if necessary I would pay her airfare. The reply was that my wife was most welcome and that they would arrange accommodation for us. It was a great joy to see the convoy arrive in Darwin. To this day, I am grateful to Tony Ashford for thanking me for my efforts in this way.

THE FINALE

THE 'Back to the Track' train was my last major effort. However, I continued, when I returned, to be Marketing Manager for 3801 Limited until December of 1995, when I finally retired from rail transport after 50 years and six months.

In this final chapter, I want to pay tribute to one special person, Mamie, my wife now for 50 years. Ours has been a good marriage that has survived many trials and tribulations that would have seen lesser unions fall apart under the stress and strain. It is undeniable

Denny and Mamie Ellis on their Golden Wedding Anniversary in 2003.

that having a child with all the problems Cathy had, is a recipe for marriage breakdown. We survived because of our love for each other, and our ability to be 'there' for one another when it was most needed. To watch a child suffer for 27 years is a burden no mother especially, or father, should have to endure.

It has been said to me on more than one occasion that the parents of children like Cathy are specially chosen by God. I am not so sure about that, but what I am sure of is, that the ability to see it through and come out the other side without too many scars is a gift from God. Our faith in God and His love has been an upholding factor through all the years.

We now have five granddaughters and one grandson. Although Shannon is now 22, I am sure she will not mind me saying,

"They are good kids."

Roy is now a District Court Judge and Faye still teaches languages at Parramatta High School.

Finally, I want to say again, writing in the first person makes it difficult on occasions not to appear to be immodest. I have tried during my writing not to put myself forward as being any better or any worse than any of my colleagues with whom I worked in a number of positions from shunting onwards. I have been a conscientious person, and although I can say today with absolute surety that I made many decisions I would have changed with the benefit of hindsight, I never once deliberately made a decision I thought would be detrimental to the department. There were areas, especially in train control, where I believe I did serve the department well, one of those being my absolute insistence that the safety of people working on the running lines was paramount. This may seem an odd choice, but I have chosen it to support a caring attitude towards those with whom I worked. I think it is reasonable to say, that any fair-minded judgment of me would say I was in the upper bracket of ability. I hope I have conveyed that. If I have conveyed more, forgive me. Beyond that, I say no more.

My final words are that The State Rail Authority, the Public Transport Commission and the New South Wales Government Railways were very good to me. I, in appreciation, never did less than my best.

THE END

APPENDIX A
SALARIED STAFF POSITIONS, COWRA — DUTY SHEETS

FIRST CLASS STATION MASTER
The duties annexed to the position were:
- Responsible for the effective management and well running of Cowra railway station.
- Responsible for the setting of the daily train running programme and the clearance of all traffic.
- Responsible for transit of all livestock and perishable traffic as listed by the District Superintendent Lithgow on Special Train Notices and by telegrams.
- Responsible for the correct compilation of the station Traffic Register, recording all tonnages and engine information as required in the register. Responsible for seeing delayed traffic given preference, after livestock and perishables.
- Responsible for liaising with the Chief Train Controller Lithgow daily (Sunday excepted) for advice of incoming trains and conveying to him the outgoing train programme.
- Responsible for advising the Mechanical Branch's steam shed inspector of the forecast train running programme for the next 24 hours and of the anticipated programme for the following 12 hours.
- Responsible for obtaining from steam shed inspector or his chargeman the steam engine allocation for the programme for the next 24 hours.
- Responsible for advising the guard's roster clerk of the programme set for 24 hours and anticipated for 36 hours.
- Responsible for setting of special trains to the branch lines with empty wheat wagons to load wheat at the direction of the Wheat Officer and for arranging transit to Glebe Island terminal silos of shipment wheat.
- Responsible for placement of inward loaded traffic in sidings and clearance of empty wagons and equipment.
- Responsible for the supply of livestock wagons at Cowra and the supply to branch line stations in accordance with directions from Esk's Stock Clerk.
- Responsible for safeguarding cash, valuables, ticket stock, COD parcels, for the collection of all money due for goods and parcels received as to-pay items prior to delivery and the issue of receipts for same.
- Responsible for the keeping of proper accounts in the goods shed, booking and parcels offices.
- Responsible for the rendition to audit of the monthly accounts within the specified time frame and for certifying their correctness.
- Responsible for ledger and bond accounts not being overdrawn.
- Responsible for ensuring unauthorised credit not allowed.
- Responsible for the correctness of the wagon book and for the collection of demurrage charges.
- Responsible for seeing penalty notices and other notices as required by the Rules and Regulations displayed for the benefit of staff and the general public.
- Responsible for the provision of all safeworking forms for emergency working, for safeguarding the staff and tickets for Cowra–Billimari–Canowindra sections and for ensuring safeworking regulations adhered to for the electric-staff working sections.
- Responsible for seeing clearance point lists and shunting limits are displayed in the signal box.
- Responsible for seeing emergency detonators regularly tested and being within time expiry date and that records are kept of tests.
- Responsible for sidings under control of Station Master Cowra and for seeing penalty notices displayed.
- Responsible for clearance of empty wagons and equipment from sidings.

- Responsible for the prompt attention to all Departmental correspondence and ensuring the accuracy and proper wording of all correspondence to superior officers.
- Responsible for the discipline and training of junior staff.
- Responsible for the overseeing of the issue of the book of Rules and Regulations to each new employee.
- Responsible for the station copies of all appendices and other authorised publications being posted with amendments and alterations, which appear in the Weekly Notices and for signing General and Local Order books.

FIRST CLASS ASSISTANT STATION MASTER
- Responsible for the safe and proper management of Cowra station during hours of duty.
- Responsible for all safeworking responsibilities being carried out in accordance with the Rules and Regulations.
- Responsible for the dispatch of telegrams to administrative officers of any safeworking irregularities or other serious breaches of the Rules and Regulations.
- Responsible for the train running programme being maintained and for adjustments where necessary to ensure maximum use of engine power and staff.
- Responsible for the compilation of shunter's lists.
- Responsible for seeing the book-outs for livestock wagons for branch trains met.
- Responsible for supplying guards with livestock wagon book-out advices.
- Responsible for seeing delayed traffic being given preference after livestock and perishables.
- Responsible for seeing to the prompt release to the locomotive depot of incoming train engines.
- Responsible for the checking of remittances made up by the booking clerk and for signing remittance notes.
- Responsible for seeing remittance dispatched in cash box.
- Responsible for on-time departure of passenger trains during shift.
- Responsible for initialling staff sign-on times in attendance books and on guards' duty sheets.
- Responsible for the compilation and transmission of all 6.00am tonnage report telegrams.
- Responsible for checking every wagon in the yard and ascertaining tonnages available for each train and ensuring the appropriate directions appear on shunters' lists.
- Responsible for keeping ongoing tonnages balances and train information in the Traffic Register.
- Other duties as directed by the station master. Peruse and sign General Order and Local Order books daily.

FOURTH CLASS COACHING CLERK – BOOKING OFFICE
- Responsible to the station master for the efficient management of all coaching and parcels business, and for the safe custody of all ticket stock, valuables, cash and excess fare receipt books.
- Responsible for the correct compilation of monthly coaching accounts and the balancing of the Station Account Current within the specified time frame and for presenting accounts for the station master's signature.
- Responsible for correct compilation of the daily blue summaries, for ticket classification sheets being brought forward daily, for checking rack ticket stock on a regular basis.
- Responsible for daily banking with the Bank of New South Wales.
- Responsible for correct compilation of the daily remittance to the Chief Cashier.
- Responsible for selling of tickets during hours of duty.
- Responsible for seeing all applications for booked seats and sleeping berths promptly dealt with.
- Responsible for seeing telegraph business conducted efficiently and for prompt despatch of all inwards and outwards telegraph business.

- Responsible for receiving cash and cheques from the parcels office and the clerk in charge of the Goods Shed and for the prompt remittance of it.
- Responsible for ordering of ticket stock and preparing requisitions for the station master's signature.
- Responsible for seeing authorised staff only permitted to enter the Booking Office. Peruse and sign General and Local Order books daily.
  * These daily summaries were known as the blue summaries because they were printed on blue paper.

SIXTH CLASS CLERK — BOOKING OFFICE
- Responsible for effective management of the Booking Office in the absence of the coaching clerk.
- Responsible for the transmission of all telegraphic business via the morse code method and for the distribution of all inward telegrams to the staff concerned.
- Responsible for prompt transmission of 6.00am traffic reports received from the assistant station master.
- Responsible for manning the ticket window between 7.00am and 8.30am and from 4.00pm to 8.30pm.
- Responsible for checking remittances and preparation of them for the assistant station master's signature.
- Responsible for the safe custody of ticket stock, cash and valuables during hours of duty.
- Responsible for compilation of balanced handover at completion of shift. Peruse and sign General and Local Order books daily.

SIXTH CLASS CLERK — PARCELS OFFICE
- Responsible to the coaching clerk for the effective management of the parcels office.
- Responsible for the delivery of parcels during hours of duty.
- Responsible for collection of all moneys owing on inwards to-pay parcels and for the issue of receipts.
- Responsible for the security of inwards cash-on-delivery parcels and for daily reconciliation between parcels on hand and inward COD book.
- Responsible for storage charges being levied on parcels not delivered within the free storage limits.
- Responsible for the entering into the Inwards Parcels and Luggage book every parcel and item of luggage received.
- Responsible for obtaining signature for every item of luggage and every parcel delivered.
- Responsible for attending to parcels office counter during hours of duty and for seeing stamps securely fixed to prepaid items.
- Responsible for seeing all parcels booked to unattended platforms booked out paid and receipt issued.
- Responsible for the correct compilation and invoicing of traffic sent 'To Pay'.
- Responsible for the daily balancing of parcels summary and completion of monthly abstracts.
- Responsible for preparing monthly parcels accounts and handing them to the officer-in-charge, booking office for his dealing and inclusion in Coaching Accounts.
- Responsible for parcel stamps stock being correctly accounted for daily and monthly.
- Responsible for ordering of parcel stamps and for preparation of requisitions for the station master's signature.
- Responsible for advising clients of parcels traffic on hand after three days.
- Responsible for seeing unauthorised credit not extended on Credit Accounts and Bond Accounts not exceeded. Peruse and sign General and Local Order books daily.

SEVENTH CLASS CLERK—STATIONS MASTER'S OFFICE
- Responsible for attending to all inward and outward correspondence.
- Responsible for addressing correspondence to employees from station master and District Superintendent Lithgow and for seeing replies promptly received.
- Responsible for preparing outwards correspondence for the signature of the station master.
- Responsible for the rostering of all guards in accordance with train running programme received from station master on a daily basis and for seeing advices in the hands of guards no later than 10.00am daily.
- Responsible for rostering station wages staff on a fortnightly basis.
- Responsible for formulating salary and wages timesheets and for rendition to timekeepers at the office of the District Superintendent Lithgow. Other duties required by the station master. Peruse General and Local Order books daily.

FOURTH CLASS CLERK—GOODS SHED
- Responsible to the station master for the effective management of the goods shed.
- Responsible for correct compiling of the Goods and Livestock Monthly Accounts and preparing for the signature of the station master within the specified time frame.
- Responsible for the safe custody of cash and valuables.
- Responsible for seeing unauthorised credit not extended.
- Responsible for seeing Bond and Ledger accounts not exceeded and for seeing monthly payments received by due dates.
- Responsible for seeing signature obtained for all goods delivered, money collected for freight and receipts issued.
- Responsible for compiling daily balance and for paying into the hands of the coaching clerk remittance cash and cheques.
- Responsible for seeing all outward traffic promptly invoiced and correct charges levied and receipts issued for goods booked out paid.
- Responsible for supervising wagon book and seeing entries made and referenced on a daily basis.
- Responsible for raising demurrage charges and for collection of them.
- Responsible for the raising and collection of storage charges where due.
- Responsible for seeing station master advised daily of shunting required to place traffic for unloading at crane, at goods shed stage and direct truck access, and clearance of empty and load outward traffic. Other duties as required by the station master. Peruse General and Local Order books daily.

SIXTH CLASS CLERK—GOODS SHED
- Responsible to the goods clerk-in-charge for the carrying out of documented duties.
- Responsible for the correct compilation of the Office Receipt book on a daily basis.
- Responsible for correct entries in Ledger and Bond Accounts.
- Responsible for compiling Ledger and Bond Monthly Accounts and forwarding to clients.
- Responsible for livestock orders and for advising station master and District Superintendent Lithgow of livestock wagon requirements.
- Responsible for correctly invoicing livestock consignments and dispatching telegrams for stock consigned from open sales. Other duties and assistance as required by the goods clerk-in-charge. Peruse General and Local Order books daily.

JUNIOR CLERK—GOODS SHED
- Work under the direction of the goods clerk.
- Responsible for consigning and invoicing all outwards traffic and for correct freight charges being levied.
- Responsible for issue of receipts for money received. Other duties as required by the goods clerk. Peruse General and Local Order books daily.

APPENDIX B
WAGES STAFF POSITIONS, COWRA — DUTY SHEETS

SENIOR SHUNTER CLASS 2
- Sign-on duty in the station master's office and peruse General and Local Order books.
- Responsible for collecting from station master 'the shunter's list' of directions for ensuing shift.
- Responsible for shunting incoming trains and forming outgoing trains during shift.
- Responsible for forming outgoing trains in sufficient time to allow on-time departure.
- Responsible for marshalling outgoing trains in accordance with the directions of the Engine Loads and Instruction book, the Local Appendix and the Working Timetable.
- Responsible for the prompt release of incoming train engines to the locomotive depot.
- Responsible for seeing incoming trains are properly secured before release of locomotives.
- Responsible for the prompt placement at stockyards of incoming loaded stock wagons.
- Responsible for seeing stock wagons and other empty wagons supplied in accordance with station master's advice in shunting list.
- Responsible for seeing wagons marshalled in station order and for cattle and sheep wagon book-outs marshalled in correct order for straight detach at loading stations.
- Responsible for seeing composite brakevans with gas lighting fully gassed before departure.
- Responsible for placing brakevans for branch and mainline pick-up trains in goods shed as required by the goods clerk for the loading of small consignments.
- Responsible for shunting of and placing traffic to sidings without delay.
- Responsible for the correct marshalling of stock on outgoing stock trains by seeing cattle and sheep wagons for Flemington marshalled separately.
- Responsible for segregating Clyde area traffic and forwarding on nominated train.

PORTER — SHUNTERS
- Sign-on duty in the station master's office. Peruse General and Local Order books. Obtain list of incoming and outgoing trains during ensuing shift.
- Responsible for the prompt admittance to shunting yard of incoming trains when senior shunter not on duty and for release of all incoming locomotives and for securing trains.
- Responsible for the piloting of outgoing locomotives to trains during hours of duty when senior shunter not on duty and for seeing locomotives attached without delay.
- Responsible for assisting with the transhipping of all parcels and luggage from incoming passenger trains to branch line services or to parcels and luggage office.
- Responsible for assisting with loading of footwarmers for *Cowra Mail* in the winter months.
- Responsible for assisting with filling of and placing in train water bottles in summer months. Other duties as required by the station master or assistant station master on duty.

LEADING PORTER — PLATFORM
- Sign-on duty in station master's office. Peruse General and Local Order books daily.
- Responsible to the station master for the cleanliness of Cowra railway station and surrounds.
- Responsible for the supervising of all transhipment of goods, parcels and luggage traffic during hours of duty.
- Responsible for seeing carriages detached from *Cowra Mail* watered and cleaned to the required standard.
- Responsible for seeing footwarmer boiler temperature maintained in winter months.
- Responsible for seeing carriage water bottles emptied and cleaned in summer months.
- Responsible for preparing requisition book orders for all cleaning and associated equipment required and presenting to the station master for approval and signature.

LEADING PORTER—GOODS SHED

- Sign-on duty in goods shed office.
- Responsible to the goods clerk for the delivery of all inwards loaded traffic and for obtaining signatures. Responsible for seeing freight paid on all inwards to-pay traffic before delivery.
- Responsible for seeing all outward truck loads of general goods, grain, baled hay and wool loaded to loading diagrams and within the limits of the loading gauge.
- Responsible for seeing all trucks loads correctly roped and tarpaulins properly secured.
- Responsible at close of day for advising the goods clerk of shunting required to place yard traffic at stage, crane and open yard for next day's requirements.
- Responsible for seeing all spare ropes rolled up and tarpaulins correctly folded and placed on stage for distribution to stations as required by the Wagon Clerk, Lithgow.
- Responsible to the goods clerk for providing daily details of traffic in goods shed sidings and for advising of inwards wagon load traffic still under load 24 hours after placement, for demurrage purposes.
- Responsible for the proper and safe use of the unloading crane and for securing jib away from running line after use.
- Responsible at close of day for seeing all wagon doors are closed and for safe arrangements made for shunting.
- Responsible for seeing all livestock loaded into stock wagons for sale days and Flemington Market days and that doors are properly closed and sealed with lead seals.

PORTERS—GOOD SHED

- Sign on duty at good shed. Responsible for duties allocated by the leading porter on a daily basis.

PORTER CLASS 1—PARCELS OFFICE

- Sign-on duty in station master's office, peruse General and Local Order books daily.
- Responsible to the parcels clerk for the proper conduct of business in the parcels office after the parcels clerk has signed off duty.
- Responsible for consigning all outward parcels traffic.
- Responsible for the issue of receipts for outwards paid parcels and for the supplying to consignors the correct amounts in stamps to attach to prepaid stamped parcels.
- Responsible for delivery of parcels as required and for obtaining signature and where necessary issuing receipts for money made in payment for inwards to-pay parcels.
- Responsible for compiling cash book handover balance at close of shift.
- Responsible for daily stamp balance of stamps used during shift.
- Responsible for security of valuables and COD parcels.

APPENDIX C
GLOSSARY OF RAILWAY TERMINOLOGY

Acacia Ridge	The standard gauge rail freight centre situated in Brisbane, Queensland.
Acdep	The service centre and depot for air-conditioned passenger rolling stock at Eveleigh.
Alliance Auto-matic Coupler	The brand name of an automatic coupling. In my shunting days they were always referred to as 'alliance couplings' to distinguish them from the few 'majestic' (another brand name) couplings that were still in use.
Alliance Auto-coupling Levers	A lever connected to the coupling pin of an automatic coupling which allowed the shunter to release the pin by lifting from the side of a wagon.
ARHS	Australian Railway Historical Society.

Automatic Wagons	Wagons that are coupled by self locking jaws.
Back Shift	A term for night work beginning between 10.00 and 11.59pm.
Back-in Siding	A siding where trains need to be reversed in.
Balloon Loop	A curved length of track which returns back to itself for the loading or unloading of unit trains.
Blocking Back	A term often used by operating staff to indicate that, for some reason, a delay was being experienced. Trains approaching the area that were halted at signals because of that delay were said to have blocked back, i.e. queued up.
Book Out	Orders to a guard indicating the stations at which he was to detach empty wagons, especially livestock wagons.
Booking Office	A place where passenger tickets were sold.
CityRail	The Sydney metropolitan and interurban rail network operating on the lines bounded by Bomaderry, Goulburn, Lithgow, Scone and Dungog.
Clipping of Points	The attachment of a point clip to rail points to prevent accidental opening during a train movement.
Cloak Room	Where passengers were able to leave luggage for a charge; generally in the parcels office.
CountryLink	The long distance passenger rail and road coach services operating beyond the limits of the CityRail network.
Crib	An authorised meal allowance.
Day shift	A shift which commenced between 6.00am and 12.00pm.
Delec	The diesel-electric and electric locomotive service centre at Enfield.
Demurrage	A charge levied when a client fails to unload a wagon within the prescribed free period of time.
Double header	Two locomotives attached together.
Engine Loads and Instruction Book	A book which contained a wealth of information regarding all steam locomotives; loads for passenger trains, draw gear capacity of the various types of passenger carriages and some Westinghouse brake information.
Four Foot and Six Foot	Four foot: a colloquial term for the space between the running rails within the gauge width, i.e. 4 foot 8½ inches. Six foot: a colloquial term for the space between the adjacent rails between the Up and Down tracks, i.e. 6 foot 6 inches.
FreightRail	The freight traffic arm of the State Rail Authority.
Ganger's Length	A particular length of track under the responsibility of a ganger.
General Order Book	The directions to staff which appeared in the weekly notices issued by the Chief Traffic Manager were posted in this book for the information of all staff.
Goods Shed	A place where all goods traffic was dealt with.
Home Station	The base station of relief staff.
Hook Wagons	Wagons attached to another wagon by means of a loose link coupling.
HST	High Speed Train (British Rail).
Interlocking	The term used to describe the machinery used to manipulate the signals and points in a signal box.
Katies	A local term for the workers' passenger trains between Thirroul and Port Kembla. The 55 Class (or K Class) goods locomotives were sometimes nicknamed Katies.
Lift or Lifting	Railway terminology for attaching traffic to trains, especially Pick-Up or livestock trains.
Light Engine	A locomotive proceeding to a destination with no train attached.

Local Appendix	An instruction book which contained information for local stations throughout the system.
Local Order Book	A book similar to the General Order Book but contained local orders issued by superintendents and local station masters.
Loco	Abbreviation for locomotive; also for a Locomotive Depot.
Long hours	Excess overtime worked after a shift.
Loop Line	A line, mostly at stations, that ran off the mainline and was utilised for the crossing of trains.
Main Line	The line which connects a series of stations.
Man on the Wall	The train controller was commonly known 'the man on the wall'.
Manna Wheat	The telegraphic code address of the Wheat Officer and Clerk in charge of wheat and grain movements.
Mile End	The rail freight centre situated in Adelaide, South Australia.
Out-of	Small consignments conveyed in brake vans or in trucks with goods for several stations, unloaded without the truck being detached from the train.
Parcels Office	The place where all parcels transactions took place.

Personnel positions:

District Superintendent (DS)
The head of a designated area.

Assistant District Superintendent (ADS)
The deputy to or the head of a designated area during the absence of the district superintendent.

Traffic Inspector	An officer who had a designated area over which he had administrative control.
Station Master	The person in charge of a railway station.
Assistant Station Master	The deputy to or the person in charge of a railway station during the absence of the station master.
Parcels Clerk	A person employed in a parcels office.
Porter	A wages staff employee.
Driver	A person who operated a locomotive; now known as an *engineman*.
Fireman	A person who maintained a steam locomotive's operational status, by maintaining sufficient steam and boiler water levels.
Guard	A person responsible for a train's security.
Shunter	A person employed in a shunting yard.
Ganger	An employee in charge of a fettling gang.
Fettler	An employee engaged in rail track maintenance.

Per Way	The Permanent Way and Works Section of the Chief Civil Engineer's Branch.
Pick-up	A train which detached and attached wagons at stations and sidings between two depots.
PMG Dept	Post Masters' General Department, a Commonwealth Government department responsible for postal, telegraphic and telephone communications, which in 1974 was divided into Australia Post and Telecom Australia. Telecom Australia is now known as *Telstra*.
Points Clip	An item attached to rail points to prevent accidental opening during a train movement over those points.
Priming (of boilers)	Priming occurred when some water in the boiler had not been converted to steam. It often occurred when engines were due for a boiler washout. A large amount of smoke, water and steam issued from the exhaust stack and if working hard, the locomotive rapidly lost steam. Mixed in this smoke was a polluted amount of water that

stained whatever it came into contact with. The Railways Department paid out many claims over the years to householders whose white sheets were ruined with it.

Reducing Time A person who was employed to relieve the incumbent in a position that was a seven day occupation.

Refuge Siding Similar to a crossing loop, but usually single-ended thus requiring trains refuged to either propel into the siding or propel out.

RTM New South Wales Rail Transport Museum.

Rules and Regulations These were the guidelines used for all operating procedures. They were found in the Rule Book and the three Appendices.

Shunting The act of shunting trains to form other trains.

Sidings and Platform book
A book that listed every station and siding in the Department of Railways network.

Signalling and Safeworking:

Acceptance or Accept Signal
A signal used on double line sections; worked from an advance signal box to indicate to a driver that the line was clear to the next signal.

Automatic Signal An electrically-controlled signal in an automatic signalling area activated by the movement of trains.

Block Telegraph A safeworking system which permits only one train between given locations at a time.

Distant Signal A signal placed at safe breaking distance from a signal protecting an interlocked area. Displays either a clear or caution signal only.

Electric Staff A token authorising a driver to proceed to the signal box in advance.

Home Signal A signal protecting an interlocked area at a station or signal box.

Landmark A fixed signal mainly found on branch lines in place of a distant signal.

Line Clear Term used on Block Telegraph instruments. Station 'A' asks 'B' is line clear by means of bell signals. 'B' responds by turning his instrument to line clear and replying to bell code 'A' instrument then shows line clear. Also used in Staff and Ticket working when 'line clear' reports are necessary.

Signal Box The place from all signals, points and lock bars were manipulated from. Also contained the appropriate safeworking instruments for the area concerned.

Signal Frame The framework housing the mechanical equipment grouped together to operate a set of signals and points.

Signal Lever A lever that operates a set of points, a facing point lock, lock bar or the aspect of a signal.

Standard Lock A brass padlock to secure signal boxes or other items at railway stations, etc for use by various operational staff. The key issued to operational staff is known as a 'SL' key.

Starting Signal The signal authorising a train to enter a safeworking section.

Staff and Ticket A single line system of safeworking of trains operating on a section.

Staff Instrument Often referred to as electric staff instrument; an electro/mechanical apparatus connected to two stations allowing a staff to be withdrawn at either end of a single track section. Only one staff can be withdrawn.

Starter Controlled Refers to the fact that a starting signal can only be cleared when line clear has been obtained from the station in advance.

Swinging the Staff A breach of regulations. The term means that when a crossing was made, the incoming electric staff was handed over to the outgoing driver without having been placed in the staff instrument and a fresh staff withdrawn.

Tyers Block Instruments   An early double line system of safeworking permitting only one train at a time between two given locations.

South Dynon	The rail freight centre situated in Melbourne, Victoria.
Special Train Notices	Notices issued from the timetabling section under the signature of the Head of the Branch and contain timetabling information.
Speed A Schedule	Authorised speeds for trains. Schedules A-B-C-D-E-F-G represent timetable schedules where each schedule has a different tonnage and speed; A schedule being the fastest.
Speed Board	An indication to the driver of the speed limit of the track to the next speed board.
SRA	State Rail Authority of NSW, which was renamed from the NSW Department of Railways in 1980. Now known as *RailCorp*.
Sydney Telegraph	The main telegraph station situated above No 1 Platform at Sydney Terminal. It was an early exchange and Morse code centre, later a teleprinter point.
Thompson Lever	Spring loaded manually operated points used in shunting yards.
Track Block	A system of safeworking applying to single and double working permitting only one train between two nominated points.

Tickets:

Season	A ticket for a set term allowing unlimited travel, included yearly, half-yearly, quarterly, monthly and some concessions.
Weekly Periodical	Allowed unlimited travel during the period of a seven-day week, mostly issued for Sydney metropolitan and some tourism areas.
Workers' Weekly	Used for daily travel to and return from a place of employment; available only between Mondays to Fridays.

Track Diagrams	These are situated in signal boxes above the signal frame and cover a designated area of track either side of the signal box. A white ball indicates the area is clear of trains and a red ball indicates a train is occupying the track. More recently, coloured lights are used.
Train Controller	An officer who worked on the train control system
Transport House	The NSW Department of Railways administration building at 19 York Street, built over Wynyard station. It was also known as the *Green House* due to its painted green exterior.
Trip Train	A train used to service the Metropolitan area goods sidings, e.g. to Botany, Rozelle, etc. there were a number of trip trains that operated as the Metropolitan Goods Controller directed.
Up and Down Lines	A means of identifying lines especially on double lines; the Down line travelled away from Sydney and the Up line towards Sydney.
Weekly Notices	Issued by the Chief Traffic Manager for the information of staff.
Weekly Speed Notices	Issued by the Chief Civil Engineer, showed all the areas in the State requiring a reduction in the set speed of the track concerned while repairs were made.
Working Time Table	A book which contained the timetables for all trains and issued only to staff.
XPT	Express Passenger Train (New South Wales).
Zona	Telegraphic code word indicating excessive time on duty.
Zona Clerk	A clerk in the rostering office responsible for relieving crews before they worked excessive hours.

APPENDIX D
NSW RAILWAY TELEGRAPHIC CODES

The NSW Department of Railways possessed a comprehensive list of codes, numbering several hundreds, to cover most situations of day-to-day operation, all of which were relayed by Morse code telegraphy. The following list represents only some of them.

ABAG	Out of gauge transversely loaded car bodies.
ABEL	Chief Mechanical Engineers' staff to check load at ...
ABLA	Special stock train will leave at ...
ABUZ	Special goods train will leave at ...
ACLO	Is amended to depart.
ACME	A light engine will leave ... station at ...
AGRA	... train left here at ...
AHAB	Train (or trains) left here on time.
AJAX	Engine left here at ...
AJOW	Train (or trains) arrived on time.
AKRU	Special train notice No ...
ALTO	Train will run.
AMAL	... Train will run in two divisions as follows:
AMBA	Require following train or trains to run.
AMEX	Train will not run.
AMID	Train is running ... minutes late.
AMOZ	What is cause of delay.
AMRI	Arrange for train No ... to cross at ...
ANAK	Truck loaded with perishable goods.
ARBU	Trucks loaded with ordinary goods.
ARGO	Trucks loaded with coal or coke.
ARUM	Trucks loaded with timber.
ATTA	Trucks loaded with rails.
AWRY	Pilot working has been arranged.
AXPA	Pilot working cancelled by me at ...
AXIS	Received special train notice.
AZOR	Arrange to provide assistant engine.

PASSENGER ARRANGEMENTS

BIKO	Economy-class reserved seat (or seats) required on train.
BIMU	First-class reserved seat (or seats) required on train.
BOXO	Air-conditioned accommodation fully booked.
BYAD	First-class single room required in roomette car.
BYBI	Additional berths required between ... and ...
BYEF	First-class double berth required for married couple in twin-berth room.
BYON	First-class lower berth required in twin-berth room.
CADI	All berths let.
CAFA	If all berths let, passenger requests name be listed.
CANA	Train has the following number of passengers: First ... Economy ...
CAPO	Provide accommodation in ...
CASU	Will provide accommodation in ...
CATO	The following are the bookings from this station per excursion:
CAWT	Specially note altered time of departure for this date and inform intending passengers.
CELU	You may book ... additional tickets for excursions.

CENA	May bookings for ... excursions be continued.
CIMA	Reserved seats fully booked.
CIRY	Has correct day and date of travel been quoted?

GOODS
COMA	In addition *to* other advices, the following extra trucks will be loaded:
CONY	Important consignment for shipment.
CUJA	Is ship ready *to* receive cargo at ...
CURO	Consignment for ship ... may be received on ...

ROLLING STOCK
DABO	Number of trucks and bags of wheat loaded for shipment.
DEHY	Diesel hydraulic locomotive.
DEMO	Tarpaulins on hand.DODOChains on hand.
DYAK	Empty stock trucks on hand.
EBER	Empty goods trucks on hand.
EBON	Loaded goods trucks on hand inwards.
ECCE	Loaded goods trucks on hand outwards.
ECHO	None on hand.
EDAR	Loaded trucks on hand over 12 hours.
EDEN	Tonnage despatched for preceding 24 hours up and down separately.
EDIX	Livestock trucks in transit.
EDNA	Tonnage on hand 6am up and down separately.
EDOW	Goods Trucks in transit.
ELAH	None to spare.
ELIM	Required for use on...
ELMO	Required for tomorrow's use.
EMIR	... trucks required for station use in addition to those on hand.
EPIC	... trucks required to load on ...
ERAM	Restocking rates will apply if conditions are fully complied with.
EROS	... urgently required. Release all possible. Advise how many available.
ETAM	What is being done to supply.
ETEK	Bulk wheat loaded
EVAN	Empty bulk trucks on hand 7am today.
EVAR	Empty bulk trucks on hand 7am previous day.
EVAY	Empty trucks received at this station since last report.
EVIL	Stop supply of empty wagons to ...
EVIX	The following orders have been cancelled.
EZUK	I am arranging supply of trucks.
FAMA	Inform ... the following trucks will be supplied:
FARO	After supplying previous orders.
FOXO	Trucks loaded since last report.
FUMY	Loaded trucks outwards, waiting transit over 12 to 24 hours.
GIBY	Arrange to work forward.
GIPO	Send all spare ...
HABA	May I accept?
HAGI	You may accept.
HAKO	Do not accept.

GOODS, PARCELS AND LUGGAGE
(a) Articles Missing
| HALO | Search ... carriages of under mentioned train for the articles and if found, send as under, and reply. |

HARA   Not to hand. Trace and wire particulars. Urgently required.

HAZY   We are short of the following. If on hand, forward by first train and reply.

HEBE   If on hand at your station, send by first train.

HEGO   Said left on station premises, search and advise result.

HUVA   Give description of case or article and contents and say if any old labels or tags attached or brands appear thereon.

HYLA   Make careful inquiry and search at your station.

IBEX   Have you any trace?

IDAS   Cannot trace, wire me full particulars.

IGOL   No trace of.

IRAN   Wire how truck labelled and transit ex yours.

IROK   Give truck number and date and time of despatch.

(b) Incomplete Particulars, Errors, Damages, etc.

JUNO   Received in bad order. Say in what condition forwarded and what receipt given.

KAXA   Consignee refuses to accept. Wire instructions.

KEPA   No further address known.

KESY   Unable contact sender.

LEDA   On hand. Wire instructions for disposal.

LENO   Following trucks received here from your station without waybill. Wire all particulars and forward invoice.

LION   Sent you unentered.

LOMA   Send copy of invoice(s) or waybill(s) quickly or say if non-issued.

LUNA   Received unentered or in excess. Wire full particulars and send invoice or copy.

LYSO   Re-direct and forward to ...

MAGI   If still unable to deliver, dispose of to best advantage.

MAZY   Wire how disposed of.

MENU   Wire sender's name and address.

MICA   Said not to have been delivered.

MIRY   Delivered on ... and signed for by ...

MOVU   ... proposes removing furniture and household effects from ... to ...

MYAL   You may recharge or transfer the amount.

NERI   ... is correct as received by you.

(c) General

NOAH   The under mentioned left behind here. Will follow next train.

NODO   Consignee claims freight should be paid at your station—advise promptly.

UNIFORM AND SUPPLEMENTARY TELEGRAPH CODE WORDS

NUMA   Furnish full particulars of forwarding, following with copies of invoices.

OBAX   Following traffic urgently wanted. If with you, work forward first means, wiring particulars of forwarding.

OBOE   ... which left under mentioned station on ... is urgently wanted. Best possible despatch to be given.

OFOD   Contents perishable.

OGLE   Following loaded trucks on hand incurring demurrage.

ONUS   Stop sending traffic as under until further advised.

ONYX   Our invoice or waybill.

OPAL   Your invoice or waybill.

OZIN   Charges paid.

CORRESPONDENCE

PASI	Acknowledge immediately by wire.
PEDO	With reference to your telegram (or previous telegrams) telephone message or conversation.
PEFU	With reference to telegrams exchanged.
PEON	With reference to my previous telegram, telephone message or conversation.
PIKO	With reference to your letter.
PINA	With reference to telegram from ...
PIZA	With reference to my !etter.
PODU	Reply immediately by wire.
POLA	Reply immediately by letter.
PRAD	The following ticket (or tickets) has been surrendered for refund by ...
PREN	Certify to amount of fare collected.
PROW	Is cash refund on the usual basis agreed to?
PUCI	The matter is now in order
PUNY	Wire how matters stand.
PURA	Take up duty at ...
PYRO	Send full report at once respecting.
RAPO	Immediately on receipt of this message.
RIMY	Take special steps to get important letter by ...
ROSY	Not to hand. Send copy by first train.
ROVA	Confirming my telephone conversation.
RUBI	Cancel my advice respecting.
RULO	Am forwarding further particulars by letter.

MISCELLANEOUS

(a) Repairs, etc

SEBA	... working out of order between ... and ...
SEVO	... out of order, forward another.
SODI	Send man here at once to attend to ...
SOJA	Fault now removed.

(b) Supply and Receipt

SOLO	Can you supply?
SUSI	We are short of the following. Supply at once.
TEMA	Send on with all speed.
TEPO	Send by first available goods train.

(c) General

VIVA	Most urgently wanted.
VOCE	Serious complaint made.
WARY	See no delay occurs.
WAXY	Give matter special attention.
ZANY	Arrange accordingly.
ZEBU	Arrange and advise all concerned.
ZENO	Instruct driver and guard in writing.
ZOLY	Arrange to relieve driver and fireman.
ZONA	Expect to be on duty over ... hours on arrival at ...
ZUKA	Staffs require balancing between ... and ...